John Lingard

The History of England, from the First Invasion by the Romans to the Accession of William and Mary in 1688

Vol. V

John Lingard

The History of England, from the First Invasion by the Romans to the Accession of William and Mary in 1688
Vol. V

ISBN/EAN: 9783744677028

Printed in Europe, USA, Canada, Australia, Japan

Cover: Foto ©ninafisch / pixelio.de

More available books at **www.hansebooks.com**

THE MARRIAGE OF PHILIP AND MARY AT WINCHESTER.

CHAPTER II.

PROGRESS OF THE REFORMATION.

King's Supremacy—Its Nature—Cromwell made Vicar-General—Bishops take out new Powers.—II. Dissolution of Monasteries—Lesser Monasteries suppressed—Death of Queen Catherine—Arrest, Divorce, and Execution of Anne—Insurrection in the North—Pole's Legation—Greater Monasteries given to the King.—III. Doctrine—Henry's Connection with the Lutheran Princes—Articles—Institution of a Christian Man—Demolition of Shrines —Publication of the Bible.—IV. Persecution of Lollards—Anabaptists— Reformers—Trial of Lambert—Pole's second Legation—Execution of his Relations.—V. Struggle between the two Parties—Statute of the Six Articles —Marriage with Anne of Cleves—Divorce—Fall of Cromwell—Marriage with Catherine Howard—Her Execution—Standard of English Orthodoxy.

Nature of the supremacy	24	Destruction of shrines	53
Cromwell vicar-general	25	Tyndal's Bible	54
Bishops sue out new powers	26	Matthewe's Bible	55
Dissolution of monasteries	27	Persecution of Lollards	56
Suppression of the lesser monasteries	28	Of Reformers	ib.
Some are respited	ib.	Trial of Lambert	57
Death of Catherine	29	Arrest and execution of the brothers of Pole	60
Queen Anne's miscarriage	30	Second Legation of Pole	61
Her imprisonment	31	The pope orders the publication of the bull against Henry	ib.
Her behaviour in prison	32		
Trial of the queen	34	Arrest and execution of Pole's mother	62
Cranmer pronounces a divorce	35		
She is beheaded	38	Struggle of parties	63
Mary reconciled to her father	39	Statute of the six articles	64
Insurrection in the northern counties	40	Terror of Cranmer	65
The pilgrimage of grace	41	Acts of parliament	ib.
It is suppressed	42	King's marriage with Anne of Cleves	67
Pole's legation defeated	44	His disappointment	68
Dissolution of the greater monasteries	45	Imprudence of Barnes	ib.
Of Furness	ib.	Cromwell's speech at the opening of parliament	69
Proceedings of the commissioners	46	He is arrested	70
Monastic property vested in the king	47	And attainted	ib.
New bishoprics established	49	King divorced from Anne	71
Doctrine of the English church	ib.	Execution of Cromwell	73
Attempted union of the king with the German reformers	50	Other executions	ib.
		King marries Catherine Howard	74
It fails	51	She is accused of incontinency	ib.
Articles of doctrine	ib.	Condemned	77
Institution of a Christian man	52	And executed	ib.
Envoys from the Lutheran princes	ib.	Restraint on the reading of the Scriptures	78
		Erudition of a Christian Man	79

CONTENTS.

CHAPTER III.

Statutes respecting Wales—Transactions in Ireland—Negotiations and War with Scotland—Rupture with France—Peace—Taxes—Depreciation of the Currency—Cranmer—Gardiner—King's last Illness—Execution of the Earl of Surrey—Attainder of the Duke of Norfolk—Death of Henry—His Character—Subserviency of the Parliament—Doctrine of passive Obedience—Servility of Religious Parties.

Wales 80	Loans 95
Ireland 81	A benevolence .. .. .. ib.
Rebellion of Kildare .. .. ib.	Adulteration of the money .. ib.
Pacification of Ireland 83	Another subsidy.. 96
Scotland 84	Danger of Cranmer .. .. ib.
Marriage of James 85	And of Gardiner.. 97
Negotiations 86	Also of Queen Catherine .. 98
An interview refused by James 87	Death of Askew and others .. 99
War between the two crowns .. ib.	Henry's last speech on religion 100
A marriage proposed between Edward and Mary 88	His maladies and inquietude .. ib.
	Rivalry between the Howards and Seymours.. 101
It is agreed to on certain conditions 89	Disgrace of Gardiner and arrest of the Howards .. .. ib.
The treaty broken 90	Execution of the earl of Surrey 102
Invasion of Scotland .. .. ib.	Confession and attainder of the duke of Norfolk 103
Peace 91	
Henry is discontented with Francis .. .. ib.	King's death 104
	The king's will 105
Concludes a treaty with the emperor 92	His character 107
	House of Lords 108
War with France .. .. ib.	House of Commons 109
Siege of Boulogne 93	Flattery of the king .. .. ib.
Francis makes peace with the emperor .. .. ib.	Ecclesiastical influence of the crown 110
England insulted by the French fleet 94	Servility of the opposite parties 111
	Extraordinary statutes .. .. ib.
Peace with France .. .. ib.	Prosecutions for treason.. .. 112
Taxes 95	

CHAPTER IV.

EDWARD VI.

Hertford is made Protector and Duke of Somerset—War with Scotland—Battle of Pinkiecleugh—Progress of the Reformation—Book of Common Prayer—Lord Admiral arrested and beheaded—Discontent and Insurrections—France declares War—Protector is sent to the Tower and discharged—Peace—Deprivation of Bishops—Troubles of the Lady Mary—Foreign Preachers—Somerset arrested and executed—New Parliament—Warwick's Ambition—Death of the King.

The council of regency 114	Creation of new titles 116
The earl of Hertford protector.. 115	Coronation of Edward 117

CONTENTS.

Address of Cranmer 117	Meeting of parliament 147
The chancellor removed .. 118	Submission and discharge of Somerset 149
Somerset made independent of the council 119	Peace with France and Scotland 151
Negotiation with France .. ib.	Deprivation of Bonner.. .. 152
Treaty with the murderers of Beaton.. 121	Deprivation of Gardiner .. 153
	Of Day and Heath 154
They are reduced by the governor ib.	Troubles of the Lady Mary .. 155
The protector invades Scotland 122	Her chaplains are prevented from saying mass 157
He returns to England 123	
Religious innovations .. .. ib.	Execution for heresy 159
New commissions to the bishops 124	Burning of Bocher .. .. ib.
Visitation of dioceses .. .. ib.	Von Paris .. .. .. ib.
Opposition of Gardiner 125	Employment of foreign divines.. 160
He is imprisoned .. .. ib.	Obstinacy of Hooper 161
A parliament .. .. .. ib.	New dissensions between Somerset and Warwick .. .. ib.
Grant of chantries .. .. ib.	
Repeal of new treasons 126	Treaty of marriage between Edward and a French princess .. 162
Petition of clergy refused .. ib.	
Election of bishops 127	Arrest of Somerset and his friends 163
Suppression of mendicity .. ib.	Arrival of the dowager queen of Scotland .. .. .. ib.
Ecclesiastical injunctions .. 129	
Gardiner sent to the Tower .. 130	Depositions against Somerset .. 164
Catechism and Book of Common Prayer.. .. .. .. ib.	His trial 165
	He is condemned .. .. ib.
Marriage of the clergy 132	And executed 166
History of the lord admiral .. ib.	Fate of his adherents 167
He marries the queen dowager.. 133	Acts of parliament .. .. ib.
Wins the affection of the king . ib.	Improvement in trials for treason 168
Aspires to the hand of the lady Elizabeth 134	Prosecution of the bishop of Durham 169
He is attainted of treason .. 135	The English service introduced into Ireland .. .. .. ib.
And is executed 137	
Resumption of hostilities with Scotland 138	Articles of religion 170
	Code of ecclesiastical laws .. 171
Mary carried to France.. .. 139	Edward's last parliament .. 172
Shrewsbury in Scotland .. ib.	Northumberland's riches and ambition 173
General discontent 140	
Insurrections 141	His attempt to alter the succession 174
In Oxfordshire .. .. .. ib.	Edward consents.. 175
In Devonshire .. .. .. ib.	Reluctance of the judges .. 176
In Norfolk 142	Conduct of the archbishop .. ib.
War declared by the king of France.. 144	The counsellors sign it .. .. ib.
	The king dies 178
Dissensions in the cabinet .. ib.	His abilities .. .. .. ib.
Somerset and Warwick opposed to each other 145	His religious opinions 179
	State of the nation during his reign .. .. ib.
Somerset sent to the Tower .. 147	

CONTENTS. vii

CHAPTER V

MARY.

Lady Jane Grey proclaimed Queen—The Lady Mary is acknowledged—Her Questions to the Emperor Charles—Execution of Northumberland—Misconduct of Courtenay—Queen seeks to restore the Ancient Service—Elizabeth conforms—Cranmer opposes—Parliament—Intrigues of Noailles—Insurrection of Wyat—Failure and Punishment of the Conspirators—Elizabeth and Courtenay in Disgrace—Treaty of Marriage between Mary and Philip—Reconciliation with Rome.

Intrigues of foreign courts .. 181	Courtenay conspires against her 202
Proceedings of the council .. 182	Queen answers the address .. 203
Lady Jane Grey.. .. .. ib.	Imperial ambassadors to conclude
Proclaimed queen 183	the treaty .. .. .. ib.
Letters between Mary and the council.. 184	Rising of the conspirators .. 205
	Wyat in Kent 207
The adherents of Mary.. .. 185	Defeats the royalists 208
Ridley preaches against her .. 186	Queen's speech in the Guildhall 209
Her success 187	Progress of Wyat 210
Northumberland alarmed .. ib.	He is made prisoner 211
The council proclaims Mary ., 188	Execution of Jane Grey and her
Northumberland is arrested .. ib.	husband 212
The queen enters the capital .. 189	Other executions 213
The new council.. 190	Arrest of Elizabeth and Courtenay 214
Proclamations .. .. .. ib.	
The queen consults the emperor 191	Evidence against them 215
Respecting the traitors.. .. 192	Letters and confessions .. .. ib.
Their trials .. .. .. ib.	They are saved by Gardiner .. ib.
And punishment .. .. ib.	Queen's conduct to Noailles .. 216
Queen proposes to marry .. 193	Ratification of the treaty of marriage .. .. ib.
The emperor offers his son .. 194	
Opposition to Philip .. .. ib.	Proceedings of parliament .. 217
Orders respecting religion .. 195	Arrival of Philip 219
Riots 196	Marriage of Philip and Mary .. ib.
Elizabeth conforms .. .. ib.	Reunion with Rome 221
Cranmer's declaration 197	Assurance of abbey lands .. ib.
The pope appoints Pole his legate .. .. ib.	Meeting of parliament .. .. ib.
	Arrival of Pole 222
Meeting of parliament 198	His proceedings .. .. .. ib.
First session .. .. .. ib.	Conduct of parliament 223
Second session 199	Decree of the legate .. .. ib.
Restoration of the ancient service ib.	Alienation of church lands .. ib.
Other enactments 200	Intrigues of the French ambassador 225
Parties respecting the queen's marriage .. .. .. ib.	
	Acts of grace .. .. .. ib.
Intrigues of Noailles 201	Embassy to Rome 226
Address to the queen .. .. ib.	

of marchioness of Pembroke, with an annuity to her of one thousand pounds for life out of the bishopric of Durham, and of another thousand out of several manors belonging to the crown; but four months later she proved to be in a condition to promise him an heir; and the necessity of placing beyond cavil the legitimacy of the child induced him to violate the pledge which he had so solemnly given to the king of France. On the 25th of January, at an early hour, Dr. Rowland Lee, one of the royal chaplains, received an order to celebrate mass in a room in the west turret of Whitehall. There he found the king attended by Norris and Heneage, two of the grooms of the chamber, and Anne Boleyn, accompanied by her trainbearer Anne Savage, afterwards Lady Berkeley. We are told that Lee, when he discovered the object for which he had been called, made some opposition; but Henry calmed his scruples with the assurance that Clement had pronounced in his favour, and that the papal instrument was safely deposited in his closet.[1]

As soon as the marriage ceremony had been performed, the parties separated in silence before it was light; and the father of Anne, now earl of Wiltshire and Viscount Rochford, was despatched to announce the event, but in the strictest confidence, to Francis. At the same time he was instructed to dissuade that king from consenting to the intended marriage of his second son with the niece of Clement; or, if it could not be prevented, to prevail on him to make it a condition of the marriage that the pope should proceed no further in his censures against Henry.[2] Francis received the intelligence with sorrow. Henry's precipitancy had broken all the measures which had been planned for the reconciliation of the English king with the pontiff; but in answer to his complaints by Langey his ambassador, Henry pleaded scruples of conscience, and promised that he would conceal the marriage till the month of May, by which time the interview between Francis and Clement would have taken place. Then, if Clement did him justice, the recent proceeding would prove of no detriment; if not, he was determined to set the papal authority at defiance. But, contrary to his hopes, the interview was postponed; the pregnancy of the bride became visible; and on Easter eve orders were given that she should receive the honours due to the queen consort. The marriage was thus acknowledged; still the date of its celebration remained involved in mystery; and, to encourage the notion that the child had been conceived in wedlock, a report was artfully circulated that the nuptials had occurred at a more early period, immediately after the separation of the two kings at Calais.[3]

Archbishop Warham, who had been

[1] Burnet .reats this account as one of the fictions of Sanders: but it is taken from a manuscript history of the divorce presented to Queen Mary, thirty years before the work of Sanders was published (see Le Grand, ii. 110); and agrees perfectly with the attempt to keep the marriage secret for two or three months. Lee was made bishop of Chester, was translated to Lichfield and Coventry, and honoured with the presidentship of Wales.—Stowe, 543.
[2] Transcripts for the N. Rym. 176.
[3] Hence the marriage is dated on the 14th of November, 1532, the day when Henry and Anne sailed from Calais, by almost all our historians. But Godwin (Annal. 51) and Stowe (Annals, 543) have assigned it to the 25th January, the feast of the Conversion of St. Paul; and that they are right is incontestably proved from a letter still extant, written by Archbishop Cranmer to his friend Hawkins, the ambassador to the emperor. After an account of the coronation, he proceeds thus: " But nowe, sir, you may nott ymagyne that this coronacion was before her marriage, for she was married much about Sainte Paule's daye laste, as the condicion thereof dothe well appere by reason she ys nowe somewhat bigge with chylde. Notwithstanding yt hath byn reported thorowte a great parte of the realme that I maried her, which was plainly false: for I myself knewe not therof a fortnyght after yt was donne."—Archæologia, xviii. 81.

driven from court by the ascendancy of Wolsey, was zealously attached to the ancient doctrines and the papal authority: his death in the course of the last summer had empowered the king to raise to the first dignity in the English church a prelate of opposite principles, and more devoted to the will of his sovereign. Thomas Cranmer, at the recommendation of Henry,[1] had been taken into the family of the Boleyns, and had assisted the father and the daughter with his services and advice: his book in favour of the divorce, the boldness with which he had advocated the royal cause at Rome, and the industry with which he had solicited signatures in Italy, had raised him in the esteem of the king; and soon after his return he had been appointed orator ad Cæsarem, or ambassador attendant on the emperor. Both Henry and Anne flattered themselves that, by selecting him for the successor of Warham, they would possess an archbishop according to their own hearts. There was, however, one objection which might have proved fatal to his elevation with a prince, who till his last breath continued to enforce with the stake and the halter the observance of clerical celibacy. Cranmer after the death of his wife had taken orders; but, during one of his agencies abroad, he had suffered himself to be captivated with the charms of a young woman, the niece of Osiander or of his wife, had married her in private, and had left her in Germany with her friends.[2] Whether this marriage had come to the knowledge of Henry, or was considered by him invalid according to the canon law, is uncertain; but, "to the surprise and sorrow of many,"[3] he resolved to raise Cranmer to the archbishopric, and appointed Dr. Hawkins to succeed him in the embassy. From Mantua, where the emperor then held his court, Cranmer returned to England; the papal confirmation was asked and obtained; the necessary bulls were expedited in the usual manner, and in a very few days after their arrival the consecration followed.[4] But by what casuistry could the archbishop elect, who was well acquainted with the services expected from him, reconcile it with his conscience to swear at his consecration canonical obedience to

---

[1] So at least we are told on the very questionable authority of a long story in Foxe, and a MS. life of Cranmer, C. C. Coll. Cam. —See Fiddes, 469.

[2] There appears some doubt as to the time of this marriage. Godwin, in his Annals, says: Uxore jamdudum orbatus, quam adolescens duxerat, puellæ cujusdam amore irretitus tenebatur (hæc erat neptis uxoris Osiandri) quam etiam sibi secundo connubio jungere omnimodis decreverat (p. 49). De Præsulibus Anglicanis, he says: Quod maxime angebat, conscientia fuit ductæ uxoris, neptis ea fuit Osiandro (p. 138).

[3] Præter opinionem et sensum multorum. —Antiq. Brit. 327.

[4] Without noticing the question whether Cranmer was eager or reluctant to accept the dignity, I shall state the principal dates, for the satisfaction of the reader.—Aug. 24. Warham dies. Oct. 1. Henry signs the recall of Cranmer, and appoints Hawkins to succeed him (Transcripts for New Rymer, 174). Oct. 4. The emperor, with whom Cranmer resides as ambassador, leaves Vienna for Italy (Sandoval, 120). Nov. 6. He fixes his residence at Mantua (Id. 124). Nov. 18. He is still at Mantua, where he has received the official notification of Cranmer's recall, and of the appointment of Hawkins; and on the same day he delivers his answer into the hands of Cranmer to take with him to England. Thus seven weeks have elapsed since the date of Cranmer's recall: for which we may safely account by the supposition that, ignorant of the emperor's departure from Vienna, Hawkins proceeded towards that city, instead of going direct to Italy — Cranmer was preconized by the pope in a consistory in January (Becchetti, viii. 234), thus leaving two months only for his journey from Mantua to England, his acceptance of the archbishopric, the mission of the proctor to Rome, and his proceedings there. The different bulls were expedited on the 21st and 22nd of February and the 3rd of March, and they arrived in England in sufficient time for the consecration on the 30th of the latter month.

the pope, when he was already resolved to act in opposition to the papal authority? With the royal approbation he called four witnesses and a notary into the chapter-house of St. Stephen's at Westminster, and in their presence declared that by the oath of obedience to the pope, which for the sake of form he should be obliged to take, he did not intend to bind himself to anything contrary to the law of God, or prejudicial to the rights of the king, or prohibitory of such reforms as he might judge useful to the church of England.[1] From the chapter-house, attended by the same persons, he proceeded to the steps of the high altar, declared in their presence that he adhered to the protestation which he had already read in their hearing, and then took the pontifical oath. The consecration followed; after which, having again reminded the same five individuals of his previous protest, he took the oath a second time, and received the pallium from the hands of the papal delegates.[2]

This extraordinary transaction gave birth to an animated controversy; the opponents of the archbishop branding him with the guilt of fraud and perjury, his advocates labouring to wipe away the imputation, and justifying his conduct by the extraordinary circumstances in which he was placed. I will only observe, that oaths cease to offer any security, if their meaning may be qualified by previous protestations, made without the knowledge of the party who is principally interested.[3]

With an archbishop subservient to his pleasure, Henry determined to proceed with the divorce. The previous arrangements were intrusted to the industry of Cromwell. To prevent Catherine from opposing any obstacle to the proceedings meditated by Cranmer, an act of parliament was passed, forbidding, under the penalty of premunire, appeals from the spiritual judges in England to the courts of the pontiff;[4] and, to furnish grounds for the intended sentence, the members of the convocation were

[1] See it in the original Latin in Strype, App. p. 9, and not in the English translation, which is very unfaithful. By one clause he declared that it had never been his intention to empower his proctor to take any oath in his name contrary to the oath which he had taken or might take to the king; and yet he must have known the contents of the oath to be taken by the proctor, and have given him the usual authority to take it; otherwise the proctor would not have been admitted to act in the court of Rome.

[2] The question of the privacy or publicity of Cranmer's protest has been set at rest by an extract from the notarial instrument in Lambeth MSS., 1136, published by Mr. Todd, i. 65. It proves, beyond the possibility of doubt, that he read the protest once only, and that before witnesses privately assembled in the Chapter-house. In the church he did no more than say to the same witnesses that he would swear in the sense of the protest made by him already; but there is no evidence that any one besides them heard his words, or that any one else was acquainted with the contents of the protest. It was evidently his object to clothe it with all the canonical forms, but at the same time to conceal its purport from the public.

[3] The archbishop himself, in excuse of his duplicity, wrote afterwards to Queen Mary, that his chief object was to be at liberty to reform the church. Pole answered: "To what did this serve but to be forsworn before you did swear? Other perjurers be wont to break their oath after they have sworn; you break it before. Men forced to swear per vim et metum may have some colour of defence, but you had no such excuse."—Strype's Chron. App. 213. Some of his modern apologists think that they have found a parallel case in the protest of Archbishop Warham, who in 1532, alarmed at the ecclesiastical innovations of the court, recorded in the strongest terms his dissent in his own name and the name of his church, to every statute passed or to be passed by parliament derogatory from the authority of the Apostolic See, or subversive of the rights of the church of Canterbury.—Wilkins, Con. iii. 746. But the resemblance is only in the technical form and title of the instrument. Warham proclaims his non-participation in the *acts of others*; Cranmer his resolution not to be bound by *his own deed*, by the oath which he was about to take; the one will never give his consent to what he disapproves in conscience, the other will take the oath which he conscientiously disapproves, and will then break it.

[4] Stat. of Realm, iii. 427.

divided into two classes, of theologians and canonists, and each was ordered to pronounce on a question separately submitted to its decision. Of the former it was asked, whether a papal dispensation could authorize a brother to marry the relict of his deceased brother in the case where the first marriage had been actually consummated: of the latter, whether the depositions taken before the legates amounted to a canonical proof that the marriage between Arthur and Catherine had been consummated. The two questions were debated for some days in the absence of the new archbishop: he then took his seat: the votes were demanded; and on both questions answers favourable to the king were carried by large majorities.[1] As soon as the convocation had separated, a hypocritical farce was enacted between Henry and Cranmer. The latter, as if he were ignorant of the object for which he had been made archbishop, wrote a most urgent letter to the king, representing the evils to which the nation was exposed from a disputed succession, and begging to be informed if it were the pleasure of the sovereign that he should hear the cause of the divorce in the archiepiscopal court. This letter, though its language was sufficiently humble, and sufficiently intelligible, did not satisfy the king or his advisers; and Cranmer was compelled, in a second letter of the same date, to take the whole responsibility on himself. It was, he was made to say, a duty, which he owed to God and the king, to put an end to the doubts respecting the validity of Henry's marriage; wherefore, prostrate at the feet of his majesty, he begged permission to hear and determine the cause, and called on God to witness that he had no other object in making this petition than the exoneration of his own conscience and the benefit of the realm.[2] There was no longer any demur. The king graciously assented to his request; but at the same time reminded the primate that he was nothing more than the principal minister of the spiritual jurisdiction belonging to the crown, and that "the sovereign had no superior on earth, and was not subject to the laws of any earthly creature."[3] It was in vain that the French ambassador remonstrated against these proceedings as contrary to the engagements into which Henry had entered at Boulogne and Calais. Catherine was cited to appear before Cranmer at Dunstable, within four miles of Ampthill, where she resided; and a post was established to convey with despatch the particulars of each day's transactions to Cromwell. At the appointed time the archbishop, with the bishop of Lincoln as his assessor, and the bishop of Winchester and seven others as counsel for the king, opened the court, and hastened the trial with as much expedition as was permitted by the forms of the ecclesiastical courts. In his letters to Cromwell the primate earnestly entreated that the intention of proceeding to judgment might be kept an impenetrable secret. Were it once to transpire, Catherine might be induced to appear, and, notwithstanding the late statute, to put in an appeal from him to the pontiff,

---

[1] Among the theologians there were nineteen ayes (Burnet strangely transformed them into nineteen universities, i. 129, but acknowledged the error in his third volume, p. 123, oct.) and sixty-six noes. The majority consisted of three bishops, forty-two abbots and priors, and the rest clergymen. Of forty-four canonists, only six voted against Henry. The same questions were answered in the same manner in the convocation at York, on the 13th of May, with only two dissentient voices in each class. I may add that Carte is certainly mistaken, when he supposes this transaction to have happened some years before.
[2] See Appendix, T.
[3] State Papers, i. 390—3. Collier, a. Records, No. xxiv.

a measure which would defeat all their plans, and entirely disconcert both himself and the counsel.[1] On Saturday the service of the citation was proved, and the queen, as she did not appear, was pronounced "contumacious." On the following Monday, after the testimony of witnesses that she had been served with a second citation, she was pronounced "verily and manifestly contumacious;" and the court proceeded in her absence to read depositions, and to hear arguments in proof of the consummation of the marriage between her and Prince Arthur. On the Saturday she received a third citation to appear, and hear the judgment of the court. Catherine took no notice of these proceedings; for she had been advised to abstain from any act which might be interpreted as an admission of the archbishop's jurisdiction. Cranmer waited for the first open day (it was Ascension week), and on the Friday pronounced his judgment, that the marriage between her and Henry was null and invalid, having been contracted and consummated in defiance of the divine prohibition, and therefore without force or effect from the very beginning.[2]

This decision was communicated to the king in a letter from the primate, who with much gravity exhorted him to submit to the law of God, and to avoid those censures which he must incur by persisting in an incestuous intercourse with the widow of his brother.[3] But what, it was then asked, must be thought of his present union with Anne Boleyn? How could he have lawfully effected a new marriage before the former was lawfully annulled? Was the right of succession less doubtful now than before? To silence these questions Cranmer held another court at Lambeth, and having first heard the king's proctor, officially declared that Henry and Anne were and had been joined in lawful matrimony; that their marriage was and had been public and manifest; and that he moreover confirmed it by his judicial and pastoral authority.[4] These proceedings were preparatory to the coronation of the new queen,[5] which was performed with unusual magnificence, attended by all the nobility of England, and

[1] Heylin's Reformation, p. 177, edition of 1674.
[2] Rym. xiv. 467. Wilk. Con. 759. Cranmer's letter to Hawkyns, Archæol. xviii. 78. Ellis, ii. 36. Stat. Pap. i. 394—7. Both in the archbishop's judgment and the two statutes confirming it, the disputed fact of the nonsummation of the marriage between Arthur and Catherine is taken as proved.—Rym. ibid. Stat. 25 Hen. VIII. c. 12, 22. It appears from Bedyl's letter to Cromwell, that the whole process had been "devysed afore the kinge's grace," and that "my lord of Cauntrebury handled himself very well, and very uprightly without eny evydent cause of suspicion to be noted in him by the counsel of the lady Katerine, if she had had any present."—Stat. Pap. i. 395.
[3] Quid vero? says Pole in a letter to Cranmer, an non tecum ipse ridebas, cum tanquam severus judex regi minas intentares?—Poli Epist. de Sac. Euch. p. 6. Cremonæ, 1581.
[4] I conceive that, immediately after judgment pronounced by Cranmer, Henry and Anne were married again. Otherwise, Lee archbishop of York, and Tunstall bishop of Durham, must have asserted a falsehood, when they told Catherine, that "after his highness was discharged of the marriage made with her, he contracted new marriage with his dearest wife, Queen Anne."—Stat. Pap. i. 419. It is plain from all that precedes and follows this passage, that they mean, after the divorce publicly pronounced by Archbishop Cranmer. Of a private divorce preceding the marriage in January, neither they nor any others, their contemporaries, had any notion. But a second marriage, after the judgment of the court, was necessary, otherwise the issue of Anne could not have been legitimate. Henry had, indeed, been aware of the irregularity of marrying her before a divorce from Catherine; but he justified his conduct by declaring that he had examined the cause in "the court of his own conscience, which was enlightened and directed by the Spirit of God, who possesseth and directeth the hearts of princes;" and as he was convinced that "he was at liberty to exercise and enjoy the benefit of God for the procreation of children in the lawful use of matrimony, no man ought to inveigh at this his doing."—Burn. iii. Rec. 64. [5] Stat. Pap. i. 396.

celebrated with processions, triumphal arches, and tournaments. The honours paid to his consort gratified the pride of the king; her approaching parturition filled him with the hope of what he so earnestly wished, a male heir to the crown. He was under promise to meet Francis again in the course of the summer; but, unwilling to be absent on such an occasion, he despatched Lord Rochford to the French court, who, having first secured the good offices of the queen of Navarre, the sister of the king, solicited him in the name of Anne—for Henry wished to appear ignorant of the proceeding—to put off the intended interview till the month of April.[1] In the eighth month after the performance of the nuptial ceremony Anne bore the king a child; but that child, to his inexpressible disappointment, was a female, the princess Elizabeth, who afterwards ascended the throne.[2]

As soon as Cranmer had pronounced judgment, Catherine received an order from the king to be content with the style of dowager princess of Wales; her income was reduced to the settlement made on her by her first husband, Arthur; and those among her dependants who gave her the title of queen, were irrevocably dismissed from her service. Still to every message and menace she returned the same answer; that she had come a clean maid to his bed; that she would never be her own slanderer, nor own that she had been a harlot for twenty years; that she valued not the judgment pronounced at Dunstable at a time when the cause was still pending "by the king's license" at Rome; pronounced too, not by an indifferent judge, but by a mere shadow, a man of the king's own making; that no threats should compel her to affirm a falsehood; and that "she feared not those which have the power of the body, but Him only that hath the power of the soul." Henry had not the heart to proceed to extremities against her. His repudiated wife was the only person who could brave him with impunity.[3]

In foreign nations the lot of Catherine became the object of universal commiseration; even in England the general feeling was in her favour. The men, indeed, had the prudence to be silent; but the women loudly expressed their disapprobation of the divorce; till Henry, to check their boldness by the punishment of their leaders, committed to the Tower the wife of the viscount Rochford, and the sister-in-law of the duke of Norfolk. At Rome, Clement was daily importuned by Charles and Ferdinand to do justice to their aunt, by his own ministers to avenge the insult offered to the papal authority; but his irresolution of mind, and partiality for the king of England, induced him to listen to the suggestions of the French ambassadors, who advised more lenient and conciliatory measures. At length, that he might appear to do something, he annulled the sentence given by Cranmer, because the cause was at the very time pending before himself, and excommunicated Henry and Anne, unless they should separate before the end of September, or show cause by their attorneys why they claimed to be considered as husband and wife. When September came, he prolonged the term, at the request of the cardinal of Tournon, to the end of October; and embarking on board the French fleet, sailed to meet Francis at Marseilles, where he was assured, a reconciliation between

---

[1] Transcripts for N. Rymer, 178.
[2] State Pap. i. 407. Hall, 212. Cranmer's letter to Hawkyns, Archæol. xviii. 81. I may here observe that this was the last coronation during Henry's reign. Of his four following wives not one was crowned.
[3] State Pap. i. 397—404, 415—420. Collier, ii. Rec. xxv.

Henry and the church of Rome would be effected.[1] By the French monarch this reconciliation was most ardently desired, as a preliminary step to an offensive alliance against the emperor, under the sanction of the Holy See. But the mind of Henry perpetually wavered between fear and resentment. Sometimes his apprehension that Clement, in a personal conference, might debauch the fidelity of his ally, induced him to listen to the entreaties and remonstrances of Francis; at other times his love of wealth and authority, joined to his resentment for the repeated delays and refusals of the pontiff, urged him to an open breach with the see of Rome. In conformity indeed with the promise given at Calais, the duke of Norfolk had proceeded to France accompanied by the lord Rochford and Pawlet, Brown and Bryan, with a retinue of one hundred and sixty horsemen; but he was bound by secret instructions to dissuade the king from the intended interview, and to offer him a plentiful subsidy, on condition that he would establish a patriarch in his dominions, and forbid the transmission of money to the papal treasury. Francis replied that he could not violate the solemn pledge which he had already given; and doubted not that at Marseilles, with a little condescension on each side, every difficulty might be surmounted. The duke took his leave, assuring the king that the only thing which Clement could now do to reconcile himself with Henry was to annul the marriage with the lady Catherine; yet he was so impressed with the arguments of Francis, that he prevailed on his sovereign to send two ambassadors, the bishop of Winchester, and Bryan, to supply his place at the interview. They professed that they came to execute th orders of the French monarch; but were in reality unfurnished with powers to do any act, and only commissioned to watch the progress of the conferences, and to send the most accurate information to their own court. The truth was, that both Henry and Anne began to suspect the sincerity of Norfolk, and were ignorant whom to trust, or what measures to pursue.[2]

About the middle of October Clement made his public entry into Marseilles, and was followed the next day by the king of France. The two sovereigns met with expressions of respect and attachment; but the king pertinaciously refused to entertain any other question till he had received from the pope a promise that he would do in favour of Henry whatever lay within the extent of his authority. To his surprise and disappointment he now learned that the ambassadors were not authorized to treat either with the pontiff or himself; but at his solicitation they despatched a courier to request full powers; and in the interval a marriage was concluded between the duke of Orleans, the son of Francis, and Catherine of Medici, the pope's niece. In point of fortune it was a very unequal match; but the king, if we may believe his own assertion, had assented to it, in the hope of bringing to an amicable conclusion the quarrel between Henry and the Holy See.[3] The reconciliation seems to have been

---

[1] Herb. 386. Burnet, i. 132. Le Grand, iii. 569. It is remarkable that on the 9th of July, just two days before Clement annulled the judgment of Cranmer, Henry gave the royal assent to the suspended act, abolishing the payment of annates to the see of Rome.—Stat. of Realm, iii. 387. The reason assigned for the delay is—" that by some gentell wayes the said exaccions myght have byn redressed"—and the reason for the king's assent—" that the pope had made no answere of hys mynde therein."—Stat. of Realm, 462. [2] Burnet, iii. 74, 75. [3] Il se peut dire qu'il a pris une fille comme toute nue pour bailler à son second fils, chose toutes fois qu'il a si volontiers et

proposed on this basis; that each party should reciprocally revoke and forgive every hostile measure; and that the cause of the divorce should be brought before a consistory, from which all the cardinals holding preferment or receiving pensions from the emperor, should be excluded as partial judges. Clement had promised to return an answer to this project on the 7th of November; that very morning, Bonner, who had lately arrived from England, requested an audience; and the same afternoon he appealed in the name of Henry from the pope to a general council. Both Clement and Francis felt themselves offended. The former, besides the insult offered to his authority, began to suspect that he had been duped by the insincerity of the French monarch; the latter saw that he negotiated for Henry without possessing his confidence; and deemed the appeal a violation of the hospitality due to so exalted a guest under his own roof. Both yielded to the suggestions of their resentment; both afterwards relented. Clement affected to believe the assertion of the king, that the appeal opposed no new obstacle to a reconciliation; Francis despatched the bishop of Bayonne, now bishop of Paris, to Henry, to complain of his precipitation, and to request that he would consent to the renewal of the negotiation which had thus been interrupted.[2]

The reader is aware that this prelate possessed a high place in the esteem of the king of England. Henry listened to his advice, and gratefully accepted his offer to undertake the care of the royal interests in the court of Rome. Of the instructions with which he was furnished we are ignorant; but the English agents in that city were ordered to thank Clement for the assurances which he had made to the king of his friendship; to object on different grounds to the expedients which had been suggested; to propose that the royal cause should be tried in England, with an understanding that the judgment given there should receive the papal ratification; and to promise that on such conditions the kingdom should remain in full obedience to the Apostolic See. They were also informed that this was not a final resolution, but that Henry was prepared to make greater concessions in proportion to the readiness which Clement might show to serve him.[2] Stimulated by his hopes, the bishop of Paris hastened in the depth of winter to Rome; the French ambassador and the English agents seconded his endeavours; and so promising were the appearances, or so eager was his zeal, that he deceived himself with the assurances of success. To Francis he sent a list of the cardinals who would vote for the king of England; to Henry he wrote in terms of exultation, exhorting him to suspend for a few days all measures of a religious nature which might have been brought before parliament. The friends of Charles and Catherine were not less sanguine: at their solicitation a consistory was held on the twenty-third of March; the proceedings in the cause were explained by Simonetta, deputy auditor of the Rota; and out of two-and-twenty cardinals, nineteen decided for the validity of the marriage, and three only, Trivulzio, Pisani, and Rodolphi, proposed a further delay. Clement himself had not expected this result; but he acceded, though with reluctance, to the opinion of so numerous a majority; and a definitive sentence was pronounced, declaring the marriage lawful and valid, condemning the

---

si patiemment porté, par le bon gré qu'il pensoit avoir fait un grand gain en faisant cette perte.—Le Grand, iii. 581.

[1] Du Bellay's instructions, apud Le Grand, iii. 571—588. Burnet, iii. 82, 84. Records, p. 37—40. [2] Apud Burnet, iii. 84.

proceedings against Catherine of injustice, and ordering the king to take her back as his legitimate wife. The imperialists displayed their joy with bonfires, discharges of cannon, and shouts of Viva l'imperio, viva l'Espagna. The bishop and his colleagues were overwhelmed with astonishment and despair; while Clement himself forbade the publication of the decree before Easter, and consulted his favourite counsellors on the means the most likely to mollify the king of England, and to avert the effects of his displeasure.[1]

But in reality it mattered little whether Clement had pronounced in favour of Henry or against him. The die was already cast. The moment the bishop of Paris was departed, violent councils began to prevail in the English cabinet; and a resolution was taken to erect a separate and independent church within the realm. That prelate was indeed suffered to negotiate with the pontiff; but in the mean time act after act derogatory from the papal claims was debated, and passed in parliament; and the kingdom was severed by legislative authority from the communion of Rome long before the judgment given by Clement could have reached the knowledge of Henry.[2]

The charge of framing these bills, and of conducting them through the two houses, had been committed to the policy and industry of Cromwell, whose past services had been lately rewarded with a patent for life of the chancellorship of the Exchequer. 1. The submission, which during the last year had been extorted from the fears of the clergy, was now moulded into the form of a statute, while the preamble, which seemed to confine its duration to the present reign, was artfully omitted. In this state it passed the two houses, received the royal assent, and became part of the law of the land; but a most important clause had been added to it: "that all such canons and ordinances, as had been already made, and were not repugnant to the statutes and customs of the realm, or the prerogatives of the crown, should be used and enforced, till it should be otherwise determined according to the tenor and effect of the said act." To

---

[1] Le Grand, i. 273—276; iii. 630—638.
[2] It is generally believed on the authority of Fra Paolo and Du Bellay, the brother of the bishop of Paris, that this event was owing to the precipitation of Clement. We are told that the prelate requested time to receive the answer of Henry, which he expected would be favourable; that the short delay of six days was refused; and that two days after the sentence a courier arrived, the bearer of the most conciliatory despatches. Now it is indeed true that the bishop expected an answer to his letter, and probable that a courier arrived after the sentence: but, 1. It is very doubtful that he asked for a delay till the courier arrived. For in his own account of the proceedings he never mentions it; and instead of going to the consistory to demand it, was certainly absent, and went afterwards to the pope to ask the result. 2. It is certain that the answer brought by the courier was unfavourable; because all the actions of Henry about the time when he was despatched prove a determination to separate entirely from the papal communion. 3. The judgment given by Clement could not be the cause of that separation, because the bill abolishing the power of the popes within the realm was introduced into the commons in the beginning of March, was transmitted to the lords a week later, was passed by them five days before the arrival of the courier (March 20), and received the royal assent five days after his arrival in Rome (March 30).—See Lords' Journals, 75, 77, 82. It was not possible that a transaction in Rome on the 23rd could induce the king to give his assent on the 30th. There was, however, appended to the least important of these acts (that respecting the abolition of Peter-pence and licenses) a proviso that it should not be in force before the Nativity of St. John Baptist, unless the king by letters patent should so order it; and that, in the interval, he might according to his pleasure annul or modify it. The object probably was to keep open one subject of negotiation with Clement, and to prevent him from pronouncing judgment. But eight days later (April 7), as soon as the news from Rome arrived, Henry, by his letters patent, ordered that act to be put in execution.—See Stat. of Realm, iii. 471.

Henry it was sufficient that he possessed the power of modifying the ecclesiastical laws at pleasure; that power he never thought proper to exercise; and the consequence has been, that in virtue of the additional clause the spiritual courts have existed down to the present time. 2. The provisions of the late statute, prohibiting appeals to Rome in certain cases, were extended to all cases whatsoever; and in lieu of the right thus abolished, suitors were allowed to appeal from the court of the archbishop to the king in Chancery, who should appoint commissioners, with authority to determine finally in the cause. This occasional tribunal has obtained the name of the Court of Delegates. 3. In addition to the statute, by which the payment of annates had been forbidden, and which had since been ratified by the king's letters patent, it was enacted that bishops should no longer be presented to the pope for confirmation, nor sue out bulls in his court; but that, on the vacancy of any cathedral church, the king should grant to the dean and chapter, or to the prior and monks, permission to elect the person whose name was mentioned in his letters missive; that they should proceed to the election within the course of twelve days, under the penalty of forfeiting their right, which in that instance should devolve to the crown; that the prelate named or elected should first swear fealty; after which the king should signify the election to the archbishop, or, if there be no archbishop, to four bishops, requiring them to confirm the election, and to invest and consecrate the bishop elect, who might then sue his temporalities out of the king's hands, make corporal oath to the king's highness and to no other, and receive from the king's hands restitution of all the possessions and profits spiritual and temporal of his bishopric. 4. It was also enacted, that since the clergy had recognised the king for the supreme head of the church of England, every kind of payment made to the Apostolic Chamber, and every species of license, dispensation, and grant, usually obtained from Rome, should forthwith cease; that hereafter all such graces and indulgences should be sought of the archbishop of Canterbury; and that if any person thought himself aggrieved by the refusal of the archbishop, he might by a writ out of Chancery compel that prelate to show cause for his refusal. By these enactments, in the course of one short session was swept away what yet remained of the papal power in England; and that at a time when the judgment pronounced at Rome was not only not known, but probably not even anticipated by Henry.[1]

From the establishment of the king's supremacy the attention of parliament was directed to the succession to the crown; and by another act the marriage between Henry and Catherine was pronounced unlawful and null, that between him and Anne Boleyn lawful and valid; the king's issue by the first marriage was of course excluded from the succession, that by the second was made inheritable of the crown; to slander the said marriage, or seek to prejudice the succession of the heirs thereof, was declared high treason, if the offence were committed by writing, printing, or deed; and misprision of treason, if by words only; and all the king's subjects of full age, or who hereafter should be of full age, were commanded to swear obedience to the same act, under the penalty of misprision of treason.[2]

---

[1] Stat. 25 Hen. VIII. 19, 20, 21.
[2] Ibid. c. 22. Not content with exacting the submission of his own subjects, Henry ordered an instrument to be drawn up, which should be executed by the king of France, in which the latter declared that

This act deserves the particular notice of the reader. For the preservation of the royal dignity, and the security of the succession as by law established, it provided safeguards and created offences hitherto unknown; and thus stamped a new character on the criminal jurisprudence of the country. The statute itself was indeed swept away in the course of two or three years; but it served as a precedent to subsequent legislatures in similar circumstances; and regulations, of the same nature, but enforced with penalties of less severity, have been occasionally adopted down to the present times.

The king had now accomplished the two objects which had been promised by Cromwell; he had bestowed on his mistress the rights of a lawful wife, and had invested himself with the supremacy of the church. But the opposition which he had experienced strengthened his passions and steeled his heart against the common feelings of humanity. He was tremblingly alive to every rumour; his jealousy magnified the least hint of disapprobation into a crime against the state; and each succeeding year of his reign was stained with the blood of many, often of noble and innocent, victims. The first who suffered were implicated in the conspiracy attributed to Elizabeth Barton and her adherents. This young woman, a native of Aldington in Kent, was subject occasionally to fits, in the paroxysms of which she often burst into vehement and appalling exclamations, and periodically, about the beginning of December, to a trance of a few days' duration, after which she would narrate the wonders that she had seen in the world of spirits, under the guidance and tuition of an angel.[1] By the neighbours, her sufferings and sayings were attributed to some preternatural agency; she herself insensibly partook of the illusion; and Masters, the clergyman of the parish, advised her to quit the village and to enter the convent of St. Sepulchre in Canterbury. In her new situation her ecstasies and revelations were multiplied; and Archbishop Warham, at a loss to form a satisfactory judgment, appointed Bocking, a monk of Christchurch, her confessor. Bocking soon professed himself a believer in her inspired character; and both Sir Thomas More and Bishop Fisher appear to have gone over to his opinion. The maid grew less cautious in her predictions, and occasionally rose to higher and more dangerous matters. Whilst the great cause between Henry and Catherine was yet pending in the court of the legates, she informed Wolsey, at the command of her angel, that if he ventured to pronounce a divorce, God would visit him with the most dreadful chastisement; and after Wolsey's death she stated to her admirers, that God had shown to her an evil root buried in the earth, out of which three shoots had sprung; a vision interpreted to mean, that the king, and Norfolk, and Suffolk, were now carrying into execution the evil projects devised by the late cardinal. She even admonished Henry in per-

---

Henry's first marriage was null, the second valid; that Mary was illegitimate, Elizabeth legitimate; and promised most faithfully to maintain these assertions, even by force of arms if necessary, against all opponents. It is published by Burnet from a copy (iii. Rec. 84), but in all probability was never executed.

[1] A collection of these expressions had been made, and sent to the king, who showed it to Sir Thomas More, and asked his opinion:

"I told him," says More, "that in good faith I found nothing in these words that I could regard or esteem. For seeing that some part fell in rhythm, and that, God wot, full rude also, for any reason that I saw therein, a right simple woman might in my mind speak it of her own wit well enough."—More's Letter to Cromwell, apud Burnet, ii. Rec. p. 286. Another collection of her visions and prophecies may be seen in Strype, i. 177.

son, at the command of her angel, that if he were to marry Anne Boleyn, while Catherine was alive, he would no longer be looked upon as a king by God; but would die the death of a villein within a month, and be succeeded on the throne by his daughter Mary. Years had elapsed since Henry first heard of the woman, her visions, and prophecies; still he continued to treat her with ridicule and contempt. But, when he had publicly acknowledged his second marriage, he deemed it necessary to close her mouth and prevent the circulation of her predictions by severity of punishment. Barton was taken from her convent, and examined in private, first by Cranmer alone, and then by Cromwell and Cranmer together. That by dint of argument and authority they should draw from her an admission that her supposed revelations from heaven were the delusions of her own distempered brain, and that she felt a gratification in communicating them to others, is probable enough; and, in their official report, she is said to have confessed that "her predictions were feigned of her own imagination only, to satisfy the minds of them which resorted to her, and to obtain worldly praise."[1] The chief of her friends and advisers had been already apprehended: after several examinations, all were arraigned in the Star-chamber, and adjudged to stand during the sermon at St. Paul's Cross, and to confess the imposture. From the cross they were led back to prison, to await the royal pleasure. But the king was not satisfied: he determined that they should die; and thus leave behind them an awful warning to those who might feel disposed to make him the subject of their visions and prophecies.

A bill of attainder was brought into the house of lords, of attainder of treason against the maid, and her abettors, Bocking, Masters, Deering, Gold, Rich, and Risley; and of misprision of treason against Sir Thomas More, the bishop of Rochester, and others charged with having known of her predictions without revealing them to the king. To sustain the charge of treason, it was presumed, that the communicators of such prophecies must have had in view to bring the king into peril of his crown and life; and, if this were treason, it followed of course that to be acquainted with such facts, and yet conceal them, amounted to the legal offence of misprision of treason. The accused were not brought to trial. They had already confessed the imposture; and, if we may judge from similar proceedings during this reign, it would be contended that the traitorous object of such imposture could not be doubted. Still to attaint without trial, except in cases of open rebellion, was so inconsistent with men's notions, that at the third reading the lords resolved to inquire, whether it might stand with the good pleasure of the king that they should send for Sir Thomas More, and the rest of the accused, into the Star-chamber, and inquire what defence they could make. The answer is not recorded; but no defence was allowed.[2] The bill was read a fourth time and passed by the lords, and soon afterwards by the commons also. It had been written on paper; now it was delivered to the chancellor to be reduced into form, and engrossed on parchment; and in this state at the close of the session it received the royal assent. The parties attainted of treason suffered at Tyburn, where

---

[1] Stat. of Realm, iii. 448. Burnet, ii. Rec. 123, 286, 287; and Cranmer's letter in Todd, i. 89.

[2] In place of a defence, Henry permitted the name of Sir Thomas More to be scored out. So I collect, because his name is not mentioned after this.

Barton confessed her delusion, but threw the burden of her offence on her companions in punishment; she had been, she said, the dupe of her own credulity; but then she was only a simple woman, whose ignorance might be an apology for her conduct, while they were learned clerks, who, instead of encouraging, should have detected and exposed the illusion.

Among those who had been charged with misprision of treason, were two men of more elevated rank, Fisher, bishop of Rochester, and Sir Thomas More, lately lord chancellor. Fisher was far advanced in age, the last survivor of the counsellors of Henvy VII., and the prelate to whose care the countess of Richmond recommended on her death-bed the youth and inexperience of her royal grandson. For many years the king had revered him as a parent, and was accustomed to boast that no prince in Europe possessed a prelate equal in virtue and learning to the bishop of Rochester.[2] But his opposition to the divorce gradually effaced the recollection of his merit and services; and Henry embraced with pleasure this opportunity of humbling the spirit, or punishing the resistance of his former monitor.[3] It was asserted that he had concealed from the king his knowledge of Barton's predictions; and Cromwell sent to him message after message conceived in language most imperious and unfeeling, yet tempered with an assurance that he might obtain pardon by throwing himself without reserve on the royal mercy. But Fisher disdained to acknowledge guilt, when he knew himself to be innocent. He replied that, after suffering for six weeks under severe illness, he was unfit to stir from home; that to answer letters he found a very dangerous task; for let him write whatever he would, it was taken as a proof "of craft, or wilfulness, or affection, or unkindness;" and that "to touch upon the king's great matter" was to him forbidden ground. He was unwilling to give offence, or to betray his conscience. The consciences of others he did not condemn; but he knew that he could not be saved by any conscience but his own. Henry, however, was resolute; the name of Fisher was included in the bill of attainder for misprision of treason; and the bishop deemed it necessary to address to the lords a justificatory letter, in which he contended that there could be no offence against the law in believing, on the testimony of several good and learned men, that Barton was a virtuous woman; with this impression on his mind he had conversed with her, and heard her say, that the king would not live seven months after the divorce. He had not indeed communicated this discourse to his sovereign; but he had two reasons for his silence: 1. Because she spoke not of any violence to be offered to Henry, but of the ordinary visitations of Providence: 2. Because she assured him that she had already apprized the king of the revelation made to her; nor had he any reason to doubt her assertion, as he knew that she had been admitted to a private audience. He was therefore guiltless of any conspiracy. "He knew not, as he would answer before the throne of Christ, of any malice or evil that was intended by her or by any other earthly creature unto the king's highness." But the lords dared not listen to the voice of innocence in

---

[1] Lords' Journal, i. 72. Hall, 219—224. Godwin, 53, 54.

[2] Apol. Pol. p. 95. He adds that on one occasion the king turned round to him and said, "Be judicare me nunquam invenisse in universa peregrinatione mea, qui literis et virtute cum Roffense esset comparandus."—Ibid.

[3] I draw this inference from the peevish answer of Cromwell, published by Burnet, i. Records, ii. p. 123.

opposition to the royal pleasure; the bill was read a second time, and Fisher made an attempt to pacify the king by assuring him that, if he had not revealed to him the prediction of Barton, it was because he knew that Henry was already acquainted with it; and because, after "the grevouse letters and moche fearful wordes" addressed to him on account of his disapproval of the divorce, he was loth to venture into the royal presence with such a tale pertaining to the same matter; wherefore he begged this only favour, that the king would free him from his present anxiety, and allow him to prepare himself in quiet for his passage to another world. His prayers, however, and his reasoning were fruitless; he was attainted with the others, and compounded with the crown for his freedom and personalities in the sum of three hundred pounds.[1]

Sir Thomas More had ceased to fill the office of chancellor. By the king's desire he had discussed the lawfulness of the divorce with the Doctors Lee, Cranmer, Fox, and Nicholas; but the apparent weakness of their reasoning served only to convince him of the soundness of his own opinion; and at his earnest request, he was indulged in the permission to retire from the council-chamber as often as that subject was brought under consideration. Still in the execution of his office he found himself unavoidably engaged in matters which he could not reconcile with his conscience; and at length he tendered his resignation, on the ground that age and infirmity admonished him to give his whole attention to the concerns of his soul. Henry, who had flattered himself that the repugnance of More would gradually melt away, was aware how much his retirement would prejudice the royal cause in the mind of the public. But he deemed it prudent to suppress his feelings; dismissed the petitioner with professions of esteem, and promises of future favour; gave the seals to Sir Thomas Audeley, a lawyer of less timorous conscience; and ordered the new chancellor, at his installation, to pronounce an eulogy on the merits of his predecessor, and to express the reluctance with which the king had accepted his resignation.[2] From the court, More repaired to his house at Chelsea, where, avoiding all interference in politics, he devoted his whole time to study and prayer. Of Elizabeth Barton he had heard many speak with applause; once he had a short conversation with her himself in a chapel at Sion House, but refused to listen to any of her revelations; and on another occasion he wrote to her, advising her to abstain from speaking of matters of state, and to confine herself to subjects of piety in her communications with others. To her miraculous and prophetic pretensions he appears to have given no credit; but he looked upon her as a pious and virtuous woman, deluded by a weak and excited imagination. His letter, however, and the preceding interview, afforded a presumption that the ex-chancellor was also a party in the conspiracy; his name was introduced into the bill of attainder; nor was it till he had repeatedly written to the king and to Cromwell, protesting his innocence, and explaining the substance of his communication with the pretended prophetess, and till the archbishop, the chancellor, the duke of Norfolk, and Cromwell had solicited Henry on their knees, that he could appease the king's anger, and procure the erasure of his name

---

[1] See his original letters in Collier, ii. 87, and Arch. xxv. 89—93.
[2] Pole, fol. xcii. Audeley, if we may believe Marillac, the French ambassador, was grand vendeur de justice.—Le Grand, i. 224.

from the list of victims enumerated in the bill.[1]

The authority of Fisher and More was great, not only in England, but also on the continent; and the warmest opponents of the divorce were accustomed to boast that they followed the opinions of these two celebrated men. The experiment was now made, whether the danger to which they had been exposed had subdued their spirit. Within a fortnight after the attainder of Barton and her abettors, the bishop and the ex-chancellor were summoned before the council at Lambeth, and were asked whether they would consent to take the new oath of succession. But the act, the approval of which, "with all the whole effectes and contentes therof," was inserted in the oath, was not confined to the succession only; it embraced other matters of a very questionable nature; it taught that no power on earth could dispense within the degrees prohibited in the book of Leviticus, and that the marriage of Henry with Catherine had always been unlawful and of no effect. More, who was introduced the first, offered to swear to the succession alone, but not to every particular contained in the act, for reasons which prudence compelled him to suppress.[2] Fisher's answer was the same in substance. He divided the act into two parts. To that which regarded the succession he made no objection, because it came within the competence of the civil power; to the other part, of a theological nature, his conscience forbade him to subscribe. Both were remanded, that they might have more time for consideration. Cranmer advised that their oaths should be received with the limitations which they had proposed, on the ground that it would deprive the emperor and his adherents abroad, Catherine and her advocates at home, of the support which they derived from the example of Fisher and More.[3] But Henry preferred the opinion of Cromwell, and determined either to extort from them an unconditional submission, or to terrify their admirers by the severity of their punishment. The oath was therefore tendered to them a second time; and both, on their refusal to take it, were committed to the Tower.[1]

Whether it were from accident or design, the form of this oath of succession had not been prescribed by the statute; and Henry, taking advantage of the omission, modelled and remodelled it at his pleasure. From the members of parliament, and probably from the laity (it was required from both men and women),

---

[1] See his letters in his printed works, p. 1423—1428; Burnet's collection, tom.ii.p.286 —292; and Strype, i. App. 130; Ellis, ii. 48.

[2] He has given an interesting account of his examination in a letter. It was intimated to him that, unless he gave the reasons for his refusal, that refusal would be attributed to obstinacy. *More.* It is not obstinacy, but the fear of giving offence. Let me have sufficient warrant from the king, that he will not be offended, and I will explain my reasons. *Cromwell.* The king's warrant would not save you from the penalties enacted by the statute. *More.* In that case I will trust to his majesty's honour. But yet it thinketh me, that if I cannot declare the causes without peril, then to leave them undeclared is no obstinacy. *Cranmer.* You say that you do not blame any man for taking the oath. It is then evident that you are not convinced that it is blameable to take it; but you must be convinced that it is your duty to obey the king. In refusing therefore to take it, you prefer that which is uncertain to that which is certain. *More.* I do not blame men for taking the oath, because I know not their reasons and motives; but I should blame myself, because I know that I should act against my conscience. And truly such reasoning would ease us of all perplexity. Whenever doctors disagree, we have only to obtain the king's commandment for either side of the question, and we must be right. *Abbot of Westminster.* But you ought to think your conscience erroneous, when you have against you the whole council of the nation. *More.* I should, if I had not for me a still greater council, the whole council of Christendom.—More's Works, p. 1429, 1447.

[3] See the letters of Fisher and Cranmer to Cromwell (Strype's Cranmer, 13, 14)

he accepted a promise of allegiance to himself and his heirs, according to the limitations in the act; but from the clergy he required an additional declaration that the bishop of Rome had no more authority within the realm than any other foreign bishop, and a recognition that the king was the supreme head of the church of England, without the addition of the qualifying clause, which had been in the first instance admitted. The summer was spent in administering the oath, in receiving the signatures of the clergy and clerical bodies, and of the monks, friars, and nuns in the several abbeys and convents, and in obtaining formal decisions against the papal authority from both convocations and the two universities.[1]

In autumn the parliament assembled after the prorogation, and its first measure was to enact that the king, his heirs and successors, should be taken and reputed the only supreme heads on earth of the church of England,[2] with full power to visit, reform, and correct all such errors, heresies, abuses, contempts, and enormities, which by any manner of spiritual authority ought to be reformed or corrected. 2. To remedy the defect in the late act of succession, it was declared that the oath administered at the conclusion of the session was the very oath intended by the legislature, and that every subject was bound to take it under the penalties of the same act. 3. It was evident that the creation of this new office, of head of the church, would add considerably to the cares and fatigues of royalty: an increase of labour called for an increase of remuneration; and therefore, by a subsequent act for "the augmentation of the royal estate and the maintenance of the supremacy," the first fruits of all benefices, offices, and spiritual dignities, and the tenths of the annual income of all livings, were annexed to the crown for ever. 4. To restrain by the fear of punishment the adversaries of these innovations, it was made treason to wish or will maliciously,[3] by word or writing, or to attempt by craft, any bodily harm to the king or queen, or their heirs, or to deprive any of them of the dignity, style, and name of their royal estates, or slanderously and maliciously to publish or pronounce by words or writing that the king is a heretic, schismatic, tyrant, or infidel. 5. As an additional security, a new oath was tendered to the bishops, by which they not only abjured the supremacy of the pope, and acknowledged that of the king, but also swore never to consent that the bishop of Rome should have any authority within the realm; never to appeal, nor to suffer any other to appeal to him; never to write or send to him without the royal permission; and never to receive any message from him without communicating it immediately to the king. 6. If the reader think that Henry must be now satisfied, let him recollect the secret protest, the theological legerdemain, by which Cranmer pretended to nullify the oath of obedience which he was about to make to the pontiff. The king had been indeed privy to the artifice; but he was unwilling that it should be played off upon himself; and on that account he now exacted from each prelate a full and formal renunciation of every protest

---

[1] Wilk. Con. iii. 771, 774, 775. Rym. xiv. 487—527.

[2] Without the saving clause, "as far as the law of God will allow."

[3] It was not till after some struggle that the king yielded to the insertion of this qualification, "maliciously."—Arch. xxv. 795. It appears, however, that at More's trial the judges contrived to render it useless, by declaring that a refusal to acknowledge the supremacy was a proof of internal "malice."

previously made, which might be deemed contrary to the tenor of the oath of supremacy.[1] Penal statutes might enforce conformity; they could not produce conviction. The spiritual supremacy of a lay prince was so repugnant to the notions to which men had been habituated, that it was everywhere received with doubt and astonishment. To dispel these prejudices, Henry issued injunctions that the very word "pope" should be carefully erased out of all books employed in the public worship; that every schoolmaster should diligently inculcate the new doctrine to the children intrusted to his care; that all clergymen, from the bishop to the curate, should on every Sunday and holiday teach that the king was the true head of the church, and that the authority hitherto exercised by the popes was an usurpation, tamely admitted by the carelessness or timidity of his predecessors; and that the sheriffs in each county should keep a vigilant eye over the conduct of the clergy, and should report to the council the names, not only of those who might neglect these duties, but also those who might perform them indeed, but with coldness and indifference.[2] At the same time he called on the most loyal and learned of the prelates to employ their talents in support of his new dignity; and the call was obeyed by Sampson and Stokesley, Tunstall and Gardiner;[3] by the two former, as was thought, from affection to the cause, by the latter through fear of the royal displeasure. But though an appearance of conformity was generally obtained, there still remained men, chiefly among the three religious orders of Carthusians, Brigittins, and Franciscan Observants, who were neither to be reclaimed by argument, nor subdued by terror. Secluded from the commerce and the pleasures of the world, they felt fewer temptations to sacrifice their consciences to the command of their sovereign; and seemed more eager to court the crown, than to flee from the pains of martyrdom. When to

---

[1] St. 26 Hen. VIII. 1, 2, 3, 13. Wilk. Con. iii. 780, 782. It would appear that some of the prelates submitted with reluctance to this oath, and that threats were employed to enforce obedience.—See Archbishop Lee's letter to Cromwell (St. Pap. i. 428). He will do anything the king wishes, "So that our Lord bee not offended, and the unitie of the faiethe and of the Catholique Chyrche saved;" and with this he hopes "his highness wolbe content."

[2] Ibid. 772. Cranmer, as the first in dignity, gave the example to his brethren, and zealously inculcated from the pulpit what his learning or fanaticism had lately discovered, that the pontiff was the antichrist of the Apocalypse (Poli Ep. i. 444): an assertion which then filled the Catholic with horror, but at the present day excites nothing but contempt and ridicule.

[3] Reginald Pole, that he might take no share in these transactions, had retired to the north of Italy; but Henry sent him Sampson's work, and commanded him to signify his own sentiments on the same subject. Pole obeyed, and returned an answer in the shape of a large treatise, divided into four books, and afterwards entitled Pro Ecclesiasticæ Unitatis Defensione. Not content with replying to the theological arguments of Sampson, he described, in that style of declamatory eloquence in which he excelled, the vicious parts of the king's conduct since the commencement of his passion for Anne Boleyn. His Italian friends disapproved of this portion of the work; but he justified it on the ground that the fear of shame was more likely to make impression on the mind of Henry than any other consideration. In this perhaps he argued correctly; for the king, suppressing his resentment, made him advantageous offers if he would destroy the work; and Pole himself so far complied, that none of the injuries which he afterwards received from Henry could ever provoke him to publish it. That he wrote in this manner from affection, as he asserts, may be true: but it subjected him to the severe censures of his English friends, which have been followed by many writers since his death. On the other hand, he defended himself ably, and has found many defenders.—See his Epistles, i. 436, 441, 456, 471; his Apologia ad Angl. Parliamentum, i. 179; his Epistle to Edward VI. Ep. iv. 307 – 321, 340; Burnet, iii. Rec. 114—130; Strype, i. 188—223; and Quirini, Animadversio in Epist. Shelbornii, i—lxxx.

the reprimand which two Friars Observants, Peyto and Elstow, had received for the freedom of their sermons, Cromwell added, that they deserved to be inclosed in a sack, and thrown into the Thames, Peyto replied, with a sarcastic smile, "Threaten such things to rich and dainty folk, which are clothed in purple, fare deliciously, and have their chiefest hopes in this world. We esteem them not. We are joyful that for the discharge of our duty we are driven hence. With thanks to God we know that the way to heaven is as short by water as by land, and therefore care not which way we go."[1] Peyto and Elstow were dismissed; but it soon appeared that the whole order was animated with similar sentiments; and Henry deemed it necessary to silence, if he could not subdue, its opposition. All the Friars Observants were ejected from their monasteries, and dispersed, partly in different prisons, partly in the houses of the Friars Conventuals. About fifty perished from the rigour of their confinement; the rest, at the suggestion of Wriothesley, their secret friend and patron, were banished to France and Scotland.

But Henry soon proved that the late statute was not intended to remain a dead letter. The priors of the three charter-houses of London, Axeholm, and Belleval, had waited on Cromwell to explain their conscientious objections to the recognition of the king's supremacy. From his house he committed them to the Tower, and contended at their trial that such objections, by "depriving the sovereign of the dignity, style, and name of his royal estate," amounted to the crime of high treason.[2] The jury, however, would not be persuaded that men of such acknowledged virtue could be guilty of so foul an offence. When Cromwell sent to hasten their determination, they demanded another day to deliberate: though a second message threatened them with the punishment reserved for the prisoners, they refused to find for the crown; and the minister was compelled to visit them himself, to argue the case with them in private, and to call intimidation to the aid of his arguments, before he could extort from their reluctance a verdict of guilty. Five days later, the priors, with Reynolds, a monk of Syon, and Haile, a secular clergyman, suffered at Tyburn; and they were soon afterwards followed by three monks from the Charterhouse, who had solicited in vain that they might receive the consolations of religion previously to their deaths.[3] On all these the sentence of the law was executed with the most barbarous exactitude. They were suspended, cut down alive, embowelled, and dismembered.[4]

The reader will have observed that

[1] Stowe, 543. Collect. Anglo-Minoritics, p. 233. Pole observes that the three orders of Carthusians, Brigittins, and Observants (by this name the reformed Franciscans were meant) had at that period the greatest reputation for piety. Quosnam, he asks, habes, cum ab iis tribus discesseris, qui non prorsus ab instituti sui authoribus degeneraverint?—Pole, fol. ciii. He notices the banishment of the Observants, ibid.

[2] By the 26 Henry VIII. c. 1, the king was declared supreme head of the church, with the *style* and *title* thereof; by the same, c. xiii., it was made high treason to attempt by *words* or writing to deprive him "of the dignity, *style*, or *name*, of his royal estate."

[3] That the offence for which they suffered was the denial of the king's supremacy, is not only asserted by the ancient writers, but proved by the true bill found against two of them, John Rochester and James Whalworth, which is still extant.—Cleop. E. vi. f. 204. See Archæol. xxv. 84.

[4] The reader may see the sufferings of these, with those of the other Carthusian monks, in Chauncey's Historia aliquot nostr sæculi Martyrum, Moguntiæ, 1550. Also in Pole's Defensio Eccles. Unit. fol. lxxxiv; and his Apology to Cæsar, p. 98. He bears testimony to the virtue of Reynolds, with whom he was well acquainted, and who quod in paucissimis ejus generis hominum reperitur, omnium liberalium artium co-

the form of the oath, for the refusal of which More and Fisher were committed, had not then obtained the sanction of the legislature. But the two houses made light of the objection, and passed against them a bill of attainder for misprision of treason, importing the penalty of forfeiture and perpetual imprisonment.[1] Under this sentence More had no other resource for the support of life than the charity of his friends, administered by the hands of his daughter, Margaret Roper.[2] Fisher, though in his seventieth year, was reduced to a state of destitution, in which he had not even clothes to cover his nakedness. But their sufferings did not mollify the heart of the despot; he was reolved to triumph over their obstinacy, or to send them to the scaffold. With this view they were repeatedly and treacherously examined by commissioners, not with respect to any act done or any word uttered by them since their attainder, but with regard to their private opinions relative to the king's supremacy. If they could be induced to admit it, Henry would have the benefit of their example; should they deny it, he might indict them for high treason. Both answered with caution; the bishop, that the statute did not compel any man to reveal his secret thoughts; More, that under the attainder he had no longer any concern with the things of this world, and should therefore confine himself to the preparation of his soul for the other. Both hoped to escape the snare by evading the question; but Henry had been advised that a refusal to answer was proof of malice, and equivalent to denial; and a special commission was appointed to try the two prisoners on a charge of high treason. In the mean time news arrived that the pontiff, at a general promotion of cardinals, had named Fisher to the purple. To the person who brought him the intelligence the prisoner replied, that, "If the hat were lying at his feet, he would not stoop to take it up; so little did he set by it."[3] Henry, on the other hand, is reported to have exclaimed, "Paul may send him the hat, but I will take care that he have never a head to wear it on." Previously to trial more examinations took place, but nothing criminal was elicited; and therefore the searching and fatal questions were put to each: "Would he repute and take the king for supreme head of the church? Would he approve the marriage of the king with the most noble queen Anne to be good and lawful? Would he affirm the marriage with the lady Catherine to have been unjust and unlawful?" More replied, that to questions so dangerous he could make no answer: Fisher, that he should abide by his former answer to the first question; and that with respect to the second, he would obey the act, saving his conscience, and defend the succession as established by law; but to say absolutely Yea or No, from that he begged to be excused.[4] These replies sealed their doom.

The bishop was the first placed at the bar, and charged with having "falsely, maliciously, and traitorously wished, willed, and desired, and by craft imagined, invented, practised, and attempted to deprive the king of the dignity, title, and name of his

---

gnitionem non vulgarem habebat, eamque ex ipsis haustam foutibus (fol. ciii.)—See also Strype, i. 196.
[1] Stat. of Realm, iv. 527, 528.
[2] From the petition of More's "poore miserable wyffe and children," it appears that Henry at first allowed her to retain the moveables and the rents of the prisoner for their common support; but that after the passing of the last act, everything was taken from them.—See it in Mr. Bruce's inedited documents relating to Sir Thomas More (App. p. 11). [3] Archæol. xxv. 99.
[4] State Papers, i. 431—6.

royal estate, that is, of his title and name of supreme head of the church of England, in the Tower, on the 7th day of May last, when, contrary to his allegiance, he said and pronounced, in the presence of different true subjects, falsely, maliciously, and traitorously, these words: *The kyng oure soveraign lord is not supreme hedd yn erthe of the cherche of Englande.*"[1] If these words were ever spoken, it is plain, both from his habitual caution and the place where the offence is stated to have been committed, that they were drawn from him by the arts of the commissioners or their instruments, and could not have been uttered with the malicious and traitorous intent attributed to him.[2] He was, however, found guilty and beheaded. Whether it was that Henry sought to display his hatred for his former monitor, or to diffuse terror by the example of his death, he forbade the body to be removed from the gaze of the people. The head was placed on London Bridge; but the trunk, despoiled of the garments, the perquisite of the executioner, lay naked on the spot till evening, when it was carried away by the guards and deposited in the churchyard of All Hallows Barking.[3]

The fate of Fisher did not intimidate his fellow victim. To make the greater impression on the people, perhaps to add to his shame and sufferings, More was led on foot, in a coarse woollen gown, through the most frequented streets, from the Tower to Westminster Hall. The colour of his hair, which had lately become grey, his face, which, though cheerful, was pale and emaciated, and the staff, with which he supported his feeble steps, announced the rigour and duration of his confinement. At his appearance in this state at the bar of that court in which he was wont to preside with so much dignity, a general feeling of horror and sympathy ran through the spectators. Henry dreaded the effect of his eloquence and authority; and therefore, as if it were meant to distract his attention and overpower his memory, the indictment had been framed of enormous length and unexampled exaggeration, multiplying the charges without measure, and clothing each charge with a load of words, beneath which it was difficult to discover its real meaning. As soon as it had been read, the chancellor, who was assisted by the duke of Norfolk, Fitzjames the chief justice, and six other commissioners, informed the prisoner that it was still in his power to close the proceedings and to recover the royal favour by abjuring his former opinion. With expressions of gratitude he declined the favour, and commenced a long and eloquent defence. Though, he observed, it was not in his power to recollect one-third part of the indictment, he would endeavour to show that he had not offended against the statute, nor sought to oppose the wishes of the sovereign. He must, indeed, acknowledge that he had always disapproved of the king's marriage with Anne Boleyn, but then he had never communicated that disapprobation to any other person than the king himself, and not even to the king till Henry had commanded him on his

---

[1] I quote these words of the indictment from Archæol. xxv. 94, because it has been sometimes asserted that Fisher suffered, not for the denial of the supremacy, but for other, though unknown, acts of treason.

[2] It is possible that the words charged in the indictment may have been extracted from the "certain answer which he had once given, and to which, if it were the king's pleasure, he was yet content to stand."—State Papers, i. 431. That answer prudence forbade him to repeat before the commissioners.

[3] Mortui corpus nudum prorsus in loco supplicii ad spectaoulum populo relinqu. mandaverat.—Poli Apol. ad Cæs. 96. Hall, 230. Fuller, 205. In this account of Bishop Fisher, I am greatly indebted to a very interesting memoir by Mr. Bruce in Archæologia, vol. xxv.

allegiance to disclose his real sentiments. In such circumstances to dissemble would have been a crime, to speak with sincerity was a duty. The indictment charged him with having traitorously sought to deprive the king of his title of head of the church. But where was the proof? That, on his examination in the Tower he had said, he was by his attainder become civilly dead; that he was out of the protection of the law, and therefore could not be required to give an opinion of the merits of the law; and that his only occupation was and would be to meditate on the passion of Christ, and to prepare himself for his own death. But what was there of crime in such an answer? It contained no word, it proved no deed against the statute. All that could be objected against him was silence; and silence had not yet been declared treason. 2. It was maintained that in different letters written by him in the Tower he had exhorted Bishop Fisher to oppose the supremacy. He denied it. • Let the letters be produced; by their contents he was willing to stand or fall. 3. But Fisher on his examination had held the same language as More, a proof of a conspiracy between them. What Fisher had said, he knew not: but it could not excite surprise if the similarity of their case had suggested to each similar answers. This he could affirm with truth, that, whatever might be his own opinion, he had never communicated it to any, not even to his dearest friends.

But neither innocence nor eloquence could avert his fate. Rich, the solicitor-general, afterwards Lord Rich, now deposed, that in a private conversation in the Tower, More had said: "The parliament cannot make the king head of the church, because it is a civil tribunal without any spiritual authority." It was in vain that the prisoner denied this statement, showed that such a declaration was inconsistent with the caution which he had always observed, and maintained that no one acquainted with the former character of Rich would believe him even upon his oath; it was in vain that the two witnesses, who were brought to support the charge, eluded the expectation of the accuser by declaring that, though they were in the room, they did not attend to the conversation; the judges maintained that the silence of the prisoner was a sufficient proof of malicious intention; and the jury, without reading over the copy of the indictment which had been given to them, returned a verdict of guilty. As soon as judgment of death had been pronounced, More attempted, and, after two interruptions, was suffered to address the court. He would now, he said, openly avow, what he had hitherto concealed from every human being, his conviction that the oath of supremacy was unlawful. It was, indeed, painful to him to differ from the noble lords whom he saw on the bench; but his conscience compelled him to bear testimony to the truth. This world, however, had always been a scene of dissension; and he still cherished a hope that the day would come when both he and they, like Stephen and Saul, would be of the same sentiment in heaven. As he turned from the bar, his son threw himself on his knees and begged his father's blessing; and as he walked back to the Tower, his daughter Margaret twice rushed through the guards, folded him in her arms, and, unable to speak, bathed him with her tears.

He met his fate with constancy, even with cheerfulness. When he was told that the king, as a special favour, had commuted his punishment to decapitation, "God," he he replied, "preserve all my friends from such favours." On the scaffold the executioner asked his forgiveness. He kissed him, saying, "Thou wilt render me to-day the greatest service in the power of any mortal: but" (putting an angel into his hand) "my neck is so short that I fear thou wilt gain little credit in the way of thy profession." As he was not permitted to address the spectators, he contented himself with declaring that he died a faithful subject to the king, and a true Catholic before God. His head was fixed on London Bridge.[1]

By these executions the king had proved that neither virtue nor talent, neither past favour nor past services, could atone in his eyes for the great crime of doubting his supremacy. In England the intelligence was received with deep but silent sorrow; in foreign countries with loud and general execration.[2] The names of Fisher and More had long been familiar to the learned; and no terms were thought too severe to brand the cruelty of the tyrant by whom they had been sacrificed. But in no place was the ferment greater than in Rome. They had fallen martyrs to their attachment to the papal supremacy; their blood called on the pontiff to punish their persecutor. Clement died ten months before, and Paul had hitherto followed the cautious policy of his predecessor; but his prudence was now denominated cowardice; and a bull against Henry was extorted from him by the violence of his counsellors. In this extraordinary instrument, in which care was taken to embody every prohibitory and vindictive clause invented by the most aspiring of his predecessors, the pontiff, having first enumerated the offences of the king against the Apostolic See, allows him ninety, his fautors and abettors sixty days to repent, and appear at Rome in person or by attorney; and then, in case of default, pronounces him and them excommunicated; deprives him of his crown; declares *his* children by Anne, and *their* children by their legitimate wives, incapable of inheriting for several generations; interdicts his and their lands and possessions; requires all clerical and monastic bodies to retire out of Henry's territories; absolves his subjects and their tenants from the oaths of allegiance and fidelity; commands them to take up arms against their former sovereign and lords; dissolves all treaties and alliances between

---

[1] Ep. Gul. Corvini in App. ad Epist. Erasmi, p. 1768. Pole, lxxxix–xciii. Roper, 48. More, 242. Stapleton, Vit. Mor. 335. Lettere di Princ. i. 134. State Trials, i. 59, edit. 1730. His death spread terror through the nation. On the 24th of August Erasmus wrote to Latomus, that the English lived under such a system of terror, that they dared not write to foreigners, nor receive letters from them. Amici, qui me subinde literis et muneribus dignabantur, metu nec scribunt nec mittunt quicquam, neque quicquam a quoquam recipiunt, quasi sub omni lapide dormiat scorpius (p. 1509).

[2] Ipse vidi multorum lacrymas, qui nec viderant Morum, nec ullo officio ab eo affecti fuerant.—Ep. Corvini, p. 1769. See also Pole, Ep. iv. 317, 318. The king of France spoke also of these executions with great severity to the ambassador, and advised that Henry should banish such offenders rather than put them to death. Henry was highly displeased. He replied that they had suffered by due course of law; and "were well worthy, if they had a thousand lives, to have suffered ten times a more terrible death and execution than any of them did suffer."—Burnet, iii. Rec. 81. Several letters were written to the ambassadors abroad, that they might silence these reports to the king's prejudice, by asserting that both Fisher and More had been guilty of many and heinous treasons. But in no one instance were these treasons particularized. That they amounted in fact to nothing more than a refusal of acknowledging the king's supremacy, is plain from the indictment of Fisher already noticed, and from that of More, which is in the inquisitio post mortem, lately edited by Mr. Bruce, App. 12—16, and Archæol. xxv. 370—4. That indictment charges him with saying, in answer to the question of the king's supremacy, "that it was lyke a swerde with two edges," on May 7th and June 3rd, and of denying it to Sir Richard Rich on June 12th, and thus attempting regem de dignitate, titulo et nomine supremi capitis in terra Anglicanæ ecclesiæ penitus deprivare. No treason on any other subject is mentioned.

Henry and other powers as far as they may be contradictory to this sentence: forbids all foreign nations to trade with his subjects, and exhorts them to capture the goods, and make prisoners of the persons, of all such as still adhere to him in his schism and rebellion.[1]

But when Paul cast his eyes on the state of Europe, when he reflected that Charles and Francis, the only princes who could attempt to carry the bull into execution, were, from their rivalry of each other, more eager to court the friendship than to risk the enmity of the king of England, he repented of his precipitancy. To publish the bull could only irritate Henry and bring the papal authority into contempt and derision. It was therefore resolved to suppress it for a time; and this weapon, destined to punish the apostasy of the king, was silently deposited in the papal armoury, to be brought forth on some future opportunity, when it might be wielded with less danger and with greater probability of success.[2]

[1] Bullar. Rom. i. 704, edit. 1673.
[2] Bullar. Rom. i. 708, edit. 1673.

CHAPTER II.

PROGRESS OF THE REFORMATION.

I. KING'S SUPREMACY—ITS NATURE—CROMWELL MADE VICAR-GENERAL—BISHOPS TAKE OUT NEW POWERS——II. DISSOLUTION OF MONASTERIES—LESSER MONASTERIES SUPPRESSED—DEATH OF QUEEN CATHERINE—ARREST, DIVORCE, AND EXECUTION OF ANNE—INSURRECTION IN THE NORTH—POLE'S LEGATION—GREATER MONASTERIES GIVEN TO THE KING——III. DOCTRINE—HENRY'S CONNECTIONS WITH THE LUTHERAN PRINCES—ARTICLES—INSTITUTION OF A CHRISTIAN MAN—DEMOLITION OF SHRINES—PUBLICATION OF THE BIBLE——IV. PERSECUTION OF LOLLARDS—ANABAPTISTS—REFORMERS—TRIAL OF LAMBERT—POLE'S SECOND LEGATION—EXECUTION OF HIS RELATIONS——V. STRUGGLE BETWEEN THE TWO PARTIES—STATUTE OF THE SIX ARTICLES—MARRIAGE WITH ANNE OF CLEVES—DIVORCE—FALL OF CROMWELL—MARRIAGE WITH CATHERINE HOWARD—HER EXECUTION—STANDARD OF ENGLISH ORTHODOXY.

I. HENRY had now obtained the great object of his ambition. His supremacy in religious matters had been established by act of parliament; it had been admitted by the nation at large—the members of every clerical and monastic body had confirmed it by their subscriptions, and its known opponents had atoned for their obstinacy by suffering the penalties of treason. Still the extent of his ecclesiastical pretensions remained subject to doubt and discussion. That he meant to exclude the authority hitherto exercised by the pontiffs was sufficiently evident; but most of the clergy while they acknowledged the new title assumed by the king, still maintained that the church had inherited from her founder the power of preaching, of administering the sacraments, and of enforcing spiritual discipline by spiritual censures,—a power which, as it was not derived from, so neither could it be dependent on, the will of the civil magistrate. Henry himself did not clearly explain, perhaps knew not how to explain, his own sentiments. If on the one hand he was willing to push his ecclesiastical prerogative to its utmost limits, on the other he was checked by the contrary tendency of those principles which he had published and maintained in his treatise against Luther. In his answer to the objections proposed to him by the convocation at York, he clothed his meaning in ambiguous language, and carefully eluded the real point in discussion. "As to spiritual things," he observed, "meaning the sacraments, being by God ordained as instruments of efficacy and strength, whereby grace is of his infinite goodness conferred upon his people, for as much as they be no worldly or temporal things, they have no worldly or temporal head, but only Christ." But then with respect to those who administer the sacraments, "the persons of priests, their laws, their acts, their manner of living, for as much as they be indeed all temporal, and concerning this present life only, in those we, as we be called, be indeed in this realm caput, and, because there is no man above us here, supremum caput."[1]

Another question arose respecting the manner in which the supremacy was to be exercised. As the king had neither law nor precedent to guide him, it became necessary to determine the duties which belonged to him in his new capacity, and to establish an additional office for the conduct of ecclesiastical affairs. At its head was placed the man whose counsels had first suggested the attempt, and whose industry had brought it to a successful termination. Cromwell already held the offices of chancellor of the exchequer and of first secretary to the king. He was, after some delay, appointed "the royal vicegerent, vicar-general, and principal commissary, with all the spiritual authority belonging to the king as head of the church, for the due administration of justice in all cases touching the ecclesiastical jurisdiction, and the godly reformation and redress of all errors, heresies, and abuses in the said church."[2] As a proof of the high estimation in which Henry held the supremacy, he allotted to his vicar the precedence of all the lords spiritual and temporal, and even of the great officers of the crown. In parliament Cromwell sat before the archbishop of Canterbury; he superseded that prelate in the presidency of the convocation. It was with difficulty that the clergy suppressed their murmurs when they saw at their head a man who had never taken orders, nor graduated in any university; but their indignation increased when they found that the same pre-eminence was claimed by any of his clerks, whom he might commission to attend as his deputy at their meetings.[3]

Their degradation, however, was not yet consummated. It was resolved to probe the sincerity of their submission, and to extort from them a practical acknowledgment that they derived no authority from Christ, but were merely the occasional delegates of the crown. We have on this subject a singular letter, from Leigh and Ap Rice, two of the creatures of Cromwell, to their master. On the ground that the plenitude of ecclesiastical jurisdiction was vested in him as vicar-general, they advised that the powers of all the dignitaries of the church should be suspended for an indefinite period. If the prelates claimed authority by divine right, they would then be compelled to produce their proofs; if they did not, they must petition the king for the restoration of their powers, and thus acknowledge the crown to be the real fountain of spiritual jurisdiction.[4]

---

[1] Wilk. Con. iii. 764.
[2] St. 31 Hen. VIII. 10. Wilk. Con. iii. 791. Collier, ii. Rec. p. 21.
[3] Collier, ii. 119.
[4] Collier, ii. 105. Strype, I. App. 144.

This suggestion was eagerly adopted; the archbishop, by a circular letter, informed the other prelates, that the king, intending to make a general visitation, had suspended the powers of all the ordinaries within the realm; and these, having submitted with due humility during a month, presented a petition to be restored to the exercise of their usual authority. In consequence a commission was issued to each bishop separately, authorizing him, during the king's pleasure, and as the king's deputy, to ordain persons born within his diocese, and admit them to livings; to receive proof of wills; to determine causes lawfully brought before ecclesiastical tribunals; to visit the clergy and laity of the diocese; to inquire into crimes, and punish them according to the canon law; and to do whatever belonged to the office of a bishop besides those things which, according to the sacred writings, were committed to his charge. But for this indulgence a most singular reason was assigned; not that the government of bishops is necessary for the church, but that the king's vicar-general, on account of the multiplicity of business with which he was loaded, could not be everywhere present, and that many inconveniences might arise, if delays and interruptions were admitted in the exercise of his authority.[1]

II. Some years had elapsed since the bishop of Paris had ventured to predict that whenever the cardinal of York should forfeit the royal favour, the spoliation of the clergy would be the consequence of his disgrace. That prediction was now verified. The example of Germany had proved that the church might be plundered with impunity; and Cromwell had long ago promised that the assumption of the supremacy should place the wealth of the clerical and monastic bodies at the mercy of the crown.[2] Hence that minister, encouraged by the success of his former counsels, ventured to propose the dissolution of the monasteries, and the motion was received with welcome by the king, whose thirst for money was not exceeded by his love of power; by the lords of the council, who already promised themselves a considerable share in the spoils; and by Archbishop Cranmer, whose approbation of the new doctrines taught him to seek the ruin of those establishments which proved the firmest supports of the ancient faith. The conduct of the business was intrusted to the superior cunning and experience of the favourite, who undertook to throw the mask of religious zeal over the injustice of the proceedings.

With this view a general visitation of the monasteries was enjoined by the head of the church; commissioners of inquiry by his lay vicar were selected; and to these in pairs were allotted particular districts for the exercise of their talents and industry. The instructions which they received breathed a spirit of piety and reformation, and were formed on the model of those formerly used in episcopal and legatine visitations; so that to men not intrusted with the secret, the object of Henry appeared, not the abolition, but the support and improvement of the monastic institute.[3] But the visitors themselves were not men of high standing or

---

[1] The suspension is in Collier, ii. Rec. p. 22; the form of restoration of episcopal powers in Burnet, i. Rec. iii. No. xiv. The latter was issued to different bishops in October (Harmer, 52). See also Collier, ii. Rec. p. 33. A similar grant was afterwards made to all new bishops, before they entered on the exercise of their authority.

[2] Poli Apol. ad Cæs. 121.

[3] The inquiries, amounting to eighty-six questions, were drawn up by Dr. Layton; and to these were added injunctions in twenty-six articles, to be left in each house by the visitors. Both are to be found in Cleop. E. iv. 12—24. The injunctions regard the papal power, the supremacy, the suc-

reputation in the church. They were clerical adventurers of very equivocal character, who had solicited the appointment, and had pledged themselves to effect, as far as it might be possible, the object of that appointment, that is, the extinction of the establishments which they should visit.[1] They proceeded at first to the lesser houses only. There they endeavoured by intimidation to extort from the inmates a surrender of their property to the king; and, when intimidation failed, were careful to collect all such defamatory reports and information as might afterwards serve to justify the suppression of the refractory brotherhood. With respect to their chief object, the visitors were unsuccessful. During the whole winter they could procure the surrender of no more than seven houses;[2] but from their reports a statement was compiled and laid before the parliament, which, while it allotted the praise of regularity to the greater monasteries, described the less opulent as abandoned to sloth and immorality. To some men it appeared contrary to experience that virtue should flourish most where the temptations to vice were more numerous, and the means of indulgence more plentiful; but they should have recollected that the abbots and priors of the more wealthy houses were lords of parliament, and therefore present to justify themselves and their communities; the superiors of the others were at a distance, unacquainted with the charges brought against them, and of course unable to clear their own characters, or to expose the arts of their accusers.

A bill was introduced, and hurried, though not without opposition, through the two houses,[3] giving to the king and his heirs all monastic establishments the clear yearly value of which did not exceed two hundred pounds, with the property belonging to them, both real and personal, vesting the possession of the buildings and lands in those persons to whom the king should assign them by letters patent, but obliging the grantees, under the penalty of ten marks per month, to keep on them an honest house and household, and to plough the same number of acres which had been ploughed on an average of the last twenty years. It was calculated that by this act about three hundred and eighty communities would be dissolved; and that an addition of thirty-two thousand pounds would be made to the yearly revenue of the crown, besides the present receipt

---

cession to the crown, the internal discipline of the monastery, its revenues, and the giving of alms. The sixteenth teaches the difference between the ceremonies and the substance of religious worship; and seems to have furnished the model for six of the surrenders published by Rymer, xiv. 610—612.

[1] I will transcribe the letter of Dr. Layton: "Pleaset yowe to understand, that whereas ye intende shortly to visite, and belike shall have many suiters unto yowe for the same, to be your commissioners, if hit might stond with your pleasure that Dr. Lee and I might have committed unto us the north contre, and to begyn in Lincoln dioces northwards here from London, Chester dioces, Yorke, and so furth to the bouder of Scotlande, to ryde downe one syde, and come up the other. Ye shall be well and faste assuryede that ye shall neither fynde monk, chanone, &c. that shall do the kyng's hygness so good servys, nether be so trusty, trewe, and faithfull to yowe. Ther ys nether monasterie, sell, priorie, nor any other religiouse howse in the north, but other Dr. Lee or I have familiar acquaintance within x or xii mylls of hyt, so that no knaverie can be hyde from us.........we know and have experience both of the fassion of the contre and rudeness of the pepul."—Cleop. E. iv. fol. 11.

[2] These were in Kent, Langdon, Folkstone, Bilsington, and St. Mary's in Dover; Merton in Yorkshire; Hornby in Lancashire; and Tiltey in Essex.—Ibid. 555-558. See a letter from the visitors in Strype, i. 260.

[3] Spelman tells us that it stuck long in the house of commons, and would not pass till the king sent for the Commons, and told them he would have the bill pass, or take off some of their heads.—Hist. of Sacrilege, p. 183.

of one hundred thousand in money, plate, and jewels.

This parliament by successive prorogations had now continued six years, and, by its obsequious compliance with every intimation of the royal will, had deserved, if any parliament could deserve, the gratitude of the king. To please him it had altered the succession, had new modelled the whole frame of ecclesiastical government, and had multiplied the prerogatives, and added to the revenue of the crown. It was now dissolved; and commissioners were named to execute the last act for the suppression of the smaller monasteries. Their instructions ordered them to proceed to each house within a particular district, to announce its dissolution to the superior and the brotherhood, to make an inventory of the effects, to secure the convent seal and the title-deeds, and to dispose of the inhabitants according to certain rules. But the statute which vested these establishments in the king, left it to his discretion to found them anew,—a provision which, while it left a gleam of hope to the sufferers, drew considerable sums of money into the pockets of Cromwell and his deputies. The monks of each community flattered themselves with the expectation of escaping from the general shipwreck, and sought by presents and annuities to secure the protection of the minister and the visitors. On the other hand, the favourites, to whom Henry had already engaged to give or sell the larger portion of these establishments, were not less liberal in their offers, nor less active in their endeavours to hasten the dissolution.[1]

The result of the contest was, that more than a hundred monasteries obtained a respite from immediate destruction; and of these the larger number were founded again by the king's letters patent, though each of them paid the price of that favour by the surrender of a valuable portion of its possessions. With respect to the suppressed houses, the superior received a pension for life; of the monks, those who had not reached the age of twenty-four were absolved from their vows, and sent adrift into the world without any provision; the others were divided into two classes. Such as wished to continue in the profession, were dispersed among the larger monasteries; those who did not, were told to apply to Cranmer or Cromwell, who would find them employments suited to their capacities. The lot of the nuns was more distressing. Each received a single gown from the king, and was left to support herself by her own industry, or to seek relief from the charity and commiseration of others.[2]

During the suppression of these establishments, the public attention had been in a great measure diverted to a succession of most important events,—the death of Catherine, the divorce and execution of Anne Boleyn, and the king's marriage with Jane Seymour.

1. During the three last years Catherine with a small establishment[3] had resided on one of the royal manors.

---

[1] Cromwell made a rich harvest during the whole time of the suppression.—See letters on the subject, Cleop. E. iv. fol. 135, 146, 205, 216, 220, 257, 264, 269.
[2] See Burnet, 192, 222, Rec. iii. p. 142, 157; Rym. xiv. 574. Stevens has published an interesting document, containing the names of those houses which had obtained a respite from instant destruction, the names of the persons to whom they had been granted, and the names of such as had been confirmed or founded again at the time when the paper was written. Forty-six had been certainly confirmed; the writer had his doubts respecting five others; and out of this number thirty-three had previously been promised by Henry to different persons.—Stevens, Monast. ii. App. p. 17. From the surrenders which were afterwards made, it appears that several more in the catalogue were confirmed after the date of the document.
[3] In one of her letters she observes, that she had not even the means of riding out.—Hearne's Sylloge, at the end of Titus Livius, p. 77

In most points she submitted without a murmur to the royal pleasure; but no promise, no intimidation could induce her to forego the title of queen, or to acknowledge the invalidity of her marriage, or to accept the offer made to her by her nephew, of a safe and honourable asylum either in Spain or Flanders. It was not that she sought to gratify her pride, or to secure her personal interests; but she still cherished a persuasion that her daughter Mary might at some future period be called to the throne, and on that account refused to stoop to any concession which might endanger or weaken the right of the princess. In her retirement she was harassed with angry messages from the king: sometimes her servants were discharged for obeying her orders; sometimes were sworn to follow the instructions which they should receive from the court. Forest, her confessor, was imprisoned and condemned for high treason; the act of succession was passed to defeat her claim; and she believed that Fisher and More had lost their lives merely on account of their attachment to her cause. Her bodily constitution was gradually enfeebled by mental suffering; and feeling her health decline, she repeated a request, which had often been refused, that she might see her daughter, once at least before her death; for Mary, from the time of the divorce, had been separated from the company,[1] that she might not imbibe the principles of her mother. But at the age of twenty she could not be ignorant of the injuries which both had suffered; and her resentment was daily strengthened by the jealousy of a hostile queen, and the caprice of a despotic father.[2] Henry had the cruelty to refuse this last consolation to the unfortunate Catherine,[3] who from her death-bed dictated a short letter to "her most dear lord, king, and husband." She conjured him to think of his salvation; forgave him all the wrongs which he had done her; recommended their daughter Mary to his paternal protection; requested that her three maids might be provided with suitable marriages, and that her other servants might receive a year's wages. Two copies were made by her direction, of which one was delivered to Henry, the other to Eustachio Chapuys, the imperial ambassador, with a request that, if her husband should refuse, the emperor would reward her servants. As he perused the letter, the stern heart of Henry was softened; he even shed a tear, and desired the ambassador to bear to her a kind and consoling message. But she died before his arrival; and was buried by the king's direction with becoming pomp in the abbey church of Peterborough.[4] The reputation which she had acquired on the throne

[1] At the commencement of their separation, Catherine wrote to her a letter of advice:—"I beseech you agree to God's pleasure with a merry heart, and be you sure, that without fail he will not suffer you to perish, if you beware to offend him......... Answer the king's message with a few words, obeying the king your father in everything save only that you will not offend God, and lose your soul.........And now you shall begin, and by likelyhood I shall follow. I set not a rush by it; for when they have done the uttermost they can, then I am sure of the amendment. I pray you recommend me unto my good lady of Salisbury, and pray her to have a good heart, for we never come to the kingdom of Heaven but by troubles."—Apud Burnet, ii. Records, p. 243.

[2] One great cause of offence was that she persisted in giving to herself the title of princess, and refused it to the infant Elizabeth, whom she called nothing but sister. On this account she was banished from court, and confined to different houses in the country.—See two of her letters in Foxe, tom. ii. lib. ix. p. 131; and in Hearne's Titus Livius, p. 144.
[3] Cum hoc idem filia cum lacrymis postularet, mater vix extremum spiritum ducens flagitaret, quod hostis nisi crudelissimus nunquam negasset, conjux a viro, mater pro filia, impetrari non potuit.—Poli Apol. ad Carol. 182.
[4] Sanders, 144. Herbert, 432. Heylin's Reform. 179. Her will is published by Strype, i. App. 160. See Appendix, U.

did not suffer from her disgrace. Her affability and meekness, her piety and charity, had been the theme of universal praise; the fortitude with which she bore her wrongs raised her still higher in the estimation of the public.

2. Four months did not elapse before Catherine was followed to the grave by Anne Boleyn. But their end was very different. The divorced queen died peaceably in her bed; her successful rival died by the sword of the headsman on the scaffold. The obstinacy of Henry had secured, as long as the divorce was in agitation, the ascendancy of Anne; but when that obstacle was removed, his caprice sought to throw off the shackles which he had forged for himself. His passion for her gradually subsided into coldness and neglect; and the indulgent lover became at last a suspicious and unfeeling master. Thus in the beginning of 1535 we accidentally discover her deeply in disgrace with him, and pitifully imploring the aid of the king of France to reconcile her with her husband. For that purpose she had employed Gontier, a gentleman belonging to the French embassy, from whose despatch we learn that on his return to England, he waited on the king and queen at Greenwich in the withdrawing-room after dinner. Having paid his compliment to Henry, he presented to Anne, who was sitting at a distance, a letter from Montmorency, the prime minister of Francis. She read it with evident marks of disappointment and alarm. Why, she asked Gontier, had he tarried so long? His stay in France had engendered doubts, suspicions, and strange imaginings in the mind of the king her husband.[1] It was necessary that Montmorency and his master should remove them immediately, for she was now on the brink of ruin. If Francis did not take her cause in hand, she was a distracted, a lost woman. She was in greater pain and distress than *before her marriage*.[2] But she could not, she said, speak to him as fully as she wished. Her agitation was too visible, and the eyes of the king and the whole company were fixed upon her. She dared not write to him, nor see him again, nor converse with him any longer. With these words, she turned aside. Henry immediately walked into the ballroom; the dancing began, and the queen remained unnoticed behind.[3] We have no clue to the misunderstanding between the parties; but it is plain from this graphic description in the despatch of Gontier, that Anne did not always enjoy, amidst the splendours of royalty, those halcyon days which she had anticipated.

But whatever were her griefs at that time, they passed away, and were forgotten. She thought no more of becoming a lost woman, and at the death of Catherine made no secret of her joy. Out of respect for the Spanish princess, the king had ordered his servants to wear mourning on the day of her burial; but Anne dressed herself in robes of yellow silk, and openly declared that she was now indeed a queen, since she had no longer a competitor. In this, however, she was fatally deceived. Among her maids was one named Jane Sey-

---

[1] Doutes, etranges pensemens—doutes et soupscons.—Le Laboureur, i. 405.

[2] Qu'elle ne demeure affolee et perdue; car elle se voit proche de cela, et plus en peine et ennuy que paravant ses espousailles. Does not this message to Francis, that "she was in greater distress now than before her marriage," seem to import that she had experienced the friendly aid of the French king on some past occasion of distress, which had been removed by her marriage. The reader will recollect how earnestly and covertly she had requested him to invite her, as it were spontaneously, to the interview of the two monarchs in 1532.—See vol. iv. p. 277.

[3] See Le Laboureur, i. 405. Palamedes Gontier was secretary to Philippes de Chabot, admiral of France.

mour, the daughter of a knight of Wiltshire, who, to equal or superior elegance of person, added a gentle and playful disposition, as far removed from the Spanish gravity of Catherine as from that levity of manner which Anne had acquired in the French court. In the midst of her joy the queen accidentally discovered Seymour sitting on the king's knee. The sight awakened her jealousy; in a few days she felt the pains of premature labour, and was delivered of a dead male child. To Henry, who most anxiously wished for a son, the birth of Elizabeth had proved a bitter disappointment; on this, the second failure of his hopes, he could not suppress his vexation. Anne is reported to have answered, that he had no one to blame but himself, that her miscarriage had been owing to his fondness for her maid.[1]

Unfortunately, if Henry had been unfaithful, she herself, by her levity and indiscretion, had furnished employment to the authors and retailers of scandal. Reports injurious to her honour had been circulated at court; they had reached the ear of Henry, and some notice of them had been whispered to Anne herself. The king, eager to rid himself of a woman whom he no longer loved, referred these reports to the council; and a committee was appointed to inquire into the charges against the queen. It consisted of the lord chancellor, the dukes of Norfolk and Suffolk, her own father, and several earls and judges; who reported that sufficient proof had been discovered to convict her of incontinence, not only with Brereton, Norris, and Weston, of the privy chamber, and Smeaton, the king's musician, but even with her own brother Lord Rochford.[2] They began with Brereton, whom they summoned on the Thursday before May-day, and committed immediately to the Tower. The examination of Smeaton followed on the Sunday, and the next morning he was lodged in the same prison. On that day the Lord Rochford appeared as principal challenger in a tilting match at Greenwich, and was opposed by Sir Henry Norris as principal defendant. The king and Anne were both present; and it is said that, in one of the intervals between the courses, the queen, through accident or design, dropped her handkerchief from the balcony; that Norris, at whose feet it fell, took it up and wiped his face with it; and that Henry instantly changed colour, started from his seat, and retired. This tale was probably invented to explain what followed: but the match was suddenly interrupted; and the king rode back to Whitehall with only six persons in his train, one of whom was Norris, hitherto an acknowledged favourite both with him and the queen. On the way Henry rode with Norris apart, and earnestly solicited him to deserve pardon by the confession of his guilt. He refused, strongly maintaining his innocence, and, on his arrival at Westminster, was conducted to the Tower.

Anne had been left under custody at Greenwich. The next morning she received an order to return by water; but was met on the river by the lord chancellor, the duke of Norfolk, and Cromwell, who informed her that she had been charged with infidelity to the king's bed. Falling on her knees, she prayed aloud that if she were guilty, God might never grant her pardon. They delivered her to Kyngstone, the lieutenant of the Tower. Her brother Rochford had already been sent there; Weston and

---

[1] Sanders, 147. Heylin, 263. Wyat in Singer's Cavendish, 443.
[2] His name was George. He had been summoned to the first parliament after her marriage with Henry by the style of George Bullen de Rochford, chevalier.

Smeaton followed; and preparations were made to bring all the prisoners to immediate trial.[1]

From the moment of her confinement at Greenwich, Anne had foreseen her fate, and abandoned herself to despair. Her affliction seemed to produce occasional aberrations of intellect. Sometimes she would sit absorbed in melancholy, and drowned in tears; and then suddenly assume an air of unnatural gaiety, and indulge in immoderate bursts of laughter. To those who waited on her she said that she should be a saint in heaven; that no rain would fall on the earth till she were delivered from prison; and that the most grievous calamities would oppress the nation in punishment of her death. But at times her mind was more composed; and then she gave her attention to devotional exercises, and for that purpose requested that a consecrated host might be placed in her closet. The apartment allotted for her prison was the same in which she had slept on the night before her coronation. She immediately recollected it, saying that it was too good for her; then falling on her knees, exclaimed, "Jesus, have mercy on me!" This exclamation was succeeded by a flood of tears, and that by a fit of laughter. To Kyngstone, the lieutenant of the Tower, she protested, "I am as clear from the company of man, as for sin, as I am clear from you. I am told that I shall be accused by three men; and I can say no more but nay, though you should open my body." Soon afterwards she exclaimed in great anguish, "O! Norris hast thou accused me? Thou art in the Tower with me; and thou and I shall die together. And thou, Mark [Smeaton], thou art here too; Mr. Kyngstone" (turning to the lieutenant), "I shall die without justice." He assured her, that if she were the poorest subject in the realm, she would still have justice; to which she replied with a loud burst of laughter.

Under the mild administration of justice at the present day, the accused is never required to condemn himself; but in former times every artifice was employed to draw matter of proof from the mouth of the prisoner by promises and threats, by private examinations in the presence of commissioners, and ensnaring questions put by the warders and attendants. Whatever was done or uttered within the walls of the Tower, was carefully recorded, and transmitted to the council. Mrs. Cosin, one of the ladies appointed to wait on the queen, asked, why Norris had said to her almoner on Saturday last, that he could swear for her that she was a good woman. Anne replied: "Marry, I bade him do so; for I asked him why he did not go through with his marriage; and he made answer that he would tarry a time. Then, said I, You look for dead men's shoes; for, if aught but good should come to the king" (Henry was afflicted with a dangerous ulcer in the thigh), "you would look to have me. He denied it; and I told him that I could undo him, if I would." But it was of Weston that she appeared to be most apprehensive, because he had told her that Norris frequented her company for *her* sake, and not, as was pretended, to pay his addresses to Madge, one of her maids; and when she reproached him with loving a kins-

---

[1] Rochford, Weston, and Norris had stood high in the king's favour. The two first often played with him for large sums at shovelboard, dice, and other games, and also with the lady Anne.—Privy Purse Expenses, passim. Norris was the only person whom he allowed to follow him into his bed-chamber.— Archæol. iii. 155. Smeaton, though of mean origin, was in high favour with Henry. He is mentioned innumerable times in the Privy Purse Expenser.

woman of hers more than his own wife, he had replied that he loved *her* better than both the others. When Mrs. Stonor, another attendant, observed to her that Smeaton was treated more severely than the other prisoners, for he was in irons, she replied that the reason was, because he was not a gentleman by birth; that he had never been in her chamber but once, and that was to play on a musical instrument; and that she had never spoken to him from that day till the last Saturday, when she asked him why he appeared so sad, and he replied that a look from her sufficed him.[1]

Of the five male prisoners four persisted in maintaining their innocence before the council. Smeaton, on his first examination, would admit only some suspicious circumstances; but on the second he made a full disclosure of guilt, and even Norris, yielding to the strong solicitation of Sir William Fitzwilliam, followed his example. Anne had been interrogated at Greenwich. With her answers we are not acquainted; but she afterwards complained of the conduct of her uncle Norfolk, who, while she was speaking, shook his head, and said, " Tut, tut." She observed enigmatically, that Mr. Treasurer was all the while in the forest of Windsor; and added that Mr. Comptroller alone behaved to her as a gentleman. At times she was cheerful, laughed heartily, and ate her meals with a good appetite. To Kyngstone she said, " If any man accuse me, I can say but nay: and they can bring no witness."[2]

I have related these particulars, extracted from the letters of the lieutenant, that the reader may form some notion of the state of the queen's mind during her imprisonment, and some conjecture respecting the truth or falsehood of the charge on which she suffered. From them it is indeed plain that her conduct had been imprudent; that she had descended from her high station to make companions of her men-servants; and that she had even been so weak as to listen to their declarations of love. But whether she rested here, or abandoned herself to the impulse of licentious desire, is a question which probably can never be determined. The records of her trial and conviction have mostly perished, perhaps by the hands of those who respected her memory; and our judgment is held in suspense between the contradictory and unauthenticated statements of her friends and enemies. By some we are told that the first disclosure was made by a female in her service, who, being detected in an unlawful amour, sought to excuse herself by alleging the example of her mistress; by others that the suspicion of the king was awakened by the jealousy of Lady Rochford, whose husband had been discovered either lying on, or leaning over, the bed of his sister. But that which wrought conviction in the royal mind was a deposition made upon oath by the lady Wingfield on her death-bed; of which the first lines only remain, the remainder having been accidentally or designedly destroyed.[3] This, however, with the depositions of the other witnesses, was

---

[1] These particulars are taken from the letters of the lieutenant, and may be seen in Herbert, 446; Burnet, i. 199; Strype, i. 280—283; and Ellis, ii. 53—62.

[2] Strype, i. 282, and the letters of Cromwell and Baynton, Heylin, 264. I have not noticed Anne's letter to the king, supposed to be written by her in the Tower; because there is no reason for believing it authentic. It is said to have been found among Cromwell's papers, but bears no resemblance to the queen's genuine letters in language or spelling, or writing or signature. — See Fiddes, 197.

[3] Burnet, i. 197. We still possess the most important of the few documents seen by Burnet, and some others of which he was ignorant, particularly Constantyne's Memoir in Archæol. xxiii.

embodied in the bill of indictment, and submitted to the grand juries of Kent and Middlesex, because the crimes laid to the charge of the prisoners were alleged to have been committed in both counties.[1] The four commoners were arraigned in the court of King's Bench. Smeaton pleaded guilty; Norris recalled his previous confession; all were convicted, and received sentence of death.[2]

But the case of the queen was without precedent in English history; and it was determined to arraign her before a commission of lords, similar to that which had condemned the late duke of Buckingham. The duke of Norfolk was appointed high steward, with twenty-six peers as assessors, and opened the court in the hall of the Tower. To the bar of this tribunal, the unhappy queen was led by the constable and lieutenant, and was followed by her female attendants. The indulgence of a chair was granted to her dignity or weakness. The indictment stated that, inflamed with pride and carnal desires of the body, she had confederated with her brother, Lord Rochford, and with Norris, Brereton, Weston, and Smeaton, to perpetrate divers abominable treasons; that she had permitted each of the five to lie with her several times; that she had said that the king did not possess her heart; and had told each of them in private, that she loved him better than any other man, to the slander of the issue begotten between her and the king; and that she had, in union with her confederates, imagined and devised several plots for the destruction of the king's life. According to her friends, she repelled each charge with so much modesty and temper, such persuasive eloquence, and convincing argument, that every spectator anticipated a verdict of acquittal; but the lords, satisfied perhaps with the legal proofs furnished by the confession of Smeaton, and the conviction of the other prisoners, pronounced her guilty on their honour; and the lord high steward, whose eyes streamed with tears whilst he performed the unwelcome office, condemned her to be burnt or beheaded at the king's pleasure. Anne, according to the testimony or the fiction of a foreign poet, instantly burst into the following exclamation:—"O! Father, O! Creator, thou knowest I do not deserve this death." Then addressing herself to the court, "My lords, I do not arraign your judgment. You may have sufficient reason for your suspicions; but I have always been a true and faithful wife to the king."[3] As soon as she was removed, her

---

[1] In the indictment the offence with Norris was laid on 12th Oct. 1533, that with Brereton on the 8th Dec. of the same year, with Weston on 20th May, 1534, with Smeaton on 26th April, 1535, with her brother on the 5th Nov. of the same year. We are indebted to the industry of Mr. Turner for the discovery both of the indictment, and the preceding commission among the Birch MSS. 4293.

[2] The records of these trials have perished; but if the reader consider with what promptitude, and on what slight presumptions (see the subsequent trials of Dereham and Culpeper) juries in this reign were accustomed to return verdicts for the crown, he will hesitate to condemn these unfortunate men on the sole ground of their having been convicted. The case of Smeaton was indeed different. He confessed the adultery; but we know not by what arts of the commissioners, under what influence of hope or terror, that confession was obtained from him. It should be remembered that the rack was then in use for prisoners of Smeaton's rank in life.

[3] It is extraordinary that we have no credible account of the behaviour of this unfortunate queen on her trial. There can be no doubt that she would maintain her innocence, and therefore I have admitted into the text that exclamation, which is generally attributed to her. It comes to us, however on very questionable authority, that of Meteren, the historian of the Netherlands, who says that he transcribed it from some verses in the Platt-Deutsch language, by Crispin, lord of Milherbe, a Dutch gentleman present at the trial: so that Burnet himself has some doubt of its truth.

brother occupied her place, was convicted on the same evidence, and condemned to lose his head, and to be quartered as a traitor.[1]

By the result of this trial the life of Anne was forfeited to the law; but the vengeance of Henry had prepared for her an additional punishment in the degradation of herself and her daughter. On the day after the arrest of the accused, he had ordered Cranmer to repair to the archiepiscopal palace at Lambeth, but with an express injunction that he should not venture into the royal presence. That such a message at such a time should excite alarm in the breast of the archbishop, will not create surprise; and the next morning he composed a most eloquent and ingenious epistle to the king. Prevented, he said from addressing his grace in person, he deemed it his duty to exhort him in writing, to bear with resignation this, the bitterest affliction that had ever befallen him. As for himself, his mind was clean amazed. His former good opinion of the queen prompted him to think her innocent; his knowledge of the king's prudence and justice induced him to believe her guilty. To him she had proved, after the king, the best of benefactors; wherefore he trusted that he might be allowed to wish and pray that she might establish her innocence; but if she did not, he would repute that man a faithless subject, who did not call for the severest punishment on her head, as an awful warning to others. He loved her formerly, because he thought that she loved the gospel;[2] if she were guilty, every man would hate her in proportion to his love of the gospel. Still he hoped that as the king had not begun the Reformation through his affection for her, but through his love of the truth, he would not permit her misconduct to prejudice that important work in his opinion. But the alarm of the archbishop was without any real foundation. Henry had no other object than to intimidate, and by intimidating to render him more ductile to the royal pleasure. He had already written, but had not despatched his letter, when he was summoned to meet certain commissioners in the Star-chamber, who laid before him the proofs of the queen's offence, and acquainted him with the duty which was expected from him. He had formerly dissolved the marriage between Henry and Catherine; he was now required to dissolve that between Henry and Anne.[3]

It must have been a most unwel-

"I leave it thus," says he, "without any other reflection upon it, but that it seems all over credible."—Burnet, iii. 181, edit. Nares.

[1] Burnet, i. 201, 202; iii. 119; St. 28 Henry VIII. 7. It is supposed that the charge of conspiracy against the king's life was introduced into the indictment merely for form; yet I observe that the lord chancellor takes it as proved in his speech to the two houses of parliament in presence of Henry. He reminds them twice of the great danger to which the king had been exposed during his late marriage, from the plots laid for his life by Anne and her accomplices.—Journals, p. 84.

[2] From this and similar expressions the queen has been represented a Protestant. She was no more a Protestant than Henry. It is plain from several circumstances that his religion was hers. The word "gospel" in the archbishop's letter meant nothing more, or the use of it would have accelerated her ruin.

[3] The letter is published by Burnet (i. 200), and certainly does credit to the ingenuity of the archbishop in the perilous situation in which he thought himself placed: but I am at a loss to discover in it any trace of that high courage, and chivalrous justification of the queen's honour, which have drawn forth the praises of Burnet and his copiers. In the postscript the archbishop adds: "They" (the commissioners) "have declared unto me such things, as your grace's pleasure was they should make me privy unto; for the which I am most bounden unto your grace. And what communication we had together, I doubt not but that they will make the true report thereof unto your grace. I am exceedingly sorry that such faults can be proved by the queen, as I heard of their relation; and I am and ever shall be your faithful subject.'

come and painful task. He had examined that marriage juridically; had pronounced it good and valid; and had confirmed it by his authority as metropolitan and judge. But to hesitate would have cost him his head. He acceded to the proposal with all the zeal of a proselyte; and, adopting as his own the objections to its validity with which he had been furnished, sent copies of them to both the king and queen, "for the salvation of their souls," and the due effect of law; with a summons to each to appear in his court, and to show cause why a sentence of divorce should not be pronounced. Never, perhaps, was there a more solemn mockery of the forms of justice, than in the pretended trial of this extraordinary cause. By the king Dr. Sampson was appointed to act as his proctor; by the queen, the doctors Wotton and Barbour were invested with similar powers; the objections were read; the proctor on one part admitted them, those on the other could not refute them; both joined in demanding judgment: and two days after the condemnation of the queen by the peers, Cranmer, "having previously invoked the name of Christ, and having God alone before his eyes," pronounced definitively that the marriage formerly contracted, solemnized, and consummated between Henry and Anne Boleyn was, and always had been, null and void.[1] The whole process was afterwards laid before the members of the convocation, and the houses of parliament. The former presumed not to dissent from the decision of the metropolitan; the latter were willing that in such a case their ignorance should be guided by the learning of the clergy. By both the divorce was approved and confirmed. To Elizabeth, the infant daughter of Anne, the necessary consequence was, that she, like her sister, the daughter of Catherine, was reputed illegitimate.[2]

On the day on which Cranmer pro-

But what was this report, which they were to make to the king from him? The sequel seems to show that it regarded the course to be pursued in pronouncing the divorce.

[1] Several questions rose out of this judgment. 1. If it were good in law, Anne had never been married to the king. She could not, therefore, have been guilty of adultery, and consequently ought not to be put to death for that crime. 2. If the same judgment were good, the act of settlement became null, because it was based on the supposition of a valid marriage; and all the treasons created by that act were at once done away. 3. If the act of settlement were still in force, the judgment itself, inasmuch as it "slandered and impugned the marriage," was an act of treason. But Anne derived no benefit from these doubts. She was executed, and the next parliament put an end to all controversy on the subject by enacting, that offences made treason by the act, should be so deemed if committed before the 8th of June; but that the king's loving subjects concerned in the prosecution of the queen in the archbishop's court, or before the lords, should have a full pardon for all treasons by them in such prosecution committed.—Stat. of Realm, iii. 658.

[2] See the record in Wilkins (Con. iii. 803). Burnet, unacquainted with this instrument, which, he asserts, was burnt, informs us that the divorce was pronounced in consequence of an alleged precontract of marriage between Anne and Percy, afterwards earl of Northumberland; that the latter had twice solemnly denied the existence of such contract on the sacrament; but that Anne, through hope of favour, was induced to confess it. That Percy denied it, is certain from his letter of the 13th of May (Burn. i. Rec. iii. 49); that Anne confessed it, is the mere assertion of the historian, supported by no authority. It is most singular that the real nature of the objection on which the divorce was founded is not mentioned in the decree itself, nor in the acts of the convocation, nor in the act of parliament, though it was certainly communicated both to the convocation and the parliament. If the reader turn to p. 232, 243, vol. iv. he will find that the king had formerly cohabited with Mary, the sister of Anne Boleyn; which cohabitation, according to the canon law, opposed the same impediment to his marriage with Anne, as had before existed to his marriage with Catherine. On this account he had procured a dispensation from Pope Clement; but that dispensation, according to the doctrine which prevailed after his separation from the communion of Rome, was of no force; and hence I am inclined to believe that the real ground of the divorce pronounced by Cranmer, was Henry's pre-

nounced judgment the companions of the queen were led to execution. Smeaton was hanged; the other four, on account of their superior rank, were beheaded. The last words of Smeaton, though susceptible of a different meaning, were taken by his hearers for a confession of guilt. "Masters," said he, "I pray you all, pray for me, for I have deserved the death." Norris was obstinately silent; Rochford exhorted the spectators to live according to the gospel; Weston lamented his past folly in purposing to give his youth to sin, and his old age to repentance; Brereton, who, says an eye-witness, was innocent if any of them were, used these enigmatical words:—"I have deserved to die, if it were a thousand deaths; but the cause wherefore I die, judge ye not. If ye judge, judge the best."[1]

To Anne herself two days more were allotted, which she spent for the most part in the company of her confessor. On the evening before her death, falling on her knees before the wife of the lieutenant, she asked her for a last favour, which was, that Lady Kyngstone would throw herself in like manner at the feet of the lady Mary, and would in Anne's name beseech her to forgive the many wrongs which the pride of a thoughtless unfortunate woman had brought upon her. We learn from Kyngstone himself, that she displayed an air of greater cheerfulness than he had ever witnessed in any person in similar circumstances; that she had required him to be present when she should receive "the good lord," to the intent that he might hear her declare her innocence; and that he had no doubt she would at her execution proclaim herself "a good woman for all but the king." If, however, such were her intention, she afterwards receded from it. The next morning the dukes of Suffolk and Richmond, the lord mayor and aldermen, with a deputation of citizens from each company, assembled by order of the king on the green within the Tower. About noon the gate opened, and Anne was led to the scaffold, dressed in a robe of black damask, and attended by her four maids. With the permission of the lieutenant, she thus addressed the spectators: "Good Christian people, I am not come here to excuse or justify myself, forasmuch as I know full well that aught which I could say in my defence doth not appertain to you, and that I could derive no hope of life for the same. I come here only to die, and thus to yield myself humbly to the will of my lord the king. And if in life I did ever offend the king's grace, surely with my death do I now atone for the same. I blame not my judges, nor any other manner of person, nor anything save the cruel law of the land by which I die. But be this, and be my faults as they may, I beseech you all, good friends, to pray for the life of the king, my sovereign lord and

---

vious cohabitation with Mary Boleyn; that this was admitted on both sides; and that in consequence the marriage with Anne, the sister of Mary, was judged invalid.—See Appendix, W.

- Constantyne's Memoir in Archæol. xxiii. 63—66. It may be observed that in none of these declarations, not even in that of Smeaton, is there any express admission, or express denial of the crime for which these unfortunate men suffered. If they were guilty, is it not strange that not one out of five would acknowledge it? If they were not, is it not still more strange, that not one of them should proclaim his innocence, if not for his own sake, at least for the sake of that guiltless woman who was still alive, but destined to suffer for the same cause in a few days? The best solution, in my opinion, is to suppose that no person was allowed to speak at his execution without a solemn promise to say nothing in disparagement of the judgment under which he suffered. We know that, if the king brought a man to trial, it was thought necessary for the king's honour that he should be convicted; probably, when he suffered, it was thought equally for the king's honour that he should not deny the justice of his punishment.

yours, who is one of the best princes on the face of the earth, and who has always treated me so well that better cannot be; wherefore I submit to death with a good will, humbly asking pardon of all the world." She then took her coifs from her head, and covered her hair with a linen cap, saying to her maids, "I cannot reward you for your service, but pray you to take comfort for my loss. Howbeit, forget me not. Be faithful to the king's grace, and to her whom with happier fortune you may have for your queen and mistress. Value your honour before your lives; and in your prayers to the Lord Jesus, forget not to pray for my soul." She now knelt down; one of her attendants tied a bandage over her eyes, and, as she exclaimed, "O Lord God, have mercy upon my soul," the executioner, with one blow of his sword, severed her head from the body. Her remains, covered with a sheet, were placed by her maids in an elm chest, brought from the armoury, and immediately afterwards buried within the chapel of the Tower.[1]

Thus fell this unfortunate queen, within four months after the death of Catherine. To have expressed a doubt of her guilt during the reign of Henry, or of her innocence during that of Elizabeth, would have been deemed a proof of disaffection. The question soon became one of religious feeling, rather than of historical disquisition. Though she had departed no further than her husband from the ancient doctrine, yet, as her marriage with Henry led to the separation from the communion of Rome, the Catholic writers were eager to condemn, the Protestant to exculpate, her memory. In the absence of those documents which alone could enable us to decide with truth, I will only observe that the king must have been impelled by some most powerful motive to exercise against her such extraordinary, and, in one supposition, such superfluous rigour. Had his object been (we are sometimes told that it was) to place Jane Seymour by his side on the throne, the divorce of Anne without her execution, or the execution without the divorce, would have effected his purpose. But he seems to have pursued her with insatiable hatred. Not content with taking her life, he made her feel in every way in which a wife and a mother could feel. He stamped on her character the infamy of adultery and incest; he deprived her of the name and the right of wife and queen; and he even bastardized her daughter, though he acknowledged that daughter to be his own. If then he were not assured of her guilt, he must have discovered in her conduct some most heinous cause of provocation, which he never disclosed. He had wept at the death of Catherine; but, as if he sought to display his contempt for the memory of Anne, he dressed himself in white on the day of her execution, and was married to Jane Seymour the next morning.

For two years Mary, his daughter

---

[1] Compare Constantyne's Memoir, who was present, with the letter of a Portuguese gentleman, who wrote soon afterwards to a friend in Lisbon, in Excerpta Hist. 264. The speech in the text is taken from him: that in Constantyne is as follows: "Good people, I do not intend to reason my death, but I remit me to Christ wholly, in whom is my trust; desiring you all to pray for the king's majesty, that he may long reign over you; for he is a very noble prince, and full gently hath handled me." In both the substance is the same; but probably what one has dilated the other has condensed. Plain, however, it is that Anne, like her fellow sufferers, chose to leave the question of her guilt or innocence problematical. I may add that the Portuguese writer is certainly in error when he supposes Smeaton to have been beheaded; and that he only relates the reports of the day, when he says that the council had pronounced the queen's daughter the child of Lord Rochford, and that the king had owned Mary for his legitimate heir.—Ibid. 265.

by Catherine, had lived at Hunsdon, a royal manor, in a state of absolute seclusion from society. Now, taking advantage of a visit from Lady Kyngstone, who had probably been allowed to deliver the message from Anne Boleyn, she solicited the good offices of Cromwell, and received from him a favourable answer.[1] It was not that the heartless politician felt any pity for the daughter of Catherine; but he had persuaded himself that both Mary and Elizabeth, though bastards by law, might, if they were treated as princesses in fact, be married, to the king's profit, into the families of some of the continental sovereigns.[2] Through his intercession she was permitted to write to her father; her letters, the most humble and submissive that she could devise, were never noticed; she again consulted Mr. Secretary, followed his advice, and adopted his suggestions and corrections;[3] but Henry was resolved to probe her sincerity, and instead of an answer, sent to her a deputation with certain articles in writing to which he required her signature. From these her conscience recoiled; but Cromwell subdued her scruples by a most unfeeling and imperious letter. He called her "an obstinate and obdurate woman, deserving the reward of malice in the extremity of mischief;" if she did not submit, he would take his leave of her for ever, "reputing her the most ungrateful, unnatural, and obstinate person living, both to God and her father;" and ended with saying, that by her disobedience she had rendered herself "unfit to live in a Christian congregation, of which he was so convinced, that he refused the mercy of Christ if it were not true."[4] Intimidated and confounded, she at last consented to acknowledge that it was her duty to observe all the king's laws; that Henry was the head of the church; and that the marriage between her father and mother had been incestuous and unlawful.[5] It was then required that she should reveal the names of the persons who had advised her former obstinacy and her present submission; but the princess indignantly replied, that she was ready to suffer death rather than expose any confidential friend to the royal displeasure. Henry relented; he permitted her to write to him; and granted her an establishment more suitable to her rank.[6] But though she was received into favour, she was not restored in blood. The king had called a parliament to repeal the last, and to pass a new act of succession, entailing his crown on his issue by his queen Jane Seymour.

---

[1] "I perceived that nobody durst speak for me as long as that woman lived, who is now gone, whom I pray our Lord of his great mercy to forgive. Wherefore now she is gone, I desire you for the love of God to be a suitor for me to the king's grace......... Accept mine evil writing; for I have not done so much this two year or more; nor could not have found the means to do it at this time but by my Lady Kyngston's being here."—Sylloge Epist. at the end of Titus Livius by Hearne, p. 140.

[2] See a memorandum by Cromwell in Ellis, Sec. Ser. ii. 123.

[3] She had said, "I have decreed simply from henceforth and wholly *next to Almighty God*, to put my state, continuance, and living in your gracious mercy." Cromwell objected to the words in italics; and she replied that she had always been accustomed to except God in speaking and writing, but would follow his advice, and copy the letter which he had sent her.—Sylloge Epist. at the end of Titus Livius, by Hearne, p. 124, 126.

[4] Sylloge Epist. at the end of Titus Livius, by Hearne, p. 137.

[5] Ibid. p. 142. State Papers, i. 455—459.

[6] From one of her letters she appears to have been intrusted with the care of Elizabeth. "My sister Elizabeth is in good health, thanks be to our Lord, and such a child toward, as I doubt not, but your highness will have cause to rejoice of in time coming, as knoweth Almighty God" (p. 131). The privy purse expenses of Mary at this period, for which we are indebted to Sir Frederick Madden, exhibit proofs of a cheerful and charitable disposition, very different from the character given of her by several writers.

But he did not rest here: in violation of every constitutional principle, he obtained a power in failure of children by his present or any future wife, to limit the crown in possession and remainder by letters patent under the great seal, or by his last will, signed with his own hand, to any such person or persons whom he might think proper.[1] It was believed that he had chiefly in view his natural son, the duke of Richmond, then in his eighteenth year, and the idol of his affection. But before the act could receive the royal assent the duke died; Henry remained without a male child, legitimate or illegitimate, to succeed him; and a project was seriously entertained, but afterwards abandoned, of marrying the lady Mary to the duke of Orleans, the second son of the French monarch, and of declaring them presumptive heirs to the crown.[2]

During the summer the king sought to dissipate his grief for the death of his son in the company of his young queen: in autumn he was suddenly alarmed by an insurrection in the northern counties, where the people retained a strong attachment to the ancient doctrines; and the clergy, further removed from the influence of the court, were less disposed to abjure their opinions at the nod of the sovereign. Each succeeding innovation had irritated their discontent; but when they saw the ruin of the establishments which they had revered from their childhood; the monks driven from their homes, and in many instances compelled to beg their bread; and the poor, who had formerly been fed at the doors of the convents, now abandoned without relief;[3] they readily listened to the declamations of demagogues, unfurled the standard of revolt, and with arms in their hands, and under the guidance of Makerel, abbot of Barlings, who had assumed the name of Captain Cobbler, demanded the redress of their grievances. Nor was the insurrection long confined to the common people. The nobility and gentry, the former patrons of the dissolved houses, complained that they were deprived of the corrodies reserved to them by the charters of foundation; and contended that, according to law, whenever these religious corporations ceased to exist, their lands ought not to fall

---

[1] Stat. of Realm, iii. 659. Strype, i. Rec. 182. A multitude of new treasons was created by this statute. It was made treason to do anything by words, writing, imprinting, or any exterior act or deed, to the peril of the person of the king or his heirs; or for the repeal of this act, or of the dispositions made by the kinge in virtue thereof; or to the slander and prejudice of his marriage with Queen Jane or any other his lawful wife; or by words, writing, imprinting, or any other exterior act, to take and believe either of the king's former marriages valid, or under any pretence to name and call his issue by either of those marriages lawful issue; or to refuse to answer upon oath any interrogatories relative to any clause, sentence, or word in this act, or to refuse to promise upon oath to keep and observe the same act. In accordance with the spirit of this enactment, the lord Thomas Howard, brother to the duke of Norfolk, was attainted of high treason, by a bill introduced, and read three times in each house on the last day of the session. His offence was that he had privately contracted marriage with the lady Margaret Douglas; a sufficient proof, in the opinion of Henry, that he aspired to the throne after the king's death. He was not executed, but suffered to die in the Tower. The lady was also committed. Her mother, the queen dowager of Scotland, begged of Henry to remember that she was his "nepotas, and oyster naturall unto the king, her derrest son." Chron. Catal. 190. Margaret was discharged on the death of the lord Thomas, and we shall meet with her again as countess of Lennox, and mother of Lord Darnley.

[2] Philip, duke of Bavaria, also made to her an offer of marriage (Privy Purse, &c. pref. xciv.); but Mary replied that she had no wish to enter that *religion*, i. e. a married life.

[3] "Whereby the service of God is not only minished, but also the poreslty of your realm be unrelieved, and many persons be put from their livings and left at large, which we think is a great hinderance to the commonwealth."—Lincolnshire remonstrance, apud Speed, 1033.

to the Crown, but should revert to the representatives of the original donors. The archbishop of York, the lords Nevil, Darcy, Lumley, and Latimer, and most of the knights and gentlemen in the north, joined the insurgents, either through compulsion, as they afterwards pretended, or through inclination, as was generally believed. The first who appeared in arms were the men of Lincolnshire; and so formidable was their force, that the duke of Suffolk, the royal commander, deemed it more prudent to negotiate than to fight. They complained chiefly of the suppression of the monasteries, of the Statute of Uses,[1] of the introduction into the council of such men as Cromwell and Rich, and of the preferment of the archbishops of Canterbury and Dublin, and of the bishops of Rochester, Salisbury, and St. David's, whose chief aim was to subvert the church of Christ. Several messages passed between the king and the insurgents: at length a menacing proclamation created dissension in their counsels; and, as soon as the more obstinate had departed to join their brethren in Yorkshire, the rest accepted a full pardon on the acknowledgment of their offence, the surrender of their arms, and the promise to maintain all the acts of parliament passed during the king's reign.[2]

In the five other counties the insurrection had assumed a more formidable appearance. From the borders of Scotland to the Lune and the Humber, the inhabitants had generally bound themselves by oath to stand by each other, "for the love which they bore to Almighty God, his faith, the holy church, and the maintenance thereof; to the preservation of the king's person and his issue; to the purifying of the nobility; and to expulse all villein blood, and evil counsellors from his grace and privy council; not for any private profit, nor to do displeasure to any private person, nor to slay or murder through envy, but for the restitution of the church, and the suppression of heretics and their opinions." Their enterprise was quaintly termed the "pilgrimage of grace;" on their banners were painted the image of Christ crucified, and the chalice and host, the emblems of their belief; and, wherever the pilgrims appeared, the ejected monks were placed in the monasteries, and the inhabitants were compelled to take the oath, and to join the army.[3] The strong castles of Skipton and Scarborough were preserved by the courage and loyalty of the garrisons; but Hull, York, and Pontefract admitted the insurgents; and thirty thousand men, under the nominal command (the real leaders seem not to have been known) of a gentleman named Robert Aske, hastened to obtain possession of Doncaster. The earl of Shrewsbury, though without any commission, ventured to arm his tenantry, and throw himself into the town; he was soon joined by the duke of Norfolk, the king's lieutenant, with five thousand men; a battery of cannon protected the bridge over the river, and the ford was rendered impassable by an

---

[1] By the Statute of Uses was meant the statute for transferring uses into possession, by which persons who before had the use only of their lands, and thus lay in a great measure at the mercy of the feoffees, became seised of the land in the same estate of which they before had the use.—St. 27 Hen. VIII. 10.

[2] Speed, 1033. Herbert, 474. State Papers, i. 462—466, 468—470.

[3] As an instance I will add the summons sent to the commons of Hawkside:—"We command you, and every of you to be at the Stoke-green beside Hawkside kirk on Saturday next by eleven of the clock, in your best array, as you will answer before the high Judge at the great day of doom, and in the pain of pulling down your houses, and the losing of your goods, and your bodies to be at the captain's will."—Speed, 1033.

accidental swell of the waters. In these circumstances the insurgents consented to an armistice, and appointed delegates to lay their demands before Henry, who had already summoned his nobility to meet him in arms at Northampton, but was persuaded by the duke to revoke the order, and trust to the influence of terror and dissension.

To the deputies the king gave a written answer, composed by himself;[1] to Norfolk full authority to treat with the insurgents, and to grant a pardon to all but ten persons, six named, and four unnamed. But this exception caused each of the leaders to fear for his own life: the terms were refused; another negotiation was opened; and a numerous deputation, having previously consulted a convocation of the clergy sitting at Pontefract,[2] proposed their demands to the royal commissioners. They required that heretical books should be suppressed, and that heretical bishops and temporal men of their sect, should either be punished according to law, or try their quarrel with the pilgrims by battle; that the statutes of uses, and treason of wards, with those which abolished the papal authority, bastardized the princess Mary, suppressed the monasteries, and gave to the king the tenths and first-fruits of benefices, should be repealed; that Cromwell the vicar-general, Audeley the chancellor, and Rich the attorney-general, should be punished as subverters of the law, and maintainers of heresy; that Lee and Layton, the visitors of the northern monasteries, should be prosecuted for extortion, peculation, and other abominable acts; that no man residing north of the Trent should be compelled by subpœna to appear at any court but at York, unless in matters of allegiance; and that a parliament should be shortly held in some convenient place, as at Nottingham or York. These demands were instantly rejected by the duke, as was an offer of pardon, clogged with exceptions, by the insurgents. The latter immediately recalled such of their partisans as had left their camp; their numbers multiplied daily; and Norfolk, who dreaded the result of an attack, found it necessary to negotiate both with his sovereign and his opponents. At length he subdued the obstinacy of each; and Henry offered, the insurgents accepted, an unlimited pardon, with an understanding that their grievances should be shortly and patiently discussed in the parliament to be assembled at York.[3] But the king, freed from his apprehensions, neglected to redeem his promise; and within two months the pilgrims were again under arms. Now, however, the duke, who lay with a more numerous force in the heart of the country, was able to intercept their communications, and to defeat all their measures. They failed in two successive attempts to surprise Hull and Carlisle; the lord Darcy, Robert Aske, and most of the leaders were taken, sent to London, and executed,[4] the others were hanged by scores at York, Hull, and Carlisle;

---

[1] It is characteristic of the author. He marvels that such ignorant churls should talk of theological subjects to him who "something had been noted to be learned;" or should complain of his laws, as if, after the experience of twenty-eight years, he did not know how to govern a kingdom; or should oppose the suppression of monasteries, as if it were not better to relieve the head of the church in his necessity, than to support the sloth and wickedness of monks.—It is printed in Speed, 1038, and Herbert, 480.

[2] Their answers to the questions proposed to them may be seen in Strype, i. App. 170; Wilk. iii. 812.

[3] See Hardwicke, State Papers, p. 28, 29, &c. Henry "thought his honour would be much touched if he granted them a free pardon." On this account he was very peevish with the duke.

[4] Mr. Tytler, in his history of Henry (p. 382), refers to a curious paper in the State Papers (i. 583), entitled "The saying of Robert Aske to me Richard Coren, out of confession afore his death," as "illustrative

and at length, when resistance had ceased, and the royal resentment had been satisfied, tranquillity was restored by the proclamation of a general pardon.[1]

From the insurgents Henry directed his attention to the proceedings of his kinsman, Reginald Pole. That young nobleman, after his refusal of the archbishopric of York, had obtained permission to prosecute his studies on the continent; and, aware of the storm which was gathering in England, had silently withdrawn to the north of Italy, where he devoted himself exclusively to literary pursuits. But the jealousy of the king, or the malice of his enemies, followed him into this peaceful asylum; and he received a royal order to state in writing his opinion on the two important questions of the supremacy and the divorce. For months Pole declined the dangerous task. But the execution of Anne Boleyn, and a repetition of the order from Henry, induced him to obey; and in a long and laboured treatise, which was conveyed in secrecy by a trusty messenger to the king, he boldly condemned the divorce from Catherine as unlawful, and the assumption of the supremacy as a departure from the unity of the church. Of this Henry could not reasonably complain.

Pole had done his duty: he had obeyed with sincerity the royal command; but in addition he proceeded, in that style of rhetorical declamation which was habitual to him, to arraign the misconduct of the monarch in the marriage of a second wife pending the life of the first, and in the judicial murder of Fisher, More, and the other sufferers, for their conscientious refusal to swear to his supremacy.[2] Irritable as the king was, he dissembled; and, in language singularly mild and gracious, ordered his kinsman to return, that they might discuss these questions in private to their mutual satisfaction. Pole instantly saw the danger. Were he to set foot in England, as long as the new statutes continued in force, he must either abjure his opinion, or forfeit his life. He replied, therefore, in humble and supplicatory terms, expressive of a hope that the king would not be offended if he accepted an invitation from the pontiff to visit him in Rome. Henry disdained to return an answer; but he employed Pole's mother and brothers, and Cromwell and his friends in England, to deter him from the journey; and afterwards the two houses of parliament joined in a letter to dissuade him from the acceptance of office in Rome.[3] The advice from the first

---

of the revealing of confessions in this reign." The mistake might be easily made by a writer unacquainted with the peculiar language of Catholics. By "out of confession" was meant "not in confession;" and Coren employed the phrase to show that he was *not* betraying the sacramental confession of the convict.

[1] Herbert, 489.

This epistle was kept secret during the life of Henry; after his death it was published from a pirated copy by a bookseller in Germany, which induced Pole to give a correct edition of it himself, under the title of "Pro Ecclesiasticæ Unitatis Defensione Libri IV." The asperity of his language to the king was reprehended by his friends in Italy, and his English correspondents: his apology was that he deemed it a service to Henry to lay before him a representation of

his conduct in all its deformity. Some on this account have called in question the accuracy of his statements; but in his answer to the English parliament, he boldly defies any man to point out a single instance of falsehood or misrepresentation in it.— Apologia ad Angliæ Parl. i. 179.

[3] Neve (Animad. on Philips, 249) ridicules the idea of such a letter; but Pole in his answer directed to the parliament says expressly, Literas omnium vestrum nominibus subscriptas (Pol. Ep. i. 179). As no parliament was then sitting, I conceive that, like the letter formerly sent to Clement VII., it was subscribed by the lords, and by a few commoners in the name of the lower house. Pole's answer was addressed to parliament, because he understood that it was to assemble at York, as had been promised, on the 30th of March.

shook, but did not subdue the resolution of Reginald; that from the latter reached him too late. Aware, indeed, that he should make the king his implacable enemy, and expose his family to the resentment of an unprincipled sovereign, he had at first refused every offer; but he yielded after a long resistance to the persuasion of his friend Contarini, and the command of the pontiff; accepted about Christmas the dignity of cardinal; and, before two months had elapsed, was unexpectedly named to a very delicate but dangerous mission.

When Paul first heard of the insurrection in the north of England, he thought that the time was come in which he might give publicity to the bull of excommunication and deposition, which he had subscribed about two years before; but from this measure, which at that moment might have added considerably to the difficulties of Henry, he was withheld by the arguments and entreaties of the young Englishman. Still a notion prevailed in the Roman court, that the rising, even after it had been quelled, might have left a deep impression on the mind of the king, and that during the parliament, which he had promised to convene at York, means might be successfully employed to reconcile him with the Apostolic See. The imperial cabinet strongly recommended that the charge of opening and conducting this negotiation should be intrusted to Pole; the French ambassador concurred;[1] and the English cardinal was appointed legate beyond the Alps. His instructions ordered him first to exhort Charles and Francis to sheath their swords against each other, and employ them only against the Turks, then to announce the pope's intention of convoking a general council, and lastly to proceed to the Netherlands, where he should fix his residence, unless circumstances should induce him to visit his own country. Of this appointment, and of the tenor of his instructions, Pole also informed the king. But Cromwell, his personal enemy, possessed the ear of the monarch; and was soon enabled to fulfil the prediction which he had uttered to Latimer, that he would make the cardinal through vexation "eat his own heart."[2] As soon as Pole had entered France, the English ambassador, in virtue of an article in the alliance between the two crowns, required that he should be delivered up, and sent a prisoner to England; and the king, though he indignantly rejected the demand, requested Pole, by a private messenger, not to ask for an audience, but to prosecute his journey with the utmost expedition. He soon reached Cambray; but Henry's agent had already terrified the court of Brussels, and the queen-regent refused him permission to enter the imperial territory. At the same time the king proclaimed him a traitor, fixed a price of fifty thousand crowns on his head, and offered to the emperor in exchange for the person of the cardinal an auxiliary force of four thousand men during his campaign against France.[3] Alarmed by the danger to which he was exposed at Cambray, Pole repaired, under the protection of an escort, to Liege, and in August was recalled to Rome. It has been said that, in accepting this mission, he sought to induce the

---

[1] Pol. Ep. ii. 31, 35, 42.

[2] "I herde you say wons that you wold make hym to ete hys owne hartt, which you have now, I trow, brought to passe, for he must nedes now ette hys owne hartt, and becum as hartlesse as he is gracelesse."—Bishop Latimer to Cromwell, Wright, Suppres. of Monast. p. 150.

[3] Dudith. Vit. Pol. No. x. xi. Besattelli, inter Ep. Poli, v. 366. Ep. Pol. ii. p. 43, 48, 55.

emperor and the king of France to make war upon Henry, and that he even indulged a hope of being able to obtain the crown for himself, as a descendant of the house of York. These charges are satisfactorily refuted by his official and confidential correspondence;[1] but at the same time it is plain that one object of his mission was to confirm by his residence in Flanders the attachment of the northern counties to the ancient faith; to supply, if it were necessary, the leaders of the malcontents with money, and to obtain for them the favour and protection of the neighbouring powers.[2] Hence it will not excite surprise if Henry, who had formerly been the benefactor of Pole, looked on him from this moment as an enemy, and pursued him ever afterwards with the most implacable hatred.

The northern insurrection, instead of securing the stability, accelerated the ruin of the remaining monasteries. The more opulent of these establishments had been spared, as was pretended, on account of their superior regularity; and of the many convents of friars no notice at all had been taken, probably because, as they did not possess landed property, little plunder was to be derived from their suppression. A charge, however, was now made, that the monks in the northern counties had encouraged their tenants to join in the pilgrimage of grace; and a commission, under the presidency of the earl of Sussex, was appointed to investigate their conduct. As a fair specimen of the proceedings, I will describe the surrender of the great monastery of Furness. All the members of the community, with the tenants and servants, were successively examined in private; and the result of a protracted inquiry was, that though two monks were committed to Lancaster Castle, nothing could be discovered to criminate either the abbot or the brotherhood. The commissioners proceeded to Whalley; and a new summons compelled the abbot of Furness to reappear before them. A second investigation was instituted, and the result was the same. In these circumstances, says the earl in a letter to Henry, which is still extant, "devising with myself, yf one way would not serve, how and by what means the said monks might be ryd from the said abbey, and consequently how the same might be at your graceous pleasur, I determined to assay him as of myself, whether he would be contented to surrender giff and graunt unto (you) your heirs and assigans the sayd monastery: which thing so opened to the abbot farely, we found him of a very facile and ready mynde to follow my advice in that behalf." A deed was accordingly drawn for him to sign, in which, having acknowledged "the misorder and evil rule both unto God and the king of the brethren of the said abbey," he, in discharge of his conscience, gave and surrendered to Henry all the title and interest which he possessed in the monastery of Furness, its lands and its revenues. Officers were immediately despatched to take possession in the name of the king; the commissioners followed with the abbot in their company; and in a few days the whole community ratified the deed of its superior. The history of Furness is the history of

---

[1] See his letter to the cardinal of Carpi (ii. 33), to the pope (ii. 46), to Edward VI. (tom. iv. 337), to Cromwell or Tunstall, from Cambray (Burnet, iii. 125; Strype, i. App. 218); and another from Throckmorton, a gentleman in his suite, but at the same time in the pay of Cromwell (Cleop. E. vi. 382). The reports of Throckmorton were so favourable to the cardinal, that his sincerity was suspected, and he was attainted the next year.

[2] Pol. Ep. ii. Monim. prælim. cclxvii.—cclxxix. and Ep. p. 52.

Whalley, and of the other great abbeys in the north. They were visited under pretext of the late rebellion; and by one expedient or other were successively wrested from the possessors, and transferred to the crown.[1]

The success of the earl of Sussex and his colleagues stimulated the industry of the commissioners in the southern districts. For four years they proceeded from house to house, soliciting, requiring, compelling the inmates to submit to the royal pleasure; and each week, frequently each day of the week, was marked by the surrender of one or several of these establishments. To accomplish their purpose, they first tried the milder expedient of persuasion. Large and tempting offers were held out to the abbot and the leading members of the brotherhood; and the lot of those who had already complied, the scanty pittances assigned to the refractory, and the ample pensions granted to the more obsequious, operated on their minds as a warning and an inducement.[2] But where persuasion failed, recourse was had to severity and intimidation. 1. The superior and his monks, the tenants, servants and neighbours, were subjected to a minute and rigorous examination: each was exhorted, was commanded, to accuse the other; and every groundless tale, every malicious insinuation, was carefully collected and recorded. 2. The commissioners called for the accounts of the house, compared the expenditure with the receipts, scrutinized every article with an eye of suspicion and hostility, and required the production of all the moneys, plate, and jewels. 3. They proceeded to search the library and the private rooms for papers and books; and the discovery of any opinion or treatise in favour of the papal supremacy, or of the validity of Henry's first marriage, was taken as a sufficient proof of adhesion to the king's enemies, and of disobedience to the statutes of the realm.[3] The general result was a real or fictitious charge of immorality, or peculation, or high treason. But many superiors, before the termination of

---

[1] See the original papers in the British Museum (Cleop. E. iv. 111, 224, 246), copied and published by West in his History of Furness, App. x. (4, 5, 6, 7).

[2] The pensions to the superiors appear to have varied from 266*l*. to 6*l*. per annum. The priors of cells received generally 13*l*. A few, whose services had merited the distinction, obtained 20*l*. To the other monks were allotted pensions of six, four, or two pounds, with a small sum to each at his departure, to provide for his immediate wants. The pensions to nuns averaged about 4*l*. It should, however, be observed, that these sums were not in reality so small as they appear, as money was probably at that period of six or seven times greater value than it is now. It was provided that each pension should cease, as soon as the pensioner obtained church preferment of equal value.

[3] These transactions are thus described by Catherine Bulkeley, abbess of Godstow, in a letter to Cromwell:—"Dr. London is soddenlye commyd unto me with a great rowte with him, and doth threten me and my sisters, saying that he hath the king's commission to suppress this house spyte of my tethe. When I shewyd him playne that I wolde never surrender to his haude, being an awncyent enemye, now he begins to intrete me, and invegle my sisters one by one, otherwise than I ever herde tell that the king's subjects had been handelyd; and here taryeth, and contynueth to my grete coste and charges, and will not take my answere, that I will not surrender, till I know the king's gracious commandment, or your good lordship's.........And notwithstanding, that Dr. London, like an untrewe man, hath informed your lordship that I am a spoiler and a waster, your good lordship shall know that the contrarie is trewe; for I have not alienatyd one halporthe of the goods of this monasterie movable or immovable."—Cleop. E. iv. p. 238. Of this Dr. London, Fuller says, "He was no great saint; for afterwards he was publicly convicted of perjury, and adjudged to ride with his face to the horse-tail at Windsor and Ockingham" (p. 314): to which may be added that he was also condemned to do public penance at Oxford for incontinency with two women, the mother and daughter. —Strype, i. 377.

the inquiry, deemed it prudent to obey the royal pleasure: some, urged on the one hand by fear on the other by scruples, resigned their situations, and were replaced by successors of more easy and accommodating loyalty; and the obstinacy of the refractory monks and abbots was punished with imprisonment during the king's pleasure. But the lot of these was calculated to terrify their brethren. Some of them, like the Carthusians, confined in Newgate, were left to perish through hunger, disease, and neglect;[1] others, like the abbots of Colchester, Reading, and Glastonbury, were executed as felons or traitors.[2]

During these proceedings, the religious bodies, instead of uniting in their common defence, seem to have awaited singly their fate with the apathy of despair. A few houses only, through the agency of their friends, sought to purchase the royal favour with offers of money and lands; but the rapacity of the king refused to accept a part when the whole was at his mercy; and a bill was brought into parliament, vesting in the crown all the property, moveable and immoveable, of the monastic establishments, which either had already been, or should hereafter be suppressed, abolished, or surrendered.[3] The advocates of the measure painted its advantages in the most fascinating colours. It would put an end to pauperism and taxation; it would enable the king to create and support earls, barons, and knights; to wage war in future without any additional burden to the people; and to free the nation from all apprehension of danger from foreign enmity or internal discontent.[4]

The house of lords at that period contained twenty-eight abbots, and the two priors of Coventry and of St. John of Jerusalem. Though they could not be ignorant of the real object of the bill, not one dared to open his mouth against it, and before the next session their respective houses, and with the houses their right to sit as lords of parliament, had ceased to exist. The abolition of the latter was a matter of no consequence; but the suppression of the

---

[1] Ellis, ii. 98. The fate of these Carthusians is thus announced to Cromwell in a letter from Bedyl, one of the visitors:—"My very good lord, after my most hearty commendations—It shall please your lordship to understand that the monks of the Charter-house here at London committed to Newgate for their treacherous behaviour continued against the king's grace, be almost dispatched by the hand of God, as it may appear to you by this bill inclosed. Wherefore, considering their behaviour, and the whole matter, I am not sorry; but would that all such as love not the king's highness, and his worldly honour, were in like case. There be departed, Greenwood, Davye, Salte, Peerson, Greene. There be at the point of death, Scriven, Reading. There be sick, Jonson, Horne. One is whole, Bird."—Cleop. E. iv. fol. 217. Ellis, ii. 76.

[2] Whiting, abbot of Glastonbury, "a very sick and weakly old man," was sent to the Tower, examined by Cromwell, and brought to confess that he had been privy to concealment of some of the plate belonging to the abbey. He was then sent back, and on Nov. 16, Lord Russell wrote to Cromwell—"My Lorde, thies shal be to asserteyne that on Thursdaye the xiiij. daye of this present moneth the abbot was arrayned, and the next daye putt to execution with ij other of his monkes for the robbyng of Glastonburye churche, on the Torre Hyll, the seyde abbottes body beyng devyded in fower partes, and heedd stryken off, whereof oone quarter stondyth at Welles, another at Bathe, and at Ylchester and Brigewater the rest, and his hedd upon the abbey gate at Glaston."—State Papers, i. 621.

[3] It should be observed that the transfer of the monastic property, and the suppression of the monastic orders, were not in the first instance effected by legislative enactment. It had been artfully devised that both should proceed from the monastic bodies themselves, who successively surrendered their property to the king, and thus in fact dissolved their own establishments. It might, however, be argued, that as each member possessed only a life-interest in the property, they could not singly or collectively confer anything more on the sovereign; and, therefore, the legislature came to his assistance, and by positive enactment vested in him for ever all monastic property which then was, or afterwards might be, actually in his possession.

[4] Coke, Inst. iv. 44. Strype, i. 211, 272.

religious houses failed to produce the benefits which had been so ostentatiously foretold. Pauperism was found to increase; the monastic property was lavishly squandered among the parasites of the court; and the king, instead of lightening the national burthens, demanded compensation for the expense which he had incurred in the reformation of religion. Within twelve months a subsidy of two-tenths and two-fifteenths was extorted by him from the reluctant gratitude of his parliament.[1]

By the spring of the year 1540, all the monastic establishments in the kingdom had been torn from the possession of the real owners by forced and illegal surrenders.[2] To soften the odium of the measure, much has been said of the immorality practised, or supposed to be practised, within the monasteries. It is not in human nature that in numerous societies of men, all should be equally virtuous. The monks of different descriptions amounted to many thousands; and in such a multitude there must have existed individuals whose conduct was a disgrace to their profession. But when this has been conceded on the one hand, it ought to be admitted on the other, that the charges against them are entitled to very little credit. They are ex parte statements, to which the accused had no opportunity of replying, and were made to silence inquiry and sanctify injustice. Of the commissioners, some were not very immaculate characters themselves;[3] all were stimulated to invent and exaggerate, both by the known rapacity of the king, and by their own prospects of personal interest.[4] There is, however, one fact, which to me appears decisive on the subject. Of all the monastic bodies, perhaps the monks of Christ-church have suffered the most in reputation; they are charged with habitually indulging the most immoral and shameful propensities. Yet, when Archbishop Cranmer named the clergy for the service of his cathedral, he selected from these very men no fewer than eight prebendaries, ten minor canons, nine scholars, and two choristers. From his long residence in Canterbury he could not be ignorant of their pre-

---

[1] Journals, 110, 111, 135. See also the preface to Stowe by Howes. According to Bale, an ardent reformer, "A great part of this treasure was turned to the upholding of dice-playing, masking, and banqueting; yes," he adds, "(I would I could not by just occasion speak it) bribing, wh.........., and swearing."—Bale, apud Strype, i. 346.

[2] As soon as an abbey was surrendered, 1. The commissioners broke its seal, and assigned pensions to the members. 2. The plate and jewels were reserved for the king; the furniture and goods were sold; and the money was paid into the Augmentation Office, lately established for that purpose. 3. The abbot's lodgings and the offices were left standing for the convenience of the next occupant; the church, cloisters, and apartments for the monks were stripped of the lead and every saleable article, and then left to fall in ruins.—Burnet, i. Rec. 151. 4. The lands were by degrees alienated from the crown by gift, sale, or exchange. From a commission in Rymer (xiv. 653) it appears that the lands sold at twenty, the buildings at fifteen years' purchase; the buyers were to hold of the crown, paying a reserved rent, equal to one-tenth of the usual rent. 5. The annual revenue of all the suppressed houses amounted to 142,914l. 12s. 9¼d., about the one-and-twentieth part of the whole rental of the kingdom, if Hume be correct in taking that rental at three millions.

[3] As London, mentioned in note p. 46, and Bedyl, mentioned in note, p. 47, who, from a letter of one of his colleagues (Fuller, 315), appears to have been an artful but profligate man. If we believe the northern insurgents, Layton and Lee were not much better.

[4] MS. Cleop. E. iv. 106, 213. When Gifford gave a favourable character of the house, the king maintained that he had been bribed. The reader may see the vices ascribed to the monks of some houses in Strype, i. 252—257; or Cleop. E. iv. 124, 127, 131, 134, 147; and letters in favour of others, ibid. 203, 209, 210, 213, 257, 269. Much has been written about the "blood of Hales."—See the vindication of the monks on that head by Hearne in App. to Benedictus Abbas, p. 761.

vious conduct; from respect for his own character, he would not surround himself with men addicted to the most disgraceful vices.[1] To lull his own conscience, or to silence the murmurs of his subjects, Henry resolved to appropriate a portion of the spoil to the advancement of religion; and for that purpose was authorized by act of parliament to establish new bishoprics, deaneries, and colleges, and to endow them with adequate revenues out of the lands of the suppressed monasteries. He seems to have frequently amused himself with this project. From papers extant, in his own hand, it appears that plans were devised, the revenues fixed, the incumbents appointed on paper; but when he attempted to execute the design, unforeseen difficulties arose; his donations to others had already alienated the greater part of the property; and his own wants required the retention of the remainder. Out of eighteen, the number originally intended, only six episcopal sees, those of Westminster, Oxford, Peterborough, Bristol, Chester, and Gloucester, were established; and even these were at first so scantily endowed, that the new prelates for some years enjoyed little more than a nominal income.[2] At the same time the king converted fourteen abbeys and priories into cathedral and collegiate churches, attaching to each a dean and a certain number of prebendaries; but was careful to retain for himself a portion of the original possessions, and to impose on the chapters the obligation of contributing annually a certain sum to the support of the resident poor, and another for the repair of the highways.[3] Thus he continued to the end of his reign, taking from the church with one hand, and restoring with the other but taking largely and restoring sparingly, extorting from the more wealthy prelates exchanges of lands and advowsons, and in return occasionally endowing a rectory or re-establishing a charitable foundation. Still his treasury was empty; the only individuals who profited by the pillage were the men whom he had lately raised to office and rank, whose importunities never ceased, and whose rapacity could never be satisfied.

III. From the time of the abolition of the papal authority to the close of Henry's reign, the creed of the church of England depended on the theological caprice of its supreme head. The clergy were divided into two opposite factions, denominated the men of the old and the new learning. The chief of the former was Gardiner bishop of Winchester, who was ably supported by Lee archbishop of York, Stokesley bishop of London, Tunstall of Durham, and Clarke of Bath and Wells. The latter acknowledged for their leaders, Cranmer archbishop of Canterbury, Shaxton of Sarum, Latimer of Worcester, and Fox of Hereford. These could depend on the powerful interest of Cromwell the vicar-general, and of Audeley the lord chancellor; the others on that of the duke of Norfolk, and of Wriothesley the premier secretary. But none of the prelates on either side, warmly as they might be attached to their own opinions, aspired to the palm of martyrdom. They possessed little of that firmness of mind, of that high and unbending spirit, which generally characterizes the leaders of religious

---

[1] See Stevens, Monast. i. 386; also Brown Willis, i. 37; Harmer, 47; Hearne, pref. to sec. Append. to Lel. Collect. p. 84.
[2] Journals, 112. Strype, i. Rec. 275. Rym. xiv. 709, 717—736, 748, 754.
[3] They were Canterbury, Rochester, Westminster, Winchester, Bristol, Gloucester, Worcester, Chester, Burton-upon-Trent, Carlisle, Durham, Thornton, Peterborough, and Ely. The dean and chapter of Canterbury were enjoined to give annually to the poor 100l., towards the highways 40l. The others were rated in proportion.—Rym. xv. 77.

parties; but were always ready to suppress, or even to abjure, their real sentiments at the command of their wayward and imperious master. If, on the one hand, Gardiner and his associates, to avoid the royal displeasure, consented to renounce the papal supremacy, and to subscribe to every successive innovation in the established creed, Cranmer and his friends on the other submitted with equal weakness to teach doctrines which they disapproved, to practise a worship which they deemed idolatrous or superstitious, and to consign men to the stake for the open profession of tenets, which, there is reason to suspect, they themselves inwardly believed. Henry's infallibility continually oscillated between the two parties. If his hostility to the court of Rome led him to incline towards the men of the new learning, he was quickly brought back again by his attachment to the doctrines which he had formerly maintained in his controversy with Luther. The bishops on both sides acted with equal caution. They carefully studied the inclinations of the king, sought by the most servile submission to win his confidence, and employed all their vigilance to defeat the intrigues and to undermine the credit of their adversaries.

Though the refusal of the German reformers to approve of the divorce had not contributed to efface that unfavourable impression which had been originally made on the king's mind by the writings of Luther, his subsequent defection from the see of Rome prompted him to seek an union with those who for so many years had set at defiance the authority and censure of the pontiff. The formation of the confederacy at Torgau[1] had been followed by the diet of Spires; and six princes with fourteen cities had signed a formal protest against the decree of that assembly.[2] It was in vain that at the next diet of Augsburg, Charles endeavoured to appease the Protestants by condescension, or to intimidate them by menaces. They presented to him a confession of their faith, refused to submit to his determination, concluded a new confederacy at Schmalcalden, and wrote a defence of their proceedings to the kings of England and France. Both returned complimentary answers; and the latter, in 1535, invited to his court Melancthon, the most learned and moderate of the new teachers. The moment the intelligence was communicated to Henry, he despatched letters and messengers first to Germany, and in the next place to Paris; those to intercept Melancthon on his journey, these to prevail on him, if he had reached France, to come forward without interruption to England.[3] What might be the king's object, it were idle to conjecture; but the elector of Saxony was persuaded by the policy or jealousy of Luther to detain Melancthon within his own territory. Soon afterwards, Henry sent to the Protestant princes at Schmalcalden an embassy, consisting of the bishop of Hereford, Archdeacon Heath, and Dr. Barnes, to represent to them that, as both he and they had defied the authority of the pontiff, it might be for their mutual interest to join in one common confederacy. But

---

[1] See vol. iv. p. 230.

[2] This instrument displays in strong colours the intolerance of the first reformers. The decree, among other things, forbade any person, layman or ecclesiastic, to employ violence and constraint in matters of religion, to abolish the mass by force, or to prohibit, command, or compel any one to assist at it. They replied, that they could not consent to this article; that conscience forced them to abolish the mass; nor would they permit any of their subjects to be present at it.—Sleidan, l. vi. p. 80. It was from this protestation that the reformers acquired the name of Protestants.

[3] Mr. Coxe has printed the original letters in his Life of Melancthon, p. 371, 384.

the Germans, assuming a lofty tone, required that he should subscribe to their confession of faith, and should advance, partly as a loan, partly as a present, the sum of one hundred, or if it were necessary, of two hundred thousand crowns; and, as a reward for his compliance, offered to him the title of head of the league, and promised not to obey any decrees of the bishop of Rome, nor to acknowledge any council convoked by the pontiff without the consent of the king. Henry took a long interval to reply, and consulted Gardiner, at that time his ambassador in France, who, anxious to wean his sovereign from this heterodox connection, opposed the demands of the princes with much art and ability. Why was Henry, he asked, to subscribe to their confession of faith? Had he emancipated himself from the usurped authority of the pontiff, to put his neck under the yoke of the German divines? "It would be rather a change of a bond of dependence, than a riddance thereof." The word of God authorized the king to make all necessary reformation in religious matters; but now his hands were to be tied, till he should ask and obtain the consent of the princes at Schmalcalden. In the next place, those princes were incompetent to conclude such a league. The emperor was the head of the German, on the same grounds as Henry was the head of the English church; nor could the subjects of the one lawfully make religious treaties with a foreign prince, with greater right than those of the other. At all events, the king ought to require from them, as preliminary concessions, the approbation of his divorce, and the acknowledgment of his supremacy; two points to which Gardiner well knew that the Germans would never accede. Had he been present, there can be little doubt that, by thus appealing to the king's favourite prejudices, he would have broken off the negotiation altogether; as it was, Henry replied by thanking them for their good will, and consenting to aid them with money on certain conditions; but he required that a deputation of German divines should previously repair to England, and, in conjunction with the English theologians, should fix the firm basis of a thorough reformation. After some discussion, Melancthon, with certain divines, received an order to visit Henry; but the order was revoked as soon as the unfortunate end of Anne Boleyn was known in Germany. The reformers suspected that the king was not sincere in his religious professions; and that now, when the original cause of dissension was removed, he would seek a reconciliation with both the emperor and the pontiff.[1]

Soon afterwards, the lower house of convocation denounced to the higher fifty-nine propositions extracted from the publications of different reformed writers. The subject instantly attracted the notice of the head of the church; and Henry, with the aid of his theologians, compiled a book of "Articles," which was presented to the convocation by Cromwell, and subscribed by him and the other members. It may be divided into three parts. The first declares that the belief of the Apostles' Creed, the Nicene Creed, and the Athanasian Creed, is necessary for salvation; the second explains the three great sacraments of baptism, penance, and the altar, and pronounces them the ordinary means of justification; the third teaches that, though the use of images,

---

[1] See Collier, ii. Records, p. 23; and Strype, i. Rec. 157—163. In a letter written by Cromwell on this occasion, he says, "The king, knowing himself to be the learnedest prince in Europe, he thought it became not him to submit to them, but he expected they should submit to him."—Burnet, iii. 112.

the honouring of the saints, the soliciting of their intercession, and the usual ceremonies in the service, have not in themselves the power to remit sin, or justify the soul, yet they are highly profitable, and ought to be retained.—Throughout the work, Henry's attachment to the ancient faith is most manifest; and the only concession which he makes to the men of the new learning, is the order for the removal of abuses, with perhaps the omission of a few controverted subjects. The vicar-general immediately issued injunctions, in the name of the king, that "the Articles" should be read to the people in the churches without any comment; and that, until the next Michaelmas, no clergyman should presume to preach in public unless he were a bishop, or spoke in the presence of a bishop, or were licensed to teach in the cathedral, at the peril of the bishop.[1]

By these articles, Henry had now fixed the landmarks of English orthodoxy; for the better information of his subjects, he ordered the convocation "to set forth a plain and sincere exposition of doctrine." The task was accomplished by the publication of a work entitled, "The godly and pious Institution of a Christian Man," subscribed by the archbishops, bishops, archdeacons, and certain doctors of canon and civil law, and pronounced by them to accord "in all things with the very true meaning of Scripture."[2] It explains in succession the creed, the seven sacraments, which it divides into three of a higher, and four of a lower order, the ten commandments, the Paternoster and Ave Maria, justification, and purgatory. It is chiefly remarkable for the earnestness with which it refuses salvation to all persons out of the pale of the Catholic church, denies the supremacy of the pontiff, and inculcates passive obedience to the king. It teaches that no cause whatever can authorize the subject to draw the sword against his prince; that sovereigns are accountable to God alone; and that the only remedy against oppression is to pray that God would change the heart of the despot, and induce him to make a right use of his power.[3]

The design of a conference between the English and German divines was soon afterwards revived, chiefly at the instigation of Cranmer. Had the archbishop openly called in question any of "the Articles" lately determined by Henry, he would probably have paid with his head the forfeit of his presumption; but he conceived that foreigners might venture to defend their own creed without giving offence; and flattered himself with the hope that their reasoning might make impression on the theological obstinacy of the king. Burkhard, vice-chancellor to the elector of Saxony, Boyneburg, doctor of laws, and Myconius, superintendent of Saxe-Gotha, arrived in England in the spring of 1538; and frequent conferences were held between them and a commission of divines appointed by Henry. But the policy of Cranmer was disappointed. His German missionaries were not deficient in zeal or learning, but it was their lot to labour on an ungrateful soil. As a last effort, they laid before the king a detailed statement of the reasons on which they grounded their demand of the concession of the cup to the laity, of the abrogation of private masses, and of the permission of marriage to the priesthood; but Henry, having, with the aid of the bishop of Durham, condescended to answer their arguments, thanked them for their trouble, granted them permission to return

---

[1] Wilk. Con. iii. 804—608, 817—823.   [2] Ibid. 830.   [3] Collier, ii. 139—143.

home, and promised to bear honourable testimony to their learning, zeal, and talents.[1]

Their departure was a severe mortification to the men of the new doctrine. Still, however, the spirit of innovation continued to make a slow but steady progress; and though it might not keep pace with their wishes, afforded them grounds to hope for a favourable result. The king redeemed his pledge of "the removal of abuses." By his order, a number of holidays were abolished, which he considered superfluous, as far as regarded religion, and injurious, inasmuch as they restrained the industry of the people. The clergy were enjoined to admonish their parishioners, that images were permitted only as books for the instruction of the unlettered; that to abuse them for any other purpose was idolatry; and that the king intended to remove whatever might be the "occasion of so great an offence to God, and so great a danger to the souls of his loving subjects."[2] For this purpose shrines were demolished; genuine or supposititious relics were burnt; and the most celebrated roods and images were broken into fragments, or given to the flames. To make the greater impression, the royal agents conducted their operations with much parade and solemnity, and employed every engine to detect and expose the real or pretended frauds by which the devotion of the people had been attracted towards particular churches. Whatever credit may be due to reports originating with men whose great object it was to bring the religious orders into disrepute, and to terrify them into the surrender of their property,[3] there is one proceeding, which, on account of its singularity and absurdity, deserves the attention of the reader. It had been suggested that, as long as the name of St. Thomas of Canterbury should remain in the calendar, men would be stimulated by his example to brave the ecclesiastical authority of their sovereign. The king's attorney was therefore instructed to exhibit an information against him; and "Thomas Becket, some time archbishop of Canterbury," was formally cited to appear in court and answer to the charge. The interval of thirty days, allowed by the canon law, was suffered to elapse; still the saint

[1] Both papers are printed by Burnet, i. Addenda, p. 332—360. See others on the subject in Strype, i. Rec. 258—263.

[2] Wilkins, Con. iii. 816, 823, 826. One of the principal roods, called Darvel Gatheren, was brought from Wales to London to be employed at the execution of Dr. Forest; because there was an old saying, that Darvel Gatheren would one day burn a forest. The doctor belonged to the convent of Observant Friars at Greenwich, and was confessor to Queen Catherine, a fact of itself sufficient to set aside all the ill-defined charges against him in the letters of Lyst, a discontented lay brother, to Cromwell and the lady marquess (Anne Boleyn) in 1532 and 1533. (See them in Ellis, 3rd series, ii. 245—270.) Forest was a powerful opponent of the divorce, and sent away by the king's order from Greenwich to a convent in the north. In 1538 he was brought back to London, and condemned (in what court is not mentioned) to suffer as a traitor and a heretic. For this purpose a double gallows was erected in Smithfield. In the midst, Forest was suspended by chains passed round his waist and under his arms; in front, on a platform, sat the lord mayor, and several of the privy council; and from a pulpit on the side, preached Latimer, bishop of Worcester. The bishop ended with an offer of pardon from the king to Forest, if he would recant. This the friar refused: a slow fire was kindled under him: he remained constant in his resolution; and was consumed with the rood. The heresy for which he was burnt is plain from the lines affixed to the gallows:—

" Forest the friar,
That infamous liar,
That wilfully will be dead,
In his contumacy,
The gospel doth deny,
The king to be supreme head."

See Sanders, 138, 163; Hall, 232; Burnet, i. 358; Wood, Athenæ, i. 42.

[3] Most of these tales depend at present on the very questionable authority of William Thomas, the author of Il Pelerino Inglese, who has led Burnet into a multitude of errors.—See Collier, ii. 149.

neglected to quit the tomb in which he had reposed for two centuries and a half; and judgment would have been given against him for default, had not the king, of his special grace, assigned him a counsel. The court sat at Westminster; the attorney-general and the advocate of the accused were heard; and sentence was finally pronounced, that Thomas, some time archbishop of Canterbury, had been guilty of rebellion, contumacy, and treason; that his bones should be publicly burnt, to admonish the living of their duty by the punishment of the dead; and that the offerings which had been made at his shrine, the personal property of the reputed saint, should be forfeited to the crown.[1] A commission was accordingly issued; the sentence was executed in due form; and the gold, silver, and jewels, the spoils obtained by the demolition of the shrine, were conveyed in two ponderous coffers to the royal treasury. Soon afterwards a proclamation was published, stating that, forasmuch as it now clearly appeared, that Thomas Becket had been killed in a riot excited by his own obstinacy and intemperate language, and had been afterwards canonized by the bishop of Rome as the champion of his usurped authority, the king's majesty thought it expedient to declare to his loving subjects, that he was no saint, but rather a rebel and traitor to his prince, and therefore strictly charged and commanded that he should not be esteemed or called a saint; that all images and pictures of him should be destroyed; the festivals in his honour be abolished, and his name and remembrance be erased out of all books, under pain of his majesty's indignation, and imprisonment at his grace's pleasure.[2]

In another, and more important point, the archbishop proved equally fortunate. Some years had passed since William Tyndal, a tutor in a family of Gloucestershire, but of suspicious orthodoxy, had fled into the Netherlands, where he printed a version of the New Testament, of his own composition. The zeal of Warham was alarmed; he admonished the provincial bishops to destroy all the copies of this version to be found in their dioceses, and purchased, at his own cost, the copies remaining in the hands of the publisher.[3] But the destruction of one impression led only to the production of many. Editions in different forms, some with, some without notes, were issued on speculation, from different presses in the Netherlands; and Tyndal, continuing his labours, published a version of some parts of the Old Testament. Henry now deemed it proper to come forward as defender of the faith. His first object was to get into his possession the translator himself; overtures were made to the exile, to induce him to return to his country, and orders were sent to the king's agents to seize his person and hurry him by force on board a ship bound to England. When these attempts failed, a consultation was held with the bishops and certain divines

---

[1] Wilk. Con. iii. 835, 636. As we have only translations of the citation and judgment made by foreigners, I might have doubted the authenticity of these instruments, were they not alluded to by the king in his proclamation of Nov. 16: "Forasmuch as it appeareth *now clearly* that Thomas," &c. (ibid. 848); and by Paul III. in his bull of Dec. 17: In judicium vocari, et tanquam contumacem damnari, ac proditorem declarari fecerat.—Ibid. 841.

[2] Wilk. Con. iii. 841. Another proclamation of similar import was issued in the next month.—Burnet, iii. Rec. 152.

[3] The expense was 66l. 9s. 4d.—Ellis, 3rd ser. ii. 86—92. I suspect that the stories in Hall, Burnet, and others, respecting the purchase of an edition by Bishop Tunstall in 1529, have no other foundation than this purchase by Archbishop Warham in 1527. Tunstall's commission to the archdeacons was issued in obedience to Warham's letter, and is dated on the same day Oct. 24, 1526.

from the two universities, and a royal proclamation was published, ordering all copies of the versions of the New or Old Testaments to be delivered up; declaring that in respect of the malignity of the times, it was better that the Scriptures should be explained by the learned than exposed to the misapprehension of the vulgar; and promising that, if it should hereafter appear that erroneous opinions were forsaken, and the present version was destroyed, the king would provide a new translation by the joint labours of great, learned, and Catholic persons[1]

This promise was not forgotten by Cranmer, who had witnessed the success with which so powerful a weapon had been wielded by the reformers in Germany. He often ventured to recall it to the royal recollection; his endeavours were seconded by the petition of the convocation and the recommendation of Cromwell; and Grafton and Whitechurch, two printers, obtained the royal license to publish a folio edition of the Bible, in English. It bore the name of Thomas Matthewe, a fictitious signature; and was made up of the version by Tyndal, and of another by Coverdale, printed very lately, as it was thought, at Zurich. Injunctions were now issued, that a Bible of this edition should be placed in every church at the joint expense of the incumbent and the parishioners, and that any man might have the liberty of reading in it at his pleasure, provided he did not disturb the preacher in his sermon, nor the clergyman during the service. Soon afterwards this indulgence was extended from the church to private houses; but Henry was at all times careful to admonish the readers, that when they met with difficult passages they should consult persons more learned than themselves; and to remind them, that the liberty which they enjoyed was not a right to which they possessed any claim, but a favour granted "of the royal liberality and goodness."[2]

IV. The king, like all other reformers, made his own judgment the standard of orthodoxy; but he enjoyed an advantage, which few besides himself could claim, the power of enforcing obedience to his decisions. That the teachers of erroneous doctrine ought to be repressed by the authority of the civil magistrate, was a maxim which at that period had been consecrated by the assent and practice of ages. No sooner had Constantine the Great embraced Christianity, than he enacted against dissenters from the established creed the same punishments which his pagan predecessors had inflicted on those who apostatized from the religion of their fathers.[3] His example was repeatedly followed by succeeding emperors;[4] it was adopted without hesitation by the princes of the northern tribes, who, after their conversion, were accustomed to supply from the imperial constitutions the deficiencies of their own scanty legislation. Hence religious intolerance became part of the public law of Christendom: the principle was maintained, the practice enforced, by the reformers themselves;[5] and whatever might be the predominant doctrine, the dissenter from it invariably found himself subject to civil restrictions, perhaps to imprisonment and death. By Henry the laws against

---

[1] Wilk. Con. iii. 706, 735, 740.
[2] Wilk. Con. iii. 776, 811, 843, 847, 856.
[3] Socrat. p. 32. Sozom. p. 38, 72, 90, edit. Vales. 8. Aug. contra ep. Parmen. l. i. c. 7.
[4] Leg. 51, 56. Cod. Theod. de Hæret.

Leg. 5, 11, 12, 14, 16. Cod. Just. de Hæret.
[5] Calvin in refut. Error. Mich. Serveti, p. 587, and in his letter to the duke of Somerset. Merentur gladio ultore coerceri, quem tibi tradidit Deus.—Ep. Calvini Protect. Aug. p. 65.

heresy were executed with equal rigour both before and after his quarrel with the pontiff. In his third and thirteenth years the teachers of Lollardism had awakened by their intemperance the zeal of the bishops; and the king by proclamation charged the civil magistrates to lend their aid to the spiritual authorities. Of the numbers brought before the primate and the bishops of London and Lincoln, almost all were induced to abjure; a few of the more obstinate forfeited their lives.[1] Lollardism, however, presented but little cause for alarm; it was the progress of Lutheranism in Germany which first taught the bishops to tremble for the security of their church. Curiosity led men to peruse the writings of the reformer and his partisans; the perusal occasionally made converts, and the converts laboured to diffuse the new light with all the fervour of proselytism. They were not content to propagate their doctrine by preaching: the Bible, as the reader, has just seen, was translated and printed beyond the sea; and books were published which condemned the creed of the established church, ridiculed the ceremonies of its worship, and satirized the lives of its ministers. Henry, as defender of the faith, thought himself bound in honour to protect with the sword those doctrines which he had supported with his pen. When the convocation condemned Tyndal's Bible as an unfaithful version, and the other works as teeming with errors and slander, the king by proclamation forbade them to be imported, sold, or kept; and ordered the chancellor, justices, and inferior officers to make oath that "they would give their whole power and diligence to destroy all errors, and would assist the bishops and their commissaries as often as they should be required."[2] Numerous arrests and abjurations followed; and four or five unfortunate men, who, having obtained a pardon, reverted to their former practice of selling the prohibited works, were on the second conviction, condemned to the flames.[3] In 1533, the elevation of Cranmer to the archiepiscopal dignity, the divorce of Catherine, and the subsequent abolition of the papal authority, inspired the advocates of innovation with the hope of impunity; but experience taught them, to their cost, that they had as much to fear now from the head of the church, as they had before from the defender of the faith; and that the prelates of the new learning were not less eager than those of the old to light the fagot for the punishment of heresy. The first victims were, John Frith, who maintained that it was not necessary to believe or deny the doctrine of the real presence, and Hewet, a tailor, who had determined to believe and speak, to live and die, with John Frith.[4] The succeeding years were employed chiefly in the punishment

---

[1] Fox, ii. 19. Burnet, i. 27. I have not noticed the legend of Hunn, who was found dead in prison. To the account given by Hall and Fox may be opposed that by Sir Thomas More (Supplic. of Soules, 297—299).
[2] Wilk. Con. iii. 727—739. In consequence of this oath, Sir Thomas More frequently gave his aid in causes of heresy. Fox from the reports of the reformers accuses him of unnecessary cruelty, and has induced some modern writers to brand him with the name of persecutor. It is, however, but fair to hear his defence. "Of al that ever came into my hand for heresye, as helpe me God, had never any of them any stripe or stroke given them, so much as a fylyppe on the forehead."—Apol. c. 36, p. 901.
[3] With Fox (ii. 223, 237—240) should be read Sir Thomas More's Confutation of Tyndal, 344—350.
[4] Fox, ii. 251, 256. Hall, 225. Person's Three Conversions, part iii. 45—59. Cranmer gives the following account of Frith and Hewet, in his letter to Mastyr Hawkins (Archæol. xviii. p. 81). "One Fryth which was in the Tower in pryson, was appoynted by the kyng's grace to be examyned befor me, my lorde of London, my lorde of Wynchester, my lorde of Suffolke, my lorde

of those who denied the king's supremacy, and in the contest with the northern insurgents; but when, in 1535, a colony of German Anabaptists landed in England, they were instantly apprehended; and fourteen, who refused to recant, were condemned to the flames. The fate of these adventurers did not alarm their brethren abroad; in 1538, more missionaries followed: and the king ordered Cranmer, with three other prelates, to call them before him, to admonish them of their errors, and to deliver the refractory to the secular magistrate. Four of the number abjured; one man and a woman expiated their obstinacy at the stake.[1]

But of all the prosecutions for heresy, none excited greater interest than that of Lambert, alias Nicholson, a clergyman in priest's orders, and schoolmaster in London; nor is it the least remarkable circumstance in his story, that of the three men who brought him to the stake, Taylor, Barnes, and Cranmer, two professed, perhaps even then, most certainly later, the very doctrine for which they prosecuted their victim, and all three suffered afterwards the same or nearly the same punishment.[2] Lambert had been imprisoned on a charge of heresy by Archbishop Warham, and had escaped by the timely death of that prelate: but his zeal despised the warning; and, urged by an unconquerable passion for controversy, he presented to Dr. Taylor a written paper containing eight reasons against the belief of the real presence. Taylor consulted Barnes; Barnes disclosed the matter to Cranmer; and Cranmer summoned the schoolmaster to answer for his presumption in the archiepiscopal court. The particulars of his examination have not been preserved; but he appealed from the metropolitan to the head of the church; and the king gladly embraced the opportunity of exercising in person the judicial functions attached to his supremacy. On the appointed day he took his seat on the throne, clothed in robes of white silk; on his right were placed the bishops, the judges, and the sages of the law; on his left the temporal peers and the officers of the household. The proceedings were

chancelloure, and my lorde of Wyltshire, whose opynion was so notably erroneouse, that we culde not dispatche hym; but was fayne to leve hym to the determynacion of his ordinarye, which ys the bishop of London. His said opynion ys of such nature, that he thoughte it not necessary to be beleved as an article of our faythe, that ther ys the very corporall presence of Christe within the oste and sacramente of the alter; and holdeth of this poynte moste after the opynion of Oecolampadious. And suerly I myself sent for hym iii or iiii tymes to perswade hym to leve that his imaginacion; but for all that we culd do therein, he woulde not apply to any counsaile: notwithstandyng he ys nowe at a fynall ende with all examinacions for my lorde of London hathe gyven sentance, and delyvered hym to the secular power, where he looketh every day to go to the fyer. And ther ys condempned with hym one Andrewe a tayloure of London for the said self-same opynion."

[1] Stowe, 570, 575. Collier, ii. Records, 46. Wilk. Con. iii. 836. It is remarkable that Barnes, who was burnt soon afterwards, was one of the commissioners.

[2] It is not easy to ascertain the real sentiments of the English reformers at a time when the very suspicion of heteroloxy might have cost them their lives. Knowing the king's attachment to the doctrine of the real presence, they deemed it prudent to elude, and, if possible, to suppress all controversy on that subject. Thus Cranmer conjured Vadianus to be silent; because "dici non potest, quantum hæc tam cruenta controversia.........maxime apud nos bene currenti verbo evangelii obstiterit."—Strype's Cran. App. p. 47, anno 1537. And Fox observes of Barnes, that "although he did otherwise favour the gospel, he seemed not greatly to favour this cause, fearing peradventure that it would breed some let or hindrance among the people to the preaching of the gospel."—Fox, ii. 355. Cranmer's promptitude to reject the doctrine of the real presence, when he could do it with safety, has provoked a suspicion that he did not sincerely believe it before: but Burnet and Strype conceive that he held the Lutheran tenet of consubstantiation at this period; and I am inclined to think the same from the tenor of the two letters already quoted,—that to Hawkins, and the other to Vadianus.

opened by Sampson, bishop of Chichester, who said that though the king had abolished the papal authority, ejected the monks and friars, and put down superstition and idolatry, he neither meant to trench on the ancient doctrines, nor to suffer the faith of his fathers to be insulted with impunity. Henry rose, and in a mild and conciliatory tone, inquired of the accused whether he were still attached to his former opinion. Having received an answer in the affirmative, he made a long and argumentative harangue against the first of the reasons contained in the writing which Lambert had presented to Taylor. He was followed by the bishops, seven in number, to each of whom had been allotted the refutation of one of the remaining objections. Lambert occasionally attempted to answer his opponents; but he seemed overpowered with terror, and gave no proof of that ability and learning for which he had been extolled by his partisans. Five hours were employed by the several disputants, Henry, Cranmer, Gardiner, Tunstall, Stokesley, Sampson, and two others; when the king asked him, "What sayest thou now, after the instructions of these learned men? Art thou satisfied? Wilt thou live or die?" The prisoner replied, that he threw himself on the mercy of his majesty. "Then," said the king, "thou must die, for I will not be the patron of heretics;" and Cromwell, as the vicar-general, arose, and pronounced the usual judgment in cases of heresy.[1] Lambert met his fate with the constancy of a man who was convinced that he suffered for the truth; Henry, who had expected to make him a convert, was consoled for his disappointment by the praise which his flatterers lavished on his zeal, his eloquence, and his erudition.[2]

But while the king was employing his authority in support of the ancient doctrines, the court of Rome threatened to visit his past transgressions with the severest punishment in its power. Paul had formerly indulged a hope that some fortunate event might bring Henry back to the communion of the Apostolic See; and that expectation was encouraged by a succession of occurrences which seemed to favour his views. The publication of "the Articles" showed that the king was not disposed to dissent from the pontiff on doctrinal matters: the death of Catherine and the execution of Anne Boleyn removed the first and principal cause of the schism; and it was thought that the northern insurrection would convince Henry of the danger of persisting in his apostasy. But if his passion for Anne originally provoked, his avarice, ambition, and

---

[1] If any thing after this exhibition can surprise the reader, it will be the praise which is bestowed on it by Cromwell himself in a letter to Wyatt, the ambassador in Germany. "The king's majesty presided at the disputation, process, and judgment of a miserable heretic sacramentary, who was burnt the 20th of November. It was wonderful to see how princely, with how excellent gravity, and inestimable majesty, his highness exercised there the very office of supreme head of the church of England; how benignly his grace essayed to convert the miserable man; how strong and manifest reasons his highness alleged against him. I wish the princes and potentates of Christendom to have had a meet place to have seen it."—Collier, ii. 152.

[2] Godwin (67) and Fox (ii. 355—358) have given long accounts of this trial; but I have deserted them, where I could obtain better authority. Lambert's arguments were eight, not ten, as appears from the speech of Sampson (not Day), bishop of Chichester, published by Strype (App. 43); Henry's tone was not intimidating but conciliatory, if we may believe Cromwell in the last note; and the prisoner showed no ability, but considerable terror, according to Hall, who was present (Hall, 233). The story told by Fox of Cromwell sending for Lambert to his house, and asking his pardon, is irreconcilable with his letter to Wyatt.

resentment now conspired to perpetuate the quarrel. Far from accepting offers of reconciliation, he appeared to seek opportunities of displaying his hostility, and by his agents at different courts laboured to withdraw all other sovereigns from the communion of Rome. Paul was perplexed by the opposite opinions of his advisers. Many condemned the suspension of the censures against Henry as inconsistent with the honour and the interest of the pontiff, while others continued to object the disgrace and impolicy of publishing a sentence without the power of carrying it into execution. The great obstacle arose from the difficulty of appeasing the resentments, and reconciling the claims of the emperor and the king of France. After years of contention in the cabinet and in the field, neither had obtained the mastery over the other; and if Charles had defeated the attempts of his adversary on Milan and Naples, Francis, by allying himself with the Protestants of Germany, and calling to his aid the naval forces of Turkey, had been able to paralyze the superior power of Charles. Wearied at length by hostilities without victory, and negotiations without peace, they listened to the entreaties and exhortations of Paul; a truce of ten years was concluded under the papal mediation at Nice; and the pontiff embraced the favourable opportunity to sound the disposition of the two monarchs relatively to the conduct of Henry. From both he received the same answer, that if *he* would publish the bull, *they* would send ambassadors to England to protest against the schism; would refuse to entertain the relations of amity with a prince who had separated himself from the Catholic church; and would strictly forbid all commercial intercourse between their subjects and the English merchants.[1]

The substance of these negotiations was soon conveyed to Henry by the spies whom he maintained at different courts; and, to disconcert the counsels of his enemies, he instructed his ambassadors abroad to excite by tempting offers the hopes, and inflame by artful suggestions the jealousy of both Francis and Charles; while at home, that he might be provided for the event, he ordered his navy to be equipped, the harbours to be put in a state of defence, and the whole population to be called under arms.[2]

Among those who had accompanied the pontiff to Nice, was Cardinal Pole, whom both the emperor and the king had received with marked distinction, and whom Henry believed to be the original author of the present combination against him. The cardinal, indeed, under the protection of foreign powers, might defy the malice of his persecutor; but his mother, and brothers, and relatives, remained in England; and these were now marked out for victims by the jealousy, or the resentment, of the monarch. Becket, usher, and Wrothe, sewer of the royal chamber, proceeded on a mission to Cornwall, ostensibly to visit their friends, in reality to collect matters for accusation against Henry Courtenay, marquess of Exeter, and his adherents and dependants.[3] In a short time Sir Geoffrey Pole, a brother of the cardinal, was brought before the council and committed. His arrest

---

[1] Though the cardinals Farnese and Pole repeatedly mention the protestation in their letters, they do not explain its object, because it was sufficiently known to their correspondents. I have, however, collected it from detached passages, and have no doubt that it is faithfully represented above.

[2] Hall, 234.

[3] See the instructions to Becket and Wrothe in Arch. xxii. 24. All doubt respecting the lines between the 3rd and 4th articles may be removed by reference to the letter in Ellis, ii. 104.

was followed by that of another brother, the lord Montague, of their mother the countess of Salisbury, of the marquess and marchioness of Exeter, and of Sir Edward Neville, the brother of Lord Abergavenny.[1] Courtenay was grandson to Edward IV., his mother being Catherine, daughter of that monarch; and the Poles were grandsons to George, duke of Clarence, the brother of Edward, their mother being Margaret, the daughter of Clarence and the countess of Salisbury. On this account both families were revered by the ancient adherents of the house of York; and had not their loyalty been proof against ambition, they might have taught the king, during the northern insurrection, to tremble for the security of his crown.[2] On the last day of the year the marquess and the lord Montague were arraigned before their peers, and three days later the commoners, before juries of their equals, on a charge of having devised to maintain, promote, and advance one Reginald Pole, late dean of Exeter, the king's enemy beyond the seas, and to deprive the king of his royal state and dignity. The overt act charged against the marquess (probably the case of the others might be similar) was, that he had been heard to say, "I like well of the proceedings of Cardinal Pole: I like not the proceedings of this realm. I trust to see a change in the world. I trust once to have a fair day on the knaves which rule about the king. I trust to give them a buffet one day."[3] It would require some ingenuity to extract treason from these words, even if they had been proved; but both peers and jury had only to do the bidding of their imperious master; and all the accused, being found guilty, received judgment of death. Geoffrey Pole saved his life, as it was supposed, by revealing the secrets of his companions in misfortune;[4] the rest were beheaded, as was also Sir Nicholas Carew, master of the horse, for being of counsel to the marquess. A commission then proceeded to Cornwall, and two Cornish gentlemen, Kendall and Quintrell, suffered death on the charge of having said, some years before, that Exeter was the heir apparent, and should be king, if Henry married Anne Boleyn, or it would cost a thousand lives.[5] These executions, particularly of noblemen so nearly allied to Henry in blood, on a charge so ill defined and improbable, excited a general horror; and the king in his own vindication, ordered a book to be published containing the proofs of their real or pretended treason.[6]

The pontiff, encouraged by the promises of Charles and Francis, to which had now been joined those of the king of the Romans and of the king of Scotland, revoked the suspension, and ordered the publication of the bull.[7]

---

[1] Ellis, ii. 96.

[2] Maximo erant numero, et illorum sanguini et nomini plusquam deditissimi. Quo tempore non solum illi in suo malo resistere facultatem maximam habuissent, sed illum cum omnium commodo si voluissent, oppugnandi, et tyrannide ejiciendi.—Apol. Poli ad Car. p. 112.

[3] Howell's State Trials, iii. 367.

[4] He was probably sent out of the kingdom; for he obtained a full pardon and permission to return in the next reign.—Burnet, iii. 186.   [5] Ellis, ii. 107.

[6] Lord Herbert observes that he could never discover the particular offences of these lords; only that the secretary in a letter to one of the ambassadors says that the accusations were great, and duly proved, and that another person says they had relieved the cardinal with money.—Herb. 502. See one of these letters in Ellis, ii. 109. Such circulars were always sent on similar occasions in vindication of the king's conduct. The cardinal himself maintains that if they had entertained any designs against the king, they would have shown them during the insurrection; and adds that he had sought in vain in the king's book for some proof against them;—sed nihil tandem invenire potui, nisi id quod liber tacet, et quod ipse diu judicavi, odium tyranni in virtutem et nobilitatem.—Apol. Poli, 118.

[7] Bullar. Rom. 708.

At the same time Cardinal Pole was despatched on a secret mission to the Spanish and French courts; but his arrival had been anticipated by the English agents: neither Charles nor Francis would incur the hostility of Henry by being the first to declare himself; and both equally prohibited the publication of the bull within their dominions.[1] To the cardinal at Toledo, Charles replied, that there were other matters which more imperiously required his attention; the progress made by the Turks in Hungary, and the hostile disposition of the Protestants in Germany; that the latter, were he to provoke Henry, would solicit and obtain pecuniary aid out of those treasures which the king of England had acquired by the suppression of the monasteries; that nevertheless he was willing to fulfil his engagements, to make the protestation, and to interrupt all commercial intercourse, but on this condition, that the king of France should cordially join in the undertaking, and adopt at the same time the same measures. Pole returned, and from Avignon sent a confidential messenger to Francis, from whom he received an answer equally cold and unpromising, that he was indeed anxious to perform his promise to the pontiff, but he could not rely on the mere word of the emperor; that he requested the legate not to enter his dominions till he could bring with him some certain document as a pledge of the imperial sincerity; and that in such case he should be willing to join his forces with those of Charles and the king of Scotland, to attempt the conquest of England; and in event of success, to divide it among the three powers, or to establish a new sovereign in the place of Henry.[2] The negotiation continued for some months; Francis persisting in his refusal to receive the legate without the pledge demanded from Charles, and Charles to give that pledge till the legate had been received by Francis as well as by himself. The pontiff, who saw that he was deluded by the insincerity of the two monarchs, recalled Pole to Rome; and the papal court, abandoning all hope of succeeding by intimidation, submitted to watch in silence the course of political events.[3]

The part which the cardinal had taken in the negotiation inflamed the hatred of Henry. Judgment of treason was pronounced against him; foreign princes were solicited to deliver him up; and he was constantly beset with spies, and, as he believed, with ruffians hired to take his life. At home, to wound him in the most tender part,

---

[1] I cannot find any proof that it was ever published at all.

[2] If this suggestion had been thrown out before, and come to the knowledge of Henry, it would account for the late executions. He could fear no competitor whom they might set up, unless he were of the house of York.

[3] For these particulars consult the letters of Cardinal Pole (ii. p. 142—199, 232); those of Cardinal Farnese, from Toledo (ibid. cclxxxiv. cclxxxvii.); Pole's instructions, cclxxix.; Beccatelli's life of Pole in the same work (v. 365); and Pallavicini's account, drawn from the letters of different legates and nuncios (Pallav. i. 309). Pole, to excuse his conduct in this legation, assures Edward VI. that his chief object was, to induce these princes to employ all their interest with Henry in favour of religion; but acknowledges that he wished them, in case the king refused to listen to them as friends, to add menaces, and to interrupt the commerce with his subjects. He asserts, however, that he had no desire to injure him in reality, nor ever attempted to excite them to make war upon him—hoc ego nunquam profecto volui, neque cum illis egi.—Ep. ad Edvard. tom. iv. p. 337. He might, indeed, have hoped that these measures would persuade or intimidate Henry; but he must also have known, that if they had been pursued, they would lead to discontent within the kingdom, and to war without; and that such results were contemplated by those who employed him. Che tutti d'accordo levariano il commertio d'Inghilterra, con la qual via pensavasi, che le genti, di quel regno havessero a tumultuare.—Beccat. 367. That there was some expectation of war, appears also from the letter of Farnese, supra.

Henry ordered his mother, the venerable countess of Salisbury, to be arrested and examined by the earl of Southampton and the bishop of Ely; but she behaved with such firmness of character, such apparent consciousness of innocence, as completely disconcerted her accusers. Unable to extract from her admissions sufficient matter for a criminal prosecution, Cromwell consulted the judges, whether a person accused of treason might not be attainted without a previous trial or confession. They replied, that it would form a dangerous precedent; that no inferior tribunal would venture on so illegal a proceeding; but that the court of parliament was supreme, and an attainder by parliament would be good in law.[1] This was sufficient for the king, who sought not justice but revenge; and in a bill of attainder, containing the names of several individuals who had been condemned in the lower courts, were introduced those of Pole's mother the countess, of his nephew the son of Lord Montague,[2] and of Gertrude, relict of the marquess of Exeter, though none of them had confessed any crime, or been heard in their own defence. With the fate of the young man we are not acquainted; the marchioness obtained a pardon at the expiration of six months;[3] and it was hoped that the king would extend the same mercy to the countess. She was more than seventy years of age, the nearest to him in blood of all his relations, and the last in a direct line of the Plantagenets, a family which had swayed the English sceptre through so many generations. Henry kept her in the Tower, probably as a hostage for the behaviour of her son, or her friends; but at the end of two years, on account of some provocation in which she could have had no share, ordered her to be put to death. In the prison and on the scaffold she maintained the dignity of her rank and descent; and when she was told to lay her head on the block, "No," she replied, "my head never committed treason; if you will have it, you must take it as you can." She was held down by force; and while the executioner performed his office, exclaimed, "Blessed are they who suffer persecution for righteousness' sake." Her death, or rather murder, which seemed to have no rational object, proclaimed to the world that the heart of the king was not less steeled to the feelings of relationship and humanity, than it was inaccessible to considerations of justice and honour; and proved an awful admonition to his subjects, that nothing short of unlimited obedience could shield them from the vengeance of their sovereign.[4]

V. For some time Cromwell and Cranmer had reigned without control in the council. The duke of Norfolk, after the submission of the insurgents, had retired to his estates in the country; and Gardiner, on his return from an honourable exile of two years in foreign courts, had repaired, without even seeing the king, to his bishopric of Winchester.[5] But the general understanding between the pontiff and the Catholic sovereigns, and the mission of Pole to the emperor and the

---

[1] Coke, Inst. iv. 37.
[2] I observe that our historians are ignorant of the attainder, and even of the existence, of the son of Lord Montague. Yet Pole could not have been mistaken. Nec vero solam damu: tam mulierem septuagenariam, qua nullam, excepta filia, propinquiorem habet; et, ut ille ipse, qui eam damnavit, sæpe dicere solebat, neo regnum illud sanctiorem habuit feminam, sed cum nepote suo, filio fratris mei puero, spe reliqua stirpis nostræ.—Ep. Poli, ii. 197.
[3] Rym. xiv. 652.
[4] See Pole's letter to the cardinal of Burgos. He concludes, quod autem ad me ipsum attinet, etiam honore auctus hujus mortis genere videor, qui deinceps martyris me filium (quod certe plus est quam ullo regio genere ortum esse) nunquam verebor dicere (iii. 36, 70). [5] Le Grand, ii. 223.

king of France, had awakened serious apprehensions and new projects in the mind of Henry. He determined to prove to the world that he was the decided advocate of the ancient doctrines: Gardiner was recalled to court, and ordered to preach during the Lent at St. Paul's Cross; and the duke of Norfolk was commissioned to conduct the business of the crown as the prime minister, in the house of peers. As soon as the parliament assembled, a committee of spiritual lords was appointed to examine the diversity of opinions on religious subjects; but on every question the members divided five against four, the bishops of York, Durham, Carlisle, Bath, and Bangor, against Cromwell and the prelates of Canterbury, Salisbury, and Ely. The king waited eleven days for their decision; his patience was exhausted; and the duke, having remarked that no result was to be expected from the labours of the committee, proposed to the consideration of the house six questions respecting the eucharist, communion under one kind, private masses, the celibacy of the priesthood, auricular confession, and vows of chastity. The debate was confined to the spiritual peers, while the others, even Cromwell and Audeley, observed a prudent and respectful silence. On the second day the king himself came down to the house, and joined in the debate. To resist the royal theologian required a degree of courage unusual in the prelates of that day; and Cranmer and his colleagues, who had hitherto led the opposition, now, with the exception of the bishop of Salisbury, owned themselves vanquished and convinced by the superiority of his reasoning and learning.[1]

Immediately after a short prorogation, Henry, flattered with his victory, sent a message to the lords, congratulating them on the unanimity which had been obtained, and recommending the enactment of penalties against those who should presume to disturb it by preaching the contrary doctrines. Two separate committees were appointed, with the same instructions to each, to prepare a bill in conformity with the royal suggestion. One consisted, and it must appear a most singular selection, of three converts to the cause, the prelates of Canterbury, Ely, and St. David's, and the other of their warmest opponents, the bishops of York, Durham, and Winchester. Instead of choosing between the two bills, which they presented, the lords submitted both to the king, who gave the preference to that which had been drawn by the second committee;[2] and this, as soon as the clergy

---

[1] On the testimony of Fox we are told that the archbishop persisted in his opposition to the last (Fox, ii. 372. Burnet, i. 258); but this statement not only seems irreconcilable with the Journals, but is contradicted by a document of far higher authority. We know not the name of the writer, but he was a lord of parliament, had been present at the discussions, and thus describes the proceedings, at the very time when they took place:—" Notwithstanding my lord of Canterbury, my lord of Ely, my lord of Salisbury, my lords of Worcester, Rochester, and St. Davyes, defended the contrary a long time, yet finally his highness confounded them all with goodlie learning. York, Durham, Winchester, London, Chichester, Norwiche, and Carlisle have showed themselves honest and well learned men. We of the temporalty have been all of one opinion; and my lord chancellor (Audeley) and my lord privy seal (Cromwell) as good as we can devise. My lord of Canterbury and all his bishops have given their opinions, and have come in to us, save Salisbury, who yet continueth a lewd fool."—Cleop. E. v. p. 128. It was probably Cranmer's consciousness of having on this occasion sacrificed his own convictions to the will of the king, and his knowledge that others had done the same, which induced him to assert to the Devonshire insurgents that "if the king's majesty had not come personally into the parliament house, those laws had never passed" (Strype, App. 92); and to remind Gardiner, that " how that matter was enforced by some persons, they knew right well, that were there present."—Defence against Gardiner, 286.

[2] It is supposed that it had been drawn up with the privity of the king, as there is

in the lower house of convocation had reported their assent to the articles, was introduced by the chancellor, passed by the lords and commons, and received the royal assent.[1] It begins by reciting the six articles to which the parliament and convocation had agreed: 1. That in the eucharist is really present the natural body of Christ, under the forms, and without the substance, of bread and wine; 2. That communion under both kinds is not necessary ad salutem; 3. That priests may not marry by the law of God; 4. That vows of chastity are to be observed; 5. That private masses ought to be retained; 6. That the use of auricular confession is expedient and necessary. Then follow the penalties: 1. If any person write, preach, or dispute against the first article, he shall not be allowed to abjure, but shall suffer death as a heretic, and forfeit his goods and chattels to the king; 2. If he preach in any sermon or collation, or speak openly before the judges against any one of the other five, he shall incur the usual penalties of felony; but if he only hold contrary opinions, and publish them, he shall for the first offence be imprisoned at the king's pleasure, and shall forfeit his lands during life, and his goods for ever; for the second he shall suffer death; 3. The act pronounces the marriages of priests or nuns of no effect, orders such persons so married to be separated; and makes it felony if they cohabit afterwards; 4. It subjects priests, living carnally with women, or nuns with men, to imprisonment and forfeiture on the first conviction, and to death on the second: and lastly, it enacts that persons contemptuously refusing to confess at the usual times, or to receive the sacrament, shall for the first offence be fined and imprisoned, and for the second be adjudged felons, and suffer the punishment of felony.[2]

Such were the enactments of this severe and barbarous statute. It filled with terror the teachers and advocates of the new doctrines, who saw from the king's temper that their only security was silence and submission to the royal will. Latimer and Shaxton, the bishops of Worcester and Salisbury, who by the intemperance of their language had given offence, resigned spontaneously, or at the king's requisition, their respective sees.[3] But no one had greater cause of alarm than Cranmer. The reader will recollect that before his promotion to the archiepiscopal dignity, he had married a kinswoman of Osiander, in Germany. At a convenient time she followed him to England, where she bore him several children. He was too prudent to acknowledge her publicly; but the secret quickly transpired; and many priests, emboldened by the impunity, imitated the example of the metropolitan. As the canons, which imposed celibacy on the priesthood, had never been

---

extant a bill nearly similar in Henry's own hand. It is published by Wilkins, iii. 848.

[1] As a week intervened between the appointment of the committee and the introduction of the bill, Burnet supposes that it met with great opposition in the council (i. 258). But this is a gratuitous supposition. The committees sat on Saturday, May 31. On Monday, June 2, their bills were probably offered to the king; on Tuesday, Cromwell submitted the six articles to the consideration of the clergy; on Thursday their answer was returned; and on Saturday the chancellor brought the bill into the house of Lords.—See Journals, 113, 114, 116; and the acts of the convocation, Wilk. Con. iii. 845. [2] Stat. of Realm, iii. 739—741.

[3] Godwin, Annals, p. 70. De Præsul. Ang. i. 353; ii. 49. The French ambassador says that both refused their assent. Et deux eveques, principaux auteurs des......... et doctrines nouvelles, pour n'avcir voulu souscrire à edits, ont esté privez de leurs evechez.—Le Grand, ii. 199. Latimer asserted in 1546 that "he left his bishoprick beeng borne in hande by the Lord Crumwel that it was his Majestes pleasure he shuld resigne it, which his Majesty aftre denyed, and pitied his condicion."—State Pap. i. 849.

abrogated, the head of the church thought it his duty to notice these transgressions, and by a circular letter ordered the bishops to make inquiries in their dioceses, and either to imprison the offenders, or to certify their names to the council.[1] Two years later appeared a proclamation, ordering all priests, " who had attempted marriages that were openly known," to be deprived of their benefices, and reputed as laymen; and threatening that all who should marry after that notice should suffer punishment and imprisonment at his grace's pleasure.[2]

Though neither of these orders reached the archbishop, they convinced him that he stood on very slippery ground. To save himself, he had recourse to every expedient which his ingenuity could supply. First, with becoming humility he submitted to the superior judgment of Henry such reasons against the law of clerical celibacy as had occurred to his mind; he then suggested the expediency of a royal declaration imposing silence on the subject, and leaving every man to the dictates of his own conscience; and at length he boldly proposed, that the lawfulness of the marriage of priests should be debated in the universities before impartial judges, on the condition that, if judgment were given against his opinion, its advocates should suffer death; if in its favour, the canonical prohibition should be no longer enforced. To these solicitations of Cranmer was added the reasoning of his friend Melancthon, who, in a long and declamatory epistle, undertook the difficult task of convincing the obstinacy of the king.[3] But neither argument, nor solicitation, nor artifice, could divert Henry from his purpose. The celibacy of the priesthood was made one of the six articles and Cranmer saw with dismay that his marriage was reputed void in law, and that subsequent cohabitation would subject him to the penalty of death. In haste he despatched his children with their mother to her friends in Germany, and wrote to the king an apology for his presumption in having opposed the opinion of his majesty. Henry, appeased by his submission, returned a gracious and consoling answer by the duke of Norfolk, and Cromwell the vicar-general.[4]

Cromwell, who had been created a baron in 1536, still continued to possess considerable influence in the royal councils. His services were still wanted to perfect the great work of the dissolution of monasteries; and[3] by professing himself an early convert to the doctrine of the six articles, and labouring to procure proselytes among the bishops,[5] he had avoided the displeasure of his sovereign. It has been already noticed, that before the prorogation of parliament, all the property, real or moveable, of the religious houses " which had been already or might be hereafter dissolved, suppressed, or surrendered, or had or might by any other means come into the hands of the king," was vested in Henry and his heirs for ever, with authority to endow new bishoprics out of it according to his or their pleasure. This act affected the interests of only one class of subjects; but to it was added another, which lay prostrate at the foot of the throne the liberties of the whole nation It declared that the king for the time being should possess the right of issuing, with the advice of his council, proclamations which ought to have

---

[1] Wilk. Con. iii. 826.
[2] Strype's Cranmer, App. No. viii.
[3] Burnet, i. Records, Nos. iv. vi.

[4] Antiq. Brit. 333.
[5] Constantyne's Memoir, Archæol. xxiii. 63.

the effect of acts of parliament; adjudged all transgressors of such proclamations to suffer the imprisonment, and pay the fines expressed in them; and made it high treason to leave the realm in order to escape the penalty.[1] It was not without considerable difficulty that this act was carried through the two houses; but both the men of the old and of the new learning, jealous of each other, concurred in every measure which they knew to be pleasing to the sovereign; and the consent of the other members was obtained by the introduction of a nugatory exception in favour of statutes then in being, and saving the inheritances, offices, liberties, goods, chattels, and lives of the king's subjects.[2] At the same time Henry celebrated his triumph over the court of Rome by a naval exhibition on the Thames. Two galleys, decorated with the royal, the other with the pontifical arms, met on the river; a stubborn conflict ensued; at length the royalists boarded their antagonist; and the figures of the pope and the different cardinals were successively thrown into the water, amidst the acclamations of the king, of his court, and of the citizens.[3]

Notwithstanding these appearances, Cromwell, when he considered his real situation, discovered abundant cause for alarm. Henry in public had affected to treat him always with neglect, sometimes with insult; but these affronts he had borne with patience, knowing that they proceeded not from displeasure on the part of the king, but from unwillingness to have it thought that he stood in need of the services of the minister. Now, however, it was plain that the ancient doctrines had assumed a decided ascendancy in the royal mind; the statute of the Six Articles had been enacted contrary to his wish, and, as far as he dared disclose himself, contrary to his advice; his friends were disgraced and dispirited; his enemies active in pursuit of the king's favour; and it was useless for him to seek support from the ancient nobility, who had long borne his superior elevation with real though dissembled impatience. In these circumstances, he turned his eyes towards the Lutheran princes of Germany, with whom he had long maintained a friendly though clandestine correspondence; but the plan which he adopted to retrieve his credit served only, from the capricious disposition of the king, to accelerate his downfal.

Henry had been a widower more than two years. In 1537, Jane Seymour, his third queen, bore him a male child, afterwards Edward VI.,

---

[1] St. 31 Hen. VIII. 8. Thus Cromwell nearly accomplished his favourite doctrine, which he had formerly inculcated to Pole, and frequently maintained before Henry. "The Lord Cromwell," says Gardiner in one of his letters, "had once put in the king's head to take upon him to have his will and pleasure regarded for a law; and thereupon I was called for at Hampton Court. And as he was very stout, Come on, my lord of Winchester, quoth he, answer the king here, but speak plainly and directly, and shrink not, man. Is not that, quoth he, that pleaseth the king, a law? Have ye not that in the civil laws quod principi placuit, &c.? I stood still, and wondered in my mind to what conclusion this would tend. The king saw me musing, and with gentle earnestness said, Answer him whether it be so or no. I would not answer the Lord Cromwell, but delivered my speech to the king, and told him, that I had read of kings that had their will always received for law; but that the form of his reign to make the law his will was more sure and quiet, and by this form of government ye be established, quoth I, and it is agreeable with the nature of your people. If you begin a new manner of policy, how it may frame no man can tell. The king turned his back, and left the matter."—Fox, ii. 65.

[2] Stat. of Realm, iii. 726. Marillac, in his account of it to the king of France, says, Laquelle chose, Sire, a esté accordé avec grandes difficultez, qui ont esté debattues long tems en leurs assemblées, et avec peu de contentment, par ce qu'on voit de ceux qui y ont prété leur consentment.—Apud Le Grand, ii. 206.

[3] It was, says Marillac, un jeu de pauvre grace, et de oindre invention.—Ibid. 205.

and in less than a fortnight expired. His grief for her loss, if he were capable of feeling such grief, seemed to be absorbed in joy for the birth of a son;[1] and in the very next month he solicited the hand of Marie, the duchess dowager of Longueville. He was enamoured with her gentleness, her mental acquirements, and, above all, with the largeness of her person; not that he had seen her himself, but that he gave full credit to a confidential agent, who had artfully insinuated himself into her family. Marie, however, preferred a more youthful lover, James, king of Scotland; but Henry would admit of no refusal, nor believe the king of France, who assured him that she was contracted to James. During five months he persecuted her with his suit, and when she sailed from the shores of France to join her husband, betrayed his chagrin by refusing the permission which she asked, to land at Dover, and travel through his dominions. A daughter of Vendome was then offered; but Henry deemed it beneath him to take for a wife a woman who had been previously rejected by his nephew of Scotland; and he was prevented from marrying one of the two sisters of Marie, because Francis would not gratify his caprice by exhibiting them before him at Calais, and allowing him to make his choice.[2] These attempts of the English king to procure a wife from France alarmed the jealousy of the emperor, who, to divert him from this purpose, proposed to him to marry Christina, relict of Sforza, late duke of Milan, and to give his daughter Mary to Don Louis, infant of Portugal. The suggestion was received with pleasure. Ambassadors hastened to Spain, but could not prevail on Charles to settle Milan on the infant, a condition required by Henry. Other ambassadors repaired to the Low Countries, where Christina resided with Anne, queen of Hungary, and regent of the Netherlands. The duchess was "a goodly personage, of stature higher than either of the envoys, a very good woman's face, and competently fayre, very well favored, and a lyttle browne." But the regent was so slow and dilatory in the negotiation, that Henry put an end to it abruptly, because he suspected the offer to have been a mere feint; and aware, "that time slippeth and flyeth marvellously away," he would not defeat his object of procuring, if possible, "more increase of issue to the assurance of his succession."[3] Under these repeated disappointments, he was the more ready to listen to the suggestions of Cromwell, who proposed to him Anne, sister of William, the reigning duke of Cleves, and one of the Protestant princes of Germany. The English envoys reported to the king that Anne was both tall and portly, qualifications which he deemed essential in his wife: of her beauty he was satisfied by a flattering portrait from the pencil of Hans Holbein;[4] and his assent to their union was readily obtained by a splendid embassy from the German princes. On the day on which Anne was expected to land at Dover, the king rode in disguise to meet her at Rochester, that he might steal a first glance, and, as he expressed it, "might nourish

---

[1] To Francis, who had congratulated him on the birth of a son, he announced her death in the following unfeeling manner: "Il a semblé bon à la divine providence, de mealer cette ma grande joye avec l'amaritude du tréspas de celle qui m'avoit apporté ce bonheur. De la main de votre bon frere, Henry."—Le Grand, ii. 185.

[2] Disant qu'il semble qu'on veuille par delà faire des femmes comme de leurs guilledins, qui est en assembler une bonne quantité et les faire trotter pour prendre celuy qui ira le plus à l'aise.—Lettre à M. de Castillon, apud Le Grand, iii. 638.

[3] Chron. Catal. 204—212.

[4] He painted both Anne and her sister Emily, that the king might make his choice. —Herb. 221. Ellis, ii. 122.

love." His disappointment was evident. She was indeed tall and large as his heart could wish; but her features, though regular, were coarse, her manners ungraceful, her figure ill-proportioned. He shrunk back, and took time to compose himself before he was announced. As she bent her knee, he raised her up, and saluted her; but he could not prevail upon himself to converse with her, or to deliver the presents which he had brought for her; and after a few minutes, retiring to his chamber, sent for the lords who had accompanied her from Dover.[1] The next morning he hastened back to Greenwich; a council was summoned; and Cromwell received orders to devise some expedient to interrupt the marriage. Two days passed in fruitless consultation; Anne was required to swear that she was not pre-engaged to any other person; her conductors were subjected to repeated interrogatories; and the king at length, unprovided with any reasonable excuse, and afraid of adding the German princes to his other enemies, after the passionate exclamation, "Is there no other remedy, but that I must needs against my will put my neck into the noose?" was persuaded by Cromwell to submit to the ceremony. They cohabited for some months; but Anne had none of those arts or qualifications which might have subdued the antipathy of her husband. He spoke only English or French; she knew no other language than German. He was passionately fond of music; she could neither play nor sing. He wished his consort to excel in the different amusements of his court; she possessed no other acquirements than to read, and write, and sew with her needle. His aversion increased; he found fault with her person; persuaded himself that she was of a perverse and sullen disposition; and openly lamented his fate in being yoked for life with so disagreeable a companion.[2]

This unfortunate marriage had already shaken the credit of Cromwell · his fall was hastened by a theological quarrel between Dr. Barnes, one of his dependants, and Gardiner, bishop of Winchester. In a sermon at St. Paul's Cross, the prelate had severely censured the presumption of those preachers, who, in opposition to the established creed, inculcated the Lutheran tenet of justification by faith without works. A fortnight later, Dr. Barnes, an ardent admirer of Luther, boldly defended the condemned doctrine from the same pulpit, and indulged in a scurrilous invective against the bishop. The king summoned the preacher before himself and a commission of divines, discussed with him several points of controverted doctrine, prevailed on him to sign a recantation, and enjoined him to preach on the same subject a second time on the first Sunday after Easter. Barnes affected to obey. He read his recantation before the audience, publicly asked pardon of Gardiner, and then, proceeding with his sermon, maintained in still stronger terms the very doctrine which he had recanted. Irritated by this insult, the king committed him to the Tower, with Garret and Jerome, two preachers, who, placed in similar circumstances, had thought proper to follow his example.[3]

---

[1] "He was marvaillously astonied and abashed." He sent the presents the next morning, viz. a partlet, sable skins to wear ound the neck, and a muffley furred, with a cold a message as might be.—Strype. i. 307. On the ring which he gave her was inscribed the following allusion to the fate of Anne Boleyn: "God send me well to kepe."—Loseley MSS.

[2] See the depositions of the king and Cromwell in Burnet, i. Rec. 193—197; and of several lords in Strype, i. Rec. 307—315; and the letter of Wotton, Ellis, ii. 122.

[3] Fox, ii. 441—443. Hall, 241. Burnet, i. 296. Rec. iii. No. xxii.

It was generally believed that Henry's resentment against Barnes would beget suspicions of the orthodoxy of the minister, by whom Barnes had hitherto been protected; and so confidently did Cromwell's enemies anticipate his disgrace, that his two principal offices, those of vicar-general and keeper of the privy seal, were already, according to report, shared between Tunstall, bishop of Durham, and Clarke, bishop of Bath, prelates of the old learning, who had lately been introduced into the council.[1] The king, however, subdued or dissembled his suspicions; and, to the surprise of the public, Cromwell, at the opening of parliament, took his usual seat in the house of Lords, and delivered a royal message. It was, he said, with sorrow and displeasure that his majesty beheld the religious dissensions which divided the nation; that on the one hand presumption and liberty of the flesh, on the other attachment to ancient errors and superstitions, had generated two factions, which reciprocally branded each other with the opprobrious names of papists and heretics; that both abused the indulgence which of his great goodness the king had granted them, of reading the Scriptures in their native tongue, these to introduce error, those to uphold superstition; and that to remedy such evils, his majesty had appointed two committees of prelates and doctors, one to set forth a pure and sincere declaration of doctrine, the other to determine what ceremonies ought to be retained, what to be abolished; had strictly commanded the officers of the crown, with the judges and magistrates, to put in execution the laws already made respecting religion; and now required the aid of the two houses to enact penalties against those who should treat with irreverence, or explain rashly and erroneously, the holy Scriptures.[2]

The vicar-general now seemed to monopolize the royal favour. He had obtained a grant of thirty manors belonging to suppressed monasteries; the title of earl of Essex was revived in his favour;[3] and the office of lord chamberlain was added to his other appointments. He continued, as usual, to conduct in parliament the business of the crown. He introduced two bills, vesting the property of the Knights Hospitallers in the king, and settling a competent jointure on the queen; and he procured from the laity the almost unprecedented subsidy of four tenths and fifteenths, besides ten per cent. on their income from lands, and five per cent. on their goods; and from the clergy a grant of two tenths, and twenty per cent. on their incomes for two years.[4] So far indeed was he from apprehending the fate which awaited him, that he committed to the Tower the bishop of Chichester and Dr. Wilson, on a charge of having relieved prisoners confined for refusing the oath of supremacy, and threatened with the royal displeasure his chief opponents, the duke of Norfolk, and the bishops of Durham, Winchester, and Bath.[5]

But Henry in the mean time had ascertained that Barnes was the confidential agent of Cromwell; that he had been employed in secret missions to Germany; and that he had been the real negotiator of the late marriage with Anne of Cleves. Hence the king easily persuaded himself that the insolence of the agent arose from con-

---

[1] Le Grand, i. 285. [2] Journals, 129.

[3] The last earl, Henry Bourchier, had been killed by a fall from his horse, March 13, 1540.—Stowe, 579.

[4] Wilk. Con. 850, 863. Stat. of Realm, iii. 812.
[5] Le Grand, i. 286. See also a letter from the bishop of Chichester in the Tower to Cranmer, dated June 7, in Strype, Rec. 257.

fidence in the protection of the patron; that his vicar-general, instead of watching over the purity of the faith, had been the fautor of heretics; and that his own domestic happiness had been sacrificed by his minister to the interests of a religious faction. He now recollected that when he proposed to send Anne back to her brother, he had been dissuaded by Cromwell; and he moreover concluded, from the sudden change in her behaviour, that his intention of procuring a divorce had been betrayed to her by the same minister.[1] The earl seems to have had no suspicion of his approaching fate. On the morning of the tenth of June he attended in his place in the house of Lords; at three the same afternoon he was arrested at the council-board on a charge of high treason.[2] The offences of which he was afterwards accused may be ranged under three heads. As minister, it was said, that he had received bribes, and encroached on the royal authority by issuing commissions, discharging prisoners, pardoning convicts, and granting licenses for the exportation of prohibited merchandise; as vicar-general, he was charged with having betrayed his duty by not only holding heretical opinions himself, but also by protecting heretical preachers, and promoting the circulation of heretical books; and lastly, to fix on him the guilt of treason, it was alleged, that on one particular occasion he had expressed a resolution to fight against the king, if it were necessary, in support of his religious opinions.[3] He was confronted, at his request, with his accusers in presence of the royal commissioners, but was refused the benefit of a public trial before his peers.[4] The court preferred to proceed against him by bill of attainder; a most iniquitous measure, but of which he had no right to complain, as he had been the first to employ it against others. Cranmer alone ventured to interpose in his behalf; but his letter to the king was penned with his usual timidity and caution, rather enumerating the past services of Cromwell, than attempting to vindicate him from the charge on which he had been arrested.[5] Five days later the archbishop deemed it prudent to go along with the stream, and on the second and third readings gave his vote in favour of the attainder. The bill passed through the house of Lords, and probably through the house of Commons, without a dissentient voice.[6]

The disgrace of Cromwell was quickly followed by the divorce of the queen. On the first communication of Henry's intention she fainted to the ground; but recovering herself, was persuaded by degrees to submit the question to the decision of the clergy, and to be satisfied with the new title of the king's adopted sister. In the council several consultations were held, and different resolutions were taken. At first great reliance had been placed on a precontract of marriage between the

---

[1] Cromwell acknowledged that he had advised the change in her conduct; but denied that he had done so after the king had confided his secret to him.—See his letter in Burnet, iii. Rec. 161. [2] Journals, 143.
[3] Burnet, Rec. iii. No. 16. Mount was instructed to inform the German princes that Cromwell had threatened to strike a dagger into the heart of the man who should oppose the Reformation; which was interpreted to mean the king.—Burnet, iii. 162.
[4] See the duke of Norfolk's letter, Burnet, iii. Records, 74. It is remarkable that Cromwell was the first who perished in consequence of his own practice. He had first introduced condemnation by act of attainder, without trial, in the case of the countess of Salisbury; but she was still alive, and was not executed till the year after the execution of Cromwell. In the same letter the duke tells us that Catherine Howard, though his niece, was his great enemy; an assertion which does not confirm the supposition of Hume, that he employed her to ruin Cromwell by her insinuations to Henry. [5] Herbert, 519.
[6] Journals, 146. The act is published by Burnet, i. Rec. iii. xvi.

princess and the marquess of Lorraine; but when it was considered that both parties were children at the time, and had never since ratified the act of their parents, this plea was abandoned; and it was determined to rest the king's case on the misrepresentation which had been made to him as to her person, and the want of consent on his part both at the celebration, and ever since the celebration of the marriage.[1] In pursuance of this plan the chancellor, the archbishop, and four other peers successively addressed the house of Lords. It had been their lot, they said, to be instrumental in negotiating the late marriage; it was now their duty to state that from more recent information they doubted its validity. In such a case, where the succession to the crown was concerned, too great security could not be obtained; wherefore they moved that all the particulars should, with the royal permission, be laid before the clergy in convocation, and their decision as to the validity or invalidity of the marriage should be required. A deputation was next requested and obtained from the lower house; and the temporal lords and commoners proceeding to the palace, humbly solicited the king's permission to submit to his consideration a subject of great delicacy and importance. Henry assented, being aware that they would propose to him nothing which was unreasonable or unjust. Having heard their petition from the mouth of the chancellor, he replied, that it was indeed an important question; but that he could refuse nothing to the estates of the realm; that the clergy were learned and pious, and would, he had no doubt, come to an upright decision; and that, as far as regarded himself, he was ready to answer any question which might be put to him, for he had no other object in view but the glory of God, the welfare of the realm, and the triumph of truth.[2]

By the convocation the inquiry was referred to a committee, consisting of the two archbishops, of four bishops, and eight divines, who either found the materials ready to their hands, or were urged to extraordinary diligence by the known wish of the monarch. To receive depositions,[3] to examine witnesses, to discuss the merits of the case, to form their report, and to obtain the approbation of the whole body, was the work of but two short days. Not a voice was heard in favour of the marriage; it was unanimously pronounced void on the following grounds:—

1. There was no certainty that the alleged precontract between Anne and the marquess of Lorraine had been revoked in due form of law; and in consequence the validity of her subsequent marriage with Henry was, and the legitimacy of her issue by him would be, doubtful.

2. The king had required that this difficulty should be removed previously to his marriage. It might be considered as an indispensable condition; whence it was inferred that as the condition had failed, the marriage, which depended on that condition, must be void.

3. It was contended that, if Henry had selected Anne for his wife, he had been deceived by exaggerated accounts of her beauty; if he had solemnized his nuptials with her, he

---

[1] Dr. Clarke had been sent to open the business to the duke of Cleves; and on his journey received no fewer than three sets of instructions, each differing from the other.—See Herbert, 520, 521.

[2] Lords' Journals, p. 156. It is amusing that the whole of this farce is described, just as it was afterwards acted, in a letter from the council to Clarke, dated July 3, three days before it took place.—Herbert, 521.

[3] They have been published partly by Burnet, i. Rec. 193, 197, and partly by Strype, i. Rec. 307—315.

had been compelled by reasons of state; but he had never given that real consent which was necessary to impart force to the contract, either by any internal act of the will during the ceremony, or after the ceremony by the consummation of the marriage. It is not possible that such arguments could satisfy the reason of the members. From the benefit of the two first Henry had excluded himself by his own act in proceeding to the celebration of the ceremony; and the last, were it admitted in its full extent, would at once deprive of force every treaty between sovereigns. But the clergy in convocation, like the lords and commons in parliament, were the obsequious slaves of their master. The first decided in obedience to his will; the second passed an act confirming that decision; and then assimilating the marriage of Henry with Anne to his former marriages with his first and second queens, they subjected to the penalties of treason every man who should by writing, imprinting, or any exterior act, word or deed, directly or indirectly, accept, believe, or judge, that it was lawful and valid.[1] The German princess—she had neither friend nor adviser—submitted without complaint to her lot. By Henry's command she subscribed a letter to him, in which she was made to admit the non-consummation of the marriage, and to acquiesce in the judgment of the convocation. But the letter was written in English; and it was possible that subsequently, as Henry expressed it, "she might play the woman," revoking her assent, and pleading in justification her ignorance of the language. She was, therefore, assailed with presents from the king, and with advice from his commissioners; a version of her former letter in German, and a letter to her brother written in the same language, and containing the same admissions, were laid before her; and she was induced to copy both with her own hand, and to forward them to those to whom they were addressed.[2] He then demanded back the ring which he had given to her at their marriage, and on the receipt of it professed himself satisfied. They now called each other brother and sister, and a yearly income of three thousand pounds, with the palace of Richmond for her residence, amply indemnified the degraded queen for the loss of a capricious and tyrannical husband.[3]

The session was now hastening to a close, and little progress had been made by the committees, appointed at the recommendation of Cromwell, to frame a declaration of doctrine for the belief, and an order of ceremonies for the worship, of the English church. To give the authority of parliament to their subsequent labours, it was enacted that such ordinances as they or the whole clergy of England should afterwards publish with the advice and approbation of the king, should be fully believed, obeyed, and performed, under the penalties to be therein expressed. At the same time the rigour of the statute of the Six Articles was mitigated in that clause which regarded the incontinence of priests or nuns; and forfeiture of lands and goods was sub-

---

[1] Wilk. Con. iii. 850—855. Stat. of Realm, iii. 781.
[2] State Pap. i. 635—646. Henry attached great importance to the German letters. "Oneles," he writes to the duke of Suffolk, "these letters be obteyned, all shall remayn uncerteyn, upon a woman's promise that she wilbe no woman; the accomplissement whereof in her behalf is as difficile in the refrayning of a woman's will upon occasion, as in chaunging of her womanyssh nature, which is impossible."—Ibid. 640.
[3] Rym. xiv. 710. Her income was made to depend on her remaining within the realm.—Ibid. She died at Chelsea, July 16, 1557. See her will, in which she professes to die a Catholic, in Excerp. Hist. 295.

stituted in the place of the penalty of death.[1]

From the moment of his arrest, Cromwell had laboured without ceasing to save his life. He denied with the strongest asseverations that he was a traitor, or a sacramentary, or a heretic; he admitted that he had occasionally transgressed the limits of his authority, but pleaded in excuse the number of the offices which he held, and the impropriety of troubling at every moment the royal ear; he descended with seeming cheerfulness to every submission, every disclosure which was required of him; he painted in striking colours his forlorn and miserable condition, and solicited for mercy in terms the most pathetic, and perhaps more abject than became his character.[2] Unfortunately, among his papers had been found his clandestine correspondence with the princes of Germany;[3] the king would listen to no plea in favour of a man who had betrayed his confidence to strangers; and on the fourth day after the bill of attainder had received the royal assent he was led to execution. On the scaffold he asked pardon of his sovereign, and admitted that he had been seduced by the spirit of error; but protested that he had returned to the truth, and should die in the profession of the Catholic faith, meaning probably that faith which was now established by law.[4] If a tear were shed at his death, it was in secret, and by the preachers who had been sheltered under his protection. The nobility rejoiced to be freed from the control of a man who by cunning and servility had raised himself from the shop of a fuller to the highest seat in the house of Lords; the friends of the church congratulated themselves on the fall of its most dangerous enemy; and the whole nation considered his blood as an atonement for the late enormous and impolitic tax, imposed at a time when the king had incurred no extraordinary expense, and when the treasury was filled, or supposed to be filled, with the spoils of the suppressed monasteries.

Two days later, the citizens were summoned to behold an execution of a more singular description. By law the Catholic and the Protestant were now placed on an equal footing in respect to capital punishment. If to admit the papal supremacy was treason, to reject the papal creed was heresy. The one could be expiated only by the halter and the knife; the other led the offender to the stake and the fagot. It was in vain that the German reformers pleaded in favour of their English brethren; and that Melancthon, in a long letter, presumed to question the royal infallibility. The king continued to hold with a steady hand the balance between the two parties. During the parliament, Powel, Abel, and Featherstone, had been attainted for denying the supremacy; Barnes, Garret, and Jerome, for maintaining heterodox opinions.[5] They were now coupled,

---

[1] St. 32 Henry VIII. 10, 26.
[2] See his letters to Henry, Burnet, i. Rec. 193; iii. Rec. 161. The reader will be astonished at the number of oaths, &c. with which he maintains his innocence. "May God confound him; may the vengeance of God light upon him; may all the devils in hell confound him," and similar imprecations continually recur.
[3] Marillac, apud Le Grand, ii. 215.
[4] Hall, 242. Stowe, 580. His speech, like others on similar occasions, left his guilt or innocence as problematical as before. He came to die, not to clear himself. He thanked God for having brought him to that death for his offences; for he had always been a sinner. He had offended his prince, for which he asked forgiveness, and God, of whom he prayed all present to ask forgiveness for him.
[5] These three did not maintain any doctrines against the six articles, but (if we may judge from their recantation) that the man who has been justified, cannot fall from grace; that God is the author of sin, that it is not necessary to pardon offences; that good works are not profitable to salvation, and that the laws are not to be obeyed for

Catholic and Protestant, on the same hurdles; drawn together from the Tower to Smithfield, and while the former were hanged and quartered as traitors, the latter were consumed in the flames as heretics. Still, if we consider the persecuting policy of the age, and the sanguinary temper of the king, we shall perhaps find that from this period fewer persons suffered than might have been expected. The commissions, indeed, which Cromwell had mentioned at the opening of parliament, were issued, inquests were taken, and informations laid; but terror had taught men to suppress their real sentiments; and of those whose imprudence brought them under suspicion, the least guilty were dismissed on their recognizances for each other; and most of the rest embraced the benefit of abjuration granted by the law.[1]

Henry did not long remain a widower after his divorce from Anne of Cleves. The Lords humbly besought him, as he tendered the welfare of his people, to venture on a fifth marriage, in the hope that God would bless him with more numerous issue; and within a month Catherine, daughter to the late Lord Edmund Howard, and niece to the duke of Norfolk, appeared at court with the title of queen. Catherine had been educated under the care of the dowager duchess of Norfolk, and first attracted the royal notice at a dinner given by the bishop of Winchester. She possessed nothing of that port and dignity which Henry had hitherto required. But her figure, though small, was regular; her manner easy and graceful, and "by a notable appearance of honour, cleanness, and maidenly behaviour, she won the king's heart."[2] For more than twelve months he lavished on her tokens of his affection; but the events to which she owed her elevation, had rendered the reformers her enemies, and a discovery, which they made during her absence with the king in his progress as far as York, enabled them to recover their former ascendancy, and deprived the young queen of her influence and her life.[3]

A female, who had been one of her companions under her grandmother's roof, but was now married in Essex, had stated to Lascelles, her brother that to her knowledge, Catherine had admitted to her bed, "on an hundred nights," a gentleman of the name of Dereham, at that time page to the duchess. Lascelles—at whose instigation, or through what motives, is unknown—carried this most extraordinary tale to Archbishop Cranmer. Cranmer consulted his friends the chancellor and the lord Hertford; and all three determined to secure the person of Lascelles, and to keep the matter secret till the return of the royal party. Henry and Catherine reached Hampton Court against the feast of All Saints; on that day "the king received his maker, and gave him most hearty thanks for the good life he led and trusted to lead with his wife;"[4] on the next, whilst he was at mass, the archbishop delivered into his hands a paper containing the information obtained in his absence. He read it with feelings of pain and distrust; an inquiry into its truth or

---

conscience sake.—See the recantation, Burnet, i. Rec. iii. No. xxii.

[1] During the remainder of Henry's reign, Fox reckons ten Protestants, Dodd fourteen Catholics, who suffered, after those mentioned above.

[2] Letter of Council in Herb. 532. She is called parvissima puella (Burnet, iii. 147). What then was the age of this very little girl?

[3] I am aware that there is no direct evidence of any plot; but, if it be considered with whom the following inquiry originated, and with what art it was conducted, it is difficult to resist the suspicion of a political intrigue, having for its object to effect the downfal of the dominant party, by procuring, not indeed the death, but the divorce of the queen.

[4] Letter of Council, Herb. 532.

falsehood was immediately ordered; first Lascelles was examined; then his sister in the country; next Dereham himself; and afterwards several other persons. All this while Catherine was kept in ignorance of the danger which threatened her; but one morning the king left the court; and the council, waiting on her in a body, informed her of the charge which had been made against her. She denied it in their presence with loud protestations of innocence; but on their departure fell into fits, and appeared frantic through grief and terror. To soothe her mind, the archbishop brought her an assurance of mercy from Henry; and, repeating his visit in the evening, when she was more tranquil, artfully drew from her a promise to reply to his questions "faithfully and truly, as she would answer at the day of judgment, and by the promise which she made at her baptism, and by the sacrament which she received on All Hallows day last past." Under this solemn adjuration she admitted that, notwithstanding the precautions taken by the duchess, Dereham had been in the habit of coming at night or early in the morning to the apartment allotted to the females; that he brought with him wine and fruit for their entertainment; and he often behaved with great freedom and rudeness, and that on three occasions he had offered some violence to her person. This was the result of two examinations, in which Cranmer laboured to procure evidence of a precontract between Catherine and Dereham. Had he succeeded, she might have saved her life by submitting to a divorce; but the unfortunate queen deprived herself of this benefit by constantly maintaining that no promise had been made, and that "al that Derame dyd unto her, was of his importune forcement and in a maner violence, rather than of her fre consent and wil."[1]

The following day the judges and counsellors assembled in the Starchamber, where the chancellor announced to them the presumed guilt of the queen, read in support of the charge select passages from the evidence already procured, and intimated, in addition, that more important disclosures were daily expected.[2] At Hampton Court the same course was followed in the presence of all persons of "gentle birth," male and female, who had been retained in her service. Catherine herself was removed to Sion House, where two apartments were reserved exclusively for her accommodation, and orders were given that she should be treated with the respect due to her rank. In anticipation of her attainder, the king had already taken possession of all her personal property; but he was graciously pleased to allow her six changes of apparel, and six French hoods with edgings of goldsmiths' work, but without pearl or diamond.[3]

If there was no pre-contract between Catherine and Dereham, nothing but her death could dissolve the marriage between her and the king. Hence it became necessary to prove her guilty of some capital offence; and with this view a rigorous inquiry was set on foot respecting her whole conduct since she became queen. It was now discovered that not only had she admitted Dereham to her presence, but had

---

[1] See the archbishop's letter to the king in State Pap. l. 691; her confession in Burnet, App. lxxi., and the letter in Herbert, 532.
[2] He suppressed all the passages which might be construed in favour of pre-contract, and that because "they might serve for her defence."—State Pap. 692, 694. It was now the king's intention to proceed against her for adultery, which was incompatible with a pre-contract.
[3] State Papers, 695.

employed him to perform for her the office of secretary; and that at Lincoln, during the progress, she had allowed Culpepper, a maternal relation and gentleman of the privy chamber, to remain in company with her and Lady Rochford from eleven at night till two in the morning. The judges were consulted, who replied, that considering the persons implicated, these facts, if proved, formed a satisfactory presumption that adultery had been committed. On this and no better proof, the two unfortunate gentlemen, were tried, and found guilty of high treason. Their lives were spared for ten days, with the hope of extorting from them additional information respecting the guilt of the queen. But they gave none, probably had none to give. Dereham was hanged and quartered; Culpepper, out of regard for his family, was beheaded.[1]

But these were not the only victims. The king's resentment was extended to all those individuals who had been, or might have been, privy to the intimacy between Catherine and Dereham in the house of the duchess. He argued that, contrary to their duty, they had allowed their sovereign to marry a woman guilty of incontinence; they had thus exposed his honour to disgrace, his life to danger from the intercourse which might afterwards take place between her and her paramour; and had therefore, by their silence, committed an offence amounting at least to misprision of treason. On this charge the duchess herself, with her daughter the countess of Bridgewater,[2] the lord William Howard and his wife, and nine other persons of inferior rank, in the service of the duchess, were committed to the Tower; where the royal commissioners laboured by frequent and separate examinations, by menaces and persuasion, and, in one instance at least, by the application of torture, to draw from them the admission that they had been privy to Catherine's incontinence themselves, and the charge of such privity in their companions. The duchess and her daughter, who persisted in the denial of any knowledge or even suspicion of misconduct in their young relative, were reserved, in punishment of their obstinacy, to be dealt with by the justice of parliament; the commoners were brought to trial on the same day; among whom all the females confessed the offence with many tears and supplications for mercy; the lord William boldly put himself on his country, but was induced by the court to withdraw his plea before the conclusion; his fellow-prisoner, Damport, refusing to follow his example, was tried and found guilty. All were condemned to forfeiture and perpetual imprisonment.[3]

For some time we have lost sight

---

[1] Ibid. 701. It has been sometimes said that both confessed the adultery. But of that there is no proof; and it cannot be doubted that, if it were so, their confession would have been distinctly stated in the bill of attainder, as the best evidence of their crime. That it is false, as far as regards Dereham, will be plain from the next note.

[2] The duchess had taken some papers out of Dereham's trunks in her house. Henry was so irritated, that he charged her with treason: the judges dissented: he replied that there was as much reason to convict her of treason as there had been to convict Dereham. "They cannot say that they have any learning to maynteign that they have a better ground to make Deram's case treason, and to *presume* that his comyng agayn to the queene's servyce was to an ill intent of the renovacion of his former noughtie lif, then they have in this case to *presume* that the brekyng of the coffres was to th'intent to conceile letters of treason." —State Pap. 700.

[3] State Pap. 726. "We have finished our worke this daye moche to his majestes honor:" that is, we have procured the conviction of all the accused. From these letters it appears that the moment an individual was committed, the king's officers discharged his household, and seized his clothes, furniture, money, jewels, and cattle, that they might be secured for the crown in

of Catherine; at the beginning of the year we meet with her again at Sion House, with a parliament sitting, and a sweeping bill of attainder before it, including both the queen and all her companions in misfortune. If we consider that the attainder against her could be sustained only on the ground of adultery, we shall not be surprised that the Lords sought to learn from her what she could say to that particular charge. For this purpose they appointed a committee to wait on her with Henry's permission, and to exhort her to speak the truth without fear or reservation; to remember that the king was merciful, as the laws were just; and to be persuaded that the establishment of her innocence would afford joy, and that even the knowledge of the truth would afford relief to the mind of her husband. But of this the privy council disapproved; another plan was proposed; and after some delay the bill was read again, hastened through the two houses, and brought to the Lords by the chancellor signed by the king, with the great seal appended to it. Whilst the officer proceeded to summon the attendance of the Commons, the duke of Suffolk with some others reported, that they had waited on the queen, who "acknowledged her offence against God, the king, and the nation," expressed a hope that her faults might not be visited on her brothers and family, and begged as a last favour that she might divide a part of her clothes among her maids.[1] By this time the Commons had arrived, and the royal assent was immediately read in due form. The act attainted of treason the queen, Dereham and Culpepper as her paramours, and Lady Rochford as aider and abettor; and of misprision of treason both all those who had been convicted of concealment in court, and also the duchess of Norfolk and the countess of Bridgewater, though no legal proceedings whatsoever had been taken against them.[2]

The tragedy was now drawing to a close. Catherine had already been conducted to the Tower; two days after the passing of the act, and six months after her marriage, she was led to execution, together with her companion, the lady Rochford. They appeared on the scaffold calm and resigned, bidding the spectators take notice that they suffered justly for "their offences against God from their youth upward, and also against the king's royal majesty very dangerously." The meekness and piety of their demeanour seem to have deeply interested the only person present who has transmitted to us any account of their last moments. "Theyer sowles," he writes, "I doubt

---

the event of his attainder; that no time was lost in bringing him to trial, because, if he died before conviction, the king would lose the forfeiture; that in the present case the accused were indicted almost immediately, "that the parliament might have better grownde to confyske theyr gooddes, if any of them should chawnce before theyre atteyndour to die" (ibid. 705); and that the proofs brought at the trial consisted of copies of confessions made by others, and the testimonies of the commissioners themselves. Thus at the trials of the lord William and Damport, the witnesses examined were not persons originally acquainted with the facts, but the master of the Rolls, the attorney and solicitor general, and three of the king's counsel, who had taken the examinations.

[1] The reader will observe that in this confession, which is entered on the Journals (i. 176), there is no direct mention of adultery, the only treason that Catherine was charged with having committed. Can we believe that, if she could have been brought to confess it, Suffolk would not have stated it broadly and unequivocally? Again, why was this statement withheld till the house had passed the bill; and, when it was made, why did not Suffolk wait for the presence of the Commons? It is also singular that the statement of the earl of Southampton, who had accompanied Suffolk to the queen, is omitted. The clerk has begun the entry with these words, " hoc etiam adjiciens;" but, unaccountably, adds nothing.

[2] Journals, i. 168, 171, 172, 176. Stat. of Realm, iv. 854.

not, be with God; for they made the moost godly and Christyan's end that ever was hard tell of, I thinke, since the world's creation."[1]

To attaint without trial had of late become customary; but to prosecute and punish for that which had not been made a criminal offence by any law, was hitherto unprecedented. To give, therefore, some countenance to these severities, it was enacted in the very bill of attainder that every woman, about to be married to the king or any of his successors, not being a maid, should disclose her disgrace to him under the penalty of treason; that all other persons knowing the fact and not disclosing it, should be subject to the lesser penalty of misprision of treason; and that the queen, or wife of the prince, who should move another person to commit adultery with her, or the person who should move her to commit adultery with him, should suffer as a traitor.[2]

The king's attention was next directed to his duties as head of the church. He had formerly sanctioned the publication of an English version of the Bible, and granted permission to all his subjects to read it at their leisure; but it had been represented to him, that even the authorized version was disfigured by unfaithful renderings, and contaminated with notes calculated to mislead the ignorant and unwary; and that the indiscriminate lecture of the holy volumes had not only generated a race of teachers who promulgated doctrines the most strange and contradictory, but had taught ignorant men to discuss the meaning of the inspired writings in alehouses and taverns, till, heated with controversy and liquor, they burst into injurious language, and provoked each other to breaches of the peace. To remedy the first of these evils, it was enacted, that the version of Tyndal should be disused altogether as "crafty, false, and untrue," and that the authorized translation should be published without note or comment; to obviate the second, the permission of reading the Bible to others in public was revoked; that of reading it to private families was confined to persons of the rank of lords or gentlemen; and that of reading it personally and in secret was granted only to men who were householders, and to females of noble or gentle birth. Any other woman, or any artificer, apprentice, journeyman, servant, or labourer, who should presume to open the sacred volume, was made liable for each offence to one month's imprisonment.[3] The king had already issued a proclamation forbidding the possession of Tyndal's or Coverdale's versions, or of any book or manuscript containing matter contrary to the doctrine set forth by authority of parliament; ordering all such books to be given up before the last day of August, that they might be burnt by order of the sheriff

---

[1] Otwell Johnson's letter to his brother, in Ellis, ii. 128. In this confession on the scaffold the queen evades a second time all mention of the alleged adultery. She employs the very same ambiguous and unsatisfactory language which Suffolk had employed in the house of Lords. Could this be accidental? or was not that particular form enjoined by authority, that she might not seem to impeach "the king's justice?" On a review of the original letters in the State Papers, of the act of attainder, and of the proceedings in parliament, I see no sufficient reason to think her guilty; and, if she was innocent, so also must have been the lady Rochford. Like her predecessor Anne Boleyn, she fell a victim to the jealousy or resentment of a despotic husband; but in one respect she has been more fortunate. The preservation of documents respecting her fate enables us to estimate the value of the proofs brought against her; our ignorance of those brought against Anne renders the question of *her* guilt or innocence more problematical.

[2] Stat. of Realm, iv. 859.

[3] St. 34 Hen. VIII. 1. The king at the same time was authorized to make any alterations in this act which he might deem proper.

or the bishop; and prohibiting the importation "of any manner of Englishe booke concernyng any matter of Christin religion" from parts beyond the sea.

It was not, however, the king's intention to leave the flock committed to his charge without a competent supply of spiritual food. The reader will recollect that Cromwell in 1540 had announced the appointment of two committees of prelates and theologians to compose a new code of doctrine and ceremonies. Certain questions had been proposed to each person separately, and their answers were collated and laid before the king.[2] To make the new work as perfect as was possible, three years were employed; it was at last published with the title of "A necessary Doctrine and Erudition for any christned Man:" and, to distinguish it from "the Institution," the former exposition of the same subject, it was called the King's Book. It is more full, but teaches the same doctrines, with the addition of transubstantiation, and the sufficiency of communion under one kind. The new creed was approved by both houses of convocation;[3] all writings or books in opposition to it were prohibited; and by the archbishop it was ordered to be published in every diocese, and studied and followed by every preacher.[4] From that period to the accession of the next sovereign, "the King's Book" continued to be the only authorized standard of English orthodoxy.

---

[1] Chron. Catal. 228. The persons whose writings are condemned by name are Frythe, Tyndall, Wiclif, Joye, Roye, Basyle, Beale, Barnes, Coverdale, Tournour, and Tracy.—Ibid.

[2] Of these answers some have been published; others are to be found in the British Museum (Cleop. E. 5). Those by Cranmer prove that on every subject he had made a greater proficiency in the new learning than any of his coadjutors; but his opinion respecting orders appears extremely singular, when we recollect that he was archbishop of Canterbury. The king, he says, must have spiritual as well as civil officers, and of course has a right to appoint them; in the time of the apostles the people appointed, because they had no Christian king, but occasionally accepted such as might be recommended to them by the apostles, "of their own voluntary will, and not for any superiority that the apostles had over them;" in the appointment of bishops and priests, as in that of civil officers, some ceremonies are to be used, "not of necessity, but for good order and seemly fashion:" nevertheless, "he, who is appointed bishop or priest, needeth no consecration by the Scripture; for election or appointing thereto is sufficient." Aware, however, that it was difficult to reconcile these principles with the declaration which he had signed in the preceding year (Wilk. Con. iii. 832), or with such as he might be compelled to sign hereafter, he very prudently added, "this is mine opinion and sentence at this present; which nevertheless I do not temerariously define, but refer the judgment thereof to your majesty."—Strype, 79, App. p. 48, 52. Burnet, i. Coll. p. 201. Collier, ii. Records, xlix.

[3] Wilk. Con. iii. 868. As if it were meant to probe to the quick the sincerity of the prelates suspected of leaning to the new doctrines, the chapters on the two obnoxious tenets of transubstantiation, and communion under one kind, were subjected to the revision and approbation of the archbishop, and the bishops of Westminster, Salisbury, Rochester, and Hereford, three of whom were reformers. Per ipsos exposita, examinata, et recognita.—Ibid.

[4] Strype. 100.

CHAPTER III.

STATUTES RESPECTING WALES—TRANSACTIONS IN IRELAND—NEGOTIATION AND WAR WITH SCOTLAND—RUPTURE WITH FRANCE—PEACE—TAXES—DEPRECIATION OF THE CURRENCY—CRANMER—GARDINER—KING'S LAST ILLNESS—EXECUTION OF THE EARL OF SURREY—ATTAINDER OF THE DUKE OF NORFOLK—DEATH OF HENRY—HIS CHARACTER—SUBSERVIENCY OF THE PARLIAMENT—DOCTRINE OF PASSIVE OBEDIENCE—SERVILITY OF RELIGIOUS PARTIES.

That the reader might follow without interruption the progress of the Reformation in England, I have confined his attention in the preceding pages to those occurrences which had an immediate tendency to quicken or restrain the spirit of religious innovation. The present chapter will be devoted to matters of foreign and domestic policy: 1. The extension of the English jurisprudence throughout the principality of Wales: 2. The rebellion and pacification of Ireland: 3. The negotiations and hostilities between the crowns of England and Scotland: and 4. The war, which Henry declared against "his good brother, and perpetual ally," the king of France. These events will lead to the close of the king's reign.

1. As Henry was descended from the Tudors, a Welsh family, he naturally directed his attention to the native country of his paternal ancestors. It might be divided into two portions, that which had been originally conquered by the arms of his predecessors, and that which had been won by the courage and perseverance of the individuals afterwards called the lords marchers. The former had been apportioned into shires, and was governed by the laws of England; the latter comprised one hundred and forty-one districts or lordships, which had been granted to the first conquerors, and formed so many distinct and independent jurisdictions. From them the king's writs, and the king's officers were excluded. They acknowledged no other laws or customs than their own. The lords, like so many counts palatine, had their own courts, civil and criminal, appointed their own officers and judges, punished or pardoned offences according to their pleasure, and received all the emoluments arising from the administration of justice within their respective domains. But the great evil was, that this multitude of petty and separate jurisdictions, by holding out the prospect of impunity, proved an incitement to crime. The most atrocious offender, if he could only flee from the scene of his transgression, and purchase the protection of a neighbouring lord, was sheltered from the pursuit of justice, and at liberty to enjoy the fruit of his dishonesty or revenge.

The king, however, put an end to this mischievous and anomalous state of things. In 1536 it was enacted, that the whole of Wales should thenceforth be united and incorporated with the realm of England; that all the natives should enjoy and inherit the same rights, liberties, and laws, which were enjoyed and inherited by others the king's subjects; that the custom of gavel-kind should cease; that the several lordships' marchers should be annexed to the neighbouring counties; that all judges and justices of the peace should be appointed by the king's letters patent; that no lord should have the power to pardon any treason, murder, or felony committed within his lordship; and that the different shires in Wales, with one borough in each, should return members to parliament. Most of these regulations were extended to the county palatine of Chester.[1]

2. When Henry ascended the throne, the exercise of the royal authority in Ireland was circumscribed within very narrow limits, comprising only the principal seaports, with one-half of the five counties of Louth, Westmeath, Dublin, Kildare, and Wexford; the rest of the island was unequally divided among sixty chieftains of Irish, and thirty of English origin, who governed the inhabitants of their respective domains, and made war upon each other, as freely and as recklessly as if they had been independent sovereigns.[2] To Wolsey it appeared that one great cause of the decay of the English power was the jealousy and the dissension between the two rival families of the Fitzgeralds and the Butlers, under their respective chiefs, the earls of Kildare, and of Ormond or Ossory. That he might extinguish or repress these hereditary feuds, he determined to intrust the government to the more impartial sway of an English nobleman, and the young earl of Kildare, who had succeeded his father, was removed from the office of lord deputy, to make place for the earl of Surrey, afterwards duke of Norfolk. During two years the English governor overawed the turbulence of the Irish lords by the vigour of his administration, and won the esteem of the natives by his hospitality and munificence. But when Henry declared war against France, Surrey was recalled to take the command of the army; and the government of Ireland was conferred on Butler, earl of Ossory. Ossory was soon compelled to resign it to Kildare; Kildare transmitted it to Sir William Skeffington, an English knight, deputy to the duke of Richmond; and Skeffington, after a short interval, replaced it in the hands of his immediate predecessor. Thus Kildare saw himself for the third time invested with the chief authority in the island; but no longer awed by the frowns of Wolsey, who had fallen into disgrace, he indulged in such acts of extravagance, that his very friends attributed them to occasional derangement of intellect.

The complaints of the Butlers induced Henry to call the deputy to London, and to confine him in the Tower. At his departure the reins of government dropped into the hands of his son, the lord Thomas, a young man in his twenty-first year, generous, violent, and brave.[3] His credulity was deceived by a false report that his father had been beheaded; and his resentment urged him to the fatal resolution of bidding defiance to his sovereign. At the head of one hundred and forty followers he presented himself before the council, resigned the sword of state, the emblem of his authority, and in a loud tone declared war against Henry VIII., king of England. Cromer, archbishop of Armagh, seizing him by the hand, most earnestly besought him not to plunge himself and his family into irremediable ruin; but the voice of the prelate was drowned in the strains of an Irish minstrel, who, in his native tongue, called on the hero to revenge the blood of his father; and the precipitate youth, unfurling the standard

---

[1] Stat. of Realm, 536, 555, 563. In the county of Merioneth there was no borough which returned a member; but in that of Pembroke there were two, Pembroke and Haverfordwest.
[2] See a contemporary memoir in St. Pap. ii. 1—31. [3] Hall, 226. Herbert, 415.

of rebellion, commenced his career with laying waste the rich district of Fingal. A gleam of success cast a temporary lustre on his arms; and his revenge was gratified with the punishment of the supposed accuser of his father, Allen, archbishop of Dublin, who was surprised and put to death by the Geraldines. He now sent an agent to the emperor, to demand assistance against the man who, by divorcing Catherine, had insulted the honour of the imperial family; and wrote to the pope, offering to protect with his sword the interests of the church against an apostate prince, and to hold the crown of Ireland of the Holy See by the payment of a yearly tribute. But fortune quickly deserted him. He was repulsed from the walls of Dublin by the valour or despair of the citizens; Skeffington, the new deputy, opposed to his undisciplined followers a numerous body of veterans; his strong castle of Maynooth was carried by assault, and the lord Leonard Gray hunted the ill-fated insurgent into the fastnesses of Munster. Here by the advice of his friends he offered to submit; but his simplicity was no match for the subtlety of his opponent; he suffered himself to be deceived by assurances of pardon, dismissed his adherents, accompanied Gray to Dublin, and thence sailed to England, that he might throw himself at the feet of his sovereign.[1] Henry was at a loss in what manner to receive him. Could it be to his honour to allow a subject to live who had taken up arms against him? But then, was it for his interest to teach the Irish that no faith was to be put in the promises of his lieutenants?[2] He committed Fitzgerald to the Tower; soon afterwards Gray, who had succeeded Skeffington, perfidiously apprehended the five uncles of the captive at a banquet; and the year following all six, though it is said that three had never joined in the rebellion, were beheaded in consequence of an act of attainder passed by the English parliament.[3] Fitzgerald's father had already died of a broken heart, and the last hopes of the family centred in Gerald, the brother of Thomas, a boy about twelve years old. By the contrivance of his aunt, he was conveyed beyond the reach of Henry, and intrusted to the fidelity of two native chieftains, O'Neil and O'Donnel. Two years later he had the good fortune to escape to the continent, but was followed by the vengeance or the policy of the king, who demanded him of the king of France, and afterwards of the governor of Flanders, in virtue of preceding treaties. Expelled from Flanders, he was, at the recommendation of the pope, Paul III., taken under the protection of the prince bishop of Liege, and afterwards into the family of his kinsman Cardinal Pole, who watched over his education, and provided for his support till at length he recovered the honours and the estates of his ancestors, the former earls of Kildare.[4]

Henry's innovations in religion

---

[1] Sponte se in regis potestatem, accepta impunitatis fide dedit.........fidem publicam qua se tueri jure potest, habet.—Poli Ep. i. 431. Skeffington, indeed, says that he had surrendered "without condition."—St. Pap. 274. But that he was prevailed upon to do so by assurances of pardon is plain from the letter of the Irish council (p. 275), that of Norfolk (277), and the answer of Henry, "if he had beene apprended after suche sorte as was conveanable to his deservynges, the same had beene much more thankfull, and better to our contentacion."—Ibid. 280.
[2] See Audeley's advice, St. Pap. i. 446; Norfolk's, ii. 277.
[3] Stat. of Realm, iii. See a letter of Fitzgerald from the Tower, stating his miserable condition, and that he must have gone naked, "but that pore prysoners of ther gentylnes hathe sumtyme gevyn me old hosyn, and shoys, and old shyrtes."—St. Pap. 403.
[4] Godwin, 62, 63. Herbert, 415—417, 191. Raynald, xxxii. 592.

were viewed with equal abhorrence by the indigenous Irish and the descendants of the English colonists. Fitzgerald, aware of this circumstance, had proclaimed himself the champion of the ancient faith;[1] and after the imprisonment of Fitzgerald, his place was supplied by the zeal of Cromer, archbishop of Armagh. On the other hand, the cause of the king was supported by a more courtly prelate, Brown, who, from the office of provincial of the Augustinian friars in England, had been raised to the archiepiscopal see of Dublin, in reward of his subserviency to the politics of Cromwell. But Henry determined to enforce submission. A parliament was summoned by Lord Gray, who had succeeded Skeffington; and, to elude the opposition of the clergy, their proctors, who had hitherto voted in the Irish parliaments, were by a declaratory act pronounced to be nothing more than assistants, whose advice might be received, but whose assent was not required.[2] The statutes which were now passed were copied from the proceedings in England. The papal authority was abolished; Henry was declared head of the Irish church; and the first-fruits of all ecclesiastical livings were given to the king. But ignorance of the recent occurrences in the sister island gave occasion to a most singular blunder. One day the parliament confirmed the marriage of the king with Anne Boleyn; and the next, in consequence of the arrival of a courier, declared it to have been invalid from the beginning. It was, however, more easy to procure the enactment of these statutes, than to enforce their execution. The two races combined in defence of their common faith; and repeated insurrections exercised the patience of the deputy, till his brilliant victory at Bellahoe broke the power of O'Neil, the northern chieftain, and confirmed the ascendancy of the royal cause. This was the last service performed by Lord Gray. He was uncle by his sister to the young Fitzgerald, and therefore suspected of having connived at his escape. This, with numerous other charges from his enemies, was laid before the king; and he solicited permission to return, and plead his cause in the presence of his sovereign. The petition was granted; but the unfortunate deputy soon found himself a prisoner in the Tower, and was afterwards arraigned under the charge of treason for having aided and abetted the king's rebels. Oppressed by fear, or induced by the hope of mercy, he pleaded guilty; and his head was struck off by the command of the thankless sovereign, whom he had so often and so usefully served.[3]

After the departure of Gray, successive but partial insurrections broke out in the island. They speedily subsided of themselves; and the new deputy, Sir Anthony Saintleger found both the Irish chieftains and the lords of the pale anxious to outstrip each other in professions of obedience to his authority. A parliament was assembled; Ireland from a lordship was raised to the higher rank of a kingdom; Henry was declared head of the church, regulations were made for the administration of justice in Connaught and Munster; and commissioners were appointed with power to hear and determine all causes which might be brought before them from the other provinces.[4] The

---

[1] Pro pontificis authoritate in Hibernia arma sumpserat.—Pole, ibid.
[2] Irish St. 28 Henry VIII. 12.
[3] Godwin, 73. "As he was come of high lineage, so was he a right valiant and hardy personage; although now his hap was to lose his head."—Stowe, 582. See the charges in State Papers, iii. 249.
[4] Irish St. 33 Henry VIII. 1. Chron. Catal. p. 232.

peerage of the new kingdom was sought and obtained, not only by the lords who had hitherto acknowledged the authority of the English crown, but even by the most powerful of the chieftains, who, though nominally vassals, had maintained a real independence; by Ulliac de Burg, now created earl of Clanricard; by Murrogh O'Brian, made earl of Thomond; and by the redoubted O'Neil, henceforth known by his new title of earl of Tyrone.[1] These, with the chief of their kindred, swore fealty, consented to hold their lands by the tenure of military service, and accepted from their sovereign houses in Dublin for their accommodation, as often as they should attend their duty in parliament. Never, since the first invasion of the island by Henry II., did the English ascendancy in Ireland appear to rest on so firm a basis as during the last years of Henry VIII.

3. To explain the several causes which successively contributed to produce the rupture between Henry and his nephew the king of Scotland, it will be necessary to revert to the period of the great battle of Pavia. The intelligence of the captivity of Francis extinguished at once the hopes of the French faction in Scotland; and the earl of Angus, with the aid of the English monarch, obtained possession of the young king James V., and with him the exercise of the royal authority. Margaret, the queen-dowager, had long ago forfeited the confidence of her royal brother; an intercepted letter, which she had lately written to the duke of Albany, estranged him from her for ever. He willingly suffered her to be deprived even of the nominal authority which remained to her; Angus consented to a divorce; she married her paramour, afterwards created Lord Methven, and silently sunk into the obscurity of private life. But her son, though only in his seventeenth year, felt the thraldom in which he was detained by the Douglases, and anxiously sought to obtain his liberty, and exercise his authority. At length, he eluded the vigilance of his keepers, levied an army, and drove his enemies beyond the borders; where Angus remained for years, an exile from his own country, and the pensioner of England. The young king, notwithstanding his relationship to Henry, seems to have inherited the political sentiments of his fathers, and sought to fortify himself against the ambition of his powerful neighbour by the friendship of the emperor and of the king of France. In 1532 the two crowns were unintentionally involved in hostilities by the turbulence of the borderers; tranquillity was restored by the good offices of Francis, the common friend of the uncle and nephew; and James was even induced to solicit the hand of the princess Mary. But it was at a time when only a few months had elapsed since the divorce of Henry from Catherine; and the king, who had formerly offered, now refused his consent to a marriage which might afterwards lead the king of Scots to dispute the succession with the children of Anne Boleyn. This refusal induced James to seek a wife from some of the foreign courts, while the English monarch vainly endeavoured to make his nephew a proselyte to his new doctrine of the ecclesiastical supremacy of princes within their respective kingdoms. For this purpose he sent to James a treatise on that subject, with a request that he would seriously weigh its contents; and solicited at the same time permission for his agent Barlow, bishop elect of St. David's, to preach to the Scottish court. The present was received with an air of indifference, and instantly delivered to one of the

---

[1] Rym. xiv. 797—801; xv. 7.

prelates; and the English missionary, finding every pulpit closed against him, vented his discontent in letters to Cromwell, in which he denominated the clerical counsellors of James, "the pope's pestilent creatures, and very limbs of the devil."[1]

Henry now requested a personal interview at York; but James, who feared to trust himself in the hands of his uncle, eluded the demand by proposing a meeting of the three kings of England, France, and Scotland, at some place on the continent.[2] Soon afterwards, he concluded a treaty of marriage with Marie de Bourbon, a daughter of Vendome; but unwilling to rely on the report of his ambassadors, he sailed to Dieppe, and visited his intended bride, whose appearance disappointed his expectations. Disguising his feelings, he hastened to be present at the expected battle between the French and Imperial armies in Provence; but was met by Francis on Mount Tarare, in the vicinity of Lyons. The two monarchs repaired to Paris; Marie was forgotten; and James married Madeleine, the daughter of the French king, a beautiful and accomplished princess, who was even then in a decline, and died within fifty days after her arrival in Scotland. During some time her husband appeared inconsolable for her loss; the next year he married another French princess, Marie, duchess dowager of Longueville, and daughter to the duke of Guise; the same lady who had declined the offer of the king of England.[3]

The king of Scots, satisfied with his own creed, refused to engage in theological disputes; and the pontiff, to rivet him more closely to the communion of the Apostolic See, bestowed a cardinal's cap on the most able and most favoured of his counsellors, David Beaton, abbot of Arbroath, afterwards bishop of Mirepoix, and lastly archbishop of St. Andrew's. During his journey James had noticed the terms of execration in which foreigners reprobated the rapacity and cruelty of his reforming uncle; and his gratitude for the attentions and generosity of Francis inclined him to espouse and support the politics of the French court. When Paul had at last determined to publish the sentence of deprivation against Henry, James signified his assent, and promised to join with Charles and Francis in their endeavours to convert or punish the apostate monarch.[4]

Henry, whose pensioners swarmed in every court, was quickly apprized of these dispositions, and, as soon as he had learned the real object of Cardinal Pole's legation to the emperor and the king of France, despatched Ralph Sadler, one of the gentlemen of his privy chamber, as his ambassador to Edinburgh. This minister assured the king of Scots, that the warlike preparations in England were not designed against him, but against the pope and his associates; exhorted him, instead of giving credit to the assertions of his clergy, to examine the foundations of the papal claims, which he would find to be nothing more than an usurpation of the rights of sovereigns; re-

---

[1] Pinkerton, ii. 327. "The Doctrine of a Christian Man" was not published till after this period; the book sent was probably either Gardiner's treatise De Vera Obedientia, or another, De Vera Differentia Regiæ Potestatis et Ecclesiasticæ; both of which had been printed the year before.

[2] According to a minute of the English council, "he not only brake with th' appoyntment made for the entrevue, but for the pretence of his cause therein alleaged that it was said, he shuld be betrayed, if he proceded in the same."—St. Pap. 535.

[3] Leslie, 426.

[4] Habebit regem Scotiæ, et hic novum creatum cardinalem Scotum.—Instruc. pro Card. Polo apud Quirini, ii. Mon Præl. cclxxix.

quested him not to permit the bull against his uncle to be published, or executed within his dominions; and reminded him, that Henry was a nearer relation to him than any other prince, and that, though it was not required of him to renounce his engagements with the king of France, it was his interest to abstain from measures, of which he might afterwards repent.[1]

What effect these remonstrances might have produced is uncertain; but as neither Charles nor Francis attempted to enforce the papal bull, their inactivity induced the king of Scots to preserve the relationship of amity with his uncle. Henry, however, continued to grow more jealous both of the religious opinions of James, and of his connection with the French court. If a few Scottish refugees, the partisans of the new doctrine, flattered him with the hope that their sovereign would imitate him in assuming the supremacy of the church, he was harassed on the other hand with reports, that the king of Scots urged with assiduity the improvement of his artillery; that he had promised support to the malcontents in the northern counties; and that he suffered ballads derogatory from the honour of Henry, and prophecies predictive of his downfal, to be circulated on the borders. Another effort to convert James was made through the agency of Sadler. The ostensible object of that minister was to present to the king half a dozen stallions, sent to him by his uncle; but he was ordered to solicit a private audience, and a promise that the conversation should not be divulged. Sadler then read to James an intercepted letter from Beaton to his agent at Rome, from which he inferred that it was the aim of the cardinal to subject the royal authority to that of the pope.[2] But the king laughed at the charge, and said that the cardinal had long ago given him a copy of the letter. The envoy then observed that Henry was ashamed of the meanness of his nephew, who kept large flocks of sheep, as if he were a husbandman, and not a sovereign. If he wanted money, let him supply himself from the riches of the church; he need only make the experiment, and he would find in the dissolute lives of the monks and churchmen reasons to justify himself in following the example of England. James replied that he had sufficient of his own, without invading the property of others; that if he wanted more, the church would cheerfully supply his wants; that, if among the clergy and monks there were some who disgraced their profession, there were also many whose virtues deserved praise; and that it did not accord with his notions of justice to punish the innocent equally with the guilty. Sadler proceeded to show the advantage which the king would derive from the friendship of Henry, in preference to that of Francis; to hold out a prospect of his being inserted in the act of succession after Prince Edward; and to exhort him to meet his uncle at York, and enter into a more particular

---

[1] Sadler's State Papers, 50—56. Mr. Clifford, on the authority of Mr. Pinkerton (Hist. ii. p. 374), has allotted this negotiation to the year 1541; but it is evident from Sadler's instructions, that they were composed after Cardinal Pole had failed with the emperor, and while it was doubtful whether he would succeed or not with the king of France (Sadler's Papers, p. 53); i. e. between the end of January and the beginning of April, 1539.

[2] James had committed two clergymen to prison. Beaton, in his letter, said he should labour to have them delivered to him, as their ordinary judge. — Sadler's Papers, p. 14. This, and a petition for that purpose, were the foundation of the charge. James replied, "As for those men, they are but simple, and it was but a small matter; and we ourselves made the cardinal the minister both to commit them, and to deliver them" (p. 43).

discussion of these subjects. He answered with general expressions of affection and gratitude, but adroitly declined the meeting. The envoy in his letters ascribed the failure of his mission to the jealousy of the clergy. The principal of the nobility were, if we may believe him, sufficiently inclined to enrich themselves at the expense of the church. But their ignorance excluded them from the royal councils; and James was compelled to give his confidence to clergymen, who naturally opposed every measure which might lead to the loss of their privileges, or to the diminution of their incomes.[1]

In the next year the Scottish parliament, as if it meant to stigmatize the proceedings of that of England, passed several laws in support of the ancient doctrines and of the papal supremacy. The cardinal soon afterwards left Scotland, to proceed through France to Rome. If his departure revived the jealousy of the king of England, who suspected that a league was in agitation against him, it suggested at the same time a hope that the obstinacy of James might be subdued, when it was no longer upheld by the presence and counsels of the prelate. An interview at York was proposed for a third time; the lord William Howard, the English envoy, flattered his master with a prospect of success; and Henry left London on his road into Yorkshire. But James, who feared that, if he once put himself in the power of his uncle, he should not be permitted to return without either renouncing his alliance with France, or abjuring the authority of the pope, refused to leave his own kingdom; and Henry, having waited more than a week for his arrival at York, returned in discontent to London, and would scarcely condescend to hear the apology offered by the Scottish ambassadors.[2]

The English cabinet now determined to accomplish by force what it had in vain attempted by artifice and persuasion. Paget was first employed to sound the disposition of the king of France; whose answer, though unsatisfactory to Henry, showed that, in the present circumstances, little aid could be expected by Scotland from her ancient ally. In August forays were reciprocally made across the borders; and each nation charged the other with the first aggression; but the Scots had the advantage, who at Haldenrig defeated three thousand cavalry under the earl of Angus and Sir Robert Bowes, and made most of the captains prisoners. Enraged at this loss, the king published a declaration of war, in which he claimed the superiority over the Scottish crown, and ordered the duke of Norfolk to assemble a numerous army at York; but James, who had made no preparation for war, arrested his march by opening a negotiation; and detained Norfolk at York, till Henry, impatient of delay, sent him a peremptory order to enter Scotland. The duke crossed the borders, and gave to the flames two towns and twenty villages; but on the eighth day, constrained by want, or by the inclemency of the season, he returned to Berwick. James with thirty thousand men had advanced as far as Fala, to meet th invaders. On the intelligence of their retreat, he proposed to follow them into England; but it was objected that he had yet no heir, and that, if

---

[1] Sadler's Papers, 3—49.

[2] Hall, 248. Leslie, 432, 433. The refusal of James was nobilium consiliis (id.). Lethington says that Henry intended to have limited the succession to James and his heirs, but was so irritated by the answer of that prince, that he passed over the Scottish line entirely in his will.—Haynes, 373. It appears, however, from a minute in council, that as early as in 1537 Henry was desirous of "taking awaye the remayndre hanging on the king of Scottes."—State Papers, 546.

the same misfortune were to befall him which had deprived Scotland of his father at Flodden, the kingdom would be exposed to the ambition of his uncle. Compelled to dismiss his army, he repaired to the western marches, and ordered Lord Maxwell to enter England with ten thousand men, and to remain there as many days as the duke of Norfolk had been in Scotland. Maxwell crossed the borders; and the next day was opposed by Sir Thomas Wharton, the English warden. Whether it was that the Scots, as their historians say, refused to fight, because the command had been taken from Maxwell and given to Sinclair, the royal favourite; or that, as was reported in England, they believed the attack to proceed from the whole of Norfolk's army, both the men and their leaders fled in irremediable confusion; twenty-four pieces of artillery, the whole of the royal train, fell into the hands of the enemy; and two earls, five barons, and two hundred gentlemen, with eight hundred of their followers, were made prisoners. This cruel and unlooked-for stroke subdued the spirit of James. From the neighbouring castle of Carlaveroc he hastened to Edinburgh, and thence to the solitude of Falkland, where a fever, aided by anguish of mind, overcame the strength of his constitution. A week before his death, his queen was delivered of a female child, who, under the name of Mary, was proclaimed his successor on the Scottish throne.[1]

These unexpected events opened a new scene to the ambition of Henry, who determined to marry his son Edward to the infant queen of Scotland; and, in consequence of that marriage, to demand, as natural tutor of the young princess, the government of the kingdom. He communicated his views to the earl of Angus, and to his brother, Sir George Douglas, who had long been pensioners on his bounty; and to the earls of Cassilis and Glencairn, the lords Maxwell, Fleming, Somerville, Oliphant, and Gray, who had been made prisoners at the late battle of Solway Moss. The first through gratitude, the others through the hope of liberty, promised their concurrence; and both, as soon as the latter had given hostages for their return into captivity, if the project should fail, proceeded with expedition to Edinburgh.

There, soon after the death of the king, Cardinal Beaton had published a will of the deceased monarch, by which the regency was vested in himself and three other noblemen; but this instrument, whether it was real or supposititious, was disregarded by the lords assembled in the city. James Hamilton, earl of Arran, and presumptive heir to the throne, was declared governor during the minority of the queen; and the cardinal appeared to acquiesce in an arrangement, which he had not the power to disturb. But this seeming tranquillity vanished on the arrival of the exiles and captives from England: by whose agency the Scottish nobility was divided into two powerful factions. The English faction consisted of Angus and his associates, with their adherents; but most of these cared little for the interests of Henry, provided they could recover their sons and relatives, whom they had delivered as hostages. Their opponents were guided by the queen mother, the cardinal, and the earls of Huntley, Murray, and Argyle, and could depend on the aid of the clergy, the enemies of religious innovation, and on the good wishes of the people, hostile from education and interest

[1] Hall, 248—255. Holins. 957. Herb. 542, 545, 546. Leslie, 432—437. James, in a letter to Paul III., quoted by Mr. Pinkerton, ii. 383, says that the real cause of the war was his refusal to abandon the communion of Rome.

to the ascendancy of England.[1] The new governor wavered between the two parties. The opposition which he had experienced from the cardinal threw him at first into the arms of the English faction; his conviction that the success of their plans would endanger his chance of succeeding to the throne, naturally led him to seek a reconciliation with their adversaries. Henry, indeed, to fix him in his interest, offered to the son of Arran the hand of his daughter Elizabeth; but the penetration of the governor easily discovered that the real object of the king was to prevent, what otherwise might in all probability be accomplished, the marriage of that young nobleman with the infant queen. At first, however, he declared in favour of Henry, and imprisoned the cardinal on a fictitious charge of having persuaded the duke of Guise to levy an army for the support of his daughter, the queen dowager, against the claim of the governor.[2] A parliament was then called, which, though it approved the proposal of peace and marriage, refused, as unwarrantable, the other demands of Henry; which were, that he should have the custody of the young queen, the government of the kingdom, and the possession of the royal castles during the minority. The king had received the proposals of the Scottish envoys with indignation and scorn; and despatched again his agent, Sir Ralph Sadler, to reprimand Angus and his associates, for their apathy in the royal service, and their breach of promise. They replied that they had obtained as much as in the present temper of the nation it was possible to obtain; that if the king would be content for the present, he might afterwards effect his purpose step by step; but that, if his impatience refused to wait, he must invade the kingdom with a powerful army, and would find them ready to assist him to the extent of their power. Henry endeavoured to shake by bribes and threats the resolution of the governor; but Arran was not to be diverted from the strict line of duty. He then called on his Scottish adherents to seize the person of the infant queen and convey her to England; but the strength of the fortress and the vigilance of the governor bade defiance to both force and treachery. The king's obstinacy at last yielded to the conviction, that every day added to the strength of his enemies; and after three months of angry altercation, he condescended to sign two treaties. By the first, peace was concluded between the kingdoms; by the second, it was agreed that Mary should marry Edward; that, as soon as she had completed her tenth year, she should be sent into England; and that in the meanwhile six noblemen should be surrendered as hostages to Henry.[3]

During this protracted negotiation Cardinal Beaton had by private treaty procured his liberty; and the hopes of the French party were kept alive by repeated supplies of ammunition and money from France. But nothing created greater alarm in the governor than the arrival of Matthew Stuart, earl of Lennox, who, on the ground that Arran was an illegitimate child,

---

[1] Sir George Douglas told Sadler, that to obtain the government for Henry was impossible. "For," quoth he, "there is not so little a boy but he will hurl stones against it; and the wives will handle their distaffs, and the commons universally will rather die in it, yea, and many noblemen and all the clergy be fully against it."—Sadler's State Papers, 70. "The whole realm murmureth, that they would rather die than break their old league with France."—Ibid. 163.

[2] This fictitious charge disproves the story so often repeated of the late king's will having been forged by the cardinal. Had there been the least proof of such a crime, it would have been eagerly brought forward in justification of his imprisonment.

[3] Rym. xiv. 786, 797; xv. 4. Sadler's State Papers, 62—275.

claimed the regency for himself as the next in the line of succession. With his aid the cardinal secured the northern division of Scotland, obtained possession of the young queen, and removed her from Linlithgow to the strong castle of Stirling.[1] Arran now began to seek a reconciliation; the terms were easily arranged with Beaton; nine days after the ratification of the English treaty they met as friends; and the next week assisted together at the coronation of Mary. Henry instantly determined upon war;[2] and his cause received an accession of strength from the hesitation and subsequent defection of Lennox, whose enmity to the governor dissolved his connection with the cardinal; and whose passion for Margaret Douglas, the daughter of Angus, and niece of Henry, ultimately impelled him to join the friends of the king of England.[3] These had bound themselves by a common instrument to live and die in defence of each other; but the lords Maxwell and Somerville were arrested by the governor, and on the latter was found a copy of the bond, and a letter to Henry in which they solicited his assistance. Urged by the representations of Marco Grimani, the papal legate, and of La Brosse, the French ambassador, the governor determined to make war on his opponents; and convened a parliament, in which the adherents of England were accused of treason, and the late treaty was pronounced void, because Henry had not only delayed to ratify it, but had sanctioned incursions across the borders, and had seized several merchant-ships, the property of the citizens of Edinburgh.[4]

Though Arran solicited a renewal of the negotiation, the English king was determined to make him feel the weight of his resentment. In May, Seymour, earl of Hertford, and uncle of Prince Edward, arrived in the Frith with an army of ten thousand men, and required the immediate surrender of the young queen. On the refusal of Arran, he landed his troops at Leith; marched to Edinburgh, where he was joined by five thousand horse from Berwick; and the next morning forced open one of the gates. Four days were devoted to plunder and conflagration: but the castle defied his efforts; the governor, with Angus, Maxwell, and Sir George Douglas, whom he had released from confinement, was actively employed in collecting troops; and Hertford deemed it prudent to return before his retreat should be interrupted by a superior force. The fleet having set fire to Leith, demolished the pier, and swept the coast on each side the Frith as far as Stirling, sailed for Newcastle; the army directing its route through Seton, Haddington, and Dunbar, gave these towns to the flames, and reached Berwick with inconsiderable loss.[5]

The war from this period continued for two years. Ivers, the English warden of the middle marches, lost his life with many of his followers in an unsuccessful action at Ancram; and the governor, though aided by five thousand French troops, was compelled to retire from the fortress of Wark. Lennox had obtained the

---

[1] Henry, who had before attempted to get possession of her person by stratagem, and now feared she might be carried away to France, offered the governor the aid of an English army, and promised, in case Arran's son should marry Elizabeth, to make the father "by force of our title and superiority, the king of the rest of Scotland beyond the Firth."—Sadler, p. 248. But the governor replied, that "Marry, all his lands and living lay on this side of the Firth, which he would not gladly exchange for any living beyond the Firth" (p. 256).

[2] Ibid. 308.   [3] Sadler, p. 314.

[4] Ibid. 275–351. Leslie, 445–448.

[5] Leslie, 450, 451. Holins. 962, 963. Journal of expedition, in "Illustrations of Reign of Queen Mary," [printed for the Maitland Club, and edited by Mr. Stevenson,] p. 3.

hand of Margaret Douglas, on condition that he should surrender to Henry his castle of Dumbarton; but the governor and garrison expelled him with ignominy, and afterwards delivered it up to his rival. This circumstance, added to the submission of several of the English partisans in the western counties of Scotland, so irritated Henry, that, in a moment of passion, he ordered the hostages at Carlisle to be put to death, and clandestinely gave his sanction to a conspiracy for the assassination of the cardinal.[1] At length the Scots were comprehended in the treaty of peace between England and France, and though the conditions of that comprehension became the subject of dispute, the remaining six months of Henry's reign were not disturbed by open hostilities.[2]

III. The reader will recollect, that the king of France had complained of Henry's marriage with Anne Boleyn, as of a violation of his promise; and that Henry retorted, by objecting to Francis the support which he gave to the papal authority.[3] This dissension, though it might weaken, did not dissolve, the friendship which had so long subsisted between them; but fresh bickerings ensued; the tempers of the two princes became reciprocally soured; each wished to chastise what he deemed the caprice, the ingratitude, and the perfidy of the other; and it was at last evident that war would be declared by the first who could persuade himself that he might do it with impunity.

The emperor had watched, and nourished by his ambassadors, this growing disaffection of the king of England. After the death of his aunt Catherine, and the execution of her rival Anne Boleyn, he contended that as the original cause of the misunderstanding between the two crowns had ceased to exist, nothing ought to prevent the renewal of their former friendship. There was, however, an objection, which for some years opposed an insuperable barrier to his wishes. The honour of the imperial family demanded that the Princess Mary should be restored in blood, as the legitimate child of her father; and the pride of Henry refused to bend to an act which would be a tacit acknowledgment that he had wronged her mother. An expedient was at length adopted to the satisfaction of both parties. Mary was restored by act of parliament to her place in the succession, but without any formal mention of her legitimacy; an accommodation which was brought about by the necessities of the emperor on the one hand, and by the resentments of the king on the other. The former, induced by his losses in the campaign of 1542, and the latter, eager to punish the interference of Francis in the affairs of Scotland, concluded a treaty, by which it was agreed, 1. That they should jointly require the French king to recede from his alliance with

---

[1] "His highness reputing the fact not meet to be set forward expressly by his majesty, will not seem to have to do in it; and yet, not misliking the offer, thinketh good that they be exhorted to proceed." We owe our knowledge of this fact to Mr. Tytler, v. 389.

[2] Rym. xv. 94, 98. Epist. Reg. Scot. ii. 354.

[3] Burnet (iii. Rec. 84) had published an instrument, in which Francis is made to declare, that in his opinion, the marriage with Catherine has been void from the beginning, but that with Anne is valid; that all the judgments pronounced by the pope are false, unjust, and of no effect; and then to bind himself and his successors, under the forfeiture of his or their goods or chattels, to maintain the same opinion on all occasions. It has, however, neither signature nor date; and is evidently nothing more than a mere form, "devised," as is said on the back of it, in England, but never executed in France. From Cardinal Pole we learn, that to Henry's most earnest solicitations, the French monarch replied, that he would still be his true and faithful friend, "but only as far as the altar."—Pole, fol. cviii.

the Turks; to make reparation to the Christians for all the losses which they had suffered in consequence of that alliance; to pay to the king of England the arrears of his pension, and to give to him security for the faithful payment of it in future: 2. And that, if Francis did not signify his assent within forty days, the emperor should reclaim the duchy of Burgundy, Henry the possessions of his ancestors in France, and that each should be ready to support his right at the head of a powerful army.[1]

In consequence of these engagements, two heralds, Garter and Toison d'or, received instructions to proceed to the French court; but Francis refused to listen to demands which he deemed insulting to his honour; the messengers could not obtain permission to cross the borders; and the allied sovereigns resolved to consider the conduct of their adversary as a denial of justice, and equivalent to a declaration of war. The Imperialists in Flanders having received a reinforcement of six thousand Englishmen under Sir John Wallop, formed the siege of Landreci; while Charles, with a more numerous force, overran the duchy of Cleves, and compelled the duke, the partisan of France, to throw himself at the feet of his natural sovereign. From Cleves the emperor proceeded to the camp before Landreci; and Francis hastened at the same time to relieve the place. The grand armies were in presence of each other; and a general and decisive engagement was daily expected; but the French monarch, having amused the attention of the enemy with an offer of battle, threw supplies of men and provisions into the town, and immediately withdrew. The Imperialists were unable to make any impression on the rear of the retreating army; the English, who pursued with too much precipitation, suffered a considerable loss.[2]

The allies derived little benefit from this campaign; but Henry promised himself more brilliant success in the next, in which he intended to assume the command at the head of a numerous and disciplined army. During the winter he was visited by Gonzaga, the viceroy of Sicily, with whom it was arranged that the emperor should enter France by Champaign, the king of England by Picardy; and that both, instead of besieging towns, should march with expedition to Paris, where they should unite their forces, and from the capital dictate the law to their adversary. The Imperialists were the first in the field; Luxembourg and Ligny opened their gates; and St. Dizier surrendered after a siege of six weeks.[3] In June the first division of the English army landed at Calais; and in the middle of July, Henry saw himself within the French frontier, at the head of 30,000 Englishmen and of 15,000 Imperialists. Had he complied with his engagement to advance towards the capital, the French monarch would have been at the mercy of the allies: but the king was seduced by the prospect of conquest; the example of Charles, who had already taken three fortresses, seemed to offer an apology for his conduct; and he ordered the army to form at the same time the two sieges of Boulogne and Montreuil. It was in vain that the imperial ambassador during eleven days urged him to advance; or that the emperor, to give him the example, avoiding the fortified towns, hastened along the right bank of the Marne towards Paris. Henry persisted in his resolution, and was detained more than two months before the walls of Boulogne.

It chanced that in the Dominican

[1] Rym. xiv. 768—780. Chron. Catal. 232.
[2] Godwin, 76. Stowe, 585. Du Bellay, 547.
[3] Godwin, 578, 581.

convent at Soissons was a Spanish monk, called Guzman, of the same family as the confessor of Charles. Through him Francis conveyed to the emperor his secret wish for an accommodation. That prince immediately assented; conferences were opened; and a courier was sent to receive the demands of Henry. But when the terms of the allies were made known, they appeared so exorbitant, that the French council advised their sovereign to prefer the risk of continuing the war. Charles, during the negotiation, had not slackened the rapidity of his march, and was now arrived at Château Thierri, almost in the vicinity of Paris. Francis, alarmed for the fate of his capital, solicited a renewal of the conferences; and separate ambassadors were appointed to treat with the emperor and with Henry. The former of these princes had many reasons to wish for peace. His ally, the king of England, showed no disposition to join him; the French army between him and Paris daily increased, and his own forces were without pay or provisions. In these circumstances he consented to renew the same offers which he had made, and which Francis had refused, before the war. During the negotiation the news of the surrender of Boulogne arrived. The king of France hastened to accept the conditions; and the moment they were signed, recalled his ambassadors from the English camp. By the treaty of Crespi the two princes agreed to forget all former injuries, to restore their respective conquests, to join their forces for the defence of Christendom against the Turks, and to unite their families by the marriage of Charles, the second son of Francis, with a daughter of the emperor, or of his brother Ferdinand king of the Romans. Had Charles lived to complete this marriage, it might have been followed by the most important results; but he died within a few months, and the treaty of Crespi made little change in the existing relations among the great powers of Europe. Henry having garrisoned Boulogne, raised the siege of Montreuil, and returned to England.[1]

During the winter Francis had leisure to attend to the war with his only remaining adversary. The plan which he formed embraced two objects; to acquire such a superiority by sea as might prevent the transmission of succour to the English forces in France; and with a numerous army by land to besiege and reduce, not only Boulogne, which he had so lately lost, but also Calais, which for two centuries had been severed from the French crown. With this view, he ordered every ship fit for war to assemble in the ports of Normandy, while a fleet of twenty-five galleys was conducted by the baron De la Garde from the Mediterranean to the mouth of the Seine. To oppose his design, fortifications had been raised on the banks of the Thames, and on the coasts of Kent, Sussex, and Hampshire; and sixty ships of war had been collected at Portsmouth by Dudley Lord Lisle, high admiral of England. The French fleet, amounting to one hundred and thirty-six sail, under the command of Annebaut, left the coast on the 16th of July, and on the second day anchored at St. Helen's. Lisle, who had been forbidden to risk a close engagement with so superior a force,

---

[1] See the king's letter, and his Journal, in Rymer, xv. 50—58; Du Bellay, 590, 591; Sepulveda, ii. 503—510; Godwin, 77—79; Mém. de Tavannes, 70. A general order was given to return thanks to God for the taking of Boulogne "by devoute and generall procession in all the towns and villages." —The council to Lord Shrewsbury, Sept. 19, 1544.

after a brisk but distant cannonade, retired into the harbour; and Henry, who had repaired to Portsmouth, had the mortification to behold a foreign fleet braving him to the face, and riding triumphant in the Channel. The next day the French admiral formed his line in three divisions, and sent his galleys to insult the enemy in the mouth of the port. During the cannonade, the Mary Rose, carrying seven hundred men, was sunk under the eyes of the king; but the moment the tide turned, the English bore down on the aggressors, who instantly fled towards their own fleet. Annebaut was prepared to receive them; but Lisle, faithful to his instructions, recalled his ships, and, safe within the port, bore with patience the taunts and the triumph of his enemy.

Foiled in these attempts to provoke a battle, the French admiral summoned a council of war, in which a proposal to seize and fortify the Isle of Wight was made and rejected; and the next morning the whole armament stood out to sea, made occasional descents on the coast of Sussex, and at length anchored before Boulogne. Lisle, having received a reinforcement of thirty sail, was ordered to follow. The hostile fleets soon came in presence of each other; some time was spent in manœuvring to obtain the advantage of the wind; and at length, after the exchange of a few shots, they separated, and retired into their respective harbours.[1]

This expedition might gratify the vanity of the French monarch; but it did not secure to him what he expected, an overwhelming superiority by land. He had indeed prevented the junction of a body of lansquenets in the pay of Henry, had laid waste the Pays d'Oie, and had gained the advantage in a few rencounters. Yet he had been unable to erect the fortresses, with the aid of which he expected to reduce the garrisons of Calais and Boulogne; and during the winter his army had been thinned by the ravages of a pestilential disease. Both princes became weary of a war which exhausted their treasures without any return of profit or glory. A short armistice was employed in negotiations for peace; and it was finally agreed that Francis should pay to Henry and his successors the pension due by the treaty of 1525; that commissioners should be appointed by the two monarchs to determine the claim of the latter to a debt of 512,022 crowns; that at the termination of eight years, the king of England should receive the sum of two millions of crowns as a compensation for arrears of pensions, and the charges of repairing and preserving the fortifications of Boulogne; and that on the payment of these sums, that town, with its dependencies, should be restored to the king of France.[2]

It had been hitherto the general opinion, that Henry was the most opulent monarch in Europe; his late wars with Scotland and France revealed the inexplicable secret of his poverty. The plate and jewels which he had collected from the religious houses, and the enormous sums which he had raised by the sale of their property, seemed to have been absorbed in some invisible abyss: the king daily called on his ministers for money; and the laws of the country, the rights of the subject, and the honour of the crown, were equally sacrificed to supply the increasing demands of the treasury. In 1543 he had obtained a subsidy almost unprecedented in its amount. The clergy

---

[1] Du Bellay, 596. Mém. de Montluc, xxii. 304—344. State Papers, i. 782—834.

[2] Rymer, xv. 94. Mém. de Tavannes, xxvi. 80.

had given him for three years ten per cent. on their incomes, after the deduction of the tenths already vested in the crown; and the laity granted him a tax on real and personal property, to be paid by instalments in three years, rising gradually from fourpence to three shillings in the pound.[1] But the returns had disclosed the value of each man's estate; and soon afterwards all persons rated at fifty pounds per annum, received a royal letter demanding the advance of a sum of money by way of loan. Prudence taught them to obey; but their hope of repayment was extinguished by the servility of parliament, which at once granted to the king all those sums that he had borrowed from any of his subjects since the thirty-first year of his reign.[2] After this act of dishonesty, it would have been idle to solicit a second loan; he therefore demanded presents under the name of a benevolence, adopting again some of the expedients which had been attempted under the administration of Wolsey, and had failed through the spirited opposition of the people. But in the course of a few years the bloody despotism of Henry had quenched that spirit; the benevolence was raised without difficulty; and the murmurs of the sufferers were effectually silenced by the timely punishment of two of the aldermen of London, who had presumed to complain. One of them, Richard Reed, was immediately sent to the army in Scotland, where he was made prisoner in the first engagement, and was compelled by his captors to pay a heavy fine for his ransom; the other, Sir William Roach, was on a charge of seditious words committed to prison, whence he was liberated after a confinement of three months, but probably not before he had appeased the king by a considerable present.[3]

With the same view, Henry adulterated the purity of the coin; a plan by which, while he defrauded the public, he created numberless embarrassments in the way of trade, and involved his successors in almost inextricable difficulties. At his accession the ounce of gold, and the pound of silver, were each worth forty shillings: having raised them by successive proclamations to forty-four, forty-five, and forty-eight shillings, he issued a new coinage with a considerable quantity of alloy, and contrived at the same time to obtain possession of the old money, by offering a premium to those who would bring it to the Mint. Satisfied with the result of this experiment, he rapidly advanced in the same career. Before the end of the war his coins contained equal quantities of silver and of alloy; the year after, the alloy exceeded the silver in the proportion of two to one. The consequence was, that his successors found themselves compelled to lower the nominal value of his shillings, first from twelvepence to ninepence, and then to sixpence, and finally to

---

[1] The rates were as follows :—

	s.	d.		s.	d.
From 1*l*. to 5*l*. in goods	0	4	in lands, fees, and annuities	0	8
Do. 5 to 10	0	8		1	4
Do. 10 to 20	1	4		2	0
Do. 20 and upwards	2	0		3	0

All foreigners paid double rates.—St. 34 Henry VIII. 27.

[2] Sanders, 203. State Pap. i. 766. Lords' Journals, 265. Even if the king had paid all, or any part, of these sums, the money so paid was to be refunded; but the present holders of the royal securities could recover from the sellers the consideration which had been given for them.—St. 45 Henry VIII. 12.

[3] Sanders, 203, 204. Stowe, 588. Herbert, 587. The sum thus raised amounted to 70,723*l*. 18s. 10d.—Strype, i. App. 333. London, York, Durham, Northumberland and Westmoreland are not included.

withdraw them from circulation altogether.[1] During these operations in debasing the coin, the three years allotted for the payment of the last subsidy expired; and the king again laid his wants before his parliament, and solicited the aid of his loving subjects. The clergy granted fifteen per cent. on their incomes, during two years; the laity two tenths and fifteenths, with an additional subsidy from real and personal property, which they begged him to accept, "as it pleased the great king Alexander to receive thankfully a suppe of water of a poor man by the high way side."[2] As this, however, did not satisfy his rapacity, parliament subjected to his disposal all colleges, chantries, and hospitals in the kingdom, with all their manors, lands, and hereditaments, receiving from him in return a promise that he would not abuse the confidence of his subjects, but employ the grant to the glory of God and the common profit of the realm. This was the last aid given to the insatiate monarch. As early as the twenty-sixth year of his reign, it was asserted by those who had made the calculation from official documents, that the receipts of the Exchequer under Henry had even then exceeded the aggregate amount of all the taxes upon record, which had been imposed by his predecessors. But that sum, enormous as it must have been, was more than doubled before his death, by subsidies and loans which he was careful not to repay, by forced benevolences and the debasement of the currency, and by the secularization of part of the clerical, and of the whole of the monastic possessions.[3]

During these transactions the court of Henry was divided by the secret intrigues of the two religious parties, which continued to cherish an implacable hatred against each other. The men of the old learning naturally looked upon Cranmer as their most steady and most dangerous enemy; and, though he was careful not to commit any open transgression of the law, yet the encouragement which he gave to the new preachers, and the clandestine correspondence which he maintained with the German reformers, would have proved his ruin, had he not found a friend and advocate in his sovereign. Henry still retained a grateful recollection of his former services, and felt no apprehension of resistance or treason from a man who, on all occasions, whatever were his real opinions or wishes, had moulded his conscience in conformity to the royal will. When the prebendaries of Canterbury lodged an information against him, the king issued a commission to examine, not the accused, but the accusers; of whom some were imprisoned; all were compelled to ask pardon of the archbishop.[4] In the house of Commons Sir John Gostwick, representative for Bedfordshire, had the boldness to accuse him of heresy; but the king sent a message to the "varlet," that if he did not immediately acknowledge his fault, he should be made an example for the instruction of his fellows. On another occasion Henry had consented

---

[1] Sanders, 204. Stowe, 587. Herbert, 191, 572. Folkes, 27. Fleetwood, 53.
[2] St. of Realm, 1016.
[3] Etenim interfui ipse, cum fide dignissimi, qui tabulas publicas, in quas rationes tributorum sunt relatæ vidissent, et rationem iniissent, hoc mihi ante aliquot annos sanctissime asseverarent, ita se rem habere; quæ ille unus accepit, majorem summam efficere, quam omnia omnium tot retro sæculis tributa.—Apol. Reg. Poli, p. 91. Defen. Eccl. Unit. fol. lxxxii. Barbaro (Report to Venetian Senate, ann. 1551) gives the particulars of his receipts from his thirty-fourth to his forty-seventh year, amounting to the gross sum of 10,320,000l.
[4] Strype's Cranmer, 110—122.

to the committal of the archbishop; but afterwards he revoked the permission, telling the council that Cranmer was as faithful a man towards him as ever was prelate in the realm, and one to whom he was many ways beholden; or, as another version has it, that he was the only man who had loved his sovereign so well as never to have opposed the royal pleasure.[1] In like manner Gardiner, from his acknowledged abilities and his credit with the king, was to the men of the new learning a constant object of apprehension and jealousy. To ruin him in the royal estimation, it was pretended that he had communicated with the papal agents through the imperial ministers; and that, while he pretended to be zealously attached to the interests of the king, he had in reality made his peace with the pontiff. But it was in vain that the accusation was repeatedly urged, and that Gardiner's secretary was even tried, convicted, and executed, on a charge of having denied the supremacy; the caution of the bishop bade defiance to the wiles and the malice of his enemies. Aware of the danger which threatened him, he stood constantly on his guard; and though he might prompt the zeal, and second the efforts of those who wished well to the ancient faith, he made it a rule never to originate any religious measure, nor to give his opinion on religious subjects, without the express command of his sovereign.[2] Then he was accustomed to speak his mind with boldness; but though he might sometimes offend the pride, still he preserved the esteem, of Henry,[3] who, unmoved by the suggestions of adversaries, continued to employ him in affairs of state, and to consult him on questions of religion. As often indeed as he was absent on embassies to foreign courts, Cranmer improved the favourable moment to urge the king to a further reformation. He was heard with attention; he was even twice desired to form the necessary plan, to subjoin his reasons, and to submit them to the royal consideration; still, however, Henry paused to receive the opinion of Gardiner; and, swayed by his advice, rejected or sus-

---

[1] Ibid. 123—126. Sanders, p. 78. Unum esse tam suarum partium amantem, qui nulla unquam in re ipsius defuerit voluntati. Neque id solum præstitit in iis rebus, quæ Lutheranis jucunde acciderent, verum sive quem comburi oportebat hæresis nomine, sive sacerdotem uxore spoliari, nemo erat Cranmero in ea re exequenda diligentior.— Vit. Cran. MS. apud Le Grand, ii. 103.

[2] Modern writers have ascribed to his counsels all the measures adopted by Henry against the reformers. Yet Gardiner often denies it in his letters. "The earl of Southampton [Wriothesley] did," he says, "many things, while he was chancellor, touching religion, which misliked me not. But I did never advise him so to do, nor made on him the more for it, when he had done. He was one of whom by reason I might have been bold; but I left him to his conscience." —Apud Fox, ii. 60.

[3] On this subject I will transcribe a passage from one of his letters, because it serves to elucidate the character of the king. "This fashion of writing his highness (God pardon his soul) called whetting: which was not at all the most pleasant unto me, yet when I saw in my doings was no hurt, and sometime by the occasion thereof the matter was amended, I was not so coy as always to reverse my argument: nor, so that his affairs went well, did I ever trouble myself whether he made me a wanton or not. And when such as were privy to his letters to me, were afraid I had been in high displeasure (for the terms of the letters sounded so), yet I myself feared it nothing at all; I esteemed him, as he was, a wise prince, and whatsoever he said or wrote for the present, he would afterwards consider the matter as wisely as any man, nor either hurt or inwardly disfavour him that had been bold with him. Whereof I serve for a proof: for no man could do me hurt during his life. And when he gave me the bishopric of Winchester, he said he had often squared with me, but he loved me never the worse: and for a token thereof he gave me the bishopric.........I was reported unto him, that I stooped not, and was stubborn: and he commended unto me certain men's gentle nature, as he called it, that wept at every of his words: and methought that my nature was as gentle as theirs; for I was sorry when he was moved. But else I know, when the displeasure was not justly grounded in me, I had no cause to take thought."— Ap. Fox, ii. 60.

pended the execution of the measures proposed by the metropolitan.[1]

At the death of Lord Audeley, a zealous partisan of the new teachers, the office of chancellor was given to Lord Wriothesley, who, though he affected an equal friendship for the two parties, was in reality attached to the ancient faith. But, if the power of the reformers was weakened by this change, their loss had been amply compensated by the influence of Henry's sixth queen, Catherine Parr, relict of the late Lord Latimer;[2] who with her brother, now created earl of Essex, and her uncle, created Lord Parr of Horton, zealously promoted the new doctrines. But her zeal, whether it was stimulated by confidence in her own powers, or prompted by the suggestions of the preachers, quickly transgressed the bounds of prudence. She not only read the prohibited works; she presumed to argue with her husband, and to dispute the decisions of the head of the church. Of all men, Henry was the least disposed to brook the lectures of a female theologian, and his impatience of contradiction was exasperated by a painful indisposition which confined him to his chamber. The chancellor and the bishop of Winchester received orders to prepare articles against Catherine; but the intelligence was immediately, perhaps designedly, conveyed to the queen, who, repairing to a neighbouring apartment, fell into a succession of fits, and during the intervals made the palace ring with her cries and lamentations. Henry, moved with pity, or incommoded with the noise, first sent his physician, and was afterwards carried in a chair, to console her. In the evening she waited on him, in the company of her sister, and adroitly turning the conversation to the subject of religion, took occasion to express her admiration of his learning, and the implicit deference which she paid to his decisions. "No, no, by St. Mary," he exclaimed, "I know you too well. Ye are a doctor, Kate." She replied, that if she had sometimes presumed to differ from him, it had not been to maintain her own opinions, but to amuse his grace; for she had observed, that, in the warmth of argument, he seemed to forget the pain which tormented him. "Is it so, sweetheart?" said Henry; "then we are friends again." The following morning the chancellor came with a guard to take her into custody, but was remanded with a volley of reproaches; and the queen, taught by her past danger, was afterwards careful not to irritate the theological sensibility of her husband. It is, however, a question among the more ancient writers, whether the king was in earnest. By some the proceeding has been represented as a scheme of his own contrivance, to wean his wife from an attachment to doctrines which might in the sequel conduct her to the stake or the scaffold.[3]

The books, the perusal of which had led the queen into danger, had been introduced to the ladies at court through the agency of two females, Anne Bocher, and Anne Kyme. With Bocher we shall meet again in the next reign, when she will be condemned to the flames by Archbishop Cranmer. Kyme, who had abandoned her husband to exercise the office of an apostle under her

---

[1] Herbert, 565, 591. Strype's Cranmer, 130, 136.
[2] The king married her, after a widowhood of more than a year, on the 12th of July, 1543. The ceremony was performed by Gardiner, bishop of Winchester, in the queen's privy closet at Hampton Court, under license from the archbishop, who had dispensed with the publication of banns and all contrary ordinances for the honour and weal of the realm.—See Chron. Catal. 238.   [3] Herbert, 622.

maiden name of Askew, had been committed to Newgate by the council, "for that she was very obstinate and heady in reasoning on matters of religion."[1] There she might perhaps have escaped further notice, had not the theological jealousy of the king been provoked by the imprudent and contumacious conduct of Dr. Crome. He had given offence by a sermon, in which he maintained that no one could approve of the dissolution of monasteries, and at the same time admit the usefulness of prayers for the dead. Henry considered this assertion as a censure on himself; and Crome, to appease the king, offered to recant at St. Paul's Cross. There he disappointed the royal expectation by a reassertion of the obnoxious doctrine; was called before the council on that account, and subsequently accused several of his friends and advisers.[2] Numerous examinations followed; those who submitted to a recantation were remanded to prison; the more obstinate were sent before the ecclesiastical court, of which the archbishop was probably the chief judge;[3] and that court excommunicated them as incorrigible heretics, and delivered them over to the civil power. Among the former were Latimer, and Crome himself, who by submission escaped the flames; the sufferers were Askew,[4] Adlam a tailor, Otterden a priest, and Lascelles a gentleman at court. Shaxton, the deprived bishop of Salisbury, was to have shared with them the honour of martyrdom; but his courage shrunk from the fiery ordeal, and he not only recanted, but preached the sermon at the execution of his former associates, pitying their blindness, and exhorting them to follow his example. His conformity was rewarded with the mastership of St. Giles's hospital in Norwich.[5]

As long as Henry enjoyed health, he was able, by the interposition of his authority, and by occasional acts of severity, to check the diffusion of the new doctrines; but as his infirmities increased, he found it a more difficult task, and, in his last speech to the parliament, he complained bitterly of the religious dissensions which pervaded every parish in the realm. It was, he observed, partly the fault of the clergy, some of whom were "so stiff in their old mumpsimus, and others so busy in their new sumpsimus," that instead of preaching the word of God, they were employed in railing at each other; and partly the fault of the laity, whose delight it was to censure the proceedings of their

---

[1] See Council Book, Harl. MSS. 256, fol. 224.

[2] State Papers, i. 842—851. Burnet, ii. 572. This persecution has been attributed by some writers to the king's advisers; but from the official correspondence it appears that they were only agents under him, carefully apprizing him by letter of the daily proceedings, and never venturing to take any step but by his express order.

[3] See Anne Bocher's address to Cranmer at her trial in the next reign.

[4] In the narrative transmitted to us by Fox as the composition of this unfortunate woman, she is made to say: "My lord chancellor and Master Rich [why the name of Bishop Gardiner has since been substituted for Master Rich, in several editions, I know not] took pains to rack me with their own hands, till I was nigh dead."—Fox, ii. 578. Fox himself adds, that when Knivet the lieutenant, in compassion to the sufferer, refused to order additional torture, the chancellor and Rich worked the rack themselves. To me neither story appears worthy of credit. For, 1. Torture was contrary to law, and therefore was never inflicted without a written order subscribed by the lords of the council. 2. The person who attended on such occasions to receive the confession of the sufferer was always some inferior officer appointed by the council, and not the lord chancellor or other members of that body. 3. There is no instance of a female being stretched on the rack, or subjected to any of those inflictions which come under the denomination of torture.—See Mr. Jardine's "Reading on the use of Torture."

[5] Ellis, iii. 177. Collier, ii. 212. Stowe, 592. Fox, ii. 578. State Pap. i. 868, 875.

bishops, priests, and preachers. "If you know," he added, "that any preach perverse doctrine, come and declare it to some of our council, or to us, to whom is committed by God the authority to reform and order such causes and behaviours; and be not judges yourselves of your own fantastical opinions and vain expositions; and although you be permitted to read holy scripture, and to have the word of God in your mother tongue, you must understand it is licensed you so to do, only to inform your conscience, and inform your children and families, and not to dispute, and to make scripture a railing and taunting stock against priests and preachers. I am very sorry to know and hear, how irreverently that precious jewel, the word of God, is disputed, rhymed, sung, and jingled in every alehouse and tavern, contrary to the true meaning and doctrine of the same; and yet I am as much sorry that the readers of the same follow it in doing so faintly and coldly. For of this I am sure, that charity was never so faint among you, and virtuous and godly living was never less used, nor God himself among Christians never less served. Therefore, as I said before, be in charity with one another, like brother and brother, and love, dread, and serve God, to which I, as your supreme head and sovereign lord, exhort and require you."[1]

The king had long indulged without restraint in the pleasures of the table. At last he grew so enormously corpulent, that he could neither support the weight of his own body, nor remove without the aid of machinery into the different apartments of his palace. Even the fatigue of subscribing his name to the writings which required his signature, was more than he could bear; and to relieve him from this duty three commissioners were appointed, of whom two had authority to apply to the paper a dry stamp, bearing the letters of the king's name, and the third to draw a pen furnished with ink over the blank impression.[2] An inveterate ulcer in the thigh, which had more than once threatened his life, and which now seemed to baffle all the skill of his surgeons, added to the irascibility of his temper; and his imagination was perpetually haunted with apprehensions for the future safety of Edward, his son and heir, a young prince who had scarcely completed his ninth year. The king had no near relation of the blood royal, to whom he could intrust the care of the boy; nor could Edward's natural guardians, his uncles, boast of any other influence than what they derived from the royal favour. Two of these, Thomas and Edward, had for some years resided at court: but the former had risen to no higher rank than that of knight; the latter, though he had been created earl of Hertford, and appointed lord chamberlain, was possessed of little real power, and unsupported by family alliances. They enjoyed, however, one advantage, of which the king himself was probably ignorant. They were known to favour the new doctrines; and all those who bore with reluctance the yoke of the Six Articles, looked impatiently to the commencement of the new reign, when they hoped that the young king, under the guidance of his uncles,

---

[1] Hall, 160.
[2] Rym. xv. 100, 102. The names of the commissioners were A. Denny, John Gate, and W. Clerc, and their authority was to last from August 31, 1546, to May 10, 1547.

They were ordered to deliver to the king at the end of every month, a schedule of the instruments stamped, which schedules are in the State Paper Office.

would not only sheath the sword of persecution, but also adopt the reformed creed.

There had for some time existed a spirit of acrimonious rivalry between the Seymours and the house of Howard. The aged duke of Norfolk witnessed with indignation their ascendancy in the royal favour, and openly complained that the kingdom was governed by new men, while the ancient nobility were trampled in the dust. His son Henry, earl of Surrey, could not forgive the earl of Hertford for having superseded him in the command of the garrison of Boulogne; and had been heard to foretell that the time of revenge was not far distant. On the one hand the father and son were the most powerful subjects in the realm, and allied by descent to the royal family; on the other, though they had strenuously supported the king in his claim of the supremacy, they were on all other points zealous patrons of the ancient doctrines. Hence the ruin or depression of the Howards became an object of equal importance to the uncles of the prince and the men of the new learning; to those, that they might seize and retain the reins of government during the minority of their nephew; to these, that they might at length throw from their necks that intolerable yoke, the penal statute of the Six Articles.[1]

The rapid decline of the king's health in the month of November admonished the Seymours and their associates to provide against his approaching death. Repeated consultations were held; and a plan was adopted to remove out of their way the persons whose power and talents they had the greatest reason to fear, the duke of Norfolk with his son, and Gardiner bishop of Winchester. Of the charge brought against the bishop, we are ignorant. But he prudently threw himself on the king's mercy; and Henry, though he did not immediately receive him into favour, was pleased, to the disappointment of his enemies, to accept his submission.[2] The fate of the two Howards was more calamitous. While the royal mind, tormented with pain, and anxious for the welfare of the prince, was alive to every suggestion, their enemies reminded the king of their power and ambition, of their hatred of the Seymours, and of the general belief that Surrey had refused the hand of the daughter of Hertford because he aspired to that of the lady Mary.

Henry's jealousy was alarmed; the council received orders to inquire into their conduct; their enemies were invited to furnish charges against them; and every malicious insinuation was accepted by the credulity, and exaggerated by the fears, of the sick monarch, till at last he persuaded himself that a conspiracy existed to place the reins of government in the hands of the Howards during his illness, and to give them the custody of the prince in the event of his death.[3] The earl was examined before the council on the same day with the bishop of Winchester. He defended himself with spirit, and offered in scorn to fight his accuser in his shirt. Soon afterwards the duke was summoned

---

[1] Norfolk himself in the Tower, and ignorant of the cause of his imprisonment, seems to attribute it to the reformers. "Undoubtedly," he says to the king, "I know not that I have offended any man, or that any man was offended with me, unless it were such as are angry with me, for being quick against such as have been accused for sacramentaries."—Apud Herbert, 628.

[2] The occasion of the king's displeasure appears to have been a refusal of the bishop to assent to an exchange of lands of his bishopric.—St. Pap. i. 883. Gardiner afterwards maintained that this was the work of a conspiracy formed against him; and offered to prove his assertion by witnesses in a court of justice.—Burnet, ii. 165.

[3] The ambassadors at foreign courts were instructed that such was their crime.—Herbert, 617.

to court; and, on his arrival, both father and son, ignorant of each other's arrest, were conveyed about the same time to separate cells in the Tower.

The next day the duke's houses, his plate and all his personal property, were seized by the royal commissioners. Not only several of his servants, but his mistress Elizabeth Holland, and even his daughter the duchess of Richmond, relict of the king's natural son, were sent in custody to London to be examined before the council; and after a long investigation, conducted with all that inquisitorial rigour common in this reign, the charges selected out of the depositions were laid before Henry. Of these the principal were, that the duke bore on his escutcheon in the first quarter the arms of England with a label of silver, which belonged of right to the king's son; that the earl had introduced into *his* the armorial bearings of Edward the Confessor, which had never been borne by his ancestors; that both had sought to marry the duchess of Richmond to the brother of the earl of Hertford, "wishing her to endear herself into the king's favour, that she might rule as others had done;"[1] and that Surrey had said, "If the king die, who should have the rule of the prince but my father or I?" In the judgment of Henry the two first articles proved an intention on the part of the Howards of claiming the crown, when occasion might serve, to the disherison of the prince; the others, an attempt to rule the king and his son, and thus possess themselves of the government of the realm.

The judges agreeing with the king, pronounced them sufficient to sustain an indictment for high treason; and despatches, according to custom, were forwarded to the ambassadors in foreign parts, stating that the duke and his son had conspired to assume the government during the king's life, and to seize the person of the prince on the king's death.[2]

The nation had witnessed with surprise the arrest and imprisonment of these two noblemen. There was no individual in the realm who possessed more powerful claims on the gratitude of Henry than the duke of Norfolk. He had devoted a long life to the service of his sovereign; and had equally distinguished himself in the cabinet and in the field—in embassies of importance abroad, and in employments of difficulty and delicacy at home. His son was a nobleman of the highest promise. To hereditary courage and the accomplishments of a court, Surrey added—at that period no ordinary praise—a refined taste, and a competent knowledge of the polite arts. His poems which delighted his contemporaries, will afford pleasure to the reader of the present day. But services and abilities weighed as nothing in the scale against the interests of the opposite party. As soon as the holidays were over, the earl as a commoner, was arraigned at Guildhall on a charge of having quartered on his shield the arms of Edward the Confessor. In an eloquent and spirited defence, he showed that he had long borne those arms without contradiction, and that they had been assigned to him by a decision of the heralds. But the fact was admitted;

---

[1] If the reader recollect that the duchess was the duke's daughter, the earl's sister, and widow of the king's son, will he believe that her father and brother would advise her "to become Henry's harlot?" Yet this is the interpretation put on her words in the paper laid before the king! Probably she had been a great favourite during her husband's life, and therefore they wished her to return again to court. It was eight years since this marriage was thought of.—St. Pap. 676.

[2] Ibid. i. 889—891. Herb. 264. But see, in justification of the earl, the patents of the 20th Richard II. to his ancestor Thomas Mowbray.

the court pronounced it sufficient evidence that he aspired to the throne; and the jury found him guilty. Six days later this gallant and accomplished nobleman perished on the scaffold.[1]

But it was still more difficult to discover matter against the father. For some weeks after his arrest the duke was ignorant of the charge to be adduced against him. It was in vain that by repeated letters he requested to be confronted with his accusers, whoever they might be, in presence of the king, or at least of the council.[2] At length, after many private examinations, he consented to sign a confession, which, to every unprejudiced mind, will appear a convincing proof of his innocence. In it he acknowledged that, during his service of so many years, he had communicated occasionally to others the royal secrets, contrary to his oath; that he had concealed the treasonable act of his son in assuming the arms of Edward the confessor; and that he had himself treasonably borne on his shield the arms of England, with the difference of a label of silver, the right of Prince Edward.[3]

If by this submission the duke hoped to appease the royal displeasure, he deceived himself; in another attempt to defeat the rapacity of his enemies, he proved more successful. They had already elicited a promise from Henry, that the spoils of their victim should in certain proportions be shared among them.[4] But Norfolk, sensible that his estate, if it were preserved entire, might be more easily recovered by his family, sent a petition to the king, representing it as "good and stately gear," and requesting, as a favour, that it might be settled on Prince Edward and his heirs for ever. The idea pleased the sick monarch. He assented to the petition; and, to satisfy his favourites, promised them an equivalent from some other source. This disappointment, however, did not retard their proceedings against their prisoner. Instead of arraigning him before his peers, they brought into the house of Lords a bill of attainder, founded on his confession. It had been customary

---

[1] See the indictment in Nott's Life of Surrey.

[2] "I am sure," he says to the king "some great enemy of mine hath informed your majesty of some untrue matter against me. Sir, God doth know that in all my life I never thought one untrue thought against you, or your succession; nor can no more judge or cast in my mind what should be laid to my charge, than the child that was born this night."—"Most noble and sovereign lord, for all the old service I have done you in my life, be so good and gracious a lord unto me, that either my accusers and I together may be brought before your royal majesty, or if your pleasure shall not be to take that pains, then before your council."—Herb. 627, 628. In another he repeats his request to be confronted with his accusers. "My desire is to have no more favour showed to me, than was showed to Cromwell, I being present. He was a false man; but surely I am a true poor gentleman."—Burnet, iii. Records, 190. He was examined whether he had not written in cipher to others, whether he had not said that the bishop of Rome could dissolve the leagues between princes, whether he was not privy to an overture for an accommodation with the bishop of Rome made by Gardiner, and what were the contents of a letter written by him formerly to the bishop of Hereford, and burnt after the death of that prelate by order of the bishop of Durham. He answered the three first questions in the negative. The letter he said contained the opinion of the northern men respecting Cromwell, but did not so much as mention the king.—Ibid. 189.

[3] The confession is in Herbert, 629. In the "Memorials," &c. of the "Howard family," by Mr. Howard of Corby, it is shown that his ancestors had borne these arms from the time of Thomas of Brotherton, son of Edward I.

[4] He ordered Paget to "tot upon the earl of Hertford" lands to the value of 666*l.* 13s. 4d. per annum; Sir Thomas Seymour 300*l.*; Sir William Herbert 266*l.* 13s. 4d.; the lords Lisle, St John, and Russell, and Sir Anthony Denny, 200*l.* each, and the lord Wriothesley 100*l.* They were all dissatisfied with the small amount of these grants —Burnet, ii. 6, out of the Council Book.

on such occasions to wait for the royal assent till the close of the session. But two days after the bill had passed, the king suddenly grew worse; the precedent established in the case of Catherine Howard was adopted; and the next morning the chancellor informed the two houses, that his majesty, anxious to fill up the offices held by the duke of Norfolk, preparatory to the coronation of the prince, had appointed certain lords to signify his assent to the act of attainder. The commission under the sign manual was then read; the royal assent was given in due form;[1] and an order was despatched to the lieutenant of the Tower to execute his prisoner on the following morning. Such indecent haste, at a time when the king was lying in the agonies of death, warranted a suspicion that there were other persons besides Henry who thirsted for the blood of the duke. But Providence watched over his life. Before the sun rose, Henry was dead. The execution was accordingly suspended; and in the reign of Mary the attainder was reversed, on the ground that the act of which he was accused was not treason, and that Henry had not *signed* the commission, in virtue of which his pretended assent had been given.[2]

Of the king's conduct during his sickness, we know little. It is said that at the commencement he betrayed a wish to be reconciled to the see of Rome; that the other bishops, afraid of the penalties, evaded the question; but that Gardiner advised him to consult his parliament, and to commit his ideas to writing. He was constantly attended by his confessor, the bishop of Rochester, heard mass daily in his chamber, and received the communion under one kind. About a month before his death he endowed the magnificent establishment of Trinity College in Cambridge, for a master and sixty fellows and scholars; and afterwards re-opened the church of the Grey Friars, which, with St. Bartholomew's Hospital, and an ample revenue, he gave to the city of London.

Of his sentiments on his death-bed nothing can be asserted with any degree of confidence. One account makes him die in the anguish of despair; according to another, he refused spiritual aid till he could only reply to the exhortation of the archbishop by a squeeze of the hand; while a third represents him as expiring in the most edifying sentiments of devotion and repentance.[3] He died on Friday, the 28th of January, about two in the morning.[4]

---

[1] Burnet (i. 348) tells us that Cranmer, though the king was so near his death, withdrew to Croydon, that he might not concur in the act of attainder, both on account of its injustice, and because he and the duke were personal enemies. These might indeed have been reasons why he should abstain from giving his vote; but that they had no weight with the archbishop, is plain from the Journals, which inform us that, instead of absenting himself, as Burnet would persuade us, he attended in his place every time the bill was read, and on the day on which it received the royal assent.—Journals, 285, 286, 287, 289.

[2] Lords' Journals, 289. Herbert, 623—631. Burnet, i. 345—348. By the act 35 Henry VIII. cap. 21, the king's signature with his own hand was required to such commission; this, however, was not signed with his own hand, but only stamped.—St. Pap. i. 898.

[3] Plusieurs gentils-hommes Anglois m'ont asseuré qu'il eut belle repentance, et entre lez autres choses de l'injure et crime commise contre la dicte royne (meaning Anne Boleyn).—Thevet, Cosmog. l. xvi. quoted by O. E. in reply to N. D. anno 1600, p. 59.

[4] Journals, 291. Rym. xv. 123. "These be to signify to you that our late sovereign lord the king departed at Westminster upon Friday last, the 28th of this instant January, about two of the clock in the morning; and the king's majesty that now is, proclaimed king this present last day of the same month."—The earl of Sussex to the countess, apud Strype, ii. 11. It is, however, plain that this is no more than a repetition of the report circulated by the council.

Here the reader may pause to notice, as far as the particulars have transpired, the secret machinations of the men who during so many weeks had surrounded the bed of the sick and dying monarch. On Christmas day the violence of his fever had abated; and the next evening, sending for his will, which had already been drawn by the chancellor, he ordered several alterations to be made in the presence of the Lord Hertford and of five others. Of these alterations the most important, whether they were the result of his own judgment, or had been suggested by the party around him, had for their object to weed out of the list of his executors the persons most obnoxious to his present favourites; namely, the duke of Norfolk, being then a prisoner in the Tower under a charge of high treason; Gardiner, bishop of Winchester, because he was "too wilful;" and Thirlby, bishop of Westminster, because he was "schooled by Gardiner."[1] After these amendments, the will might be divided into three parts. By one, the king provided for the interment of his body, the celebration of masses, and the distribution of alms for the benefit of his soul. By a second he limited the succession, in default of issue by his children Edward, Mary, and Elizabeth, to the descendants of his younger sister Mary, the French queen, tacitly excluding the Scottish line, the issue of his eldest sister Margaret, the queen of Scotland. By the third he appointed sixteen individuals, Hertford, and partisans of Hertford, executors of his will, and privy counsellors of his son Edward, giving to them full power to choose a wife for the young king, to govern the kingdom in his name, and to confer all offices in the gift of the crown, till that prince should have completed his eighteenth year. Such powers had, indeed, been conferred upon him by parliament in the twenty-eighth and thirty-fifth years of his reign; but these statutes imperatively required that the instrument by which he exercised them, should be signed by him with his own hand. When, however, the amended copy of the will was laid before him for execution, he refused, through inability perhaps, or indecision, or caprice, to affix his signature. Time rolled on, he became daily more feeble and incapable; still he persisted in the refusal till within a day or two of his death, and then gave orders that the will should be stamped by William Clerc, and delivered it in that state to the earl of Hertford.[2] As far as regarded its principal pro-

---

[1] Fox, 815, first edition.
[2] This will was deposited by order of the council in the treasury of the Exchequer on the 9th of March, 1547; and thence transferred, about fifty years afterwards, to the chapter-house, Westminster, where it still remains. It bears the signature Henry R. at the beginning and at the end. From both signatures having been marked with ink, Mr. Hallam conceived that they were made by Henry himself, and thence concluding that the will was signed in conformity with the statutes, declares "it to be of course *extremely* doubtful whether James I., or any of his posterity, were *legitimate* sovereigns in the sense which that word ought to bear."—Constit. Hist. i. c. vi.

But, 1. It cannot be inferred that the signatures were made with the king's hand, from the fact that the characters are evidently written with a pen, because it was the duty of the commissioners to trace with a pen and ink the impression previously left by the dry stamp.—See p. 100.

2. It is moreover certain that the signature was stamped. In the schedule drawn up by Clerc, one of the commissioners of the stamp, and printed at the end of vol. i. of the State Papers, with this title, "Hereafter ensueth a bridgment of all such billes, which the king's majesty caused me to stamp with his highnes secret stamp at dyverse tymes and places in this moneth of Januarie, anno 38 regni, in the presence of Sir Anthonie Dennye, knyght, and Mr. John Gate, esquier" (see p. 10), before), is the following entry:—" Your majesties last will and testament, bearing date at Westminster the thirtie day December last past, written in a book of paper, signed above in the beginning, and bereth in th

visions, the absence of his signature made it a nullity; but ten gentlemen belonging to the court had been called in as witnesses, and were artfully, perhaps to conceal the defect, led to attest that it had been signed by the king with his own hand in their presence.[1] The earl then took the will, as if it had been a personal trust, into his own custody, to the exclusion of his colleagues; and the moment that Henry expired, set out for Hertford to announce the intelligence to the young Edward, who then resided in the castle of that town.

There still remained a considerable difficulty to be surmounted. How could the executors assume the government of the kingdom, unless they openly brought forward the instrument from which they pretended to derive their authority? And if that instrument were brought forward openly, in what manner were they to guard against a discovery that the royal signature had been formed with the stamp, and not written with the king's own hand? It was resolved to prove the existence of the will without submitting it to any man's inspection, to exhibit it in parliament, and at the proclamation of the new sovereign; but to read from it those passages only which circumstances might require. A messenger was despatched the same day from the council to the earl, who signified his approval of the plan, recommended the utmost caution in the selection of extracts for publication, and transmitted to his co-executors the key of the depository in which he had placed the important instrument.[2]

By the king's death parliament was dissolved; but it did not suit the convenience of the party to make that event public. On Thursday, a few hours before the time when he is said to have died, the royal assent had been given to the attainders of the duke of Norfolk and his son; and the houses had been adjourned to the Saturday following. On that day they met as usual; the business of both was transacted after the accustomed manner; and, probably to carry on the deception, a bill was sent from the Lords to the Commons to secure a grant of lands to Sir William Paget, the king's principal secretary. Nothing had yet transpired respecting Henry's death; no suspicion of that event was hinted in parliament; and Wriothesley, the chancellor, boldly, as if he knew that the king was still living, adjourned the house to the Monday following.

On that day he sent for the Commons to the house of Lords, and

---

end, and sealed with the signet in the presence of th' erl of Hertford, Mr. secretarie Paget, Mr. Denny, and Mr. Harbert, and also in the presence of certain other persons, whose names ar subscribed with their own hands as witnesses to the same, which testament your majesty delyvered then in our sights with your own hand to the said erle of Hertforde as your owne dede, last will and testament, revoking and annulling all other your highnes former willes and testaments." This entry sets that question at rest.

I have stated that the will was not executed till a short time before the king expired. This also appears plain from Clerc's schedule; for the number of instruments which he stamped "at divers times in the month of January," and which he entered in order, amounted to eighty-six, of which eighty-four were stamped before the will, and only one afterwards, on the 27th; but a few hours before the king's death.—Lords' Journals, i. 289. State Papers, i. 892.

[1] The will concluded in the following manner:—"We have signed it with our hand in our Palys of Westminster, the thirtie day of December, in the yere of our Lord 1546.—Being present and called to be witnesses these persons which have written their names hereunder." Then follow the signatures of ten persons called in, who, ignorant of this passage, could only bear witness to what they had seen, the stamping and delivering of the will.—Rymer, xv. 117.

[2] See Hertford's letter written the next day at three in the morning, in Tytler's Edward and Mary, i. 15.

announced to them "the loss of their good master," who had died on the preceding Friday. But he could proceed no further. His utterance now failed him; the tears rolled down his cheeks; and sobs and sighs burst in sympathy from every part of the hall. After this outbreak of feeling he resumed his speech. "Their beloved monarch," he added, "had not been unmindful of them; he had amply, by his last will and testament, provided for their welfare and for the government of the kingdom during the minority of his successor."[1] Sir William Paget followed immediately, holding out the will itself, and reading from it occasional passages to gratify their curiosity: those passages principally which limited the succession, recorded the names of the individuals appointed executors to Henry and privy councillors to his son, and detailed the powers with which they were invested, the manner of discharging the personal debts of the late king, and the legacies in money which he had left to his servants. When Paget had done, the chancellor gave to the Commons license to depart, but requested the Lords to remain in the capital, that they might welcome their young sovereign on his arrival, and give their attendance at his coronation.[2] After this exhibition it could not be expected that any man would dispute the existence of the will, or venture to call for proof that it had been executed in strict conformity with the statutes.

We may now return to the defunct monarch. To form a just estimate of the character of Henry, we must distinguish between the young king, guided by the counsels of Wolsey, and the monarch of more mature age, governing by his own judgment, and with the aid of ministers selected and fashioned by himself. In his youth, the beauty of his person, the elegance of his manners, and his adroitness in every martial and fashionable exercise, were calculated to attract the admiration of his subjects. His court was gay and splendid; and a succession of amusements seemed to absorb his attention; yet his pleasures were not permitted to encroach on his more important duties; he assisted at the council, perused the despatches, and corresponded with his generals and ambassadors; nor did the minister, trusted and powerful as he was, dare to act, till he had asked the opinion, and taken the pleasure of his sovereign. His natural abilities had been improved by study; and his esteem for literature may be inferred from the learned education which he gave to his children, and from the number of eminent scholars to whom he granted pensions in foreign states, or on whom he bestowed preferment in his own. The immense treasure which he inherited from his father was perhaps a misfortune; because it engendered habits of expense not to be supported from the ordinary revenue of the crown; and the soundness of his politics may be doubted, which, under the pretence of supporting the balance of power, repeatedly involved the nation in continental hostilities. Yet even these errors served to throw a lustre round the English throne, and raised its possessor in the eyes of his own subjects and of the different nations of Europe. But as the king advanced in age, his vices gradually developed themselves; after the death of Wolsey they were indulged without restraint. He became as rapacious as he was prodigal; as obstinate as he was capricious; as fickle in his friendships, as he was merciless in his resentments. Though liberal of his confidence, he soon grew suspicious of those whom he had

---

[1] Lords' Journals, i. 260.

[2] Lords' Journals, i. 291.

trusted; and, as if he possessed no other right to the crown than that which he derived from the very questionable claim of his father, he viewed with an evil eye every remote descendant of the Plantagenets; and eagerly embraced the slightest pretexts to remove those whom his jealousy represented as future rivals to himself or his posterity. In pride and vanity he was perhaps without a parallel. Inflated with the praises of interested admirers, he despised the judgment of others; acted as if he deemed himself infallible in matters of policy and religion; and seemed to look upon dissent from his opinion as equivalent to a breach of allegiance. In his estimation, to submit and obey were the great, the paramount duties of subjects; and this persuasion steeled his breast against remorse for the blood which he shed, and led him to trample without scruple on the liberties of the nation.

When he ascended the throne, there still existed a spirit of freedom, which on more than one occasion defeated the arbitrary measures of the court, though directed by an able minister, and supported by the authority of the sovereign; but in the lapse of a few years that spirit had fled, and before the death of Henry, the king of England had grown into a despot, the people had shrunk into a nation of slaves.[1] The causes of this important change in the relations between the sovereign and his subjects, may be found not so much in the abilities or passions of the former, as in the obsequiousness of his parliaments, his assumption of the ecclesiastical supremacy, and the servility of the two religious parties which divided the nation.

I. The house of Peers no longer consisted of those powerful lords and prelates, who in former periods had so often and so successfully resisted the encroachments of the sovereign. The reader has already witnessed the successive steps by which most of the great families of the preceding reigns had become extinct, and their immense possessions had been frittered away among the favourites and dependants of the court. The most opulent of the peers under Henry were poor in comparison with their predecessors; and by the operation of the statute against liveries, they had lost the accustomed means of arming their retainers in support of their quarrels. In general they were new men, indebted for their present honours and estates to the bounty of Henry or of his father; and the proudest among the rest, by witnessing the attainders and executions of others, had been taught to tremble for themselves, and to crouch in submission at the foot of a master, whose policy it was to depress the great, and punish their errors without mercy, while he selected his favourites from the lowest classes, heaping on them honours and riches, and confiding to them the exercise of his authority.[2]

2. By the separation of the realm from the see of Rome, the dependence of the spiritual had been rendered still more complete than that of the temporal peers. Their riches had been diminished, their immunities taken away; the support which they

---

[1] Quando enim unquam, non dico in Anglia, ubi semper populi liberiores sub regum imperio fuerunt, sed omnino in aliquo Christianorum regno, auditum est, ut unus sic plus omnibus posset, et sic omnia suæ potestati ac libidini subjecta haberet, ut nullum cuiquam contra illius voluntatem præsidium in legibus constitutum esset, sed regis nutus omnia moderaretur. — Pole, fol. ci.

[2] Sic nobiles semper tractavisti, ut nullius principatu minore in honore fuerint: in quos, si quid leviter deliquissent, acerbissimus fuisti; nihil unquam cuiquam condonasti; omnes despicatui habuisti; nullum apud te honoris aut gratiæ locum obtinere passus es: cum interea semper alienissimos homines ex infima plebe assumptos circum te habueris, quibus summa omnia deferres.— Pole, fol. lxxxiii.

might have derived from the protection of the pontiff was gone; they were nothing more than the delegates of the king, exercising a precarious authority determinable at his pleasure. The ecclesiastical constitutions, which had so long formed part of the law of the land, now depended on his breath, and were executed only by his sufferance. The convocation indeed continued to be summoned; but its legislative authority was gone. Its principal business was to grant money; yet even these grants now owed their force, not to the consent of the grantors, but to the approbation of the other two houses, and the assent of the crown.[1]

3. As for the third branch of the legislature, the Commons of England, they had not yet acquired sufficient importance to oppose any effectual barrier to the power of the sovereign; yet care was taken that among them the leading members should be devoted to the crown, and that the speaker should be one holding office, or high in the confidence of the ministers.[2] Freedom of debate was, indeed, granted; but with a qualification which in reality amounted to a refusal. It was only a *decent* freedom;[3] and as the king reserved to himself the right of deciding what was or was not decent, he frequently put down the opponents of the court, by reprimanding the "varlets" in person, or by sending to them a threatening message.

It is plain that from parliaments thus constituted, the crown had little to fear; and though Wolsey had sought to govern without their aid, Henry found them so obsequious to his will, that he convoked them repeatedly, and was careful to have his most wanton and despotic measures sanctioned with their approbation. The parliament, as often as it was opened or closed by the king in person, offered a scene not unworthy of an oriental divan. The form indeed differed but little from our present usage. The king sat on his throne; on the right hand stood the chancellor, on the left the lord treasurer; whilst the peers were placed on their benches, and the commons stood at the bar. But the addresses made on these occasions by the chancellor or the speaker, usually lasted more than an hour; and their constant theme was the character of the king. The orators, in their efforts to surpass each other, fed his vanity with the most hyperbolical praise. Cromwell was unable, he believed all men were unable, to describe the unutterable qualities of the royal mind, the sublime virtues of the royal heart. Rich told him that in wisdom he was equal to Solomon, in strength and courage to Sampson, in beauty and address to Absalom; and Audeley declared before his face, that God had anointed him with the oil of wisdom above his fellows, above the other kings of the earth, above all his predecessors; had given him a perfect knowledge of the Scriptures, with which he had prostrated the Roman Goliath; a perfect knowledge of the art of war, by which he had gained the most brilliant victories at the same time in remote places; and a perfect knowledge of the art of govern-

---

[1] Journals, 156, 218, 277. The first instance which I find was in 1540.

[2] The members were in a great measure named by the Crown or the Lords. See a letter of the earl of Southampton to Cromwell, Cleop. E. iv. 176, and another from Gardiner to the council, reminding them that the house of Commons was not complete, because he had not made returns as usual for several places (Fox, ii. 69). The treasurer and comptroller of the household were accustomed to conduct the business of the crown. The former generally named the speaker. See the Journals of the Commons for the following reigns, p. 24, 27, 37.

[3] Journals, 167. This is the first time during Henry's reign that the request of freedom of speech is mentioned in the journals, anno 1542.

ment, by which he had for thirty years secured to his own realm the blessings of peace, while all the other nations of Europe suffered the calamities of war.

During these harangues, as often as the words "most sacred majesty"[1] were repeated, or any emphatic expression was pronounced, the lords rose, and the whole assembly, in token of respect and assent, bowed profoundly to the demigod on the throne. Henry himself affected to hear such fulsome adulation with indifference. His answer was invariably the same; that he had no claim to superior excellence; but that, if he did possess it, he gave the glory to God, the Author of all good gifts; it was, however, a pleasure to him to witness the affection of his subjects, and to learn that they were not insensible of the blessings which they enjoyed under his government.[2]

II. It is evident that the new dignity of head of the church, by transferring to the king that authority which had been hitherto exercised by the pontiff, must have considerably augmented the influence of the crown; but in addition, the arguments by which it was supported tended to debase the spirit of the people, and to exalt the royal prerogative above law and equity. When the adversaries of the supremacy asked in what passage of the sacred writings the government of the church was given to a layman, its advocates boldly appealed to those texts which prescribe obedience to the established authorities. The king, they maintained, was the image of God upon earth; to disobey his commands was to disobey God himself; to limit his authority, when no limit was laid down, was an offence against the sovereign; and to make distinctions, when the Scripture made none, was an impiety against God. It was indeed acknowledged that this supreme authority might be employed unreasonably and unjustly; but even then to resist was a crime; it became the duty of the sufferer to submit; and his only resource was to pray that the heart of his oppressor might be changed; his only consolation to reflect, that the king himself would hereafter be summoned to answer for his conduct before an unerring tribunal. Henry became a sincere believer in a doctrine so flattering to his pride, and easily persuaded himself that he did no more than his duty in punishing with severity the least opposition to his will. To impress it on the minds of the people, it was perpetually inculcated from the pulpit; it was enforced in books of controversy and instruction; it was promulgated with authority in the "Institution" and afterwards in the "Erudition of a Christian Man."[3] From that period the doctrine of passive obedience formed a leading trait in the orthodox creed.

III. The two great parties into which religious disputes had divided the nation, contributed also to strengthen the despotic power of Henry. They were too jealous of each other to watch, much less to resist, the encroachments of the crown. The great object of both

---

[1] The title of Majesty is given to Henry II. in two passages of the "Black Book of the Exchequer," i. 133, 255; the most ancient instances I have met with.

[2] See the Journals, 86, 101, 129, 161, 162, 164, 167.

See Gardiner's Treatise de Vera Obedientia, in the Fasciculus Rerum expetendarum, ii. 800; and Sampson's de Obedientia Regi præstanda; ibid. 820; also Strype, i. 111. Thus we are told in a sermon by Archbishop Cranmer: "Though the magistrates be evil and very tyrants against the commonwealth, and enemies to Christ's religion, yet ye subjects must obey in all worldly things as the Christians do under the truth, and ought so to do, as long as he commandeth them not to do against God."—Strype's Cranmer, Rec. 114. See also the king's books, the Articles, the Institution, and the Erudition of a Christian Man.

was the same; to win the favour of the king, that they might crush the power of their adversaries; and with this view they flattered his vanity, submitted to his caprice, and became obsequious slaves to his pleasure. Henry, on the other hand, whether it were through policy or accident, played them off against each other; sometimes appearing to lean to the old, sometimes to the new doctrines, alternately raising and depressing the hopes of each, but never suffering either party to obtain the complete ascendancy over its opponent. Thus he kept them in a state of dependence on his will, and secured their concurrence to every measure which his passion or caprice might suggest, without regard to reason or justice, or the fundamental laws of the land. Of the extraordinary enactments which followed, a few instances may suffice. 1. The succession to the crown was repeatedly altered, and at length left to the king's private judgment or affection. The right was first taken from Mary, and given to Elizabeth; then transferred from Elizabeth to the king's issue by Jane Seymour or any future queen; next restored, on the failure of issue by Prince Edward, to both Mary and Elizabeth; and lastly, failing issue by them, entailed upon any person or persons to whom it should please him to assure it in remainder by his last will.[1] 2. Treasons were multiplied by the most vexatious, and often, if ridicule could attach to so grave a matter, by the most ridiculous laws. It was once treason to dispute, it was afterwards treason to maintain, the validity of the marriage with Anne Boleyn, or the legitimacy of her daughter. It became treason to marry, without the royal license, any of the king's children, whether legitimate or natural, or his paternal brothers or sisters, or their issue; or for any woman to marry the king himself, unless she were a maid, or had previously revealed to him her former incontinence. It was made treason to call the king a heretic or schismatic, openly to wish him harm, or to slander him, his wife, or his issue.[2] This, the most heinous of crimes in the eye of the law, was extended from deeds and assertions to the very thoughts of men. Its guilt was incurred by any person who should, by words, writing, imprinting, or any other exterior act, directly or indirectly accept or take, judge or believe, that either of the royal marriages, that with Catherine, or that with Anne Boleyn, was valid, or who should protest that he was not bound to declare his opinion, or should refuse to swear that he would answer truly such questions as should be asked him on those dangerous subjects. It would be difficult to discover, under the most despotic governments, a law more cruel and absurd. The validity or invalidity of the two marriages was certainly matter of opinion, supported and opposed on each side by so many contradictory arguments, that men of the soundest judgment might reasonably be expected to differ from each other. Yet Henry, by this statute, was authorized to dive into the breast of every individual, to extort from him his secret sentiments upon oath, and to subject him to the penalty of treason, if those sentiments did not accord with the royal pleasure.[3] 3. The king was made in a great measure independent of parliament, by two statutes, one of which put his proclamations on the same footing with acts of parliament, provided they did not set aside laws actually in force, nor enjoin the penalties of dis-

---

[1] 25 Hen. VIII. 22. 28 Hen. VIII. 7. 35 Hen. VIII. 2.

[2] 25 Hen. VIII. 22. 26 Hen. VIII. 13. 28 Hen. VIII. 18. 32 Hen. VIII. 25. 33 Hen. VIII. 21. [3] 28 Hen. VIII. c. 7.

herison or death in any cases but those of heretical doctrine; the other appointed a tribunal, consisting of nine privy counsellors, with power to punish all transgressors of such proclamations.[1] 4. The dreadful punishment of heresy was not confined to those who rejected the doctrines which had already been declared orthodox, but it was extended beforehand to all persons who should teach or maintain any opinion contrary to such doctrines as the king might afterwards publish. If the criminal were a clergyman, he was to expiate his third offence at the stake; if a layman, to forfeit his personal property, and be imprisoned for life.[2] Thus was Henry invested, by act of parliament, with the high prerogative of theological infallibility, and an obligation was laid on all men, without exception, whether of the new or of the old learning, to model their religious opinions and religious practice by the sole judgment of their sovereign. 5. By an ex post facto law, those who had taken the first oath against the papal authority, were reputed to have taken, and to be bound by, a second and much more comprehensive oath, which was afterwards enacted, and which, perhaps, had it been tendered to them at first, they would have refused.[3]

But that which made the severity of these statutes the more terrible, was the manner in which criminal prosecutions were then conducted. The crown could hardly fail in convicting the prisoner, whatever might be his guilt or his innocence. He was first interrogated in his cell, urged with the hope of pardon to make a confession, or artfully led by ensnaring questions into dangerous admissions. When the materials of the prosecution were completed, they were laid before the grand inquest; and, if the bill was found, the conviction of the accused might be pronounced certain; for, in the trial which followed, the real question submitted to the decision of the petit jury was, which of the two were more worthy of credit—the prisoner who maintained his innocence, or the grand inquest which had pronounced his guilt. With this view the indictment, with a summary of the proofs on which it had been found, was read; and the accused, now perhaps for the first time acquainted with the nature of the evidence against him, was indulged with the liberty of speaking in his own defence. Still he could not insist on the production of his accusers, that he might obtain the benefit of cross-examination; nor claim the aid of counsel to repel the taunts, and unravel the sophistry, too often employed at that period by the advocates of the crown.[4] In this method of trial, every chance was

---

[1] 31 Hen. VIII. 8. 34 Hen. VIII. 23. We learn from a letter of Bishop Gardiner that these statutes originated from a decision of the judges, that the council could not punish certain merchants, who had exported grain in defiance of a royal proclamation; because they were permitted to export it by act of parliament, as long as it was below a particular price.—See Letter, apud Burnet, ii. Rec. 114. On this account it was that the king required that his proclamations should have the force of acts of parliament. The bill did not pass without "many large words."—Ibid. When it did pass, the reason assigned was, "that the king might not be driven to extend his royal supremacy." As some check on the exercise of this new prerogative, it was required that the majority of the council should advise the proclamation; and it was moreover declared, that such proclamation derived all its force "from the authority of this act,"—a declaration which preserved the superior authority of parliament.—See the statute itself.

[2] 34 Hen. VIII. 1.   [3] 35 Hen. VIII. 1.

[4] I speak with diffidence on this subject; but I conceive that the refusal to confront the accusers with the accused grew out of the ancient manner of administering justice, and was strictly conformable to the practice of the courts of law. Originally there was but one jury, that which is called the grand inquest. If the prisoner, on the presentment of this jury pleaded not guilty, the judge might allow him to prove his inno-

in favour of the prosecution; and yet it was gladly exchanged for the expedient discovered by Cromwell, and afterward employed against its author. Instead of a public trial, the minister introduced a bill of attainder into parliament, accompanied with such documents as he thought proper to submit. It was passed by the two houses with all convenient expedition; and the unfortunate prisoner found himself condemned to the scaffold or the gallows, without the opportunity of opening his mouth in his own vindication.

To proceed by attainder became the usual practice in the latter portion of the king's reign. It was more certain in the result, by depriving the accused of the few advantages which he possessed in the ordinary courts; it enabled the minister to gratify the royal suspicion or resentment without the danger of refutation, or of unpleasant disclosures; and it satisfied the minds of the people, who, unacquainted with the real merits of the case, could not dispute the equity of a judgment given with the unanimous assent of the whole legislature.

Thus it was that by the obsequiousness of the parliament, the assumption of the ecclesiastical supremacy, and the servility of religious factions, Henry acquired and exercised the most despotic sway over the lives, the fortunes, and the liberties of his subjects. Happily, the forms of a free government were still suffered to exist; into these forms a spirit of resistance to arbitrary power gradually infused itself; the pretensions of the crown were opposed by the claims of the people; and the result of a long and arduous struggle was that constitution which for more than a century has excited the envy and the admiration of Europe.

---

cence by the ordeal, afterwards by the ordeal or battle, and lastly by his country, that is, by the verdict of a petit jury, who should decide on the presentment by the grand inquest. But in this case none of the former jury, or their witnesses, technically termed accusers, and identified with them, could be produced in court; because they were an interested party, the propriety of whose proceedings was now upon trial; and on that account the names of the accusers were returned on the back of the indictment, that they might be challenged as witnesses. It was first in the reign of Edward VI. that the law allowed the accusers to be brought forward; and after that it was long before the judges could be prevailed upon to depart from the ancient practice.— See Mr. Reeves's History of English Law, ii. 268, 459; iv. 494—505. At the trial of the duke of Buckingham the witnesses or accusers were indeed brought before him. But it seems to have been a particular indulgence; "for the king had commanded that the laws should be ministered to him with favour and right." Nor does it appear that then they were cross-examined. "Their depositions were read, and the deponents were delivered as prisoners to the officers of the Tower."—Hall, fol. 85.

CHAPTER IV.

EDWARD VI.

CONTEMPORARY PRINCES.

Emp. of Germ.	*K. of France.*	*K. of Spain.*	*Q. of Sco*
Charles V.	Francis 1547	Charles V.	Mary.
	Henry II.		

Popes.
Paul III. 1549.   Julius III.

HERTFORD IS MADE PROTECTOR AND DUKE OF SOMERSET—WAR WITH SCOTLAND—BATTLE OF PINKIECLEUGH—PROGRESS OF THE REFORMATION—BOOK OF COMMON PRAYER—LORD ADMIRAL ARRESTED AND BEHEADED—DISCONTENT AND INSURRECTIONS—FRANCE DECLARES WAR—PROTECTOR IS SENT TO THE TOWER AND DISCHARGED—PEACE—DEPRIVATION OF BISHOPS—TROUBLES OF THE LADY MARY—FOREIGN PREACHERS—SOMERSET ARRESTED AND EXECUTED—NEW PARLIAMENT—WARWICK'S AMBITION—DEATH OF THE KING.

THE reader is already acquainted with the ingenious device by which, at the same time that the radical defect in the will of the late sovereign was concealed, the more important of its provisions were made public. The sixteen executors to whom Henry had confided the government of the king and kingdom, during the minority of his son Edward,—he was only nine years old,—were, Cranmer, archbishop of Canterbury; the lord Wriothesley, lord chancellor; the lord St. John, great master; the earl of Hertford, great chamberlain, and uncle to the young king; the lord Russell, privy seal; the viscount Lisle, high admiral; Tunstall, bishop of Durham; Sir Anthony Brown, master of the horse; Sir Edward Montague, chief justice of the Common Pleas; Mr. Justice Bromley; Sir Edward North, chancellor of the court of Augmentations; Sir William Paget, chief secretary; Sir Anthony Denny and Sir William Herbert, chief gentlemen of the privy chamber; Sir Edward Wotton, treasurer of Calais; and Dr. Wotton, dean of Canterbury and York. The publication of these names provoked the murmurs of many, the surprise of all. It was remarked that they were not only new men, raised to honours and office by the judgment or partiality of the late king, but for the most part the very individuals who had constantly attended him during his sickness, and had possessed exclusively the benefit of access to his person. To aid them in cases of difficulty, the will had appointed a second council, consisting of twelve persons: the earls of Arundel and Essex, Sir Thomas Cheyney, treasurer, and Sir John Gage, comptroller of the household; Sir Anthony Wingfield, vice-chamberlain; Sir William Petre, chief secretary; Sir Richard Rich, Sir John Baker, Sir Ralph Sadler, Sir Thomas Seymour, another uncle of the young king, Sir Richard Southwell, and Sir Edmund Peckham. But these were not invested with any real authority. They could only tender their advice on occasions when it might be required.¹

The new king was proclaimed immediately after the publication of the will by the chancellor—on the Monday. On the same day the executors, being assembled in the Tower, "resolved not only to stand to and maintain the last will and testament of their master, the late king, and every part and article of the same, to the uttermost of their power, wits, and cunning, but also that every one of them present should take a corporal oath upon a book, for the more assured and effectual accomplishment of the same."² Scarcely, however, had they taken this oath, when they were called upon to break it by the ambition of the earl of Hertford, whose partisans pretended that for convenience and despatch it would be necessary to appoint one of the council to transact business with the foreign envoys, and to represent on other occasions the person of the young sovereign. By Wriothesley the project was opposed with boldness and warmth. He appealed to the words and the spirit of the will, by which all the executors were invested with equal powers; and he contended that, by giving to themselves a superior, they would invalidate that which was the only foundation of their present authority. But to argue was fruitless. A majority had been previously secured; the chancellor withdrew his opposition, on an understanding that the new officer should not presume to act without the assent of the majority of the council; and the earl of Hertford was immediately appointed protector of the realm, and guardian of the king's person. His talents were perhaps unequal to the situation; but two circumstances pleaded in his favour. He was uncle to the king; and he could not boast of royal blood in his veins. The first naturally interested him in the welfare of his nephew; the second forbade him to aspire to the throne.

In the afternoon the executors conducted Edward into the chamber of presence, where all the lords temporal and spiritual waited to receive him. Each in succession approached the king, kissed his hand kneeling, and said, "God save your grace." The chancellor then explained to them the dispositions in the will of their late sovereign, and the resolution of his executors to place the earl of Hertford at their head. They unanimously signified their assent; the new protector expressed his gratitude; and Edward, pulling off his cap, said, "We heartily thank you, my lords all; and, hereafter, in all that ye shall have to do with us for any suit or causes, ye shall be heartily welcome." The appointment of Hertford was announced by proclamation, and was received with transports of joy by all who were attached to the new doctrines, or who sought to improve their fortunes at the expense of the church.³

In this instance the members of the council had been driven by the ambition of Hertford to violate the known will of their late sovereign, in another and more doubtful matter they were induced by views of personal interest to execute with scru-

---

¹ Rym. xv. 114, 116.

² Council-book, Harl. MS. 352. Bromley and the two Wottons were absent.

³ Burnet, ii. 4. Stowe, 593. Strype, 14. That the office of protector was the object of Hertford's ambition, and that he had previously intrigued to obtain it, is evident from a letter written to him afterwards by Paget. "Remember what you promised me in the gallery at Westminster, before the breath was out of the body of the king that dead is; remember what you promised me immediately after, devising with me about the place which you now occupy." July 7, 1549.—Apud Strype, ii. Rec. p. 109.

pulous exactitude certain designs, which he was said to have formed. By a clause in the body of the will, Henry had charged them with the obligation of ratifying every gift, of performing every promise, which he should have made before his death. What these gifts and promises might be, must, it was presumed, be known to Paget, Herbert, and Denny, who had stood high in the confidence, and had been constantly in the chamber, of the dying monarch. These gentlemen were therefore interrogated before their colleagues; and from their depositions it was inferred, that the king had intended to give a dukedom to Hertford; to create the earl of Essex, his queen's brother, a marquess; to raise the viscount Lisle and Lord Wriothesley to the higher rank of earls, and to confer the title of baron on Sir Thomas Seymour, Sir Richard Rich, Sir John St. Leger, Sir William Willoughby, Sir Edward Sheffield, and Sir Christopher Danby; and that, to enable the new peers to support their respective titles, he had destined for Hertford an estate in land of eight hundred pounds per annum, with a yearly pension of three hundred pounds from the first bishopric which should become vacant, and the incomes of a treasurership, a deanery, and six prebends in different cathedrals; for each of the others a proportionate increase of yearly income; and for the three deponents, Paget, Herbert, and Denny, four hundred pounds, four hundred marks, and two hundred pounds.[1] Two out of the number, St. Leger and Danby, had sufficient virtue to refuse the money and the honours which were allotted to them; Hertford was created duke of Somerset, Essex marquess of Northampton, Lisle earl of Warwick, Wriothesley earl of Southampton, and Seymour, Rich, Willoughby, and Sheffield, barons of the same names; and to all these, with the exception of the two last, and to Cranmer, Paget, Herbert, and Denny, and more than thirty other persons, were assigned in different proportions, manors and lordships out of the lands which had belonged to the dissolved monasteries, or still belonged to the existing bishoprics.[2] But Sir Thomas Seymour was not satisfied; as uncle of the king he aspired to office no less than rank; and, to appease his discontent, the new earl of Warwick resigned in his favour the patent of high admiral, and was indemnified with that of great chamberlain, which Somerset had exchanged for the dignities of lord high treasurer and earl marshal, forfeited by the attainder of the duke of Norfolk.[3] These proceedings did not pass without severe animadversion. Why, it was asked, were not the executors content with the authority which they derived from the will of their late master? Why did they reward themselves beforehand, instead of waiting till their young sovereign should be of age, when he might recompense their services according to their respective merits?

The interment of Henry was performed in the usual style of royal magnificence;[4] but at the coronation of his son, men observed with sur-

---

[1] Burnet, ex lib. Conc. ii. 7. It is observable that the deponents say:—"The king, being on his death-bed put in mind of what he had promised, ordered it to be put in his will, that his executors should perform every thing that should appear to have been promised by him."—Ibid. Such a clause, indeed, appears in the body of the will. But how could it be there, if Henry ordered it to be inserted only when he was on his death-bed, that is, about the 28th of January? The will purports to have been executed four weeks before, on the 30th of December.
[2] See the names in Strype, ii. 78.
[3] Rym. xv. 124, 127, 130. Stowe, 593.
[4] The body lay in state in the chapel or Whitehall, which was hung with black cloth. Eighty large wax tapers were kept constantly burning; twelve lords mourners

prise several departures from ancient precedent. That the delicate health of the young king might not suffer from fatigue, the accustomed ceremony was considerably abridged; and, under pretence of respect for the laws and constitution of the realm, an important alteration was introduced into that part of the form, which had been devised by our Saxon ancestors, to put the new sovereign in mind that he held his crown by the free choice of the nation. Hitherto it had been the custom for the archbishop, first to receive the king's oath, and then, having explained the obligations of that oath, to ask the people if they were willing to accept him on those terms, and to obey him as their liege lord. Now the order was inverted; and not only did the address to the people precede the oath of the king, but in that very address they were reminded that he held his crown by descent, and that it was their duty to submit to his rule. "Sirs," said the metropolitan, "I here present King Edward, rightful and undoubted inheritor, by the laws of God and man, to the royal dignity and crown imperial of this realm, whose consecration, inunction, and coronation, is appointed by all the nobles and peers of the land to be this day. Will ye serve at this time, and give your good wills and assents to the same consecration, inunction, and coronation, as by your duty of allegiance ye are bound to do?" When the acclamations of the spectators had subsided, the young Edward was led to the altar, where he took the oath, not that of former times, but one made for the present occasion, by which he bound himself,—"1. To the people of England, to keep the laws and liberties of the realm; 2. To the church and the people, to keep peace and concord; 3. To do in all his judgments equal justice; 4. To make no laws but to the honour of God, and the good of the commonwealth, and by the consent of the people as had been accustomed." He was next anointed after the ancient form; the protector and the archbishop placed on his head successively three crowns, emblematic of the three kingdoms of England, France, and Ireland; and the lords and prelates first did homage two by two, and then in a body promised fealty on their knees.[1] Instead of a sermon, Cranmer pronounced a short address to the new sovereign, telling him that the promises which he had just made could not affect his right to sway the sceptre of his dominions. That right he, like his predecessors, had derived from God; whence it followed, that neither the bishop of Rome, nor any other bishop, could impose conditions on him at his coronation, nor pretend to deprive him of his crown on the plea that he

---

sat around, within a rail; and every day masses and a dirge were performed. At the commencement of the service, Norroy king-at-arms called aloud: "Of your charity pray for the soul of the high and mighty prince, our late sovereign lord, Henry VIII." On the 14th of February, the body was removed to Sion House, on the 15th to Windsor, and the next day was interred in the midst of the choir, near to the body of Jane Seymour. Gardiner, bishop of Winchester, preached the sermon and read the funeral service. When he cast the mould into the grave, saying, Pulvis pulveri, cinis cineri, the lord great master, the lord chamberlain, the treasurer, comptroller, and gentlemen ushers, broke their staves into three parts over their heads, and threw the fragments upon the coffin. The psalm "De profundis" was then said; and Garter king at arms, attended by the archbishop of Canterbury and the bishop of Durham, immediately proclaimed the style of the new sovereign.—See Sandford, 492; Strype, ii. Rec. 3—17; Hayward, 275.

[1] Compare the ancient form in Rymer, vii. 159, with this in Burnet, ii. Records, 93; and Strype's Cranmer, 142. No notice was taken of the form of oath devised by Henry VIII. to be used "at every coronation," by which the king bound himself to keep only such rights of the church, and such customs of the realm, as were "not prejudicial to his jurisdiction and imperial duty."—See it in Ellis, vol. i. title-page.

had broken his coronation oath. Yet these solemn rites served to admonish him of his duties, which were, "as God's vicegerent and Christ's vicar, to see that God be worshipped, and idolatry be destroyed; that the tyranny of the bishop of Rome be banished, and images be removed; to reward virtue, and revenge vice; to justify the innocent and relieve the poor; to repress violence, and execute justice. Let him do this, and he would become a second Josias, whose fame would remain to the end of days." The ceremony was concluded with a solemn high mass, sung by the archbishop.[1]

As soon as Henry VI. had been crowned at the age of eight years, his uncle, the duke of Gloucester, was compelled to resign the office of protector, and to content himself with the title of prime counsellor.[2] But this precedent did not accord with the ambition of Somerset, who instead of descending from the height to which he had risen, aspired to render himself entirely independent of his colleagues. In the attempt he could rely on the cordial support of Cranmer, and of the partisans of the Reformation; but he anticipated a formidable opposition from the legal knowledge and undaunted mind of the chancellor, the new earl of Southampton. The conduct of that nobleman during the last reign was an earnest of his resistance to any measure which might tend to additional innovations in religion; and his influence had been proved on a recent occasion, when, to the mortification of Somerset, he had reduced the office of protector to a mere title without actual authority. But the imprudence of Southampton furnished his enemies with weapons against himself. Unable to attend at the same time to the daily deliberations of the council, and his duties in the Chancery, he had, without consulting his colleagues, put the great seal to a commission, empowering in the king's name four masters to hear all manner of causes in his absence, and giving to their decrees the same force as if they had been pronounced by the chancellor himself, provided that before enrolment they were ratified with his signature. A petition against this arrangement was presented by several lawyers at the secret suggestion of the protector; by the council it was referred to the judges; and the judges twice returned the same answer, that the chancellor, by affixing the great seal without sufficient warrant to the commission, had been guilty of an offence against the king, which at common law was punishable with the loss of office, and fine and imprisonment at the royal pleasure. In his own defence, Southampton argued that the commission was legal, and that he had been competent to issue it without requesting the assent of his colleagues; that, even admitting it to be illegal, they could only revoke it, to which he had no objection; that he held his office by patent from the late king; and that they, as executors, were not authorized by the will to deprive him of it. Finding, however, that it was in vain to contend against the majority, he made his submission, and was suffered to retire to his residence at Ely House. The same evening he resigned the seal, which was given to the lord St. John, and received an order to remain a prisoner in his own house, and to wait the decision of the council respecting the amount of his fine.[3] What precedent the chancellor might have for his conduct is uncertain. The commission, which he had issued without warrant, seems unjustifiable;

---

[1] Strype's Cranmer, 144.
[2] Rot. Parl. iv. 337.
[3] Burnet, ii. 15. Records, 96.

but his deprivation for a mere error in judgment was censured as harsh and tyrannical.

The next measure adopted by Somerset disclosed the real cause of Southampton's disgrace. Though the duke possessed the title of protector, he had been compelled to accept it on the condition that he should never act without the assent of the majority of the council; now he procured letters patent under the great seal, conferring on himself alone the whole authority of the crown. This extraordinary instrument confirmed his former appointment, and ratified all his acts under it; swept away the two separate councils appointed by the will; confounded the executors and their advisers under the common name of counsellors to the king; and authorized the protector to swell their number to an unlimited extent by the addition of such persons as he might think proper, and to select from the whole body a few individuals, who should form the privy council. It did not, however, bind him to follow their advice. He was still empowered to act independently, and in every case to decide according to his own judgment, till the king should have completed his eighteenth year.[1] Two months had not yet elapsed since the death of Henry; and, in that short space, the whole frame of government settled by his will had been dissolved, and the authority with which he had invested his executors had been suppressed, by the very men to whom he had given his confidence, and who had solemnly sworn to fulfil his intentions. It was asked on what principle of law or reason the present revolution had been effected. If the will possessed any force, the executors could not transfer to one person all those powers which t had confided to the joint wisdom of sixteen; if it did not, then they were unauthorized individuals, and incompetent to new-model the government of the realm.

It was observed, that the intelligence of the death of Henry had made a deep impression on the mind of the king of France. That monarch entertained a notion that the duration of their lives was limited to the same year; and sought in vain to divert his melancholy by change of residence and the pleasures of the chase. At the same time he appeared to feel an affection for the son of his former friend; a proposal was made and accepted to renew the alliance between the crowns; and messengers had already been appointed to receive the oaths of the two monarchs, when Francis expired at Rambouillet, about two months after the death of his English brother.[2] His son and successor Henry II. pursued a very different policy, under the guidance of the duke of Guise and the cardinal of Lorrain. He felt a deep interest in the fortunes of the infant queen of Scotland; and, when the treaty with England was offered to him for signature, refused to shackle himself with engagements, which might prevent him from espousing her cause. Still appearances of amity were preserved. As Francis had ordered a solemn service to be performed for Henry in the cathedral of Paris, so, to return the compliment, Cranmer was employed to sing a mass of requiem for Francis in the church of St. Paul.[3] But the sequel showed that the jealousy of the French cabi-

---

[1] Burnet, ii. 15. Records, 98. It was signed by Somerset himself, Cranmer, St. John, Russell, Northampton, Brown, and Paget, executors, and by Cheyney, one of their advisers.
[2] Rymer, xv. 139—142, 149.
[3] Stowe, 594. The name of the ambassador was Vielleville, who was so delighted with the national sports of bull-baiting and bear-baiting, that he undertook to introduce these elegant amusements among his countrymen, and took back with him a bull and bull-dogs to France. For some years bull-baiting continued to be in high favour, but

net was not without foundation. The protector was at the very time busily employed in levying troops at home; his secret agents hired bands of discharged veterans in Germany, Italy, and Spain; and an active correspondence was kept up between the council and the murderers of Cardinal Beaton in Scotland. But, to introduce these new allies to the notice of the reader, it will be necessary to revert to the year 1544.

It was in that year that Henry, foiled by the cardinal in his attempt to obtain the custody of the young queen, despatched the earl of Hertford to invade Scotland at the head of a powerful army.[1] He had repeatedly signified a wish to his Scottish adherents to have Beaton seized, and sent a prisoner to England; and now a person named Wishart came to Hertford, and by him was forwarded to Henry, the bearer of an offer from Kirkaldy, the master of Rothes, and John Charteris, "to apprehend or slee the cardinal" in one of his journeys through Fife.[2] We know not what answer he received; probably it was the same as was given the next year to the earl of Cassillis, who, having visited the king, informed Sadler, on his return to Scotland, that his friends would murder the cardinal for a reward proportioned to their services. Henry was unwilling to commit himself by the express approbation of the crime; and Sadler was instructed to reply that, if he were in the place of Cassillis, he would do the deed, and trust to the king's gratitude for the reward.[3] They, however, required the royal assurance; Crichton, laird of Brunston, repeated the offer; and, though he received the same answer, continued to correspond with Henry on the subject. At last revenge stimulated the conspirators to do that, to which they had hitherto been tempted by the prospect of pecuniary remuneration. Under their protection, George Wishart, perhaps the same who had conveyed the first offer to Henry,[4] had preached for some time the new gospel, and been the exciting cause of repeated riots. He had the misfortune, however, to fall into the hands of Beaton, by whose orders he was condemned and executed at St. Andrew's, being hanged for sedition, and burnt for heresy. To this provocation was added a private quarrel between the cardinal and the master of Rothes, respecting an estate in Fife; and only two months after the death of Wishart, that young nobleman, Kirkaldy, and others, "were stirred up by the Lord," if we may believe Fox,[5] to make the attempt which they had so long meditated. Profiting of the negligence of the warder, they entered the castle of St. Andrew's at an early hour, and slew the cardinal in his bedchamber. At the first alarm the citizens hastened to the defence of their archbishop; but at the sight of the dead body suspended from a window, they retired to their homes. The castle had been lately fortified and provi-

---

fell into disuse during the religious wars which followed.—Mém. xxviii. 331.

[1] He was instructed "to raze to the ground the castle of Edinburgh, Holyrood House, Leith, and the villages, and to put man, woman, and child to the sword, wherever resistance was offered; and then to proceed to the cardinal's town of St. Andrew's, not to leave there a stone or a stick standing, and not to spare a living creature within the same."—See these most barbarous instructions in Tytler, vi. 473.

[2] Keith, 44. Tytler, vi. 466.

[3] "His highness not reputing the fact mete to be set forward expressly by his majesty, will not seem to have to do in it, and yet not misliking the offer, thinketh good that Mr. Sadler.........should say that if he were in the curl of Cassillis place," &c. —Tytler's History of Scotland, 461. These deeds of darkness had escaped the notice of historians during three centuries, but have been lately exposed to the public eye by the industry and research of Mr. Tytler.

[4] This has been often asserted, and is rendered probable by the known connection between him and all the parties to these attempts against the cardinal. [5] Fox, 526.

sioned; Knox, the Scottish reformer, to show his approbation of "the godly fact," led one hundred and forty of his disciples to the aid of the murderers; and a resolution was formed by the whole body to defend themselves against all opponents, and to solicit the protection of the king of England. Neither did the treaty of Campes disappoint their hopes. If the Scots were included in it, yet Henry would only bind himself to abstain from hostilities, provided no additional provocation were given; and, on the other side, the earl of Arran, the governor, refused to accept of any peace, unless the Scottish fortresses, in possession of the English, were restored, and the murderers of Beaton were abandoned to their fate.

After some negotiation, Arran sat down before the castle; but though he bore with patience the severity of the winter, though he repulsed an English squadron conveying money and military stores, the obstinacy of the garrison defeated every attempt; and he was at last compelled to break up the siege, that he might preside at a convention of the three estates in the capital. The death of Henry made no alteration in the policy of the English cabinet. The protector hastily concluded two treaties with the murderers; by the first of which they bound themselves to procure, with all their power, the marriage of their infant sovereign with Edward VI., and never to surrender the castle during her minority to any Scotsman without a previous license in writing from the English king and the protector; by the second they engaged to give effectual aid to the English army which should enter Scotland for the purpose of obtaining possession of the young queen, and to deliver the castle to English commissioners, as soon as she should come into the hands of Edward VI., or the marriage between them should be solemnized. The English government in return granted pensions to each of the chiefs, and undertook to pay half-yearly the wages of a garrison of one hundred and twenty men.[1]

The second of these treaties was hardly signed before it was treacherously communicated to Arran. From it he discovered the object of the protector; and immediately published a proclamation, ordering all fensible men to assemble, on forty days' notice, at a given place, with provisions for a month, that they might be prepared to repel the threatened invasion of their country. For greater security he applied to the new king of France, who cheerfully confirmed the ancient alliance between the two kingdoms, and added a promise of succour both in men and money. The irruptions of the English marchers had called Arran to the borders, where he razed to the ground the castle of Langhope, but was called from the siege of Cawmyllis to St. Andrew's by the arrival of Strozzi, prior of Capua, with a fleet of sixteen French galleys, The combined forces besieged the castle; a considerable breach was made by the French artillery; and the garrison surrendered with a promise of their lives. The prisoners were conveyed to France, and placed at the disposal of Henry, who confined some of them in the fortresses on the coast of Bretagne, and sent the others, amongst whom was the celebrated preacher John Knox, to labour in the galleys, from which they were not released before 1550. Arran recovered his eldest son, who had been detained a captive ever

---

[1] Rym. xv. 132, 144. The pension to the master of Rothes was 280*l*.; to Kirkaldy, 200*l*. per annum. For the pay of the garrison, &c., they received in February, 1,180*l*., and in May 1,300*l*.—Burnet, ii. 8, 31.

since the assassination, and demolished the works, that the place might not hereafter fall into the hands of the English, and be held by them to the terror of the open country.[1]

Somerset, taking with him the new earl of Warwick, as second in command, crossed the Tweed[2] at the head of twenty thousand men, and directed his march upon Edinburgh; while the fleet of twenty-four galleys and an equal number of store-ships, under Lord Clinton, crept along the shore without losing sight of the army.[3] To meet this invasion Arran had despatched the fire-cross from clan to clan, and had ordered every Scotsman to join his standard at Musselburgh; but he soon found the multitude too numerous for any useful purpose, and, having selected thirty thousand men, dismissed the rest to their homes. The two armies were soon in sight, and a bloody rencounter between the Scottish and English cavalry at Falside taught them to respect each other.[4]

The next morning Arran passed the Esk; a movement which led to the great battle of Pinkiecleugh. The Scottish army, consisting almost entirely of footmen, was divided into three bodies, each of which marching in close order, presented a dense forest of pikes. The lord Grey, commander of the English gens d'armes, hoping to take advantage of some apparent confusion in the most advanced of these bodies, ordered his men to charge it in flank. They paid severely for their temerity. The bravest of them fell; their commander was wounded with a pike in the mouth; and the colours were nearly captured. This check was, however, repaired by the steadiness of the Italian and Spanish mercenaries, who, being mounted, rode towards the enemy, and halting at a short distance, discharged their fire-arms into the first ranks, whilst the archers following them sent volleys of arrows over the heads of the mercenaries into the more distant part of the hostile column. At the same time a raking fire was opened on the Scots from a galley and two pinnaces in the bay; and a battery of guns from a neighbouring eminence scattered destruction amidst the dense and exposed mass. The protector did not suffer the opportunity to escape him. Having rallied the fugitives, he led the whole army to the attack. The Scots wavered, broke, and fled. The pursuit was continued for several hours, and the slain on the part of the vanquished were said to amount at a low computation to eight thousand men. The earl of Huntley, chancellor of Scotland, the lords Yester and Wemyss, and the master of Semple, were among the prisoners.[5]

From the field of battle the conqueror marched to Leith, spent four days in plundering the town and the neighbouring villages, and hastily retraced his steps, followed by Arran at the head of a small but active body

---

[1] Epist. Reg. Scot. ii. 390. Keith, 53. Leslie, 461.
[2] Mr. Tytler has discovered in the State Papers that two hundred Scottish noblemen and gentlemen had treasonably engaged to join him in Scotland.—Hist. vi. 18–21.
[3] See the numbers in Holinshed, 980. The instructions of the admiral are in Chron. Catal. p. 294. The master of Ruthven was in the fleet, who had promised to betray Perth into the hands of the English, with the aid of his father, Lord Ruthven of Gowrie; and Sir John Luttrell was to furnish the names of the Scots "which had fayled in their fayth after assurance made," that their lands might be ravaged.—Ibid.
[4] Haywood tells us that the loss of the Scots was thirteen hundred men; of the English, one Spanish hackbutter wounded, and three cavalry officers taken in the pursuit.—Haywood, 282. Leslie, on the contrary, says that the loss was equal; about one thousand men on each side.—Leslie, 462.
[5] Leslie, 464. Buchan. l. xv. Holinsh. 994. Hayward, 285.

of cavalry. This sudden retreat, after so brilliant a victory, surprised both his friends and foes. It could not originate from want of provisions, or the intemperance of the season, or the approach of a superior enemy. By some it was said that, intoxicated with vanity, he was eager to enjoy the applause of the people, and to receive the thanks of his nephew; by others it was believed that the secret intrigues of his brother the lord admiral had induced him to forego the advantages of victory, and to hasten back to the court. The expedition was begun and ended within the short period of sixteen days.

The late king was doomed to the usual fate of despotic monarchs after their deaths. The very men who during his life had been the obsequious ministers of his will, were now the first to overturn his favourite projects. Somerset and his associates had already established a different form of government; they now undertook to establish a different religious creed. Under Henry they had deemed it prudent to conceal their attachment to the new gospel; now, freed from restraint, they openly professed themselves its patrons, and aided its diffusion with all the influence of the crown. Their zeal was the more active, as it was stimulated by the prospect of reward. For, though they were the depositaries of the sovereign authority, they had yet to make their private fortunes; and for that purpose they looked with eagerness to the possessions of the church, from which, though much had been torn during the havoc of the last reign, much still remained to be gleaned.[1] From the young king they could experience no opposition now, they feared no resentment hereafter. The men to whom his education had been intrusted by Henry were zealous though secret partisans of the reformed doctrines. They had made it their chief care to transfuse the new opinions into the mind of their royal pupil; Edward already believed that the worship so rigorously enforced by his father was idolatrous; and there could be little doubt that his early prepossessions would, as he advanced in age, acquire strength from the industry of his teachers, and the approbation of his counsellors.

Still, to change the established creed during his minority must have appeared an undertaking of some difficulty and danger. There was no certainty that the people would pay to the protector and his advisers that deference which had been extorted by the theological despotism of the late monarch; and a second pilgrimage of grace, excited by religious innovations, might speedily overturn their authority. On this account they determined to proceed with steady but cautious steps. Among their own colleagues there were only two of whose sentiments they were doubtful, Wriothesley and the bishop of Durham. The first, as the reader has seen, was already excluded from the council; pretexts were invented to confine the prelate almost entirely to his diocese; and the conduct of the business was committed to the policy and moderation of the archbishop of Canterbury.

That prelate began the attempt by giving to his brother bishops a very intelligible hint, that the possession of their sees depended on their compliance with the pleasure of the council. Arguing that his ecclesiastical authority, since it emanated from the crown, must have expired with the late king, he petitioned to be restored to his former jurisdiction, and accepted a new commission to execute the functions of an archbishop, till such commission should

---

[1] Heylin, 33. Godwin, 88, 91.

be revoked by the sovereign.[1] Many, probably all, of his colleagues, were compelled to follow the example of the metropolitan.

The next step was to establish a royal visitation. For that purpose the kingdom was divided into six circuits, to each of which was assigned a certain number of visitors, partly clergymen and partly laymen. The moment they arrived in any diocese, the exercise of spiritual authority by every other person ceased. They summoned before them the bishop, the clergy, and eight, six, or four of the principal householders from each parish, administered the oaths of allegiance and supremacy; required answers upon oath to every question which they thought proper to put, and exacted a promise of obedience to the royal injunctions.[2] These injunctions amounted in number to thirty-seven; they regarded matters of religious practice and doctrine; and were for the most part so framed, that, under the pretext of abolishing abuses, they might pave the way for subsequent innovations. With them was delivered a book of homilies to be read in every church on Sundays and holidays, with an order that each clergyman should provide for himself, and each parish for the congregation, one copy of the paraphrase of Erasmus on the New Testament. But the same policy which thus supplied books of instruction was careful to limit the number of instructors; and the power of preaching was, by successive restrictions, confined at last to such clergymen only as should obtain licenses from the protector or the metropolitan.[3] The object was evident: the people heard no other doctrines than those which were contained in the homilies, for the most part the composition of the archbishop, or which were delivered by the preachers, whose duty it was to echo his opinions, and to inveigh against the more ancient creed.

Among the prelates there was no individual whom the men of the new learning more feared, or those of the old learning more respected, for his erudition and abilities, his spirit and influence, than Gardiner, bishop of Winchester. That prelate, before the visitation of his diocese, had obtained copies of the homilies and the paraphrase, and immediately commenced a long and animated controversy with the protector and the archbishop. He maintained that the two books in several instances contradicted each other; that they inculcated doctrines irreconcilable with the creed established by act of parliament; and that they contained errors, which he deemed himself able to demonstrate to the conviction of any reasonable man. In his letter to the protector he urged with much force, that Edward was too young to understand, Somerset too much occupied to study, subjects of controversy; that it was imprudent to disturb the public peace during the king's minority, for the sole purpose of supporting the theological fancies of the metropolitan; that injunctions issued by the king could not invalidate acts of parliament; and that, as Cardinal Wolsey had incurred a præmunire, though he acted under the royal license, so every clergyman, who taught the doctrines in the homilies and paraphrase, would

---

[1] Wilkins, iv. 2.
[2] Ibid. 11, 14, 17. Collier, ii. Records.
[3] Wilk. iv. 27, 30. Even the very bishops could not preach in their own dioceses without license. — See two instances in Strype, ii. 90. Coverdale was so delighted with the injunctions, the homilies, and the paraphrase, that he pronounced the young king to be "the high and chief admiral of the great navy of the Lord of Hosts, principal captain and governor of us all under him; the most noble ruler of his ship, even our most comfortable Noah, whom the eternal God hath chosen to be the bringer of us unto rest and quietness."—Apud Strype, ii. 65.

be liable to the penalties enacted by the statute of the Six Articles, though he might plead a royal injunction in his favour. To Cranmer he wrote in a different tone, defying him to prove the truth of certain doctrines inculcated in the book of homilies, and reproaching him with duplicity in now reprobating the opinions which he had so zealously taught during the life of the late king.[1] In consequence of these letters he was summoned before the council, and required to promise obedience to the royal injunctions. He replied that he was not bound to answer, unless the injunctions were tendered to him. Let them wait till the visitors arrived in his diocese. If he should then refuse, they might determine whether that refusal were a contempt of the royal authority or not. But this objection was overruled; Cranmer gladly embraced any pretext to silence so dangerous an opponent during the approaching parliament; and Gardiner, though he could not be charged with any offence against the law, was committed to the Fleet, and detained a close prisoner till the end of the session.[2]

The proceedings of this parliament are deserving of the reader's attention. Many of the chantries, colleges, and free chapels, though given to Henry VIII. by a late act, had escaped the rapacious grasp of that monarch. It was now proposed to place these with all the funds destined for the support of obits, anniversaries, and church-lights, and all guild lands possessed by fraternities for the same purpose, at the disposal of the king, that he might employ them in providing for the poor, augmenting the income of vicarages, paying the salaries of preachers, and endowing free schools for the diffusion of learning.[3] The archbishop, aware of the real object of the bill, spoke against it at first with some warmth. But, as the harpies of the court were eager to pounce on their prey, he deemed it prudent to withdraw his opposition; and it was passed in the Lords by a triumphant majority.[4] In the Commons a strong objection was made to that clause which went to deprive the guilds of their lands; but the leaders of the opposition, the members for Lynn and Coventry, were silenced by a promise that the crown should

[1] "Which, if it had been so" (if the doctrine in the late king's book had been erroneous), " I ought to think your grace would not, for all princes christened, being so high a bishop as ye be, have yielded unto. For obedire oportet Deo magis quam hominibus. And therefore, after your grace hath four years continually lived in agreement of that doctrine, under our late sovereign lord, now so suddenly after his death to write to me, that his highness was seduced, it is, I assure you, a very strange speech."—Strype's Cranmer, App. p. 74.

[2] See the correspondence in Fox, ii. 35—70. During Gardiner's confinement, attempts were made to obtain his co-operation in the new plan of reform. On one occasion the archbishop told him that "he liked nothing unless he did it himself." He replied, that " he was not guilty of such obstinacy; and that he had never been author yet of any one thing either temporal or spiritual; for which he thanked God." A hint was given that his compliance might be rewarded with a place in the council, and an addition in his income. But he answered indignantly, that his character and conscience forbade it; and that, "if he agreed on such terms, he should deserve to be whipped in every market-town in the realm, and then to be hanged for an example as the veriest varlet that ever was bishop in any realm christened."—Ibid. 64, 65.

[3] Our law-books teach that, by the statute passed on this occasion, lands and goods subsequently given for superstitious uses, are forfeited to the king; yet the operation of the statute is expressly limited to lands and goods belonging to colleges and chantries which existed within the five last years, or given for anniversaries, obits, and lights kept or maintained within " the five yeres next before the saide first daie of this present parliament."—Stat. of Realm, iv. 25, 26. There is nothing in the act to make it prospective.

[4] On the first division in the Lords, the minority consisted of the bishops of Canterbury, London, Ely, Norwich, Hereford, Worcester, and Chichester. At the last, Canterbury and Worcester were not in the house, and Norwich voted with the court.—Journals, 308, 313.

restore to those towns the lands of which they might be deprived by the act. A saving clause was added to secure to all persons such lands, tenements, tithes, and rents, as had been already granted to them either by the late or the present king.[1]

2. But if the ministers sought to provide for the sovereign and for themselves, they were careful to repair many of those breaches in the constitution which had been made by the despotism in the last reign. All felonies created since the first of Henry VIII., and all treasons created since the twenty-fifth of Edward III., were at once erased from the statute-book; the privilege of clergy, with the exception of a few cases, was restored; in convictions of treason two witnesses were required; the laws against the Lollards, the prohibition of reading the Scriptures, and of printing, selling, or retaining certain English publications; all enactments respecting doctrine and matters of religion, and the statute which gave to the royal proclamations the force of law, were repealed; and in place of the act of the twenty-eighth of the late king, which empowered his heir, if he were a minor at the time of his accession, to annul afterwards all statutes passed before he had attained the full age of twenty-four years, was substituted another to the same effect,—but with this proviso, that though he might deprive them of all force after that term, he could not invalidate them as to their effects during the intermediate period.[2] It should, however, be observed, that if, by the repeal of so many statutes, every sort of religious restraint was removed from the men of the new learning, it was not intended to grant any additional liberty to those of the old. The claim of the spiritual supremacy was placed on an equal footing with the other rights of the crown and to deny that the present or any succeeding king was head of the church was made the same kind of capital offence, as to deny that he was head of the state. A distinction was, however, drawn between the denial by words and the denial by writing, imprinting, or deed. The latter was at once an act of high treason; the former became so only by repetition. The first offence was punishable with the forfeiture of all goods and chattels, and imprisonment at the royal pleasure; the second subjected the offender to all the penalties of a præmunire; and the third condemned him to suffer as a traitor by the knife of the executioner.[3]

3. The convocation had been assembled at the same time as the parliament; and the members of the lower house, anxious to recover their former share in the exercise of the legislative power, petitioned to be united to the house of Commons, or, if that might not be granted, to be allowed a negative on all bills respecting religion. To this petition no answer was returned; but two questions concerning the lawfulness of marriage in the clergy, and of communion under both kinds, were submitted to their consideration. The first of these was carried in the affirmative by a majority of almost two-thirds, and a bill in its favour was introduced into the house of Commons; but its advocates, whether they apprehended an obstinate opposition from the Lords, or were content with the

---

[1] Stat. of Realm, iv. 24. The chantries and free chapels were valued at 2,593l. per annum, and sold for 46,249l. 14s.—Strype, ii. Rec. 85. A great number of grammar-schools were founded chiefly out of the chantry lands.—Id. 535.

[2] Stat. of Realm, iv. 17, 19.

[3] Ibid. 19. All the same punishments were enacted against any person who should deny that the present or any succeeding king was king of France or of Ireland, or should maintain that any other person was or ought to be king of France or of Ireland. —Ibid.

advantage which they had gained, permitted the matter to sleep for the present session. The second was approved unanimously; and a bill was framed on that decision. It stated, that the ministering of the blessed sacrament to all Christian people under both kinds, of bread and wine, is more agreeable to its first institution, and more conformable to the common practice of the apostles and the primitive church for five hundred years; and therefore enacts, that the said most blessed sacrament shall be commonly delivered and ministered to the people under both kinds. It permits, however, communion under one kind, when necessity may require it; and professes not to censure any foreign church which may retain the contrary practice. To neutralize the opposition of the prelates, who were hostile to this bill, it was artfully appended to another, which they most anxiously sought to carry, prohibiting, under pain of fine and imprisonment, the application of scurrilous and offensive language to the sacrament of the eucharist. Thus coupled together as one act, they passed both houses, and received the royal assent.[1]

4. In conformity with the opinion so often inculcated by Archbishop Cranmer, it was declared that all jurisdiction, both spiritual and temporal, is derived from the king; and on that account the election of bishops was withdrawn from the deans and chapters, as a useless and unmeaning form, and vested immediately in the crown; and it was ordered that all citations and processes of archbishops and bishops, which used to run in their names, should henceforth be made in the name of the king, but tested by the bishop, and countersigned by his commissary; and that all official documents issued from their courts should be sealed, not with the episcopal, but with the royal arms.[2]

5. The mendicants, who had formerly obtained relief at the gates of the monasteries and convents, now wandered in crowds through the country, and by their numbers and importunities often extorted alms from the intimidated passenger. To abate this nuisance, a statute was enacted, which will call to the recollection of the reader the barbarous manners of our pagan forefathers. Whosoever "lived idly and loiteringly for the space of three days" came under the description of a vagabond, and was liable to the following punishment. Two justices of the peace might order the letter V to be burnt on his breast, and adjudge him to serve the informer two years as his slave. His master was bound to provide him with bread, water, and refuse meat; might fix an iron ring round his neck, arm, or leg, and was authorized to compel him to "labour at any work, however vile it might be, by beating, chaining, or otherwise." If the slave absented himself a fortnight, the letter S was burnt on his cheek or forehead, and he became a slave for life; and if he offended a second time in like manner, his flight subjected him to the penalties of felony.[3] Two years later this severe statute was repealed.[4]

6. The close of this session was

---

[1] Stat. of Realm, iv. 2. The non-contents were the bishops of London, Norwich, Hereford, Worcester, and Chichester.—Journals, 306. [2] Stat. of Realm, iv. 3.
[3] Stat. of Realm, iv. 5. With respect to clerks convicted of felony, they, if they were entitled to purgation in the bishop's court, were to be slaves for one year, if not so entitled, to be slaves for five years.—Ibid.
[4] Stat. of Realm, iv. 115. Thus the statute of 22 Hen. VIII. 12, was revived, which allowed persons to beg with the license of the magistrates, and punish beggars without license by whipping, or the stocks for three days and three nights.

marked by a transaction without parallel in our history. The duke of Somerset, preparatory to his expedition against the Scots, had received from the king letters patent explanatory of his original commission. By these it was declared that in quality of "governor of the royal person, and protector of the realm and people during the term of the king's minority," he was the king's lieutenant and captain-general of war by sea and land, possessing all the authority of a commander-in-chief, with the power of conferring the honour of knighthood, of baronage, or any other rank of nobility in reward of military service, and of declaring war against, or of concluding peace with, any foreign power, according to his own judgment and discretion."[1] Both these patents, by which the whole power of the crown was vested in his person, he had surrendered during the parliament into the hands of his nephew, and had received in place of them a new commission, which, indeed, restored to him, with an unimportant exception, all the powers of the former, but at the same time made the duration of his office dependent on the good pleasure of the king, who might at will deprive him of it by a writ under the great seal and the sign manual. What then could induce the protector, who was now in the zenith of his power, to consent to so disadvantageous an exchange? No reason is stated. But we know that great misgivings existed with regard to the validity of the first commission; because it emanated from the council, which had not the power to create such an office.[2] This was an inherent defect, which certainly could not be cured by a second commission proceeding in reality from the same source; but it seems to have been thought that the appointment would be less objectionable, if, instead of being permanent, it were made revocable at the king's pleasure; and if it were confirmed also with the signatures of almost every man of consequence in the realm. The first of these expedients might be easily attained by a change in the form of the instrument; the second was accomplished by the following contrivance.[3] At the prorogation of parliament on December 24, before the members had departed, an extraordinary meeting was called, and the new commission was read before those who attended. It bore already the sign manual, and was now subscribed by Ryche, the lord chancellor, by the other lords, both spiritual and temporal, according to the usual order of precedency in the house, and then by distinguished commoners, privy councillors, judges, and most of the civil and law officers of the crown, to the number of sixty-two individuals. It was certainly an improvement of the manner in which the protectorship had been originally conferred. Then the appointment was announced to a meeting of the Lords, who were supposed to approve, because no one objected: now all who were present testified their approbation by append-

---

[1] Rymer, xv. 174.

[2] Paget writes to Somerset: "I believe, sir, if anything chance amiss, that not only your grace shall give the account which have authority in your hands, but also such as did first assent and accord to give it you."—Strype, Rec. part ii. p. 111.

[3] From the instrument itself it appears that it was subscribed on the 24th of December. The omission of any mention of the subscription in the Journals, shows that it did not take place before the prorogation. I conclude that it took place immediately afterwards, because all the lords who, according to the Journals, were in the house, subscribed the commission in proper order, excepting the bishop of Bath and the lord Powis, who may be supposed to have departed immediately after the prorogation. Lord Seymour and the bishop of St. David's were not in the house; but subscribed the instrument. Probably they came later, for though the bishop subscribes, it is not in his proper order but in a vacant space.

ing their signatures to the commission. To these signatures Somerset frequently appealed in his subsequent troubles.[1] The session closed with a general pardon from the king, in consequence of which Gardiner obtained his liberty.[2]

The result of this meeting of parliament cheered the men of the new learning with the most flattering anticipations; but the archbishop, aware that the great majority of the nation was still attached to the ancient faith, deemed it prudent to moderate their zeal, and pursued his course with caution and perseverance. Latimer, who had resigned his bishopric in 1539, was called from his retirement, and appointed to preach at St. Paul's Cross. The character of the man, the boldness of his invectives, his quaint but animated eloquence, were observed to make a deep impression on the minds of his hearers; and a pulpit was erected for him in the king's privy garden, where the young Edward, attended by his court, listened to sermons of an hour's duration, and admired what he could not understand, the controversial superiority of the preacher.[3]

The bishops received orders to abolish in their respective dioceses, the custom of bearing candles on Candlemas-day, of receiving ashes on Ash Wednesday, and of carrying palms on Palm Sunday.[4] The late king had frequently commanded the removal from the churches of all such images as had been the occasion of superstition and abuse: a proclamation now appeared, which complained that these injunctions had given birth to dissensions among the parishioners, and required that, to restore tranquillity, all images whatsoever should be destroyed.[5] To this succeeded an order for the public administration of the sacrament under both kinds and in the English language. To avoid offence, no alteration was made in the mass itself; no expression liable to objection was introduced into the new office; but at the end of the canon, an exhortation was ordered to be made to the communicants, a prayer followed, and the eucharist was distributed first to the clergy, and then to the laity. But to appease the impatience of the reformers, the young king was made to say in the preface: " We would not have our subjects so much to mistake our judgment, so much to mistrust our zeal, as if we either could not discern what were to be done, or would not do all things in good time. God be praised! we know both what by his word is meet to be redressed, and have an earnest mind, by the advice of our most dear uncle, and others of our privy council, with all diligence to set forth the same."[6] The reader should recollect that this learned and zealous theologian was ten years old.

It was soon discovered that imprisonment had not broken the spirit of Gardiner. He was again summoned before the council, and the next day, in proof of his submission, was ordered

---

[1] The commission itself with the signatures is in the possession of William Staunton, esquire, of Longbridge House, Warwick; and has been published with valuable remarks by Mr. G. Nichols, in Archæol. xxx. 463.

[2] In one of his letters, written during the session, he hints that, if any man thought it politic to keep him from parliament, such person ought to consider whether his forcible absence, with that of those whom he had been used to name in the nether house, might not afterwards be urged as an objection to the validity of the proceeding.— Fox, ii. 69. I notice this passage, because it proves that several boroughs at that period were so dependent on the lords and bishops, that they not only returned the members named by such lords, but without such nomination made no return at all.

[3] He gave to Latimer as a reward for his first sermon 20l. The money was secretly supplied by the lord admiral.

[4] Wilk. iv. 22. [5] Ib. 23. [6] Ib. 11—13.

to preach at St. Paul's Cross, in the presence of the king, on the feast of St. Peter. To the different subjects which were prescribed to him he made no objection; but he refused to deliver a written discourse which was offered, or to submit his own composition to the correction of the council. He added that, as this was perhaps the only opportunity which the king would have of hearing the truth, he was determined, whatever might be the consequence, to explain to his young sovereign the Catholic doctrine with respect to the mass and the eucharist. The sermon was preached, and the next day the bishop was committed to the Tower. His discourse might be divided into three parts. With the first, which commended the religious innovations of the last and the present reign, even his enemies were satisfied; of the second, in which he maintained that a rightful king was as much a sovereign in his infancy as at a more mature age, they could not complain; though it disappointed the hopes of the protector, who wished him to contradict a very prevailing notion, that the authority of the council during the minority did not extend to the issuing of new injunctions, but was confined to the execution of the existing laws. It was the third part which furnished the pretext for his commitment, under the charge of disobedience. In it he had treated of the mass and the eucharist, though the protector had forbidden him in writing to touch on any controverted matter respecting these questions. In his own justification he alleged, that he had not been guilty of disobedience, because the letter was a private communication and not an order from the king in council, and because he had entered into no controversy, but had confined himself to the explication of the established doctrine of the English church, in language similar to that employed by the archbishop in the disputation with Lambert.[1] His imprisonment was evidently illegal; but his absence from parliament was not less desirable in the present than it had been in the past year. His constancy, however, encouraged the partisans of the ancient faith; and in a short time several other prelates ventured to express their disapprobation of the attempts of the metropolitan.

Cranmer had lately published a catechism "for the singular profit and instruction of children and young people;"[2] and was now employed with a committee of bishops and divines in the composition of a more important work, a liturgy in the English language, for the use of the English church; the adoption of which by authority of parliament would, it was hoped, consummate the separation of the kingdom from the communion of Rome, by destroying the similarity which still remained in the mode of religious worship sanctioned by the two churches. Taking the Latin missals and breviaries for the groundwork, they omitted such parts as they deemed superfluous or superstitious, translated others, and by numerous additions and corrections endeavoured to meet the wishes of the new teachers, without shocking

---

[1] The protector's letter is in Wilkins, iv. 28. The other particulars are extracted from the articles against Gardiner, and his answers in Fox, ii. 75—77.

[2] It is remarkable, that in this catechism the archbishop leans more than usually to the ancient doctrines. He comprises the prohibition of false gods and of images under one commandment; teaches that in the communion are received with the bodily mouth the body and blood of Christ; inculcates in strong terms the advantages of confession and absolution, and attributes the origin of ecclesiastical jurisdiction to Christ in a manner which seems to do away his former opinion on the same subject.—Burnet, ii. 71. Collier, ii. 251.

the belief or the prejudices of their opponents. Before Christmas they had compiled a book of common prayer and administration of the sacraments, and other rites and ceremonies, after the use of the church of England.[1] To the premature judgment and early piety of the king the completion of the work afforded "great comfort and quietness of mind." He hastened to recommend it to the notice of the Lords and Commons assembled in parliament, and a bill was introduced to abolish all other forms of worship, and establish this in their place. The preamble states that, whereas numerous dissensions had arisen in the kingdom from the pertinacity with which many adhered to the old, and others to new, forms of divine worship, the king, abstaining of his clemency from the punishment of the offenders, had appointed certain prelates and learned men to compose one convenient and meet order, rite, and fashion of common and open prayer; by whom that important task had been accomplished by the aid of the Holy Ghost with one uniform agreement:[2] therefore the two houses, considering the godly travail of the king and council, and the godly prayers, orders, rites, and ceremonies of the said book, and the reasons of altering those things which be altered, and of retaining those which be retained, and also the honour of God and the great quietness likely to ensue from the use of the same, do give to his highness most hearty and lowly thanks, and pray that it may be enacted that after the feast of Pentecost all ministers of the church within the realm of England shall be bound " to say and use the matins, even song, celebration of the Lord's Supper commonly called the mass, and administration of each of the sacraments, and all their common and open prayer, after the order and form of the said book," and of no other; and that if any parson, vicar, or spiritual person, shall refuse to use it, or shall preach or speak in derogation of it, or shall officiate with any other form, he shall for the first offence forfeit a year's profit of one of his preferments, with six months' imprisonment; for the second lose all his preferments, with a whole year's imprisonment; and for the third be imprisoned for life; and if any one ridicule the same form of worship, or menace the minister for using it, or prevail on him to use any other, he shall on the first conviction pay a fine of ten pounds, on the second of twenty, and on the third forfeit all his goods and chattels, and be imprisoned for life.[3] In the lower house the bill passed without much difficulty; in the higher it experienced a warm opposition; but "after a notable disputation respecting the sacrament,"[4] it was carried by a majority of thirty-one to eleven.[5]

---

[1] The principal differences between this and the present book of common prayer are to be found in the prayer of consecration (it contained, in imitation of all the ancient liturgies, these words: "Heare us, we beseeche thee, and with thy holy spirite and worde vouchsafe to bl+esse and sancti+fie these thy gifts and creatures of bread and wyne, that they maye be unto us the bodie and blood of thy most derely beloved sonne"), the unctions in baptism and confirmation, the sign of the cross in matrimony, the anointing of the sick, and prayer for the dead. The rubric also in the communion service ordered, that the bread should be unleavened, that the communicant should receive at the hand of the priest with the mouth, and that one individual at least in each family should communicate every Sunday in person or by proxy, and pay his share of the expense.

[2] This is an extraordinary assertion. There were eighteen bishops in the committee which composed the book of common prayer (Collier, ii. 243), and eight out of the number voted against it (Lords' Journals, 331). Would they disapprove in the house what they had approved in the committee?

[3] Stat. of Realm, iv. 37, 38. A provision was added, authorizing the singing of psalms "at any due time," by all men, whether in the church or in private houses.—Ibid.

[4] The King's Journal, 6.

[5] Journals 331. The non-contents were

To this important innovation in the manner of public worship, succeeded another not less important in the condition of the priesthood. In the last reign the archbishop had contended for the marriage of the clergy with a pertinacity which might have cost him his life: in the present he was assured of a safe and easy victory. The path had already been opened by the decision of the late convocation; and at an early period of the session a bill for the marriage of priests was introduced into the lower house. On the third reading it was discovered that, though it allowed laymen who had wives to take orders, it did not permit clergymen who had received orders, to take wives. A new bill was therefore brought in, and passed after a long and stormy discussion. In the Lords, however, for reasons now unknown, it remained during two months without notice, when a totally different bill was substituted in its place, and on a division was carried by a majority of thirty-nine to twelve.[1] To this bill the Commons assented. It states that, though it were to be wished that the clergy would observe perpetual continency, as more becoming their spiritual character, rendering them better able to attend to their ministry, and freeing them from worldly cares and embarrassments, yet so many inconveniences had arisen from compulsive chastity, that it was deemed better to allow to those who could not contain, the godly use of marriage; wherefore it enacts, that thenceforth all laws made by man only, and prohibitory of the marriages of spiritual persons, shall be void and of none effect; but that all divorces hitherto made (in consequence of the statute of the Six Articles) shall remain valid in law.[2]

Of these enactments it was natural that men should judge according to the bias given to their minds by their religious notions: but there was another proceeding in this parliament, which appeared to shock the feelings of the whole nation. The protector had a younger brother, Sir Thomas Seymour, whose ambition was equal, whose abilities were superior, to his own. Between them a broad distinction had been drawn by the discernment or partiality of the late king; and while Edward had risen to the rank of earl, had obtained the command of armies, and been named one of the governors of his nephew, Thomas had been left without title, and without any other office than that of counsellor to Henry's executors. If the latter bore with impatience the superiority of his brother during the last reign, his discontent was not appeased by the first measures of the present. He had indeed obtained a grant of the manor of Sudeley, and of other manors in eighteen different counties:[3] had been created a baron by the style of Lord Seymour of Sudeley, and had been appointed high admiral of England: but to his ambition these grants and preferments appeared as nothing comparatively with the rank and titles of Edward, who was protector of the realm, guardian of the royal person, lord high treasurer, earl marshal, and duke of

---

the earl of Derby, the bishops of London, Durham, Norwich, Carlisle, Hereford, Worcester, Westminster, and Chichester, and the lords Dacres and Wyndsor.—Ibid. The earl of Derby, who supposed that another temporal peer had joined in the opposition, boasted that "the way of them four would he to be seen as long as the parliament-house stood."—Strype, ii. 84.

[1] Journals of Com. iv. 5. Journals of Lords, 323, 339. The lords in the minority were the bishops of London, Durham, Norwich, Carlisle, Worcester, Chichester, Bristol, and Landaff, and the lords Morley, Dacres, Wyndsor, and Wharton.—Ibid.
[2] Stat. of Realm, iv. 67.
[3] Strype, ii. 125. Sudeley had belonged to the abbey of Winchelcombe.

Somerset. The first step towards the improvement of his fortune was his marriage with the queen dowager. Whether that princess be entitled to all the praises which have been lavished on her by her panegyrists, may fairly be doubted. Certainly she displayed no very great sense of decorum in the precipitancy with which, after the death of Henry, she sought a fourth husband, almost before the dead body of the third was deposited in the grave. We first meet with her at court, probably to offer her congratulations to the new king on his accession. There she spoke in private to Lord Seymour, who had once been her wooer. Her words did not transpire, but on her return home, she wrote to assure him that they did not proceed from any sudden impulse of passion, but from that affection which she bore to him formerly, and which was still unimpaired.[1] We next find her watching for his arrival at the postern-gate of her garden at Chelsea in the dead of the night, and stealthily introducing him into her house, on condition that he should withdraw by seven of the clock, to avoid detection.[2] From the language in her letters, it seems that some contract of espousal soon passed between them; but that contract was kept a profound secret, because, according to ancient precedents, to marry a queen dowager without the permission of the reigning sovereign was a misdemeanour subjecting the offender to fine and imprisonment. Their furtive meetings, however, could not be continued with safety; and it became a matter of the first importance to procure the royal consent to their marriage.[3] The pride of Seymour recoiled from asking the favour from his brother, the protector; but at last necessity or opportunity led him to break the matter to Somerset, not as if he spoke of a marriage already contracted, but of one to which he aspired. To carry on the deception, he solicited the good offices of the young Edward, and of the lady Mary, that they would induce the queen dowager to favour his suit. From the protector and the council he received a severe reprimand for his presumption; Mary, with a caustic remark, refused to interfere;[4] but the

---

[1] Strype, ii. 132.
[2] This appears from the following passage in her letter to him: "Whan it schal be your pleasur to repayer hether, ye must take sum payne to come erly in the mornyng, that ye may be gone agayne by seven a clocke; and so I suppose ye may come without suspect. I pray you lett me have knowlege ver nyght at what hower ye wyll come, that your porteresse may wayte at the gate to the feldes for you.—By her that ys and schalbe your humble true and lovyng wyffe duryng her lyf. Kateryn the Quene. K.P."—Ellis, ii. 152. This letter has no date; but if it mean, as it seems to mean, that till seven the darkness of the morning would help to conceal him, it cannot have been written later than the middle of February: and this inference derives confirmation from the twentieth article of the charge brought against Seymour by the council, that his cohabitation with the queen "was so soon, that if she had conceived straight after, it should have been a great doubt whether the child born should have been accounted the late king's or the admiral's."—Burnet, ii. Rec. 160.
[3] It was certainly concealed till the end of May. On the 17th of that month Seymour writes to the queen from St. James's, that her sister Anne, wife to Sir William Herbert, had joked with him about his lodging at Chelsea. He denied it: "he only went by the garden, as he went to see the bishop of London's house." But "she told him further tokens which made him change colour." He recovered, however, from his fright when he found that she had not learned it from others, but had received it in confidence from the queen herself.—See it in Tytler, i. 60; and Miss Strickland's Queens, v. 100.
[4] Mary's reply does her honour: "My lorde, in this case, if it weer for my nereste kynsman and dereste frend on lyve, of all other creatures in the worlde it standest leste with my poore honore to be a medler in this matter, consyderyng whose wief her Grace was of late—Thynke not unkyndness in me, thoughe I refuse to be a medler anywayes in this matter, assuring you that (wowyng matters set aparte, wherein I, being a mayde, am nothyng connyng), if otherwayes it shall lye in my little power to do you pleser, I shall be as gladde to do it, as you to requyre it."—Ellis, ii. 150.

simplicity of Edward was easily deceived. He not only urged his mother-in-law to marry his uncle, but later, when the council had consented to the match, thanked her for having, at his prayer, done that which she had, in fact, done long before any application was made to him.[1] With the person of Catherine, Seymour became master of her wealth and her dower; but in one thing, which he coveted, he was disappointed,—the possession of the jewels presented to her by the late king. These he induced her to claim as if they had been a gift; by the council they were reclaimed as only a loan made to her, and were still the property of the crown.[2]

The next object of the admiral was to win and monopolize the affection of his nephew. With this view he indulged the young Edward in all his wishes; secretly supplied him with large sums of money,[3] blamed the severity with which he was used by the protector, hinted that he was kept under restraint unbecoming his age and parts and dignity, and purchased with presents the good-will of his preceptors, and of the gentlemen of his chamber. From ancient precedents, he contended, that the offices of protector and guardian ought not to be joined in the same person; but that, if one belonged to the elder uncle, the other ought to be conferred on the younger. The king readily imbibed the opinions of the man whom he loved; and a resolution was taken that the nephew should write a letter of complaint; that the admiral should lay it before the two houses of parliament; and that he should attempt, with the aid of his partisans, to procure the guardianship for himself. Seymour had already composed the letter for Edward, who engaged to copy it, when the plot was betrayed to the protector, and the lord admiral was called before the council.[4] He repelled the charge with haughtiness, and treated their authority with defiance. But when the law officers declared that his offence amounted to an attempt to overturn the established government, and a hint had been thrown out of committing him to the Tower, his courage quickly subsided; he condescended to acknowledge his fault; and the two brothers mutually forgave each other. To seal their reconciliation, an addition of eight hundred pounds a year was made to his appointments.

But a new prospect soon opened to his ambition, which, as it sought for power, was not to be satisfied with money. He began to aspire to the hand of the lady Elizabeth, the king's sister, and to condemn that precipitate union with Catherine which excluded him from the pursuit of so noble a prize. His attentions to the princess were remarked; and their familiarity was so undisguised, that it afforded employment to the propagators of scandal, and awakened the jealousy of his wife, by whom he was one day surprised with Elizabeth in his arms.[5] But the queen in a short time died in childbirth; and her death happened so opportunely for his project, that by the malice of his enemies it was attributed to poison.[6] He now redoubled his court to the princess;[7] her governess was bribed;

---

[1] In Strype, ii. 133. See also Seymour's attainder, Stat. of Realm, iv. 63.
[2] Haynes, 73.
[3] See Edward's Confession, ibid. 74; Burnet, ii. Rec. 163.
[4] Burnet, ii. Rec. 158. Stat. of Realm, iv. 62.   [5] Haynes, 96, 99.
Ibid. 103, 104. Even Elizabeth notices that "she, he had before, ded so myskary."—Ibid. 101. "He holpe her to her end."—Stat. of Realm, iv. 63.
[7] From the testimony of the reluctant Mrs. Ashley, Elizabeth's governess, it appears that the courtship was not conducted in the most delicate manner. The moment he was up, he would hasten to Elizabeth's

her own affections were won; but a clandestine marriage would, by the will of her father, have annulled her right to the succession; and means were to be devised to extort what otherwise would not be granted,—the consent of the council.[1] For this purpose, as it was believed, the admiral sought the friendship of the discontented among the nobility, and by condemning the measures of the government, endeavoured to acquire the applause of the people. He censured the employment of foreign troops in the war against Scotland, as an innovation dangerous to the liberties of the country; his nephew was taught to look with a jealous eye on the ambition of the protector; a marriage was secretly projected between the young king and the lady Jane Grey,[2] the presumptive heiress to the claims of the house of Suffolk; and the riches of the admiral, the number of his retainers, and his influence in different counties, were openly vaunted and exaggerated by himself and his friends.

The protector at length determined to crush so dangerous a competitor. Sherington, master of the mint at Bristol, was examined before the council, on a charge of having amassed an enormous fortune, by clipping the coin, issuing testoons of inferior value,[3] and falsifying the entries made in his books. The admiral, who was his creditor to the amount of three thousand pounds, boldly defended the accused; but Sherington, to save his life, betrayed his advocate, and confessed that he had promised to coin money for Seymour, who could reckon on the services of ten thousand men, and intended with their aid to carry off the king, and to change the present form of the government.[4] On this confession he was found guilty, and

---

chamber "in his night gown, and barelegged;" if she were still in bed, "he wold put open the curteyns and make as though he wold come at hir;" "and she wold go farther in the bed, so that he cold not come at hir;" if she were up, he "wold ax how she did, and strike hir upon the bak or the buttocks famylearly."—Ibid. 98, 99. He sent James Seymour "to recommend him to hir, and ax hir, whither hir great buttocks were grown any less or no."—Ibid. 100. Parry, the cofferer, says, "she told me that the admirall loved her but two well; that the quene was jelowse on hir and him; and that, suspecting the often accesse of the admiral to her, she came sodenly upon them, wher they were all alone, he having her in his armes."—Ibid. 96. It was reported, not only that she was pregnant, which she declared to be "a shameful schandler" (ibid. 90); but also that she bore him a childe. "There was a bruit of a childe borne and miserably destroyed, but could not be discovered whose it was, on the report of the midwife, who was brought from her house blindfold thither, and so returned. Saw nothing in the house while she was ther but candlelight; only sayd it was the child of a very fair yong ladie."—MS. life of Jane Dormer, duchess of Feria, p. 150. Elizabeth complained of these reports, and the protector at last issued a proclamation against them.—Ellis, ii. 153, 157.

[1] Elizabeth acknowledges his proposal of marriage in a letter to the protector for the purpose of excusing Mrs. Ashley.—Ellis, ii. 154. Both Ashley and Parry were true to her on this occasion; they could not be brought to admit of anything criminal in her conduct. When she became queen, she rewarded them by making Parry comptroller of the household, and keeping Ashley as a confidential servant at court till her death.

[2] He had prevailed on the marques and the marchioness of Dorset to allow the young lady to stay with the queen dowager; after whose death he again prevailed on them to agree that their daughter should reside with him, promising to bring about a marriage between her and the king.—Tyt. i. 139.

[3] The testoons passed for twelve pence, but were not intrinsically of half the value. A new coinage was issued of sovereigns and half-sovereigns, and of crowns and half-crowns, of the value of twenty, ten, five shillings, and two shillings and sixpence. These were of gold: the silver pieces were the shilling in place of the testoons, and the half-shilling.—Strype, ii. 119, 120.

[4] I have extracted these particulars from the original depositions in the Burghley State Papers, the Records in Burnet, and the act of attainder of Sherington. Several other particulars, mentioned by historians, I have omitted, because they are not supported by these documents. Nor have I given full credit to the documents themselves; particularly as to the sum of money promised to him by Sherington, and the number of men at his disposal. It has been

attainted of high treason; the admiral was committed to the Tower, and underwent several examinations, sometimes before a deputation, once before the whole of the council. On these trying occasions he lost nothing of his usual spirit. He heard the charges against him with disdain, claimed to be confronted with his accusers, and required a copy of the information. Such demands, though consonant to the principles of justice, were contrary to the practice of the age; the young king abandoned one uncle to the jealousy or vengeance of the other, and, in imitation of the illegal precedents of the last reign, a bill of attainder against him was brought into the house of Lords. The judges and law officers of the crown gave their opinion, that some of the charges amounted to treason; and several peers, rising in their places, repeated the evidence which they had already given before the council. Somerset was present at each reading of the bill. On the third it was passed without a division, and was sent to the other house with a message that the lords, who were personally acquainted with the traitorous designs of the admiral, would, if it were required, repeat their evidence before the Commons. In that house an unexpected opposition was made. It was contended that to convict by bill of attainder was contrary to law and justice; that by the late statute the accused had a right to be confronted with his accusers; and that it was unreasonable to condemn him till he had been heard in his own defence. After the second reading, the Lords repeated their message; and, having waited for a considerable time, requested the protector to receive the answer, and to report it to the house the next day. But he preferred to put an end to the discussion in the Commons by a message from the king, declaring that it was unnecessary to hear the admiral at the bar of the house, and repeating the offer of the evidence of the lords. The opponents of the court were silenced; the bill passed, and received the royal assent at the end of the session.[1]

Three days later the warrant for

---

said that the quarrel between the two brothers was owing originally to a quarrel between their wives; but this again has been disputed by some modern historians, as depending only on the assertion of Sanders. It is, however, also mentioned by Fox, p. 96. I am indeed aware that the authority of Fox is not one jot better than that of Sanders; but, when two violent writers of opposite parties agree in the same statement, it may be presumed to have some foundation in truth. The king himself notices in his Journal (p. 4), that "the lord protector was much offended with his brother's marriage." He might also dread the influence of Seymour over the mind of the young Edward; for Somerset now held his office at the king's pleasure, who could on any day, at the admiral's persuasion, remove him from it.

[1] Lords' Journals, 345–347. Journals of Commons, 8. Stat. of Realm, iv. 61. It has been alleged, in proof of the protector's brotherly love for the admiral, "that, when the bill for the attainder was brought in, he desired for natural pity's sake to withdraw."—Tyt. i. 150. Burnet, iii. 205. Undoubtedly a sense of public decency might have drawn from him the expression of some such wish. But is there any evidence that he did withdraw? All the evidence is to the contrary. From the Journals it is certain that the bill of attainder was read on three consecutive days—the 25th, 26th, and 27th of February; that Somerset was present in his place on each of those days, and that on the 27th it was passed with the assent of *all* the lords (communi omnium procerum assensu).—Lords' Journal, i. 346. Somerset was in possession of the royal authority. He might, if he had pleased, have prevented the introduction, or arrested the progress of the bill. He might have proceeded according to law, and not by attainder, according to the worst precedents of the last reign. He might have suffered his brother to make his defence. He might have granted to him a pardon, or have commuted the punishment. Yet his brotherly love did not adopt any one of these expedients. If at a later period he complained that he had been made to believe the admiral's death necessary for his own safety, and lamented that they had not personally explained matters to each other, these were plainly after-thoughts in extenuation of conduct which he could not justify, and equivalent to a confession of consciousness

the execution of Seymour was signed by the council, and among the names appear those of Somerset and Cranmer, both of whom might, it was thought, have abstained from that ungracious office, the one on account of his relationship to the prisoner, the other because the canons prohibited to clergymen all participation in judgments of blood.[1] On the scaffold the unhappy man loudly proclaimed his innocence; nor will those who attentively peruse the thirty-three charges against him, and the depositions on which they were founded, be inclined to dispute his assertion. His enmity was not against the king but against his brother. His ambition prompted him to seek a share of that power which Somerset had arrogated to himself; his influence, his intrigues, his ascendancy over the mind of his nephew, might have been dangerous to the authority of the protector; but there is no sufficient evidence that he intended to carry off the king, or to raise a civil war within the kingdom. It was thought that, if his offence had been more clearly established, he might still have obtained pardon from the charity of a brother; and it was suspected that Sherington had been suborned to calumniate him, as the price of his own life; a suspicion which was almost converted into certainty, when that offender was not only pardoned, but restored to his former appointment, and found still to possess a considerable fortune.[2] Latimer, however, who seems to have believed in the infallibility of the council, undertook their defence. In a sermon preached before the king and a numerous audience, he severely condemned the temerity of those who presumed to judge of the conduct of men in power, without being acquainted with their motives; and justified the execution of Seymour, whom he declared to have led a sensual, dissolute, irreligious life, and to have died in a manner suitable to his life, "dangerously, irksomely, horribly;" whilst of Sherington he spoke in terms of approbation, and maintained that the fervency of his repentance entitled him to his pardon, and made him a fit example for the encouragement and imitation of sinners.[3] This tragedy has left a deep stain on the memory both of Somerset and of Latimer. Somerset sacrificed a brother to ward off the danger of a rival; Latimer prostituted his holy office to sanctify a deed of cruelty and injustice.

We may now return to the Scottish war. The defeat of the Scots had not subdued their antipathy to the projected marriage between Edward and Mary. To an unprejudiced mind, indeed, that marriage must have appeared to offer numerous and valuable benefits to the country; but in

---

that he had treated his brother cruelly and unnaturally.
[1] Burnet, ii. Rec. 164.
[2] In 1550 he bought back of the king the manors and lands which he had forfeited, for the sum of 12,860*l*. 2s. 2d. He had been already restored in blood, and had obtained his former office.—Strype, ii. 199.
[3] Latimer not only arraigned the life of the admiral, but also his death. According to the account in his sermon, as Seymour laid his head on the block, he told the servant of the lieutenant, to bid *his* servant speed the thing that he wot of. That servant was apprehended, and confessed that the admiral had by some means procured ink in the Tower, had used for a pen the aiglet of a point which he plucked from his hose, and had written two letters to the lady Mary and lady Elizabeth, which he sewed within the sole of a velvet shoe. The shoe was opened, and the letters were found. Their object was to excite the jealousy of the king's sisters against the protector as their great enemy. Hence the preacher, in full belief of this incredible story, concluded that God had clean forsaken him. "Whether," he adds, "he be saved or no, I leave it to God; but surely he was a wicked man, and the realm is well rid of him."—See Latimer's fourth sermon in the 1st edition. Later editors, ashamed of the passage, have thought proper to omit it. See also Godwin, 93; Strype, i. 120.

the opposite scale of the balance were to be weighed the hereditary hatred which divided the two nations: the idea that Scotland would become a province of that kingdom which had so often but so vainly laboured to subvert its independence; and the apprehension that the loss of the national independence would be followed by the loss of the national religion. Even among those who were not moved by these considerations, there were many who, with the earl of Huntley, condemned "the manner of the wooing." To seek the friendship of a nation by declaring war against it, to claim the affection of a woman by inflicting injuries on her friends and her possessions, were novel and doubtful experiments; and the protector soon learned that his brilliant victory at Pinkie had only accelerated the evil which it was his great object to avert. In an assembly of the Scottish lords at Stirling, it was resolved to implore the aid of France, their most ancient and faithful ally, to offer the young queen in marriage to the dauphin, and to propose that for greater security she should be educated in the French court. On the other hand, Somerset had published an address to the Scottish people in English and Latin, imputing the evils of the war to Arran and his advisers, who the last year had suppressed the favourable offers of the English government. To whom, he asked, would they marry their infant sovereign? To a foreign prince? Their country would become an appendage to a foreign crown. To a native? It would perpetuate the quarrel between England and Scotland. For eight hundred years no opportunity had risen like the present. A young king and a young queen might unite their crowns; Scotland would preserve her laws and liberties; and the two nations would live in peace and harmony under the common name of Britons.

But it was chiefly on the venality of the Scottish nobles that the protector relied for success. There were not many among them whose patriotism was proof against the gold of England. They secretly subscribed the articles which he offered; they bound themselves by oath to the service of King Edward; they delivered hostages as security for the faithful performance of their obligations.[1] Still, when the moment came, they hesitated to commit themselves; and when the lord Wharton and the earl of Lennox invaded the western marches, they successively turned against the invaders, and drove them with considerable loss across the borders. But on the eastern coast the lord Gray de Wilton, at the head of a powerful army, spread the flames of war to the gates of the capital: Dalkeith was reduced to ashes; and Haddington was taken, fortified, and garrisoned with more than two thousand men, partly English and partly Italians. Gray had scarcely begun his retreat, when a hostile squadron anchored at Leith, having on board three thousand German, and two thousand French veterans, commanded by d'Essé, a brave and experienced officer.[2] Reinforced by Arran and eight thousand Scots, d'Essé sat down before Haddington. Batteries were raised, a breach was made; but Sir John Wilford, the governor, defended himself with so much skill and obstinacy, and inflicted so many injuries on the assailants, that the Frenchman, doubtful of the result, which might have proved fatal to his fol-

---

[1] See proofs in Mr. Tytler's Hist. vi. 421; and Chron. Catal. 296.
[2] Henry II. used to say of him: Nous sommes quatre gentilshommes, qui combattrons en lice, et courrons la bague contre tous allans et venans de la France; moy, Sansac, d'Essé, et Chastaigneraye.—Brantome, vii. 203. La Haye, 1740.

lowers, refused to order an assault, and converted the siege into a blockade.[1]

About the same time the earl of Arran had convened the three estates of the kingdom in the abbey of Haddington. The determination of the lords at Stirling was solemnly ratified; treaties confirmatory of the marriage and alliance were exchanged between d'Oyselles, the French ambassador, and the Scottish governor; and de Brézé and Villegaignon, sailing with four galleys in a southern direction, unexpectedly changed their course, steered round the north of Scotland to Dumbarton, received on board the young queen and her household, and reached in safety the harbour of Brest. From Brest that princess, being in her sixth year, was conducted to St. Germain en Laye, and contracted to her destined husband, the dauphin of France. From this moment the original object of the war, the acquisition of Mary, to make her the wife of the English prince, was at an end. The French monarch, as the representative of his son and daughter, now king and queen of Scotland, required that the English government should abstain from all hostility against the Scots during the minority of the two princes.[2] Somerset returned a refusal; and, from the purport of his secret negotiations with the earl of Argyle and the lord Gray, appears to have still cherished the project of expelling the French auxiliaries and establishing the English authority in Scotland.[3]

The distress of the garrison at Haddington had been occasionally but scantily relieved by small parties from Berwick; and an attempt was made to throw a more copious supply into the town by Sir Thomas Palmer and Sir Robert Bowes, at the head of two thousand horse. By the address of the lord Home the convoy was surprised, and the escort taken or slain. To repair this disaster the earl of Shrewsbury crossed the borders with twenty-two thousand men, of whom three or four thousand were German lansquenets. But d'Essé, raising the blockade, intrenched himself at Musselburgh; the earl could not provoke him to a battle, and dared not attack him within his fortifications; and the army returned, after having supplied the garrison with men and provisions, burnt Dunbar, and ravaged the country.[4]

From this period the war continued with alternate losses and advantages to both parties; though, on the whole, the balance of success inclined in favour of Scotland. Haddington was evacuated: the allies recovered the fortresses of Home-castle and Fast-castle; they crossed the borders, burnt Ford and twenty villages, and penetrated almost to the walls of Newcastle; they even obtained, after an obstinate and bloody action, possession of the rock of Inchkeith, on which Cotterel had strongly intrenched himself.

D'Essé was recalled at his own solicitation or that of the Scots,[5] and left the command to Marshal de Termes, who had lately brought a reinforcement of thirteen hundred men. De Termes imitated the policy of his predecessor; and the English ascendancy gradually yielded, not so much to the power of its adversaries, as to the influence of a series of untoward events, which distracted the attention and exhausted the resources of the government.

---

[1] Leslie, 467. Hayward, 290.
[2] Leslie, 470. Ribier, ii. 152.
[3] See Fisher's instructions in Chron. Catal. 305. He gave a pension of 2,000 crowns to Argyle, and of 1,000 to Gray.

[4] Edward's Journal, 5, 6. Holinsh. 904.
[5] The English writers say the Scots were wearied with his vanity and insolence; Brantome, that he demanded his recall on account of his health.—Brant. vii. 211.

The depreciation of the currency during the late reign had been followed by its necessary consequence, a proportionate advance in the price of saleable commodities. The value of land rose with the value of its produce; and the rents of farms had been doubled, in many instances tripled, in the course of a few years. To the working classes this alteration would have made little difference, had their wages been raised in the same ratio. But it so happened that the demand for labour had been lessened; and the price of labour sunk with the demand. Experience had proved to the agriculturist that the growth of wool was more profitable than that of corn; whence tillage was discouraged, that a larger portion of land might be brought into pasturage; and in most counties thousands of labourers were excluded from their accustomed employments. But if scarcity of work generated distress, that distress was augmented by the interested though obvious policy of the landlords. In former times, particularly on the estates of the monks and clergy, considerable portions of land had been allotted for the common use of the labourers and of the poor inhabitants. But the present proprietors had, by repeated inclosures, added many portions of the wastes and commons to the former extent of their farms, and thus had cut off or narrowed one great source of support to the more indigent classes;[1] and in addition frequently let their lands at an advanced rent to "leasemongers" or middle-men, who on their part oppressed the farmer and cottager, that they might indemnify and benefit themselves.[2]

Men, under the pressure of distress, are always prepared to arraign the conduct of their governors. The discontented, though unable to comprehend the arguments of controversialists, felt their own misery; they saw that the new proprietors of the church lands paid not the same attention as the old to the wants of the poor; they coupled their own sufferings with the innovations in religion; and complained of that system which had diminished their resources, and now compelled them to practise a worship foreign from their habits and feelings.[3] The day approached when the use of the old liturgy was to cease, and that of the new to begin; instead of the high mass, its music and its ceremonies, with which they had been familiarized from their infancy, they were to hear what they deemed an inanimate service, a "mere Christmas play;"[4] and, as if this additional provocation had goaded them to madness, the common people rose, almost at the same time, in the counties of Wilts, Sussex, Surrey, Hants, Berks, Kent, Gloucester, Somerset, Suffolk, Warwick, Essex, Hertford, Leicester, Worcester, and Rutland. In the first of these counties, Sir William Herbert put himself at the head of a body of

---

[1] In a proclamation issued the preceding year, the king is made to complain that many villages, in which one hundred or two hundred people had lived, were entirely destroyed; that one shepherd now dwelt where industrious families dwelt before; and that the realm is wasted by "bringing arable grounds into pasture, and letting houses, whole families, and copyholds to fall down, decay, and be waste." And Hales, the commissioner, in his charge repeats these complaints, observing, that the laws which forbade any man to keep more than 2,000 sheep, and commanded the owners of church lands to keep household on the same, and to occupy as much of the demesne lands in tillage as had been occupied twenty years before, were disobeyed; whence he asserts, that the number of the king's subjects had been wonderfully diminished; as appeared by the new books of musters compared with the old, and with the Chronicles.—Strype, ii. 92, 94.

[2] Strype, ii. 141.   [3] Godwin, 93.

[4] Fox, ii. 15.

troops, dispersed the insurgents, and executed martial law on the most guilty. In the others tranquillity was restored by the exertions of the resident gentry, and the persuasions of the most moderate among the yeomanry.[1] It proved, however, a deceitful calm, the forerunner of a more dangerous storm. The protector had been alarmed. Without the concurrence of the council, he appointed commissioners to inquire into the grievances of the people, to remove the new inclosures, and to restore the ancient commons. The very intelligence revived the hopes of the discontented; they assembled again in numerous bodies, and proceeded to do themselves justice without the aid of the commissioners. In general, however, as they acted without concert and without leaders, the effervescence subsided of itself; but in the counties of Oxford, of Norfolk, and of Cornwall and Devon, the risings assumed a more dangerous shape; armies were formed which threatened defiance to the government; and, if the insurrections were finally suppressed, it was only with the aid of the foreign troops, the bands of adventurers that had been raised in Italy, Spain, and Germany, to serve in the war against Scotland.

The command in Oxfordshire and Buckinghamshire was given to the lord Grey, with a body of fifteen hundred regular troops, including Spinola with his Italians. As soon as he had been joined by the gentlemen of the county, he marched against the insurgents, of whom one part fled at his approach, the other was broken at the first charge. Two hundred were made prisoners in the pursuit, and twelve of the ringleaders were delivered to the general, by whose order they expiated their offence on the gallows.[2]

In Devonshire the new liturgy had been read for the first time in the church of Samford Courtenay on Whit Sunday; the next day the parishioners compelled the clergyman to resume the ancient service. This contravention of the law was the signal of a general insurrection. Humphrey Arundel, the governor of St. Michael's Mount, put himself at its head, and in a few days numbered under his standard ten thousand men.

To oppose the insurgents the lord Russell, lord privy seal, was furnished with a small body of troops, and with three preachers, Gregory, Reynolds, and Coverdale, who received a license from the king to declare the word of God to the people in such public places as the general should appoint.[3] But Russell, distrusting the inferiority of his force, and the eloquence of his preachers, resolved to imitate the policy of the duke of Norfolk in the late reign. He offered to negotiate; and the insurgents made fifteen demands, which were afterwards reduced to eight, requiring the restoration of the ancient service, the re-enactment of the statute of the Six Articles, the introduction of Cardinal Pole into the council,[4] and the re-establishment of two abbeys at least in every county. To the first Cranmer composed a long and elaborate reply; the second was answered by a proclamation in the king's name, refusing every article in a tone of contempt and superiority.[5] But

---

[1] Edward's Journal, 6. [2] Ibid. 7.
[3] See the commission in Strype, ii. 168. Parker, afterwards archbishop of Canterbury, was another preacher for the same purpose. He harangued the Norfolk insurgents, and narrowly escaped with his life.
[4] Evidently on account of the high rank and extensive influence which his family had possessed in the county.
[5] The king's proclamation may be seen in Fox (ii. 15, 16); the reply of the archbishop has been published by Strype (Life of Cranmer, App. p. 86). In the eighth article the Cornish men "refused the English service,

Arundel, while he treated, continued his operations, and sat down before Exeter. Without cannon to make a breach, he instructed his followers to set fire to one of the gates; but the inhabitants threw additional fuel into the flames, and, while it burnt, erected a new rampart within. A second attempt to sap the wall was defeated by the vigilance of the besieged, who discovered the mine, and filled it with water. The assailants, however, were not dismayed; by watching the gates they prevented the introduction of provisions; and during a fortnight the inhabitants suffered all the privations of famine.

In the mean time the council, instead of supplying Russell with troops, had sent him nothing but proclamations. By one a free pardon was granted to all who would submit; by a second, the lands, goods, and chattels of the insurgents were given to any man who could obtain possession; a third ordered the punishment of death to be inflicted by martial law on such persons as attempted to collect any riotous or unlawful assembly; and a fourth urged the commissioners to put down illegal inclosures, and was accompanied with a private admonition that it was time for them to look to themselves, and to reform their own conduct. At length, on the fortieth day, Lord Grey arrived with a reinforcement of German horse and Italian arquebusiers; the insurgents were immediately driven from the city with the loss of nine hundred men; an attempt to rally on Clifton Down was followed by a more sanguinary defeat; and a third and last effort to oppose the royal forces at Bridgewater completed their downfal. During the insurrection four thousand men are said to have perished in the field or by the hand of the executioner.[1]

In Norfolk the first rising was at Aldborough. It appeared in its origin too contemptible to deserve notice; but it formed the nucleus round which the discontented of the neighbouring parishes successively arranged themselves; and as soon as they amounted to a formidable number, Ket, by trade a tanner, but the lord of three manors in the county, proclaimed himself their leader. He planted his standard on the summit of Moushold Hill, near Norwich, erected for himself a throne under a spreading oak, which he called the Oak of Reformation, and established courts of Chancery, King's Bench, and Common Pleas, in imitation of the courts in Westminster Hall. In his proclamations he complained that the commons were ground to the dust by the oppression of the rich; and that a new service had been forced on the people in opposition to the conviction of their consciences; and declared, that if he and his associates had taken up arms, it was for the sole purpose of placing trusty and noble

---

because certain of them understood no English." The archbishop replied, that neither did they understand Latin: an evasive answer, for in his remarks on their third request, he had assigned their ignorance of the Latin tongue as a reason why they should not have the mass in Latin.

[1] Edward's Journal, 7. Fox, 15—17. Holinshed, 1002. Hayward, 295. Strype, ii. 170. Rec. 103—107. During these disturbances, martial law was executed in every part of the kingdom; and often, as we are told, with little attention to justice. Sir Anthony Kyngstone, provost of the western army, distinguished himself by the promptitude of his decisions, and the pleasantry with which he accompanied them. Having dined with the mayor of Bodmin, he asked him if the gallows were sufficiently strong. The mayor replied that he thought so. "Then," said Kyngstone, "go up and try;" and hanged him without further ceremony. On another occasion, having received information against a miller, he proceeded to the mill, and, not finding the master at home, ordered his servant to the gallows, bidding him be content, for it was the best service which he had ever rendered to his master.—Speed, 1113. Hayward, 295.

counsellors round the king during his minority, and of removing those "who confounded things sacred and profane, and regarded nothing but the enriching of themselves with the public treasure, that they might riot in it during the public calamity."[1] Obeyed by twenty thousand men, he treated the offer of a pardon with scorn; and when the marquess of Northampton had entered Norwich with one thousand English horse, and a body of Italians under Malatesta, he attacked the city, set one part of it on fire, killed the lord Sheffield and one hundred men, and compelled the marquess and his followers to retire out of the county. The council was alarmed and embarrassed; troops were recalled from the army in Scotland; the gentlemen of the neighbouring counties were ordered by proclamation to join the royal forces; and the command was given first to the protector, and afterwards to the earl of Warwick. That nobleman, with eight thousand men, of whom two thousand were German horse, forced his way into Norwich, yet so incessant were the insurgents in their attacks, so lavish were they of life, that they often drove the gunners from the batteries, burst open the gates, and fought with the royalists in the streets. The earl commanded his followers to swear on their swords that they would never abandon the place; and by his perseverance was at last enabled to attain his object of removing the enemy from their advantageous position. Compelled by want of provisions, Ket descended from the hill; in Dussingdale he was overtaken by the royal army, his followers were broken by the charge of a large body of regular cavalry, and about two thousand men perished in the action and the pursuit. The remainder, however, surrounded themselves with a rampart of waggons, and a trench fortified with stakes; and to an offer of pardon replied, that they knew the fate which awaited them, and that it was better to perish by the sword than by the halter. The earl, still apprehensive of the result, spoke to them himself; at his solicitation they accepted a general pardon; and the severity of the law was confined to the execution of Ket on Norwich Castle, of his brother on the steeple of Windham, and of nine others on the nine branches of the Oak of Reformation.[2] It is to these events that we owe the institution of the lords lieutenants of counties, who were now appointed to inquire of treason, misprision of treason, insurrections and riots, with authority to levy men, and lead them against the enemies of the king.[3]

So many insurrections succeeding and strengthening each other had shaken the power of the protector: his fall was accelerated by the hostile determination of the king of France. From the moment that Mary of Scotland had reached St. Germains, Somerset had proposed to make peace with the Scots, to surrender Boulogne to the French monarch for a sum of money, and to unite with him in the support of the Protestant interest in Germany against the overwhelming

---

[1] Heylin, 77. Godwin, 93.
[2] Edward's Journal, 7, 8. Strype, ii. Rec. 107. Fox, 17. Godwin, 94. Holinshed, 1035, 1039. Hayward, 299.
[3] Strype, ii. 178. At this time (July 2nd) the king by proclamation fixed the prices of cattle. I shall extract a few instances.

	From July to November.	November to Christmas.	Christmas to Shrovetide.
A fat ox of largest bone	£2 5 0	£2 6 8	£2 8 4
A steer or runt, ditto	1 5 0	1 6 8	1 8 4
A heifer, ditto	1 2 0	1 3 0	

A fat sheep, large of bone, 4s. till Michaelmas, afterwards 4s. 4d.—See Strype, ii. 151.

superiority of the emperor. But he yielded against his own conviction to the majority of the council, who pronounced the surrender of Boulogne a measure calculated to cover the king's government with disgrace. Let them rather intrust that fortress to the protection of the emperor, and offer the crown of Scotland to the ambition of Arran; France would then cease to threaten England with war, and Edward might have leisure to improve his resources, and to provide against future contingencies.[1] But the emperor refused to act against the faith of his treaty with Henry; and that prince, encouraged by the insurrections in England, sent to Edward a declaration of war. Immediately the French troops poured into the Boulognnois. Sellacques was taken by storm; Ambleteuse surrendered after a siege of some days; the garrison of Blackness capitulated at the first summons; and Montalambert was evacuated before the arrival of the enemy.[2] Boulogne, indeed, defied the efforts of the French, who were deterred by the approach of winter from forming a regular siege; but there was little doubt that at the return of spring it would fall, unless a numerous army could be collected for its relief. All these disasters were attributed to the misconduct of the protector, whose reign was now rapidly drawing to an end.[3]

1. That nobleman had sealed his own doom on the day on which he signed the warrant for the execution of his brother; a warrant that disclosed to his colleagues in the council the fate which they might expect from his vengeance, if they should afterwards incur the suspicion of being his enemies. The natural consequence was, that they began to commune with each other, and to forecast the most likely means of eschewing the danger. Somerset, on the other hand, grew every day more positive and despotic; he would not allow his pleasure or opinion to be called in question: if any man in the council ventured to hint doubt or disapprobation, he was either heard with silent scorn, or was silenced at once with the most passionate expressions. The impolicy of such conduct was represented to the protector by his friend Sir William Paget, in an expostulatory letter. "Howsoever," he writes, "it cometh to pass, I cannot tell; but of late your grace is grown in great choleric fashions, whensoever you are contraried in that which you have conceived in your head......A subject in great authority, as your grace is, using such fashion, is like to fall into great danger and peril of his own person, besides that to the commonwealth."[4] It is unnecessary to add, that this prophetic warning was treated with contempt.

2. His conduct in another respect, as it was more open to the public, was universally condemned. His very friends could offer no apology for his rapacity. Of a simple knight with a slender fortune, he had become by grants from the crown, some indeed under the late king, but most since his elevation to the protectorship, and therefore of his own dictation, the possessor of more than two hundred manors, parcels of land, and hereditaments, situate in different parts of the kingdom, but principally in the counties of Wilts and Devon.[1]

---

[1] Burnet, ii. 130, 131.
[2] See the particulars of the campaign in the memoirs of Vieilleville, xxix. 190—202; and the Lettres et Mémoires d'estat de Ribier, ii. 217, 240, 241, 245.
[3] Godwin, 95. Nothing was more felt than the want of money. It was calculated that the insurrections had cost the king 28,000l. All the war-charges of the year, including fortifications, amounted to 1,356,000l.—Strype, ii 178.
[4] Letter of 8th of May, 1549, in Strype, ii. Rec. i. 108.
[5] See grants to him 1mo Edwardi, in

On the other hand, that magnificent pile of building, which still retains from him the name of Somerset House, was a standing memorial of his vanity and extravagance. It was said that, to procure a convenient site for this structure, he had demolished the parish church of St. Mary's, and compelled the bishops of Worcester, Lichfield, and Llandaff, to convey to him the episcopal mansions belonging to their respective sees; that to furnish materials he had pulled down several chapels and religious edifices; and that, at a time when the kingdom, through the poverty of the exchequer, was left almost without a soldier for its defence, he could afford to spend the daily sum of one hundred pounds in unnecessary buildings. This insatiate accumulation of wealth, joined with so much vanity, and the recklessness with which he sought to gratify it, could not fail to detract from the popularity which he had previously enjoyed.

3. But that which gave the rudest shock to his power was his wavering and doubtful policy during the late commotions. By his proclamations and commissions for the putting down of inclosures he had appeared to give the sanction of his authority to the demands of the commons: when they were actually in arms against the royal authority, he had always lent an indulgent ear to their petitions; and after their defeat he had repeatedly sought to screen them from the vengeance of the conquerors. By this he had earned for himself among them the title of "the good duke," but had awakened a spirit of jealousy and mistrust among the landholders and all those who had reason to fear for their possessions from the turbulent and disaffected temper of the commons. The conduct of the earl of Warwick had been the very reverse. His policy was to suppress by force and intimidation; and the vigour with which he had acted against the insurgents of Norfolk, with the severe punishment which he had inflicted on their leaders, had made him the idol of the higher classes, who began to look up to him for the preservation of their rights and properties. He was now on his return from Norfolk, crowned with the laurels of victory, and welcomed with the acclamations of his admirers. In the neighbourhood of London several lords and councillors joined him with their retainers in arms and new liveries, and the whole cavalcade proceeded in martial array through the city to his house at Ely Place. The protector, who, with the archbishop, Paget, and Petro and Smith, the two secretaries, was in attendance on the king at Hampton Court, taking this hostile display for a declaration of war, called by proclamation in the king's name on all faithful subjects to repair to Hampton Court in defensible array, for the protection of the royal person against a most dangerous conspiracy; while his opponents, by circular letters published on the same day, forbade obedience to his orders, and accused him of having neglected to pay the forces, or to provision the king's fortresses; of spending the public money in extravagant erections; of fomenting divisions between the higher and the lower classes in the nation; of seeking the destruction of the nobility, and of intending ultimately to substitute himself in the place of the young sovereign.[1]

Strype, ii. 308; also the Inspeximus by Queen Elizabeth, June 2, 1572, of grants made to him by Edward. The names of more than two hundred manors and parcels of land in the counties of Wilts and Devon, and of twenty more in other shires, are recited in the schedule of the lands restored to him after his submission in 1550.

[1] Mr. Tytler, with his usual industry, has discovered several of these proclamations

For some days the war was carried on between the two parties with proclamations, placards, handbills, and demands of military aid from the city; but the advantage was plainly on the part of Warwick, who not only received from the lord mayor and aldermen promises of co-operation, but, to the surprise and dismay of his opponents, gained by threats or promises possession of the Tower. The duke by his summons had drawn multitudes of the common people into the neighbourhood of Hampton Court. One day, holding Edward by the hand, he addressed them from the gate of the base-court, in a long speech, in which he praised their loyalty, and inveighed against the treasonous designs of Warwick and Warwick's adherents. But a few hours later, in the dead of the night, with five hundred armed men, he conveyed the young king from Hampton Court to Windsor Castle, the custody of which he intrusted to his own retainers.

On the preceding day he had sent Sir William Petre to Ely Place with certain proposals. Petre (whether willingly or by compulsion is unknown) remained with his colleagues, who sent back an answer, requiring the protector to submit unconditionally, and "to be content to be ordered according to justice and reason;" words of ominous import, especially to one who could not forget in what manner he had not long ago *ordered* his own brother in almost similar circumstances.[1]

At Windsor he found little to give him confidence. Scarcely a gentleman had obeyed the summons to meet him there. The commons, indeed, in Hampshire and Wiltshire had begun to rise, and their demagogues talked of marching to the aid of the good duke: but all such projects were suddenly checked by the arrival at Wilton and Andover of the Lord Russell and Sir William Herbert with part of the army which had been doing execution on the insurgents in Devonshire. These leaders made no secret of their adhesion to the council in London, and from that moment the cause of the protector became desperate. That he might disarm the hostility of Warwick, he wrote to that nobleman, reminding him of their friendship from the time of their youth; and, to provide for his own safety, he protested before the king that he had no design to injure his opponents, but was willing to submit the quarrel between him and them to four arbitrators, two to be chosen by each party. This offer was communicated to the lords in a letter from the king, who required them " to bring these uproars to a quiet," and put them in mind that, whatever offences the protector might have committed, it was still in the power of the sovereign to grant him a pardon. Cranmer, Paget, and Smith wrote to them at the same time, recommending forbearance, and stating that if, as was reported, they sought the life of the duke, it was but reasonable that, before he resigned his office, he should know on what conditions that resignation was expected.[2] But Warwick and his friends, in the pride of victory, would listen to no

---

and hand-bills in the State Paper Office. See them in his Edward and Mary I., p. 205—211.

[1] See this letter in Ellis, 2nd series, i. p. 166. The date, the 7th of October, is of importance, as it shows that Somerset had begun to despond, and the council had assumed a decided superiority, before either the one or the other could have received the letters from Lord Russell and Sir William Herbert to which those events have been attributed. The letter from the council was written on the 7th, their letters from Andover and Wilton on the 8th and 9th of October.

[2] Stowe, 598. Burnet, iv. 298. Tytler, i. 223.

compromise. In a proclamation, consisting of eight articles, and signed by every councillor at Ely Place, they publicly charged the duke with divers high crimes and misdemeanors, and through the influence of the lord mayor and sheriffs obtained from the citizens an aid of five hundred armed men. In answer to the proposals from Hampton Court they insisted on an unconditional surrender.[1] In their reply to Edward they accused the protector of arbitrary and tyrannical abuse of his authority; and in their letter to Cranmer, Paget, and Smith, they forewarned these councillors of the peril to which they had already exposed themselves by delivering the king into the hands of armed men, not his sworn servants; it is moreover said, but on the credit of a very questionable document, that Sir Philip Hoby, the bearer of their letters, made to the duke, on their part, the most flattering promises for the express purpose of deceiving him, and inducing him to submit.[2] However that may be, the archbishop and Paget deemed it their interest to transfer their services to the more powerful party, and with much labour prevailed on Somerset and his friends to disarm their followers, to restore the custody of the king with that of the castle to the royal guards, and to place themselves without reserve at the mercy of their adversaries.[3] The next day, in consequence of a hint from Paget, Sir Anthony Wingfield, the vice-chamberlain, arrived with a numerous escort to secure the person of the duke. Warwick and his friends followed, and were received by Edward with demonstrations of pleasure, which showed that he was not unwilling to be emancipated from the control of his uncle. The Sunday passed; and on Monday morning the protector was deprived of his office in due form by a writ under the great seal, and with the sign manual of the king. He was then subjected to a searching examination before the council, and committed a prisoner to the care of the earls of Huntingdon and Southampton, who with a body of three hundred horse conducted him to the metropolis. The civic authorities had already been summoned to keep watch in every ward; and Somerset, riding between the two earls, proceeded slowly through Holborn to his prison in the Tower. Five of his confidential advisers were incarcerated with him.[4]

The confinement of Somerset filled the reformers with the most gloomy apprehensions. It was not improbable that the policy or the resentment of Warwick might induce him to send their patron to the scaffold, and to restore the ascendancy of the ancient faith. But, whatever might be his real feelings, the earl deemed it more prudent to confirm his control over the mind, by indulging the wishes of the young king, his repugnance to shed the blood of a second uncle, and his prejudices against the doctrine and the worship of his fathers. Parliament had been prorogued to the beginning of November. When it assembled, Warwick seldom attended in his place, and affected to leave the members to the unbiassed exercise of their own judgment. Their first care was to prevent the return of the dis-

---

[1] Burnet, iv. 299, 300. Ellis, 2nd series, ii. 175.

[2] See it in Tytler, i. 238. My suspicion is, that this story respecting the deception attributed to Hoby was invented afterwards by the friends of Somerset, to extenuate the pusillanimity of his submission. Nor am I able to discover the menacing allusion to the *verbal* message on which Mr. Tytler insists, p. 236.

[3] See the letter in Ellis (2nd series, ii. 171), misdescribed as an offer of terms of accommodation. It contains no such offer, but states with great satisfaction that "all things are well acquieted" by the submission of Somerset and his party.

[4] Stowe, 600.

graceful and dangerous occurrences of the last year; and a bill was passed, making it felony for any persons to assemble to the number of twelve or more for the purpose of abating the rents of farms or the price of provisions, or of destroying houses or parks, or of asserting a right to ways or commons, if they continued together one hour after they had been warned to disperse by proclamation from a magistrate, sheriff, or bailiff; and raising the offence to high treason, when the object of the meeting should be to alter the laws, or to kill or to imprison any member of the king's council.[1] At Christmas, to extinguish the hopes of those who still adhered to the ancient faith, a circular letter was sent to the clergy, informing them of the king's intention to proceed with the reformation; and commanding them to deliver up all books containing any portion of the former service, that they might be burnt or destroyed. But this proclamation did not satisfy the expectations of the more zealous among the reformers, and an act was soon afterwards passed, subjecting every individual, either clerk or layman, who should keep in his possession any such book, to a fine for the first and second offence, and to imprisonment during the king's pleasure for the third.[2] Moreover, as the church of England now possessed a new order of common prayer and administration of the sacraments, it was deemed proper that its ministers should be ordained after a new form; and it was enacted, that six prelates and six other persons learned in God's law should be appointed by the king to compose a manner of making and consecrating archbishops, bishops, priests, and deacons; and that such manner, being set forth under the great seal before the first of April, should afterwards be lawfully used and exercised, and none other.[3] In the upper house some of the prelates drew a frightful picture of the national morals, and attributed the universal prevalence of vice to the manner in which the exercise of their jurisdiction had been suspended or enervated by successive acts of parliament and proclamations of the council. At their common solicitation leave was given to introduce a bill which should restore to the episcopal courts a portion of their former authority. But its provisions were deemed to trench both on the powers now exercised by the crown, and on the liberties of the subject; the earl of Warwick attended in his place to oppose it, and on the first reading it was rejected without a division.

In the mean time the council was repeatedly occupied with the fate of the noble prisoner in the Tower. The articles prepared against him might be divided into three classes, charging him with obstinacy, incapacity, and bad faith during the late insurrection, with negligence in permitting the fortresses near Boulogne to fall into the hands of the French, and with presumption in rejecting the advice of the council, though he had been raised to the protectorship on the express condition that he should never act without its assent.[4] At length an intimation was given to him, that if he hoped for pardon, he must submit to a frank and unqualified acknowledgment of his guilt.

---

[1] Stat. of Realm, iv. 104.
[2] Stat. of Realm, iv. 110. The earl of Derby, the bishops of Durham, Carlisle, Lichfield and Coventry, Worcester, Chichester, and Westminster, and the lords Morley, Stourton, Windsor, and Wharton, voted against it.—Journals, 384.
[3] Ibid. 112. It was opposed by the bishops of Durham, Carlisle, Worcester, Chichester, and Westminster.—Journals, 384.
[4] That the last charge was so far true, may be presumed from the letters of advice previously written by Paget to Somerset, on May 8 and July 7.—Apud Strype, ii. Rec. 107—114.

The condition, though painful to his feelings, was gratefully accepted. On his knees he confessed his presumption, negligence, and incapacity, subscribed the twenty-nine charges against him, and earnestly implored for mercy. Life was promised; but on condition that he should forfeit all his offices, his goods and chattels, and a portion of his lands to the yearly value of two thousand pounds. When, however, a bill of pains and penalties was introduced for this purpose, some of the peers ventured to make an objection, which no man would have dared to suggest during the last reign. They observed that by their precipitancy in such cases precedents might be established the most dangerous to the life and liberties of the subject; that before the house could ground any proceedings on the confession of Somerset, it was its duty to ascertain the motives which had induced him to sign it; and that a deputation ought to be appointed with power to interrogate him in the Tower. To this the ministers assented; the deputation on its return reported that he had made the confession of his own free will, and to exonerate his conscience; and the bill, having passed through both houses without further opposition, received the royal assent. Somerset, however, had the courage to remonstrate against the severity of his punishment; and, in order to extenuate his offences, appealed to the testimony of his conscience and the uprightness of his intentions. But the council replied with harshness and warmth; the reprimand humbled him to the dust; and he signed a second and still more abject submission, in which he disclaimed all idea of justifying his conduct, threw himself without reserve on the mercy of his sovereign, and expressed his gratitude to the king and the council, that they had been content to take his property, when they might justly have taken his life. Having given security for the payment of a heavy fine, he was discharged from the Tower, and received a pardon drawn in the most ample form that legal ingenuity could devise, but with the exception of his debts to the king.[1] His friends, who had been imprisoned with him, recovered their liberty on similar conditions; and as if it had been resolved to execute justice with the strictest impartiality, the earl of Arundel and Sir Richard Southwell, who had been among the most active of his opponents, were severally mulcted for different offences, the first in the sum of twelve thousand, the other in that of five hundred pounds. This revolution was concluded as usual by rewards to the principal actors in it. The earl of Warwick obtained the offices of great master and lord high admiral, the marquess of Northampton that of great chamberlain, and the lords Russell and St. John, created earls of Bedford and Wiltshire, were appointed lord privy seal and lord treasurer. At the same time the earls of Arundel and Southampton, the supposed confidants of Warwick, were removed from the council: the former suffered a short confinement in his own house; the latter, after a lingering illness, died before the end of summer.[2]

While Warwick and his friends were thus employed in humbling the power of Somerset, they were harassed with apprehensions of the French war; and, notwithstanding the blame which they had thrown on the late protector, were compelled to adopt his measures, and to submit to the surrender of Boulogne. The French had interrupted the communication be-

---

[1] Lords' Journals, 374, 375. Rym. xv. 205.

[2] Stowe, 603. Rym. xv. 194, 203, 209. Strype, ii. 195.

tween that city and Calais; nor was the earl of Huntingdon able to reopen it, though he had taken with him all the bands of mercenaries, and three thousand English veterans. The treasury was exhausted:[1] the garrison suffered from want of provisions; and the enemy eagerly expected the return of spring to commence more active operations. A proposal was again made to the emperor to take Boulogne into his custody; this was followed by an offer to cede it to him in full sovereignty, on condition that it should never be restored to the crown of France. Both were refused; and, as a last resource, Antonio Guidotti, a merchant of Florence, was employed to hint to the French ministers that the English cabinet was not adverse to a peace.[2] With the aid of this unaccredited agent a secret understanding was established; ambassadors were then named; and the conferences were opened. But the French, sensible of their superiority, dictated the conditions. To the proposal, that, as an equivalent for the surrender of Boulogne, Mary of Scotland should be contracted to Edward, they answered that Henry had already determined to marry her to his own son, the dauphin; and when it was demanded that at least the perpetual pension from France should be confirmed, and the arrears discharged, they indignantly replied, that their king would never condescend to pay tribute to a foreign crown; that Henry VIII. had availed himself of the accidental necessities of Francis to extort a pension from him; and that they with equal right would avail themselves of the present distress of the king of England to make him renounce it.[3] The English ambassadors assumed a tone equally haughty and repulsive; they even threatened to terminate the discussions; but their actions did not correspond with their words; each day they receded from some or other of their demands; and at length they subscribed to the terms imposed by their adversaries.

The treaty was prefaced by a long and fulsome panegyric of the two kings; Henry and Edward were the best of princes, the two great luminaries of the Christian world; personally they had no causes of enmity against each other; and if their fathers had been divided, the relics of that hostility they were determined to suppress for ever. With this view they had agreed, 1. That there should be between the two crowns a peace, league, and union, which should last not only for their lives, but as long as time should endure; 2. That Boulogne should be restored to the king of France, with the ordnance and stores which were found in it at the time of its capture; that in return for the moneys already spent on the fortifications, Henry should pay to Edward two hundred thousand crowns at the time of its delivery, and two hundred thousand more within five months; on condition that

---

[1] From the report of the senator Barbaro to the senate of Venice (communicated by H. Howard, of Corby, esq.), it appears that the king's income greatly exceeded his ordinary expenditure in time of peace, the former being about 350,000*l*., and the latter about 225,000*l*. But the war in Scotland for three years had plunged him deeply in debt; and we find him constantly sending messengers to Antwerp to borrow money for short periods at high rates of interest.—See Strype, ii. 300, 312, 313, 323.

[2] The English writers attribute the first employment of Guidotti to the French ministry, the French to the English. "Les Anglois, lassez de la guerre, &c., m'ayant fait recherchez d'envoyer mes deputiz."—Henry, apud Ribeir, ii. 287. It is probable that it was so, for in reward of his services Guidotti obtained from Edward a pension for life of 250*l*. per annum for himself, and of 35*l*. 10s. for his son.—Rym. xv. 227. He was also knighted, and received a douceur of 250*l*.—King Edward's Journal, 11.

[3] See the letter of Paget, apud Strype, ii. Rec. p. 114.

the English should previously surrender Dunglass and Lander to the queen of Scots, or, if Dunglass and Lauder were not in their possession, should raze to the ground the fortresses of Roxburgh and Eyemouth; 3. That Scotland should be comprehended in this treaty, if the queen signified her acceptance of it within forty days; and that Edward should not hereafter make war upon her or her subjects, unless some new cause of offence was given; and lastly, that all the rights, claims, and pretensions of England against France and Scotland, or of France and Scotland against England, should be mutually reserved.[1] Though Warwick had signed the instructions to the ambassadors, he absented himself under pretence of sickness from the council on the day on which the treaty was confirmed. By the public the conditions were considered a national disgrace. The sum of two millions of crowns, which Francis had consented to give for the surrender of Boulogne at the expiration of eight years, had been cut down to one-fifth; the right of enforcing the treaty of marriage between Edward and Mary of Scotland had been abandoned; and the perpetual pension, which Henry VIII. had accepted in lieu of his claim to the crown of France, had been virtually surrendered. In fact, the pretensions of the former kings of England were after this treaty suffered to sleep in silence by their successors. They contented themselves with the sole title of kings of France, a barren but invidious distinction, which, after two centuries and a half, was wisely laid aside by the grandfather of her present majesty.

Though the partisans of the new doctrines could depend with confidence on the support of the crown, the late commotions had proved to them that the reformation still rested on a very insecure foundation. Eleven-twelfths of the nation retained a strong attachment to the creed of their fathers;[2] the order for the introduction of the new liturgy had been reluctantly and negligently obeyed; the clergy, for the most part hostile to the cause, sought only to evade the penalties threatened by the statute; and the nobility and gentry were believed to dissemble their real sentiments, that they might earn the favour, or escape the displeasure, of the court. In these circumstances the archbishop proposed to purge the church of those prelates whose disaffection was the most notorious; and to supply their places with men of approved zeal and orthodox principles. The first on whom the experiment was hazarded was Bonner, bishop of London, whose apathy had long been the subject of complaint, but whose caution had preserved him from any open violation of the law. He was summoned before the council, received a severe reprimand, and was ordered to perform the new service at St. Paul's on every festival on which he and his predecessors had been accustomed to celebrate the high mass; to proceed in his court against all reputed adulterers, and such persons as absented themselves from the English liturgy, or refused to communicate according to the parliamentary form; and that he should preach at St. Paul's Cross on the first of September, and afterwards once every three months, and should be present at every other sermon which

---

[1] Rym. xv. 211, 217. The queen regent of Scotland signified her assent in due form.—Chron. Cat. 327.

[2] This is acknowledged in a confidential letter from Paget to the protector, written July 7, 1549. "The use of the old religion is forbidden by a law, and the use of the new is not yet printed in the stomachs of eleven or [of] twelve parts of the realm, what countenance soever men make outwardly to please them in whom they see the power resteth."—Apud Strype, ii. Rec. 110.

should be made there. The subject for his first discourse was given to him in writing, and divided into three parts. He was to show, 1. That "the rebels in Devonshire, Cornwall, and Norfolk, did not only deserve death as traitors, but accumulated to themselves eternal damnation, even to be in the burning fire of hell, with Lucifer, the father and first author of rebellion;" 2. That in religion, God regards the internal disposition of the heart; that the regulation of the external service belongs to the supreme magistrate; that to disobey him is to disobey the command of God; and that of course to assist at the mass, which had been prohibited by royal authority, was not to please, but to offend the Almighty; and 3. That the right and power of the king in his tender years was not less than it had been in his predecessors, or would be in himself at a more advanced age.

At the appointed day crowds assembled to hear the prelate; many from curiosity, some for the purpose of censure. In his sermon, Bonner, whether it was from accident or design, omitted the last part; the omission was observed, and denounced to the council by Latimer and Hooper, two reformed preachers; and Cranmer and Ridley, with Petre and Smith, the king's secretaries, and May, dean of St. Paul's, were appointed to try and punish the refractory prelate. Bonner appeared before his judges, with the undaunted air of a man who feels conscious that he suffers in a just cause. He had, he told them, "three things,—a few goods, a poor carcass, and a soul; the two first were at their disposal, but the last was at his own." He objected to his accusers that they were notorious heretics; excepted against Smith as his known enemy; and, in a tone of pity and contempt, twitted the archbishop with his subserviency to men in power, and the inconstancy of his religious sentiments. Being compelled to answer upon oath the questions which were put to him, he acknowledged the omission, but attributed it to the imperfection of his memory, the loss of his notes, and the interruption caused by an unexpected order which he received, to announce from the pulpit a victory gained over the insurgents. He contended, however, that he had compensated for this involuntary error by the eagerness with which he had declaimed against the rebels; and avowed his conviction that his real crime, though carefully kept out of sight, consisted in the freedom with which he had explained the Catholic and established doctrine respecting the sacrament of the altar. It was in vain that he protested against the authority of the court, or that he appealed from it to the equity of the king. The archbishop pronounced the sentence of deprivation; and Bonner was remanded to the Marshalsea, where he remained a prisoner till the king's death.[1] To most men the sentence appeared an act of unwarrantable severity; his subsequent confinement, before he had given any new cause of offence, was certainly repugnant to law and justice. Ridley, one of his judges, succeeded him in the see of London, but on conditions which seemed to stamp a still more unfavourable character on the whole proceeding. The bishopric of Westminster was dissolved by royal authority; Ridley accepted its lands and revenues, in exchange for the lands and revenues

---

[1] Fox, ii. 20—42. Burnet, ii. 121—127. State Trials, i. 631. The pretence for his imprisonment was that "the commissioners now perceived more in the matter than they did before, and that his behaviour was a greater rebellion than he was aware of."—Fox, 41.

belonging to his own church; and these, four days later, were divided among three of the principal lords at court, Rich, lord chancellor; Wentworth, lord chamberlain; and Sir Thomas Darcy, vice-chamberlain.[1]

The deprivation of Bonner would, it was hoped, intimidate and subdue the constancy of Gardiner, who had now been for two years a prisoner in the Tower, without being able to obtain a trial, or even a copy of the charges against him.[2] He was visited by a deputation from the council, and urged to subscribe a written form of submission. To those parts of it which approved the Book of Common Prayer, and acknowledged in the king the powers with which the statute had invested him as the head of the church, he did not object; but no consideration could induce him to confess that he had offended, or to solicit the forgiveness of his sovereign. A second attempt was made; but, if on this occasion the form of submission was softened down, articles were added equally repugnant to the opinions and feelings of the bishop. He was required to approve of the dissolution of monasteries, and the secularization of ecclesiastical property, of the homilies of Archbishop Cranmer, and the paraphrase of Erasmus, and of every religious innovation which had been established by act of parliament or by order of the council. Gardiner replied, that he asked for no favour; he sought only a legal trial; he was willing to stand or fall by the law. To talk to him of subscriptions in prison was unfair.

Let them discharge him as an innocent man, and he would then do whatever his duty required; but were he to subscribe in the Tower, it would be said that he had sacrificed his conscience to purchase his liberty He was next brought before the council; the articles were read in his presence; and he was asked whether he was willing to subscribe as his majesty had commanded. He replied, that "in all things that his majesty could lawfully command, he was most ready to obey; but forasmuch as there were divers things required of him that his conscience would not bear, therefore he prayed them to have him excused." Sentence was immediately pronounced by secretary Petre, that his revenue should be sequestrated from that day, and that, if he did not submit within three months, reckoning each month for a canonical monition, he should be deprived of his bishopric. At length a commission was issued to the metropolitan, three bishops, and six laymen, to proceed against him for contempt; but he defended himself with ability and perseverance; protested against some of the judges and several of the witnesses, as accomplices in a conspiracy against him, which originated about the close of the last reign, and had been continued to that day; and brought so many proofs of his allegations, that, to prevent unpleasant disclosures, Cranmer, on the twenty-second day, cut short the proceedings, pronouncing him contumacious, and adjudging him to be deprived of his bishopric.[3] By order of the council,

---

[1] Strype, ii. 217, 218. The yearly value of the lands resigned by Ridley was 480*l*. 3s. 9¾d.; of those which he received in exchange, 523*l*. 19s. 9¼d., but out of them the king reserved rents to the amount of 100*l*. —Ibid.

[2] "Considerynge," says the Council Book, "the longe imprisonment that the bishope of Winchestere hath sustayned [since June 20th, 1549], it was now thought time he should be spokene withall." The king's book of proceedings was sent to him, to which he replied, that "he could make no direct answere, unless he were at libertie; and so beinge, he would saye his conscyence" (fol. 99).

[3] Compare Fox (ii. 74—85) and Burnet (ii. 150, 165), with the Council Book, Harl. MSS. 352, and the extracts published by Mr. Ellis, in the Archæologia, xviii. 135—146, 150—152; or State Trials, i. 551.

he was sent back to a meaner cell in the Tower, with instructions that no man should see him but one of the warders; that all his books and papers should be taken from him and examined; and that he should be refused the use of pen, ink, and paper.[1] Poynet, bishop of Rochester, succeeded him at Winchester; but on conditions similar to those to which Ridley had consented on his translation to London. The new prelate surrendered to the crown all the revenues of that wealthy bishopric, and received in return rectories and lands to the yearly value of two thousand marks. A large portion of the spoil was reserved for the friends of the earl of Warwick: Sir Thomas Wroth was gratified with a pension for life of one hundred pounds; and Gates, Hoby, Seymour, Dudley, Nevil, and Fitzwilliam obtained still more valuable grants of lordships and manors for themselves and their heirs for ever.[2]

There were two other prelates prisoners in the Tower; Heath, bishop of Worcester, and Day, bishop of Chichester, both distinguished by their learning, their moderation, and their attachment to the ancient creed. Heath, though he had voted against the bill for a new ordinal, was named one of the commissioners; probably for the purpose of procuring matter of complaint against him. He disapproved of the form devised by his eleven colleagues; and on his refusal to subscribe it, was committed to the Fleet for contempt. After an imprisonment of eighteen months, he was called again before the council; and commanded to subscribe, under pain of deprivation, in four days; but "he resolutely answered he could not fynde in his conscyence to do it; and so, as a man incorrigible, he was returned to the Fleete."[3] The bishopric was given to Hooper, and Heath remained till the king's death in prison. Day had offended in a different point. As the ancient liturgy had been commuted for the communion service, the sacrifice of the mass for the supper of the Lord, it was proposed to substitute in the churches tables in the place of the altars, which, with their plate, and jewels, and decorations, would supply a new harvest to the rapacity of the royal favourites.[4] The attempt was first made by a few unauthorized individuals; it was followed by an experiment on a larger scale in the diocese of London, under the protection of Bishop Ridley; and at last the council, alleging the danger of dissension, issued a general injunction to the bishops to remove the altars in their respective dioceses.[5] Day replied that his conscience would not permit him to obey; and though he was allowed four days to deliberate, though Cranmer and Ridley were

---

[1] The chief reason assigned for this severity was that "on the daye of his judgment given againste him, he called his judges heretiques and sacramentarya, they beinge there the kinge's commissioneres, and of his highnes counsell."—Council Book, fol. 152.

[2] Strype, ii. 273.

[3] Council Book, fol. 200. Burnet, ii. 143. This ordinal gave rise to a fierce and acrimonious controversy between the two parties; the one maintaining that, though it omitted a number of ceremonies, the inventions of later ages, it had preserved whatever according to Scripture was necessary for the ordination of bishops, priests, and deacons; the other, that it had been compiled chiefly by men who considered ordination as an unnecessary rite (see chap. ii. p. 79, note); and on that account had carefully omitted what was requisite to impart the sacerdotal character, and that it made no material distinction between the office of priest and bishop. Under Mary the statute authorizing the ordinal was repealed, and the ordinations made in conformity with it were reputed invalid: under Elizabeth it was re-enacted; and one or two improvements were added to meet some of the principal difficulties. In its favour, see Mason de Ministerio Anglicano, l. ii. c. 15, 16, 17: the chief arguments against it have been collected by Dodd, Hist. ii. 278—290.

[4] Heylin, 95.   [5] Wilk. Conc. iv. 65.

commissioned to instruct and convert him, he still answered, that he "thought it a less evil to suffer the body to perish, than to corrupt the soul with that his conscience would not bear." He was committed for this contempt to the Fleet;[1] a court of delegates the next year deprived him and Heath of their bishoprics;[2] and both, notwithstanding this punishment, were kept in custody till the commencement of the next reign.[3]

There still remained one individual whose conversion in the estimation of the reformers would have balanced the opposition of a whole host of bishops,—the lady Mary, the sister of Edward, and the presumptive heir to the crown. She had embraced the first opportunity of expressing to the protector her dislike of further innovation, and her wish that religion might, during the minority of the king, be preserved in the same state in which it had been left by her royal father; but Somerset replied, that his object was to accomplish the real intentions of Henry, who on his death-bed had deeply regretted that he could not live to complete the reformation. The statute of uniformity for worship quickly supplied him with the power of putting her constancy to the test. Its framers appear to have taken for their model the intolerance of the German reformers. Not only did they introduce the new liturgy into the national churches and chapels, but, as the reader will remember, they had invaded the secrecy of the closet, and enacted severe penalties against every priest who should celebrate, every layman or woman who should attend where a priest celebrated mass, even in a private house. Mary received an admonition that she must conform to the provisions of the statute. She replied, that she did not consider it binding in conscience; reminded the lords that they had sworn to observe the laws respecting religion which had been established by her father; hinted that they could not with decency refuse so small an indulgence as liberty of worship to the daughter of him who raised *them* from nothing to their present rank and authority, and at last appealed from their intolerance to the powerful protection of her cousin the emperor. It chanced to be the very time when the English cabinet solicited the aid of that prince for the preservation of Boulogne. After a short debate, policy prevailed over fanaticism; and at the imperial intercession the indulgence which Mary prayed for was reluctantly granted. But after the conclusion of peace with France, the friendship of Charles appeared of less importance, and she was repeatedly harassed with messages from the council, and with letters from her brother. The young king maintained that he possessed as great authority in religious matters as had been possessed by his father; and declared that his love of God, and his affection

---

[1] Council Book, fol. 140, 141.

[2] Great attempts were previously made to prevail on them to conform. But Heath told the council that "of other mynde he thought never to be, adding that there be many other thinges whereunto he would not consent, yf he were demaunded, as to take down alteres, and set up tables." He was then threatened with deprivation, if he did not submit within two days; but he replied, "that he could not fynde in his conscyence to do it, and should be well conteute to abyde such ende either by deprivacon or otherwise as pleased the kinge's matie."—Council Book, fol. 200.

[3] Day, after two years' imprisonment, petitioned for his discharge, on the ground that deprivation was sufficient punishment for a conscientious dissent from an injunction; but added, that if this indulgence "were to be bought at the hazard of his conscience, he thought it better to want it than to purchase so poor a commodity at so dear a rate." His petition was refused.—Strype, ii. 391.

for his sister, forbade him to tolerate her obstinacy; still he preferred mildness to severity, and was willing to supply her with teachers who might instruct her ignorance and refute her errors. Her reasoning, and complaints, and remonstrances, were now equally fruitless. The permission which had been granted at the request of the emperor was explained to have been limited in its duration to a few months, and to have been confined to her own person, with the exclusion of her household. The application of the ambassador in her favour was met with a prompt and peremptory refusal; and, on a rumour of her intention to retire to the continent, a fleet was equipped to intercept the communication between the coast of Norfolk and the opposite shore. Soon afterwards indictments under the statute were found against two of her chaplains; and at the royal invitation Mary herself consented to meet in person the lords of the council. They parted mutually dissatisfied with each other. She asserted that "her soul was God's, and that she would neither change her faith nor dissemble her opinion;" they replied, that "the king did not constrain her faith, but insisted that she should obey like a subject, and not rule like a sovereign."[1]

The next day the ambassador came to her aid with a denunciation of war from the emperor, if Edward should presume to violate the solemn promise which he had given in her favour. This unexpected menace perplexed the orthodoxy of the council. On the one hand, by precipitation they would expose to the mercy of an enemy the goods of the English merchants, the equipments of the gens d'armes, and fifteen hundred quintals of gunpowder in the depôt in Flanders; on the other hand, the young king had persuaded himself that he could not conscientiously suffer his sister to practise any longer an idolatrous worship, and persist in the daily commission of a sin to damnation. The metropolitan with Ridley and Poynet, the two new bishops of London and Rochester was commissioned to lay the spirit which he had raised; and they, to convince the royal theologian, strongly maintained that, "though to give license to sin, was sin, yet to suffer and wink at it for a time might be borne, so all haste possible were used." With reluctance, Edward submitted to the authority of these grave and reverend fathers, but lamented with tears the blind infatuation of his sister, whose obstinacy he could not convince by argument, nor was suffered to restrain by due course of law.[2]

The next object of the council was to gain time for the removal of the stores and ammunition in Flanders to an English port. With this view the ambassador was told that the king would return an answer by a messenger of his own; and a month later Dr. Wotton was despatched to represent to the emperor that the promise given by Edward was of a temporary nature; that the liturgy adopted in England was only a revival of the service used in the first ages; that conformity was enjoined by a statute which bound all men, even the king himself; and that to overlook disobedience in the first subject in the realm, would be to encourage disobedience in others. At the same time, to proceed with impartiality, it was determined to punish the offenders first in the royal household, then in that of the princess. Of the king's servants, Sir Anthony Brown and Serjeant Morgan were sent to the Fleet, and Sir Clement Smith received a severe reprimand; from the family

---

[1] Edward's Journal, 21.

[2] Edward's Journal, 21. Burnet, ii. 172.

of the princess, Dr. Mallet, the head chaplain, was selected for an example, and committed to close custody in the Tower.[1] An active correspondence ensued;[2] Mary demanding the enlargement of her chaplain, the council requiring that she should conform to the law. At length Rochester, Waldegrave, and Inglefield, the chief officers of her household, were commanded to prevent the use of the ancient service in the house, and to communicate this order to the servants and chaplains of their mistress. Having consulted her, they returned to the council, and offered to submit to any punishment, rather than undertake what "they could not find in their hearts or consciences to perform." They were committed to the Tower for contempt;[3] and the lord chancellor, Sir Anthony Wyngfield, and Sir William Petre, proceeding to Copped Hall, in Essex, the residence of the princess, announced to her, her chaplains, and servants, the royal pleasure. *These*, after a short demur, promised obedience; *she* replied: "Rather than use any other service than was used at the death of the late king, my father, I will lay my head on a block and suffer death. When the king's majesty shall come to such years that he may be able to judge these things himself, his majesty shall find me ready to obey his orders in religion; but now, though he, good sweet king, have more knowledge than any other of his years, yet it is not possible that he can be a judge of these things. If my chaplains do say no mass, I can hear none. They may do therein as they will; but none of your new service shall be used in my house, or I will not tarry in it."[4]

After this period we hear no more of an affair, which, trifling as it was in itself, seems to have been considered of sufficient importance to endanger the existence of the amity between England and the imperial dominions. It is probable that Mary continued to have the mass celebrated, but in greater privacy; and that the council deemed it prudent to connive at that which it soon became dangerous to notice. An attempt to marry her to the infant of Portugal had failed and the declining health of the king directed every eye towards her as his successor. She occasionally visited her sick brother; and the state which she assumed was calculated to over-

---

[1] Edward's Journal, 24. Strype, ii. 252. Chron. Cat. 323.

[2] Many of the letters which were written on this occasion are extant. The council persist in asserting that the innovations in religion do not affect its substance. "Our greatest change," they say, "is not in the substance of our faith, no, not in one article of our creed. Only the difference is that we use the ceremonies, observations, and sacraments of our religion, as the apostles and first fathers in the primitive church did. You use the same that corruption of time brought in, and very barbarousness and ignorance nourished; and seem to hold for custom against truth, and we for truth against custom." She declined entering into the controversy, and contended that the king was too young to understand such matters. "Give me leave," she says, "to write what I think touching your majesty's letters. Indeed they be signed with your own hand; and nevertheless, in my opinion, not your majesty's in effect. Because, it is well known, that although (our Lord be praised) your majesty hath far more knowledge and greater gifts than any others of your years, yet it is not possible that your highness can at these years be judge in matters of religion. And therefore I take it that the matter in your letter proceedeth from such as do wish these things to take place, which be most agreeable to themselves, by whose doings (your majesty not offended) I intend not to rule my conscience."—Fox, ii. 49, 52. Ellis, ii. 177.

[3] They were to be kept in close custody, without pen, ink, and paper, and with a servant in the cell of each prisoner to observe his conduct.—Council Book, 194. After confinement for more than six months, they were allowed to go to their own houses as prisoners, March 18th, and were set at liberty April 24th.—Strype, ii. 256.

[4] See the extracts from the Council Book by Mr. Ellis, printed in the Archæologia, xviii. 154—166, and Original Letters, ii. 179.

awe her opponents. She was attended by one hundred and fifty or two hundred knights and gentlemen on horseback; and this retinue was generally augmented by the spontaneous accession of some of the first personages both male and female in the kingdom.[1]

Though the statutes against heresy had been repealed in the first year of the king's reign, still the profession of erroneous doctrine was held to be an offence punishable by the common law of the realm. It might indeed have been hoped that men who had writhed under the lash of persecution would have learned to respect the rights of conscience. But, however forcibly the reformers had claimed the privilege of judging for themselves under the late king, they were not disposed to concede it to others when they themselves came into the exercise of power. As long, indeed, as they contended that their innovations trenched not on the substance of the ancient faith, the men of the old learning were secure from prosecutions for heresy; they could be proceeded against only for a breach of the Statute of Uniformity, or for contempt of the royal authority. But among the new teachers themselves there were several whose discoveries were calculated to excite in the breasts of their more orthodox brethren feelings of alarm and abhorrence. Some taught that the prohibition of bigamy was a papal invention; and that it was lawful for any man at his option to have one or two wives, and for any wife to have one or two husbands; others, that to admit the government of a king was to reject the government of God; and many, that children baptized in infancy should be afterwards rebaptized; that human laws were not to be obeyed; that no Christian ought to bear any office in the commonwealth; that oaths are unlawful; that Christ did not take flesh of the Virgin; that sinners cannot be restored to grace by repentance; and that all things are and ought to be in common.[2]

Of these doctrines, some by denying the incarnation, were deemed to sap the very foundation of Christianity, others tended to convulse the established order of society. The lords of the council were anxious to repel the charge of encouraging tenets which, in the eyes of Europe, would reflect disgrace on the English reformation; and commissions were repeatedly issued, appointing by letters patent the archbishop, several prelates, and certain distinguished divines and civilians, inquisitors of heretical pravity. In these instruments it was asserted to be the duty of kings, especially of one who bore the title of defender of the faith, to check the diffusion of error by the punishment of its abettors,—to prevent the gangrene from reaching the more healthy parts, by the amputation of the diseased member; and therefore, as Edward himself could not at all times attend to this important concern, he delegated to the inquisitors and commissaries power to enforce the Statute of Uniformity against all offenders, to hear and determine all causes of heresy, and to admit the repentant to abjuration, but to deliver the obstinate to the arm of the civil power.[3]

The first who appeared before the archbishop was Champneis, a priest who had taught that Christ was not God, that grace was inamissible, and that the regenerate, though they might fall by the outward, could

---

[1] See in particular Strype, ii. 372.
[2] Stat. 3 Ed. VI. 24. Strype, ii. 12, 90.
[3] Rym. xv. 181, 250. In these commissions are inserted the names of Cranmer, Ridley, Thurlby, Redman, Latimer, Coverdale, Parker, afterwards archbishop of Canterbury, secretaries Petre and Cecil, Cheke, the king's tutor, and several others.

never sin by the inward man; he was followed by Puttow, a tanner, Thumb, a butcher, and Ashton, a priest, who had embraced the tenets of Unitarianism. Terror or conviction induced them to abjure: they were sworn never to revert to their former opinions, and publicly bore fagots during the sermon at St. Paul's Cross.[1] But no fear of punishment could subdue the obstinacy of a female preacher, Joan Bocher, of Kent. During the last reign she had rendered important services to the reformers by the clandestine importation of prohibited books, which, through the agency of the noted Anne Askew, she conveyed to the ladies at court. She was now summoned before the inquisitors Cranmer, Smith, Cook, Latimer, and Lyell, and was charged with maintaining that "Christ did not take flesh of the outward man of the Virgin, because the outward man was conceived in sin, but by the consent of the inward man, which was undefiled." In this unintelligible jargon she persisted to the last; and when the archbishop excommunicated her as a heretic, and ordered her to be delivered to the secular power, she replied: "It is a goodly matter to consider your ignorance. It was not long ago that you burned Anne Askew for a piece of bread; and yet came yourselves soon afterwards to believe and profess the same doctrine for which you burned her; and now, forsooth, you will needs burn me for a piece of flesh, and in the end will come to believe this also, when you have read the scriptures and understand them."

From the unwillingness of Edward to consent to her execution, a year elapsed before she suffered. It was not that his humanity revolted from the idea of burning her at the stake: in his estimation she deserved the severest punishment which the law could inflict. But the object of his compassion was the future condition of her soul in another world. He argued that, as long as she remained in error, she remained in sin, and that to deprive her of life in that state was to consign her soul to everlasting torments. Cranmer was compelled to moot the point with the young theologian: the objection was solved by the example of Moses, who had condemned blasphemers to be stoned; and the king with tears put his signature to the warrant. The bishops of London and Ely made in vain a last attempt to convert Bocher. She preserved her constancy at the very stake; and when the preacher, Dr. Scory, undertook to refute her opinion, exclaimed that "he lied like a rogue, and had better go home and study the scripture."[2]

The next victim was Von Parris, a Dutchman, and a surgeon in London. He denied the divinity of Christ, and, having been excommunicated by his brethren of the Dutch church in that capital, was arraigned before Cranmer, Ridley, May, Coverdale, and several others. Coverdale acted as interpreter: but the prisoner refused to abjure; Cranmer pronounced judgment, and delivered him to the gaoler at the Compter, and a few days later the unhappy man was committed to the flames.[3]

But while the expression of Unitarian sentiments was thus proscribed, under the penalty of death by burning, and the exercise of the ancient

---

[1] Wilk. Con. iv. 39—42. Stowe, 596.
[2] Wilk. Con. iv. 42, 43. Edward's Journal, 12. Heylin, 89. Strype, ii. 214. Hayward, 276. Strype (473) labours to throw some doubt on the part attributed to Cranmer in this prosecution, chiefly "because he was not present at her condemnation."—Todd, ii. 149. But that he was present, and actually pronounced the judgment, appears from his own register, fol. 74, 75.
[3] Wilk. Con. iv. 44, 45. Stowe, 605. Edward's Journal, 34.

worship, under that of a long or perpetual imprisonment, a convenient latitude of practice and opinion was conceded to the strangers whom the fear of persecution or the advantages of commerce induced to settle in England. Foreign religionists, of every nation and every sect,—Frenchmen and Italians, Germans, Poles, and Scots, were assured of an asylum in the palace of the archbishop. He procured for them livings in the church and protection at court; and in return he called on them to aid his efforts in enlightening the ignorance and dispelling the prejudices of his own countrymen. John Knox was appointed chaplain to the king, and itinerant preacher throughout the kingdom; Utenhoff and Pierre Alexandre remained at Canterbury to purge the clergy from the leaven of popery; Faggio, Tremelio, and Cavalier were licensed to read lectures on the Hebrew language at Cambridge; Martyr and Bucer undertook to teach the new theology in the two universities; and Joannes a Lasco, Valerandus Pollanus, and Angelo Florio were named by patent superintendents and preachers in the congregations of strangers established in London and Glastonbury.[1] Many, however, disputed the policy of thus authorizing independent churches of foreign dissenters, at a time when conformity was so rigorously exacted from the natives; or of intrusting the education of the clergy, and the revision of doctrinal matters, to men who, whatever might be their merit and acquirements, differed in several important points from the established creed, and unceasingly laboured to assimilate in doctrine and practice the prelatic church of England to the Calvinistic churches abroad.

These foreigners, however, accommodated their consciences to the existing order of things so far as to tolerate what they hoped might be afterwards reformed;[2] but there was a native preacher of more unbending principles, whose scruples or whose obstinacy proved dangerous both to himself and to the cause which he espoused. John Hooper, by his activity, his fervid declamation, and his bold though intemperate zeal, had deserved the applause and gratitude of the well-wishers to the new doctrines. Edward named him to the bishopric of Gloucester; when the preacher himself opposed an unexpected obstacle to his own promotion. How could *he* swear obedience to the metropolitan, while it was his duty to obey no spiritual authority but that of the scriptures? How could he submit to wear the episcopal habits, the livery of that church which he had so often denominated the harlot of Babylon? Cranmer and Ridley attempted to convince him by argument, and to influence him by authority; Bucer reminded him that to the pure all things are pure; and Peter Martyr contended that the wearing of episcopal habits, though meet in his opinion to be abolished, was yet an indifferent matter, in which the most timorous might conscientiously acquiesce: on the other hand, the Helvetic divines applauded his consistency; the earl of Warwick conjured the archbishop to yield in favour of his extraordinary merit; and the king promised to protect that prelate from the penalties to which he might subject himself by swerving from the ordinal.[3] But, Cranmer was unwilling to incur the danger of a premunire; and Hooper not only

---

[1] Strype's Cranmer, 194, 234, 242. Strype's Memorials, ii. 121, 205, 240.

[2] I should except Knox, who had the honesty to refuse a living, because "many things were worthy of reformation in England, without the reformation whereof, no minister did or could discharge his conscience before God."—Strype, ii. 399.

[3] Council Book, 144, 147. Strype's Cranmer, 211. Memorials, ii. Rec. 126. Burnet,

refused to submit, but published a justification of his conduct, and from the pulpit declaimed against the habits, the ordinal, and the council. The new church was on the point of being torn into fragments by the intemperance of her own children; when the royal authority interposed, and committed the refractory preacher to the Fleet. In the confinement of a prison, the fervour of his imagination gradually cooled; the rigour of his conscience relaxed; he condescended to put on the polluted habit; he took the obnoxious oath; he accepted from the king a patent, empowering him to govern the diocese of Gloucester, and fourteen months later was transferred to the united bishopric of Gloucester and Worcester. By this union a wider field was opened for the exercise of his zeal; but at the same time an ample source was supplied for the rapacity of the courtiers. With a double diocese he retained a less income; the larger portion of the revenues of the two sees being destined for the men who at this period were actively employed in carving out of the possessions of the church fortunes for themselves and their posterity.[1]

While the nation was thus distracted by religious quarrels, the court was again thrown into confusion by a new dissension between Somerset and Warwick. The duke had come from the Tower, stripped of office, and wealth, and influence. But the vengeance of his enemies seemed to be satisfied; he was allowed to visit his nephew; that portion of his goods and chattels which had escaped the rapacity of the courtiers was restored to him; his bonds and pledges were cancelled; and he was at last re-admitted into the council, where his rank of duke gave to him the nominal precedence, though in point of power he was reduced to an equality with the meanest of his colleagues. In this state the former friendship between him and Warwick seemed to revive; and their reconciliation was apparently cemented by the union of their families, in the marriage of Lord Lisle, the earl's eldest son, with Anne, one of the daughters of Somerset. The king, accompanied by his court, graced the ceremony with his presence. He rejoiced at the restoration of harmony in his council, of friendship between an uncle whom he loved and a minister whom he prized: but his joy was quickly interrupted by the renewal of their former jealousies and dissension. Somerset could not forget what he had suffered: Warwick dared not trust the man whom he had injured. The duke aspired again to the office of protector; the earl determined not to descend from his present superiority. Their fears and suspicions led them to attribute to each other the most dangerous designs: both were beset with spies and informers; both were deceived and exasperated by false friends and interested advisers. But Warwick possessed the advantage over his adversary in the council, which was principally composed of his associates, and in the palace, where the king was surrounded with his creatures. Somerset, to aid his views, had sought, by private agents, to secure the votes of several among the peers in the next parliament; and, to recover his influence with his nephew, had requested the lord Strange, the royal favourite, to suggest to Edward a marriage with the lady Jane Seymour, his third daughter.[2] Into the first of these attempts an inquiry was insti-

---

ii. 152. Collier, ii. 293. Some have supposed that he objected not to the oath of obedience, but to the oath of supremacy.—Id. 307.

[1] Rym. xv. 297—303, 320. Strype, ii. 355—357.
[2] It appears from a letter of Warwick, dated Jan. 22, and published by Strype, (ii.

tuted, but afterwards abandoned the second was defeated by the resolution of the council to demand for their sovereign the hand of Elizabeth, the eldest daughter of the king of France. It is probable that on this occasion some menaces were thrown out. The lord Grey hastily departed for the northern counties, and Somerset had prepared to follow him, when he was detained by the asseveration of Sir William Herbert, that no injury was intended. A second reconciliation ensued; for some days costly entertainments were given alternately by the lords of each party; and the rival chiefs lavished on each other demonstrations of friendship, while the bitterest animosity was festering in their breasts.[1]

The marquess of Northampton, attended by three earls, the eldest sons of Somerset and Warwick, and several lords and gentlemen, proceeded to Paris, to invest the king of France with the order of the Garter, and to seek a wife for his sovereign. His first demand, of the young queen of Scotland, was instantly refused; his second, of the princess Elizabeth, was as readily granted. The negotiators agreed that as soon as Elizabeth had completed her twelfth year she should be married to Edward; but, when they came to the settlement of her portion, the English demanded twelve hundred thousand, the French offered two hundred thousand crowns. This difference suspended the conclusion of the treaty for eight weeks; but Edward's commissioners successively lowered their demand, and at length, accepting the offer of the opposite party, agreed to assign for her dower lands in England to the yearly amount of ten thousand marks, "the same as the dower of the most illustrious lady Catherine, daughter of Ferdinand king of Castile, or of any other queen of England, lately married to Henry of happy memory, king of England."[2] To return the compliment, the French king sent to his destined son-in-law his order of St. Michael, by the marshal St. André, who was accompanied by a numerous retinue. This minister was received on his landing by the gentlemen of the county to the amount of one thousand horsemen, and, avoiding the capital on account of the sweating sickness,[3] visited the king at Hampton Court, where he was sumptuously entertained by Edward himself, by the duke of Somerset, and by the earl of Warwick. At his departure he received several valuable presents.[4]

These tranquil and festive occupa-

---

279), that during the winter the council had deliberated on a secret matter of extreme importance: that it required the greatest "vigilance and circumspection;" that the chancellor and treasurer wished "to wrap it up in silence," because it was "not expedient it should come in question;" but that he (Warwick) wished to be "reformed, seeing it had been so far debated." He makes use of these remarkable expressions: "God preserve our master! If he should fail, there is watchers enough that would bring it in question, and would burden you and others, who will not now understand the danger, to be deceivers of the whole body of the realm with an instrument forged to execute your malicious meanings." He alludes undoubtedly to the will of Henry VIII., the sole foundation of their authority. An instrument was devised to supply the defect. By it Edward ratified all the acts of the council up to that day, reappointed the same councillors during his pleasure, and invested them with full powers to discharge their office. But it does not appear to have been adopted.—Strype, ii. Rec. 139.

[1] Edward's Journal, 22, 39.
[2] Ibid. 25. Rym. xv. 273. Chron. Catal. 318, 320, 322.
[3] "This sweat was more vehement than the old sweat: for, if one took cold, he died within three hours, and, if he escaped, it held him but nine hours, or ten at the most. Also if he slept the first six hours, as he should be very desirous to do, then he roved, and should die roving."—Edward's Journal, 30. The deaths in London, on July 10th, amounted to 100; July 11th, to 120; in eleven days, from the 8th to the 19th, to 872.—Strype, ii. 277, 279.
[4] I observe that the presents given by the English exceeded in value those given by the French monarch. St. André received

tions did not, however, harmonize with the projects of revenge and bloodshed which were secretly meditated by the two rivals. But the timidity and imprudence of Somerset were no match for the caution and decision of Warwick. That nobleman was apprized of all his designs: to cut off his hope of an asylum in the northern counties, he procured for himself the general wardenship of the Scottish marches, with all that pre-eminence and authority which had ever been possessed by any former warden since the reign of Richard II.; and within a few days he was honoured with the title of duke of Northumberland, which had long been extinct in consequence of the attainder of the lord Thomas Percy in 1537. At the same time, to strengthen the attachment of his friends, he prevailed on the king to create the marquess of Dorset duke of Suffolk,[1] the earl of Wiltshire marquess of Winchester, Sir William Herbert baron of Cardiff and earl of Pembroke, and to confer on Cecil, Cheke, Sidney, and Nevil, the honour of knighthood. Somerset gradually discovered the danger which threatened him. From the earl of Arundel he received advice "to take good heed, for his counsels and secrets were come abroad;" and on application to Cecil, hitherto his creature, but now appointed secretary to the king, he was told that, if he were innocent, he had nothing to fear; if guilty, Cecil could only lament the misfortune of his former patron. To this cold and insulting answer he returned a letter of defiance; and then closely examined Sir Thomas Palmer, who was now become to him an object of suspicion; and not without reason; for he had, in fact, already sworn an information against him. But the duke suffered himself to be deceived by the bold denial of the traitor; and on the second day afterwards was arrested at court, and hurried away to the Tower. The duchess, with her favourites Crane and Crane's wife, followed him thither the next morning; and in a few days most of his supposed friends and advisers, among whom were the earl of Arundel, the lord Paget, and the lord Dacres of the north, were safely immured in the same prison.

It now happened that the thoughts of Edward were diverted from the approaching fate of his uncle by the presence of a royal visitor, the queen-dowager of Scotland, who on her way back from France to that kingdom, had cast anchor in the harbour of Portsmouth. At the request of Henry she had obtained permission to continue her journey by land; and, to do her honour, the gentlemen of each county received orders to attend upon her as she passed. Her former hostility to the interests of England gave her no claim on the friendship of Edward; but, to please the king of France, it had been determined to treat her with extraordinary respect; she was invited to the capital, and introduced to the young king, who met her in the great Hall, kissed her, took her by the hand, and conducted her to her chamber. They dined together in state, and after her departure he sent her a valuable diamond. She left London attended by a numerous retinue of ladies and gentlemen, and at the gate received a present of one hundred marks from the city.[2]

Soon after her departure Somerset was brought to trial. By the statute

---

to the value of 3,000l.; Northampton to that of 500l.—Journ. 32.

[1] He had married Frances, the eldest daughter of Charles Brandon, duke of Suffolk, by Mary, sister of Henry VIII. Her two brothers, Henry duke of Suffolk, and the lord Charles, had died during the late sickness.—Strype, ii. 277.

[2] Edward's Journal, in Burnet by Nares, 222 223. Strype, ii. 284. Archæol. xxviii. 168.

of the third and fourth of the king it had been made treason for any persons, to the number of forty or above, to assemble in forcible manner "to the intent to murder, kill, or slay, *take* or *imprison* any of the king's most honorable privy council;" and felony without benefit of clergy to procure or stir up any persons to the committal of such offences. In the indictments against him the duke was charged with both the treason and the felony, so that to his enemies it mattered little on which he might be found guilty: since in either case, his life would be equally in jeopardy, and equally at their mercy. Before the trial, the marquess of Winchester was created lord high steward, and twenty-seven peers were summoned to attend, among whom were numbered Northumberland, Northampton, and Pembroke, the three great enemies of the accused. As it was not intended to subject the witnesses to a vivâ-voce examination in open court, twenty-two lords were called into the council chamber; before whom Sir Thomas Palmer, Hammond, Crane, and Newdigate, on whose depositions the counsel for the prosecution chiefly depended, severally made oath that in their confessions they had strictly adhered to the truth, and said nothing through fear, compulsion, envy, or malice, but had favoured the prisoner as far as their consciences would permit. Unfortunately all these depositions have perished—at least, are not known to exist.[1] We have no other knowledge of them than the little which may be gleaned from the entries in the journal of the young king, and from a narrative of the trial, which he inserted in a private letter.[2] From these sources we learn that, according to the evidence, the great object of the conspiracy was to secure the persons of Northumberland, Northampton, and Herbert, who governed in the council, and were the chief obstacles to the recovery by Somerset of his former office: that for this purpose they were to be invited by the lord Paget to an entertainment to be given at his house in the Strand; in which case, if they came slenderly attended, they might be intercepted and made prisoners in the way; otherwise, be surprised and despatched at table; that Somerset should then raise the city, and with the aid of the apprentices and populace get possession of the great seal: that Vane, with his infantry and the duke's horsemen, should attack the gens d'armes; and that the king, being now again in the hands of his

---

[1] Mr. Tytler's searches for them in the State Paper Office have proved unsuccessful. He discovered, indeed, two confessions by the earl of Arundel; which, however, were not employed on Somerset's trial; and a paper entitled "Crane's information against the duke of Somerset and the earl of Arundel," which Mr. Tytler considers as a note drawn up by one of the crown lawyers of such evidence against Somerset as could be collected from the depositions of the several prisoners (p. 41). But it is a paper of a very different character. It was both then, and for several centuries, the custom after a first examination in the Tower, to collect from the answers all such passages as seemed to clash with each other, or to call for explanation, or to provoke suspicion of concealment, and out of them to form a new series of interrogations for a second examination. Now the paper in question is plainly one of these collections. In like manner the paper published by Sir Henry Ellis, under the title of "Questions put to the duke of Somerset," is not a collection of all the charges against him, but a collection of such interrogations as had been suggested by answers to former questions, and which were now to form the basis of a second examination. The numbers 10, 12, 14 are taken from the confessions of the earl of Arundel, and of Crane.

[2] I may remark that Edward's statement in his journal, of the earl of Arundel's confessions, perfectly agrees with the original confessions discovered by Mr. Tytler. Is it not then fair to conclude that he was equally careful and correct in the accounts which he gives of other confessions and depositions, though we cannot compare them?

uncle, should publish a proclamation charging the three councillors with treason. In addition it was sworn that the duke nightly kept a guard of twenty armed men near his chamber at Greenwich.

On the following morning Somerset was arraigned before his peers, and defended himself with spirit. The witnesses, Newdigate, Hammond, and Seymour, were, he said, *his* men: they had sworn fealty to him, and therefore ought not to be believed against him. Palmer was a man of bad character, and totally unworthy of credit. Crane, if confronted with him, would not dare to repeat his evidence. With respect to himself, he denied that he ever meant to raise the city of London; if he kept a guard near his chamber at Greenwich, it was to protect himself from illegal violence: the idea of bringing men to attack the gens d'armes was too extravagant to enter into a sane mind. Of the intended banquet he knew nothing: he never determined to kill the three members of the council, though that had been made the subject of conversation. So much he would not deny, but "he had determined after the contrary."[1] He maintained with oaths that he had never desired the lord Strange to suggest a marriage between the king and his daughter. Lord Strange deposed upon oath that he had done so.

It was three in the afternoon before the lords began to deliberate on their verdict. With respect to the indictment for felony all were agreed; but with regard to the charge of treason, the three councillors, whose lives the duke is said to have sought, assumed the office of his advocates. They called upon the court "to eschew rigour and extremity," to grant to the accused "as much equity as might anywise be devised," and therefore to be content with a conviction on the minor offence.[2] It is probable that by this show of moderation and forbearance they hoped to escape the imputation of revenge and cruelty.[3] Their advice was, however, adopted. Somerset was acquitted of treason, but found guilty of the felony without a dissentient voice.[4] He was then recalled, informed of the result by the lord Steward, and received the usual sentence of death for that offence. Falling on his knees, "he gave thanks to the court for the open trial, cried mercy of Northumberland, Northampton, and Pembroke, for his illmeaning against them, and made suit for his life, wife, children, servants, and debts."[5] The axe of the Tower

---

[1] Edward's Journal, 225. The king adds, "yet he seemed to confess he went about their death." And certainly, if that was the best answer which he could make to the charge, it would not go far to remove any suspicion which previously existed.

[2] See the letter of the lord Steward, written on the following day, in Tytler, ii. 63—65.

[3] Edward's Journal, 225. According to the king, in his letter to Fitzpatrick, their motive was that "men might not think they did it of malice."—Fuller, 429. Mr. Tytler, however, is convinced that the real motive was, the inability of the prosecutors to prove that the duke intended to put the councillors to death; founding this opinion on the notion that such was the treason in question. He is evidently in error; for it was no less treason "to take or imprison" them than to kill or slay them. So that if the acquittal of treason acquitted the duke of any intention to slay, so it did also of any intention to apprehend them; of which, however, he was convicted by being found guilty of the felony.

[4] That he was found guilty by the whole body, and not by a majority only, is plain from the Record; quilibet eorum separatim dixerunt quod prædictus Edvardus nuper dux Somers.; de feloniis prædictis fuit culpabilis.—Coke's Entries, fol. 482. Neither is it true that this was only felony, when the party continued together after proclamation to separate; for, as has been already noticed, there is another part of the same act, which, without mention of any proclamation, makes it felony for any person, after the 12th of February, "to stir or move others to raise or make any traitorous or rebellious assembly, to the intent to do, or exercise, or put in use, any of the things above mentioned."—Stat. of Realm, iv. 107

[5] Edward's Journal, 225 By "it

was now turned from him, and the populace observing its direction, when he left the court, expressed their joy by repeated acclamations, under the impression that he had been acquitted of every offence.

After his condemnation, and in the solitude of his cell, Somerset had leisure to compare his situation with that of the lord admiral, in the same place, not three years before. The duke had indeed enjoyed an indulgence which he had refused to his unfortunate brother—a public trial by his peers. But could he expect that the ambition of Warwick would prove less jealous or inexorable than his own; that an enemy would extend to him that mercy, which *he* had withheld from one of his own blood? He made indeed the experiment; but every avenue to the throne was closed; his nephew was convinced of his guilt, and of the expedience of his punishment; and he received for answer that he must pay the forfeit of his life, but should have a long respite to prepare himself for death. Six weeks after his trial, the warrant for his execution was signed;[1] and at an early hour, eight in the morning, he was delivered to the sheriffs of London, and by them conducted to the scaffold on Tower Hill. An immense crowd had already assembled. The duke's attention to the poor during his protectorship, and his constant opposition to the system of inclosures, had created him many friends among the lower classes, who hastened to witness his end, but still flattered themselves with the hope of a reprieve. In his address from the scaffold, he said that he had always been a true subject to the king, and on that account was now willing to lay down his life in obedience to the law; that, on a review of his past conduct, there was nothing which he regretted less than his endeavours to reduce religion to its present state; and that he exhorted the people to profess it and practise it, if they wished to escape those visitations with which Heaven was prepared to punish their offences. At that moment a body of officers with bills and halberts, who had been ordered to attend the execution, issued from the postern; and, perceiving that they were behind their time, rushed precipitately towards the scaffold. The crowd gave way: the spectators at a distance, ignorant of the cause, yielded to the sudden impulse of terror; and, in their eagerness to escape from imaginary danger, some were trampled under foot; others, to the number of one hundred, were driven into the Tower ditch; and many, dispersing themselves through the city, ascribed their fright to an earthquake, to a sudden peal of thunder, or to some miraculous and inexplicable indication of the divine displeasure. Order had scarcely been restored, when Sir Anthony Brown, a member of the council, was seen approaching on horseback. Some one imprudently shouted, "A pardon, a pardon!" and the word was quickly echoed from mouth to mouth, till it reached the scaffold: but the duke, after a moment's suspense, learned that he had been deceived by the fond wishes of the spectators. The disappointment called up a hectic colour in his cheeks; but he resumed his address with composure and firmness of voice, repeating that he was a loyal man,

---

meaning" Edward means machinations against their lives; for in his letter to Fitzpatrick, describing the same thing, he says: "whom he confessed he meant to *destroy*, altho' before he swore vehemently to the contrary."—Fuller, 409.

[1] Rym. xv. 295. We are told that the king was kept from reflection by a continued series of occupations and amusements; yet the first of these amusements occurred on the 3rd of January, a month after the condemnation. Such things always took place during the Christmas holidays.—See Edward's Journal, 43.

exhorting his auditors to love the king, and obey his counsellors, and desiring their prayers that he might die as he lived, in the faith of Christ. Then covering his face with his handkerchief, he laid his head on the block. At one stroke it was severed from the body.[1]

Of the many individuals accused as the accomplices of this unfortunate nobleman, four only, Partridge and Vane, Stanhope and Arundel, were selected for capital punishment. All were convicted on the same evidence as the duke; all at the place of execution maintained their innocence; and Vane, in strong language, assured the spectators that as often as Northumberland should lay his head on his pillow, he would find it wet with their blood. The two first died by the hand of the hangman, the others by the axe of the executioner. Though Paget had been the confidential adviser of Somerset, though it was said that at his house the intended assassination should have taken place, he was never brought to trial. But he made his submission, confessed that he had been guilty of peculation in the offices which he held under the crown, surrendered the chancellorship of the duchy of Lancaster, was degraded from the order of the Garter, and paid a considerable fine. The earl of Arundel, after an imprisonment of twelve months, recovered his liberty, but not till he had acknowledged himself cognizant of Somerset's intention to make the councillors his prisoners, had resigned the office of warden of several royal parks, and had bound himself to pay annually to the king the sum of one thousand marks during the term of six years. The lord Grey and the other prisoners were successively discharged.[2]

The parliament met the day after the execution of Somerset. As it had been originally summoned by his order and under his influence, the lower house numbered among its members several who cherished a warm, though secret attachment to his memory. Their opposition to the court animated their debates with a spirit of freedom hitherto unknown; and by delays and amendments they retarded or defeated the favourite measures of the minister, till his impatience silenced their hostility by a hasty dissolution. Of the acts which received the royal assent, a few deserve the reader's attention. 1. Now, for the first time, was made a legal provision for the poor. For that purpose the churchwardens received authority to collect charitable contributions, and the bishop of the diocese was empowered to proceed against the defaulters.[3] 2. It was about three years since the composition of the Book of Common Prayer had been attributed by the unanimous assent of the legislature to "the aid of the Holy Ghost." But this solemn declaration had not convinced the scepticism of the foreign teachers. They examined the book with a jealous eye; they detected passages which, in their estimation, savoured of superstition, or led to idolatry; their complaints were echoed and re-echoed by their English disciples; and Edward, at the suggestion of his

---

[1] Edward's Journal, 45. Fox, 98. The fanaticism of this writer compares the tumult at the execution to what "happened unto Christ, when is the officers of the high priests and Pharisees coming with weapons to take him, being astonished, ran backwards, and fell to the ground."—Ibid. The true cause is noticed by Stowe, who was present (p. 607). See also Ellis, 2nd series, ii. 215.

[2] Council Book, fol. 259. Stowe, 607, 608. Strype, ii. 310, 383. Edward's Journal, 56. It is remarkable that all of them were by degrees taken into favour, and obtained the remission of a part, or of the whole of their fines. Arundel was again admitted into the council; and was moreover discharged of his debt to the crown, but only four days before the king's death.

[3] Stat. of Realm, iv. 131.

favourite instructors, affirmed that, if the prelates did not undertake the task, the new service should be freed from these blemishes without their assistance. Cranmer submitted the book in a Latin translation to the consideration of Bucer and Peter Martyr, whose judgment or prejudice recommended several omissions, and explanations, and improvements;[1] a committee of bishops and divines acquiesced in most of the animadversions of these foreign teachers; and the book in its amended form received the assent of the convocation. But here a new difficulty arose. It was the province of the clergy to decide on matters of doctrine and worship; how then could they submit a work approved by themselves to the revision of the lay branches of the legislature? To elude the inconvenience, it was proposed to connect the amended service and the ordinal with a bill, which was then in its progress through parliament, to compel by additional penalties attendance at the national worship. The clergy hoped that both forms would thus steal through the two houses without exciting any notice; but their object was detected and defeated; the books were read through, before the act was permitted to pass; and both without alteration were allowed and confirmed. By the new statute, to which they had been appended, the bishops were ordered to coerce with spiritual censures all persons who should absent themselves from the amended form of service, the magistrates with corporal punishment all those who should employ any other service in its place. To hear, or be present at, any manner of divine worship, or administration of the sacraments, or ordination of ministers, differing from those set forth by authority, subjected the offender on the first conviction to imprisonment during the space of six months, on the second during the space of one year, and on the third during the term of his natural life.[2]

3. An attempt was made by the crown to revive some of the most objectionable acts of the late reign, though they had been repealed in Edward's first parliament. The Lords without hesitation passed a bill making it treason to call the king or any of his heirs a heretic, schismatic, tyrant, or usurper; but the rigour of the measure was mitigated by the spirit of the Commons, who, as had been done already with respect to the denial of the supremacy, drew a broad distinction between the different manners of committing the offence. To brand the king with such disgraceful appellations "by writing, printing, carving, or graving," as it demanded both time and deliberation, might be assumed as a proof of malice, and call for the very extremity of punishment; but to do it in words only, would often proceed from indiscretion or the sudden impulse of passion, and therefore could not in justice deserve so severe a retribution. On this account they visited the first and second offence with forfeiture and imprisonment only, and reserved for the third the more grievous punishment of treason. The amendment, however, was of small importance compared with the provision with which it was accompanied. The constant complaint of accused persons, that they could not

---

[1] Strype's Cranmer, 209, 252, App. 154. Burnet, ii. 155.

[2] Stat. of Realm, iv. 120. The dissentients to this intolerant act were the earl of Derby, the bishops of Carlisle and Norwich, and the lords Stourton and Windsor.—Journ. 421. After the passing of the act the bishops laid aside the episcopal dress, and the prebendaries their hoods, because the rubric required nothing more than the surplice.—Collier, ii. 325.

establish their innocence, because they were never confronted with their accusers, had attracted the public notice. The more the question was discussed, the more the iniquity of the usual method of proceeding was condemned; and it was now enacted, that no person should be arraigned, indicted, convicted, or attainted of any manner of treason, unless on the oath of two lawful accusers, who should be brought before him at the time of his arraignment, and there should openly avow and maintain their charges against him. Thus was laid the foundation of a most important improvement in the administration of criminal justice; and a maxim was introduced which has proved the best shield of innocence against the jealousy, the arts, and the vengeance of superior power.[1]

4. The utility of the last enactment was proved even before the expiration of the session. In 1550 Nynian Mennill had accused Tunstall, bishop of Durham, of having been privy to an intended rising in the North, but had failed of proving the charge, through the loss of a letter written by the bishop. That letter was now found among the private papers of the late duke of Somerset, and Tunstall, though he maintained that it was susceptible of the most innocent interpretation, was committed by the council to the Tower, "there to abide such order as his doings by the course of the lawe should appear to have deserved." But Northumberland would not trust to the course of the law. He applied to parliament by a bill "to deprive Tunstall of his bishopric for divers heinous offences." It was passed by the Lords; but the Commons, treating it as a bill of attainder, contended that he had a right to be confronted with his accuser, and petitioned that both Tunstall and Mennill might be examined before them. Edward was advised to return no answer; and they declined to proceed any further with the cause. Still the bishop did not escape. He was called before certain judges and doctors of common law, empowered to examine him of "all conspiracies, contempts, and concealments, and, if he were guilty, to deprive him of his bishopric." By them judgment of deprivation was pronounced, and he was sent back to the Tower, where he remained a prisoner till the accession of the next sovereign.[2]

The late statute insured the adoption of the amended liturgy in every diocese of the kingdom; a French translation communicated it to the natives of Jersey and Guernsey. But were not the king's subjects in Ireland equally entitled to the benefit of a form of worship in their own tongue? Undoubtedly they were: but it had long been the object of the government to suppress the Irish language within the English pale; and, to have chosen that language for the vehicle of religious instruction and religious worship, would have been to authorize and perpetuate its use. It was, I conceive, for this reason that the royal advisers submitted to entail on themselves that reproach, which they had been accustomed to cast on the church of Rome, and enjoined by proclamation that the Irish should attend to the service in English, a language which few among them could understand.[3] By Brown, the archbishop of Dublin, and four of his brethren, the order was cheerfully

---

[1] Stat. of Realm, iv. 144.
[2] Lords' Journals, 418, 425. Archbishop Cranmer and Lord Stourton dissented (418). Journals of Commons, 21, 23. Extract from Council Book, Archæol. xviii. 170; and Strype, iii. 192, reprint of 1816.
[3] The lord deputy was, however, instructed "to cause the English to be translated into the Irish, until the people may be brought to understand the English" (Chron. Cat. 311); but this was never done.

obeyed: Dowdal, archbishop of Armagh, and the other prelates, rejected it with scorn. The consequence was that the ancient service was generally retained; the new was adopted in those places only where an armed force compelled its introduction. The lords of the council, to punish the disobedience of Dowdal, took from him the title of primate of all Ireland, and transferred it to his more obsequious brother the archbishop of Dublin.[1]

At the same time Cranmer had the satisfaction to complete two works of the highest importance to the cause of the reformation,—1. A Collection of the Articles of Religion, and 2. A Code of Ecclesiastical Constitutions. 1. During the last reign he had subscribed with the other prelates every test of orthodoxy promulgated by Henry; but after the death of that monarch a new light appears to have burst upon his mind; in the homilies, the order of communion, and the English service, he continued to recede from the opinions which he had formerly approved; and it became at last a problem of some difficulty to determine what was or was not to be considered the faith of the English church. To remedy the evil, he obtained an order from the council to compose a body of religious doctrine, which, when it had received the royal approbation, should become the authorized standard of orthodoxy. It was an arduous and invidious undertaking. Why, it might be asked, now that the Scriptures were opened to all, should the opinion of any one man, or of any particular body of men, bind the understandings of others? or why should those who had emancipated themselves from the authority of the pontiff be controlled in their belief by the authority of the king? On the other hand, the archbishop was supported by the example of the reformed churches abroad, and impelled by the necessity of enforcing uniformity among the preachers at home, who by their dissensions and contradictions perplexed and disedified their hearers. Cranmer proceeded in his task with caution and deliberation: a rough copy was circulated among his friends, and submitted to the inspection of the council; the communications of others were gratefully accepted, and carefully weighed; even Knox, by command of the king was consulted,[2] and the work, when it had received the last corrections, was laid before a committee of bishops and divines. Their approbation insured that of the king, by whose authority it was published in forty-two articles in Latin and English; and by whom, a short time before his death, it was ordered to be subscribed by all churchwardens, schoolmasters, and clergymen.[3] On this foundation rests its authority. It was never ratified by parliament; nor, though the printed title makes the assertion,[4] does it appear to have been sanctioned by the convocation.

To complete the reformation but

---

[1] Leland, lib. iii. c. 8. He left the country, and the king appointed him a successor; but the new archbishop died in a few weeks, and Dowdal recovered his see at the accession of Mary.—Strype's Cranmer, 278.

[2] To Knox was offered a living, as a reward for his services; this he refused, but accepted the sum of 40*l*.—Privy Council Book, Oct. 27th, 1552. Strype, ii. 389.

[3] Strype's Cranmer, 272, 293. Burnet, ii. 166; iii. 210—213. Wilk. Conc. iv. 79. In the universities an oath was exacted from every person who took any degree, that he would look on the articles as true and certain, and would defend them in all places as agreeable to the word of God. It will, however, require some ingenuity to reconcile with each other the following passages in that oath: Deo teste promitto ac spondeo, me scripturæ auctoritatem hominum judiciis præpositurum......et articulos......regia auctoritate in lucem editos pro veris et certis habiturum, et omni in loco, tanquam consentientes cum verbo Dei defensurum.— MSS. Col. Cor. Chr. Camb. Miscel. P. fol. 492.

[4] In the title-page the Articles are said to have been agreed to "*in the synod of London* in the year 1552."

one thing more was now wanting,—a code of ecclesiastical laws in abrogation of the canons which the realm had formerly received from the church of Rome. The idea of such a compilation had been entertained under Henry: it was reduced to practice under Edward. An act had been already passed empowering the king to give the force of law to those ecclesiastical regulations, which should be made by two and thirty commissioners appointed by his letters patent, and taken in equal proportions from the spirituality and temporality of the realm. But experience showed that the number of the commissioners was calculated to breed diversity rather than uniformity of opinion; and the task was delegated in the first instance to a sub-committee of eight persons, with the archbishop at their head. The result of their labours is in a great measure attributed to his industry and research: but it was put into a new form, and couched in more elegant language, by the pens of Cheke and Haddon. Under the title of Reformatio Legum Ecclesiasticarum, it treats in fifty-one articles of all those subjects the cognizance of which appertained to the spiritual courts; and, though its publication was prevented by the premature death of the king, it must be considered as a most interesting document, inasmuch as it discloses to us the sentiments of the leading reformers on several questions of the first importance.

It commences with an exposition of the Catholic faith, and enacts the punishment of forfeiture and death against those who deny the Christian religion. It then regulates the proceedings in cases of heresy, the ceremony of abjuration, and the delivery of the obstinate heretic to the civil magistrate, that he may suffer death according to law. Blasphemy subjects the offender to the same penalty. The marriages of minors, without the consent of their parents or guardians, and of all persons whomsoever, without the previous publication of banns, or the entire performance of the ceremony in the church according to the Book of Common Prayer, are pronounced of no effect. The seducer of a single woman is compelled to marry her, or to endow her with one-third of his fortune; or, if he have no fortune, to charge himself with the maintenance of their illegitimate offspring, and to suffer some additional and arbitrary punishment. Adultery is visited with imprisonment or transportation for life. In addition, if the offender be the wife, she forfeits her jointure, and all the advantages she might have derived from her marriage; if the husband, he returns to the wife her dower, and adds to it one-half of his own fortune. But to a clergyman, in whom the enormity of the offence increases in proportion to the sanctity of his office, the penalty is more severe. He loses his benefice, and surrenders the whole of his estate, if he be married, to the unoffending party, for the support of her and her children; if unmarried, to the bishop, that it may be devoted to purposes of charity.

Divorces are allowed not only on account of adultery, but also of desertion, long absence, cruel treatment, and danger to health or life: in all which cases the innocent party is permitted to marry again, the guilty condemned to perpetual exile or imprisonment. To these five causes is added confirmed incompatibility of temper; but this, though it may justify a separation, does not allow to either party the privilege of contracting another marriage.[1] In cases of defamation, when, from the destruction of papers or the absence of witnesses, the truth cannot be discovered, the accused is permitted to

---

[1] Reform. Leg. c. viii—xii.

clear his character by his oath, provided he can produce a competent number of compurgators, who shall swear that they give full credit to his assertion. Commutation of penance for money is conceded on particular occasions; the right of devising property by will is refused to married women, slaves, children under fourteen years of age, heretics, libellers, females of loose character, usurers, and convicts sentenced to death, or perpetual banishment or imprisonment; and excommunication is asserted to cut off the offender from the society of the faithful, the protection of God, and the expectation of future happiness; and to consign him to everlasting punishment, and the tyranny of the devil.[1]

Edward had inherited from his mother a weak and delicate constitution. In the spring of the year he was considerably reduced by successive attacks of the measles and the small-pox: in the latter part of the summer a troublesome cough, the effect of imprudent exposure to the cold, terminated in an inflammation on the lungs; and, when the new parliament assembled, the king's weakness compelled him to meet the two houses at his residence of Whitehall. In the morning, after he had heard a sermon from the bishop of London, and received the sacrament in company with several of the lords, he proceeded in state to a neighbouring chamber, in which the session was opened with a speech from the chancellor, Goodrick, bishop of Ely. Northumberland had no reason to fear opposition from the present parliament. To secure a majority in the lower house, orders had been sent to the sheriffs to return grave and able men, and to attend to the recommendations of the privy councillors in their neighbourhood; and sixteen individuals, all of them employed at court, and high in the confidence of the minister, had been nominated by the king himself, in letters addressed to the sheriffs of Hampshire, Suffolk, Berks, Bedford, Surrey, Cambridge, Oxford, and Northamptonshire.[2] The great object of Northumberland was to obtain money for the payment of the royal debts, which amounted to a considerable sum, and could not be liquidated by the annual sales of the chantry lands, and of the monastic possessions still held by the crown. A subsidy with two tenths and fifteenths, was granted: but the preamble, which attributed the king's necessities to improvident and extravagant expenditure under the duke of Somerset, is said to have given rise in the lower house to a long and animated debate. Another object, perhaps of equal importance in the opinion of the minister, was the dissolution of the bishopric of Durham. Defeated in his attempt to procure the deprivation of Tunstall in the last parliament by a bill of pains and penalties, he had erected a new court of lawyers and civilians, with power to call the prelate before them, to inquire into all conspiracies, concealments, contempts, and offences with which he might be charged, and to pronounce judgment of deprivation, if his guilt should deserve such punishment. By this new, and as it was afterwards held, illegal tribunal, he had been stripped of all his ecclesiastical preferments; and, as the see of Durham was now held to be vacant,

---

[1] See the Reformatio Legum Ecclesiasticarum, published anno 1571.

[2] Strype, ii. 394.

[3] See the great amount of these sales in Strype, ii. 362, 373, 427; App. 85—94. As an additional resource, commissions were issued to seize for the treasury all the plate, jewels, and ornaments belonging to the churches, leaving only as many chalices in each as might be necessary for the administration of the sacrament, and such ornaments as the commissioners in their discretion should think requisite.—Fuller, l. vii 417.

an act was passed for the suppression of that diocese, and the establishment of two others by the king's letters patent, of which one should comprehend the county of Northumberland, the other that of Durham. To justify this measure was alleged the enormous extent of the former diocese; a hypocritical pretext employed to turn the attention of the members from the real object of the ministers. Within a month after the dissolution, the bishopric was converted into a county palatine, annexed for the present to the crown, but destined to reward at a convenient opportunity the services of the house of Dudley.[1]

Northumberland was not only the most powerful, his rapacity had made him the most wealthy, individual in the realm. Though his former possessions were sufficiently ample to satisfy the ordinary avarice of a subject, he had, during this and the two last years, increased them by the addition of the stewardships of the east riding of Yorkshire, and of all the royal manors in the five northern counties, and by grants from the crown of Tinmouth and Alnwick in Northumberland, of Bernard Castle, and the bishopric of Durham, and of extensive estates in the three shires of Somerset, Warwick, and Worcester.[2] He was, moreover, warden of the three Scottish marches, with all the authority ever enjoyed by any warden since the reign of Richard II. Still he was aware that he held this pre-eminence by a very precarious tenure. The life of the king was uncertain, in all probability was hastening to its close; from the lady Mary, the presumptive heir, he had little reason to expect friendship or protection; and he foresaw that, if he were left to the mercy of his enemies, he must resign his offices, regorge his wealth, and perhaps atone for his ambition on the scaffold. It became his policy to provide against future danger, by increasing the number, and multiplying the resources of his adherents. His brother and sons were placed in confidential situations near the throne; every office at court was successively intrusted to one or other among his creatures, whose predecessors received yearly pensions as the reward of their resignation, and the price of their future services; and, to connect with his own the interests of other powerful families, he projected a marriage between his fourth son, Guildford Dudley, and the lady Jane Grey, the granddaughter of Mary, sister to Henry VIII.; a second between his own daughter Catherine, and the lord Hastings, the eldest son of the earl of Huntingdon; and a third between the lady Catherine Grey and Lord Herbert, the son of the earl of Pembroke, who owed both his title and property to the favour of Northumberland.[3]

Hitherto Edward, who had inherited a portion of his father's obstinacy, had paid little attention to the advice of his physicians. In the beginning of May an unexpected improvement was observed in his health; he promised to submit for the future to medical advice; and the most flattering hopes were entertained of his recovery.[4] Northumberland chose this period to celebrate the marriages by which he sought to consolidate his power. Durham

---

[1] Strype, ii. 507.

[2] See the titles of these grants in Strype, ii. 499, 504, 507, 508.

[3] Stowe, 609. There remained a third daughter, the lady Mary Grey, who in 1565 was furtively married to Martin Keys, the gentleman porter. He was the largest man, she the most diminutive woman, at court. Elizabeth threw them both into prison.—Strype, Annals of the Reformation, i. 477.

[4] See Northumberland's letter to Cecil, dated May 7; Strype, ii. App. 161; and the lady Mary's to the king, dated May 16, Strype, ii. 424.

House, in the Strand, his new residence, was a scene of continued festivity and amusement; the king, unable to attend in person, manifested his approval by magnificent presents; and at the same time, as if it were wished to conciliate the approbation of the lady Mary, a grant was made to her of the castle of Hertford, and of several manors and parks in the counties of Hertford and Essex.[1]

After a short and delusive interval, Edward relapsed into his former weakness. The symptoms of his disorder grew daily more alarming; and it became evident that his life could not be protracted beyond the term of a few weeks. His danger urged Northumberland to execute a project, which he had in all probability meditated for some time, of placing the crown, in the event of the king's death, on the head of his own son.[2] By act of parliament, and the will of the last monarch, the next heirs were the ladies Mary and Elizabeth; but, as the statutes pronouncing them illegitimate had never been repealed, it was presumed that such illegitimacy might be successfully opposed in bar of their claim. After their exclusion, the crown would of right descend to one of the representatives of the two sisters of Henry VIII.—Margaret, queen of Scotland, and Mary, queen of France. Margaret was the elder but her descendants had been overlooked in the will of the late king, and the animosity of the nation against Scotland would readily induce it to acquiesce in the exclusion of the Scottish line. There remained then the representative of Mary, the French queen, who was Frances, married to Grey, formerly marquess of Dorset, and lately created, in favour of his wife, duke of Suffolk. But Frances had no ambition to ascend a disputed throne, and easily consented to transfer her right to her eldest daughter Jane, the wife of Northumberland's fourth son, Guildford Dudley.[3] Having arranged his plan, the duke ventured to whisper it in the ear of the sick prince; and recommended it to his approbation by a most powerful appeal to his religious prejudices. Edward, he said, by the extirpation of idolatry, and the establishment of a pure system of faith and worship, had secured to himself an immortal reputation in this, everlasting happiness in the next world. The lovers of the gospel had promised to themselves the long enjoy-

---

[1] Strype, ii. 520, 521.
[2] With what view? Probably to secure himself and his colleagues from the punishment which he anticipated in a new reign, "for having been deceivers of the whole body of the realm by a forged instrument." See his letter in p. 162, note. Might not the real object of that letter be to remind the councillors of their danger, and thus predispose them to assent to the change of the succession, which he contemplated?
[3] HENRY VII.

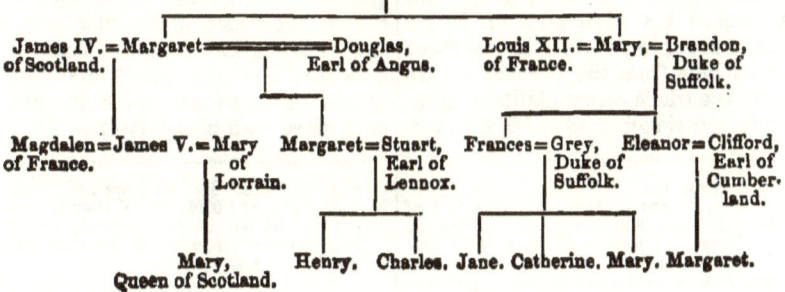

ment of so invaluable a blessing; but now the dangerous state of his health opened to them a dark and menacing prospect. He was acquainted with the bigotry of his sister Mary, which had hitherto set at defiance both his persuasion and his authority. Were she to ascend the throne, she would seize the first opportunity to undo all that he had done; to extinguish the new light, and to replunge the nation into the darkness of error and superstition. Did he not shudder at the very thought? Could he answer it to himself, would he be able to answer it before God, if by his connivance he should permit, while he had it in his power to avert, so direful an evil? Let him make a will like his father, let him pass by the lady Mary on account of illegitimacy, and the lady Elizabeth, who laboured under the same defect, and then entail the crown on the posterity of his aunt, the French queen, whose present descendants were distinguished by their piety and their attachment to the reformed worship.[1]

To these interested suggestions the sick prince, over whose mind the duke had long exercised an unlimited control, listened with feelings of approbation. Perhaps he persuaded himself that he might justly assume on his death-bed those powers which had been exercised by his father Henry; perhaps he deemed it a duty to sacrifice the rights of his sisters to the paramount interests of his religion. He was, however, taught not to expose his adversaries to the resentment of those whom he was about to exclude from the succession. He took the whole responsibility on himself; and sketched with his own pen a rough draft, by which the crown was entailed in the first place on "the Lady Fraunces's heirs masles," in the next on "the Lady Jane's heirs masles," and then on the heirs male of her sisters. But this suited not the views of Northumberland. Not one of these ladies had heirs male; and of course the crown, at the death of Edward, would not devolve on any one of that family. A slight correction was therefore made. The letter "s" at the end of "Jane's" was scored out, the words "and her" were interlined; by which change the instrument was made to read thus: "to the lady Jane and her heirs masles." Thus the wife of Guildford Dudley became the first in the succession. A fair copy was then made, and Edward put to it his signature, above, below, and on each margin.[2]

As soon as these preparations were completed, Sir Edward Montague, chief justice of the Common Pleas, Sir Thomas Bromley, another justice of the same court, and Sir Richard Baker, chancellor of the augmentations, with Gosnold and Gryffyn, the attorney and solicitor general, received a summons to attend the council at Greenwich. On their arrival they were introduced to the king, who said that he had seriously weighed the dangers which threatened the laws, and liberties, and religion of the country, if the lady Mary should inherit the crown, and marry a foreign prince; that, to prevent so great an evil, he had determined to change the order of the succession; and that he had sent for them to draw up a legal instrument, according to the instructions, which he had authorized with his signature. They

---

[1] Godwin, 103.
[2] Strype's Cran. App. 164. The fact of the correction was first made known by Dr. Nares, in his Life of Burghley, i. 452. The instructions for the rest of the will were written by Secretary Petre, and dictated by Edward. He left Mary and Elizabeth annuities of 1,000*l*., and if they should marry by advice of the council, added 10,000*l*. to the portions left them by his father.—Strype, ii. 431.

attempted to speak; but he refused to hear any objection, and with difficulty consented to a short respite, that they might peruse the different acts of succession; and deliberate on the most eligible means of accomplishing the royal pleasure.

Two days later Montague and his companions waited on the lords of the council, and informed them that such an instrument as had been required was a violation of the statute of the thirty-fifth of the late king, and would subject both those who had drawn, and those who had advised it, to the penalties of treason. At these words Northumberland entered from another room, trembling with rage; he threatened and called them traitors; and declared that he was ready to fight in his shirt with any man in so just a quarrel. They were commanded to retire, and the same evening received an order to attend the next day, with the exception of the solicitor-general.

On their admission to the royal presence, Edward sternly asked why his command had not been obeyed. The chief justice replied that to obey would have been dangerous to them, and of no service to his grace; that the succession had been settled by statute, and could be altered only by statute; and that he knew of no other legal expedient but the introduction of a bill for that purpose into the next parliament. The king replied that it was his determination to have the deed of settlement executed now, and ratified afterwards in the parliament summoned to meet in September; and therefore he commanded them on their allegiance to submit to his pleasure. Montague began to waver: his conversion was hastened by the threats and reproaches of the lords of the council, who attended in a body; and, after a short hesitation, turning to the king, he professed his readiness to obey, but requested that he might have under the great seal, first a commission to draw the instrument, and then a full pardon for having drawn it. To this Edward assented; Bromley and Baker followed the example of the chief justice; but the repugnance of Gosnold was not subdued till the following day.[1]

Among the privy councillors there were some who, though apprized of the illegality, and apprehensive of the consequences of the measure, suffered themselves to be seduced from their duty by the threats and promises of Northumberland, and by their objection to the succession of a princess who would probably re-establish the ancient faith, and compel them to restore the property which they had torn from the church. The archbishop, if we may believe his own statement, had requested a private interview with the king, but he was accompanied by the marquess of Northampton and the lord Darcy, in whose presence Edward solicited him to subscribe the new settlement, expressed a hope that he would not refuse to his sovereign a favour which had been granted by every other councillor, and assured him that, according to the decision of the judges, a king, in actual possession, had a power to limit the descent of the crown after his decease. Cranmer confesses that he had the weakness to yield against his own conviction, "and so," says he, "I granted him to subscribe his will, and to follow the same; which when I had set my hand unto, I did it unfeignedly and without dissimulation."[2]

---

[1] See Montague's statement in Fuller, l. viii. 2—5.

[2] I give his words, because their meaning has been disputed. To me he appears to say, that, when he had once subscribed, he followed the will, that is, supported it, unfeignedly and without dissimulation. The object of his letter was to beg pardon for "consenting and *following* the testament." —See Strype, App. 169.

Northumberland, whether it was that he suspected the fidelity of some among his colleagues, or that he was unwilling to trust the success of his project to the dilatory forms of office, had prepared another paper, to which at the royal command four-and-twenty of the counsellors and legal advisers of the crown affixed their signatures. By it they pledged their oaths and honour to "observe every article contained in his majesty's own device respecting the succession, subscribed with his majesty's hand in six several places, and delivered to certain judges and other learned men, that it might be written in full order;" to maintain and defend it to the uttermost of their power during their lives; and if any man should hereafter attempt to alter it, to repute him an enemy to the welfare of the kingdom, and to punish him according to his deserts.[1] As soon as the official instrument had been prepared, it was engrossed in parchment, carried to the Chancery, and authenticated with the great seal. It then received the signatures of the lords of the council, and of several peers, judges, officers of the crown, and others, to the number of one hundred and one witnesses.[2]

Northumberland's next object was to secure the person of the lady Mary. His sons had received licences to raise companies of horse; several petty fortifications on the sea-coast and the banks of the Thames had been dismantled, to provide, without exciting suspicion, a supply of powder and ammunition for the Tower; forty additional warders were introduced into that fortress; the constable, Sir John Gage, was superseded in the command by Sir James Croft, a creature of the duke; and Croft, when all was ready, surrendered his charge to the lord Clinton, lord high admiral. Then, to secure their prey, a letter was written by the council to the lady Mary, requiring her by the king's order to repair immediately to court. Had she reached London, her next removal would have been to the Tower: but she received a friendly

---

[1] The subscribers were Thomas, archbishop of Canterbury; Thomas, bishop of Ely, chancellor; Winchester, lord treasurer; Northumberland, great master; Bedford, lord privy seal; John, duke of Suffolk; Northampton, lord high chamberlain; Shrewsbury, lord president in the north; the earl of Huntingdon; the earl of Pembroke; Clinton, lord admiral; Darcy, chamberlain of the household; Lord Cobham; Cheyne, treasurer of the household; Lord Rich; Gate, vice-chamberlain; Petre, Cheke, and Cecil, principal secretaries; Montague, Baker, Gryffyn, Lucas and Gosnold.—See the instrument in Strype's Cranmer, App. p. 163; Burnet, iii. Rec. 207. In defence of the subscribers, it has been supposed that they might have been deceived; that the original draft by Edward had been exhibited to them; and that they subscribed without any knowledge of the correction to be afterwards made in it. But this is no more than an unfounded conjecture. None of them subsequently alleged any such excuse; nor could it avail them; for even the original draft was an infringement of the statute of the 35th of Henry VIII., and of his alleged will, on which the council founded their own authority.

[2] See the will in Howel' 754. We have three accounts of the transaction, one by Sir Edward Montague, another by Cranmer, and a third by Cecil. It may perhaps detract something from their credit, that they are interested statements, drawn up by the writers for the purpose of extenuating their own guilt in the estimation of Queen Mary. Neither is it easy to reconcile them with each other, or with known facts. Thus Cranmer says that both the king and his council assured him that the judges had declared in favour of the legality of the measure (Strype's Cran. App. 169): Montague, on the contrary, tells us that he repeatedly, in his own name and that of his colleagues, pronounced it illegal in the presence of the whole council, and consequently of the archbishop.—Fuller, l. viii. p. 3. Cecil said that he refused to subscribe, when none of the others refused: and that if he subscribed at last, it was not as an abettor of the measure, but merely as a witness to the king's signature.—Strype, ii. 430; iv. 347. Yet in the instrument mentioned in the last note, his name occurs in its proper place, not as of a witness, but as of one who takes his oath, and promises on his honour to maintain it. Cranmer in his statement takes credit to himself for being the last who was persuaded to subscribe.

hint of her danger on the road; and hastened back to her usual residence, Kenninghall, in the county of Norfolk.[1]

We are told that at this period the care of the king was intrusted to a female empiric, whose charms or medicines, instead of alleviating, aggravated his sufferings; and that his physicians, when they were recalled, pronounced him to be at the point of death.[2] The report originated probably with those who afterwards accused Northumberland of having taken the life of his sovereign. However that may be, on the first of July the duke pretended to entertain hopes of his recovery: on the sixth of the same month the king expired in the evening. The event had long been expected by the nation, and the vengeance of the council had already visited with stripes and imprisonment several offenders, both male and female, who had prematurely announced the intelligence.[3]

It would be idle to delineate the character of a prince who lived not till his passions could develop themselves, or his faculties acquire maturity.[4] His education, like that of his two sisters, began at a very early age. In abilities he was equal, perhaps superior, to most boys of his years; and his industry and improvement amply repaid the solicitude of his tutors. But the extravagant praise which has been lavished on him by his panegyrists and admirers must be received with some degree of caution. In the French and Latin letters, to which they appeal, it is difficult to separate the composition of the pupil from the corrections of the master;[5] and since, to raise his reputation, deceptions are known to have been employed on some occasions, it may be justifiable to suspect that they were practised on others. The boy of twelve or fourteen years was accustomed to pronounce his opinion in the council with all the gravity of a hoary statesman. But he had been previously informed of the subjects to be discussed; his preceptors had supplied him with short notes, which he committed to memory; and, while he delivered their sentiments as his own, the lords, whether they were aware or not of the artifice, admired and applauded the precocious wisdom with which Heaven had gifted their sovereign.[6]

---

[1] Strype, ii. 521. Hayward, 327.

[2] Hayward, 327. Heylin, 139. Rosso, 10.

[3] See several instances from the Council Book in Strype, ii. 428. On the first of July they wrote to the foreign ambassadors, "that his majesty was alive, whatsoever evil men did write or spread abroad; and, as they trusted and wished, his estate and towardness of recovery out of his sickness should shortly appear to the comfort of all good men."—Strype, ii. 429.

[4] One part of his education was likely to have strengthened his passions. No one was permitted to address him, not even his sisters, without kneeling to him. "I have seen," says Ubaldini, "the princess Elizabeth drop on one knee five times before her brother, before she took her place." At dinner, if either of his sisters were permitted to eat with him, she sat on a stool and cushion, at a distance, beyond the limits of the royal dais.—Ubaldini, apud Von Raumer, ii. 70. Even the lords and gentlemen who brought in the dishes before dinner were bareheaded, and knelt down before they placed them on the table. This custom shocked the French ambassador and his suite: for in France the office was confined to pages, who bowed only, and did not kneel.—See the Mémoires de Vieilleville, Mém. xxviii. 319.

[5] These letters may be seen in Fuller, l. vii. p. 423; Hearne's Titus Livius, 115; and Strype, ii. App. 162. Perhaps the character given of him by Barbaro, the Venetian ambassador, in 1551, approaches nearest to the truth. "He is of good disposition, and fills the country with the best expectations, because he is handsome, graceful, of proper size, shows an inclination to generosity, and begins to wish to understand what is going on; and in the exercise of the mind, and the study of languages, appears to excel his companions. He is 14 years of age. This is what I am able to state about him."—MS. at Greystoke Castle.

[6] See Strype, ii. 104. From a document in Raumer, it appears that Northumberland was also accustomed to prepare the king for the discussion of subjects beforehand (iii. 79).

Edward's religious belief could not have been the result of his own judgment. He was compelled to take it on trust from those about him, who moulded his infant mind to their own pleasure, and infused into it their own opinions or prejudices. From them he derived a strong sense of piety, and a habit of daily devotion, a warm attachment to the new, and a violent antipathy to the ancient doctrines. He believed it to be the first of his duties to extirpate what he had been taught to deem the idolatrous worship of his fathers; and with his last breath he wafted a prayer to Heaven for the preservation of his subjects from the infection of "papistry."[1] Yet it may be a question whether his early death has not proved a benefit to the church of England as it is at present established. His sentiments, like those of his instructors, were tinged with Calvinism; attempts were made to persuade him that episcopacy was an expensive and unnecessary institution; and the courtiers, whose appetite for church property had been whetted rather than satisfied by former spoliations, looked impatiently towards the entire suppression of the bishoprics and chapters.[2] Of the possessions belonging to these establishments, one-half had already been seized by the royal favourites: in the course of a few years their rapacity would have devoured the remainder.[3]

The governors and counsellors of the young king were so occupied with plans of personal aggrandizement, and the introduction of religious reform, that they could pay but little attention to the great objects of national polity. Under their care or negligence England was compelled to descend from the pre-eminence which she previously held among the nations of Europe; and her degradation was consummated at the conferences for the restoration of Boulogne, by the supercilious conduct of the French, and the tame acquiescence of the English ministers. For the advantage of commerce, the exclusive privileges enjoyed by the corporation of the Stilyard were abolished; and a little before the king's death an expedition was fitted out to discover a north-east passage to China and India. With this view a joint-stock company was formed under the direction of Sebastian Cabote, son of Cabote the celebrated navigator: three stout ships were built at the cost of six thousand pounds; and Sir Hugh Willoughby, a brave and experienced soldier, but probably no sailor, was intrusted with the chief command. Off the northern extremity of Norway, this little fleet

---

[1] Fox, ii. 130.

[2] On this subject the reader will be amused with the disinterested advice of Hobey. In a letter of the 10th of January, 1549, he tells the protector, that the foreign Protestants " have good hopes, and pray earnestly therefore, that the king's majesty will appoint unto the good bishops an honest and competent living, sufficient for their maintenance, taking from them the rest of their worldly possessions and dignities, and thereby avoid the vain glory that letteth them truly and sincerely to do their duty." From the bishops he proceeds to the chapters. He had been told that 1,500 horsemen had mustered at Brussels to meet the prince of "Spain: which," he adds, "when I heard, remembering what great service such a number of chosen men were able to do, specially in our country, wherein is so much lack of good horsemen, it caused me to declare, under your grace's correction, what I thought; earnestly to wish with all my heart that, standing with the king's majesty's pleasure and your prudence, all the prebends within England were converted to the like use, for the defence of our country, and the maintenance of honest poor gentlemen."—Apud Strype, ii. 88.

[3] By the extortion of grants and exchanges the incomes of the richer bishoprics were reduced about two-thirds, those of the poorer about one-half; and on the other hand eighteen free schools were founded, the endowments of which amounted to 360l. per annum.—Strype, ii. 535. Rec. 159. I may add, that in a patent for the exchange of lands to the bishop of Bath and Wells, are mentioned not only the lands, but also nativi, et nativæ, et villani cum eorum sequelis.—Id. 554. So long did villenage continue in England.

was dispersed by a violent storm. Challoner, the second in command, continued his course alone, keeping in sight of the land, till he entered an immense estuary, now called the White Sea, and found an asylum for the winter in the port of Archangel; whence he traversed Russia to Moscow, and, having been favourably received by the emperor Iwan Wasilejevitch, returned to Archangel, and thence to England, with a letter from the Czar to the king of England. Of Challoner's former companions we know nothing more than that they reached the shore of Nova Zembla, and afterwards landed somewhere on the coast of Russian Lapland, where they afterwards perished.

Within the realm poverty and discontent generally prevailed. The extension of inclosures, and the new practice of letting lands at rack rents, had driven from their homes numerous families, whose fathers had occupied the same farms for several generations; and the increasing multitudes of the poor began to resort to the more populous towns in search of that relief which had been formerly distributed at the gates of the monasteries.[1] Nor were the national morals improved, if we may judge from the portraits drawn by the most eminent of the reformed preachers. They assert that the sufferings of the indigent were viewed with indifference by the hard-heartedness of the rich; that in the pursuit of gain the most barefaced frauds were avowed and justified; that robbers and murderers escaped punishment by the partiality of juries and the corruption of judges; that church livings were given to laymen, or converted to the use of the patrons; that marriages were repeatedly dissolved by private authority; and that the haunts of prostitution were multiplied beyond measure.[2] How far credit should be given to such representations, may perhaps be doubtful. Declamations from the pulpit are not the best historical evidence. Much in them must be attributed to the exaggeration of zeal, much to the affectation of eloquence. Still, when these deductions have been made, when the invectives of Knox and Lever, of Gilpin and Latimer, have been reduced by the standard of reason and experience, enough will remain to justify the conclusion, that the change of religious polity, by removing many of the former restraints upon vice, and enervating the authority of the spiritual courts, had given a bolder front to licentiousness, and opened a wider scope to the indulgence of criminal passion.

---

[1] Thus Lever exclaims: "O merciful Lord! what a number of poor, feeble, halt, blind, lame, sickly, yea, with idle vagabonds and dissembling caitiffs mixed among them, lie and creep, begging in the miry streets of London and Westminster."—Strype, ii. 449.

[2] The industry of Strype has collected several passages on these subjects from the old preachers (369, 438—450).

CHAPTER V.

MARY.

CONTEMPORARY PRINCES.

Emp. of Germ.	*Q. of Scotland.*	*K. of France.*	*K. of Spain.*
Charles V. 1558	Mary.	Henry II.	Charles V. 1550
Ferdinand.			Philip II.

Popes.
Julius III., 1555.   Marcellus II., 1555.   Paul IV.

LADY JANE GREY PROCLAIMED QUEEN—THE LADY MARY IS ACKNOWLEDGED—HER QUESTIONS TO THE EMPEROR CHARLES—EXECUTION OF NORTHUMBERLAND—MISCONDUCT OF COURTENAY—QUEEN SEEKS TO RESTORE THE ANCIENT SERVICE—ELIZABETH CONFORMS—CRANMER OPPOSES—PARLIAMENT—INTRIGUES OF NOAILLES—INSURRECTION OF WYAT—FAILURE AND PUNISHMENT OF THE CONSPIRATORS—ELIZABETH AND COURTENAY IN DISGRACE—TREATY OF MARRIAGE BETWEEN MARY AND PHILIP—RECONCILIATION WITH ROME.

THE declining health of Edward had attracted the notice of the neighbouring courts: to the two rival sovereigns, Charles V. of Germany, and Henry II. of France, it offered a new subject of political intrigue. The presumptive heir to the sick king was his sister Mary, a princess who, ever since the death of her father, had been guided by the advice, and under persecution had been protected by the remonstrances, of the emperor. Gratitude, as well as consanguinity, must attach her to the interests of her benefactor and relative; probably she would, in the event of her succession, throw the power of England into the scale against the pretensions of France: it was even possible that partiality to the father might induce her to accept the son for her husband. On these accounts both princes looked forward with considerable solicitude to the approaching death of Edward, and to the result of the plot contrived by the ambition of Northumberland.

Charles had despatched from Brussels Montmorency, Marnix, and Renard, as ambassadors extraordinary to the English court. They came under the pretence of visiting the infirm monarch; but the real object was to watch the proceedings of the council, to study the resources of the different parties, to make friends for the lady Mary, and, as far as prudence would allow, to promote her succession to the throne.[1]

The same reasons which induced the emperor to favour, urged the king of France to oppose, the interest of Mary. Aware of the design of his rival, Henry despatched to London the bishop of Orleans, and the Chevalier de Gye, with instructions to counteract the attempts of the imperial envoys; but the slow progress of these ministers was anticipated by

---

[1] From their instructions in the collection of the papers of the ambassador Renard, in the library of Besançon, tom. iii. fol. 1, it appears that they were sent "devers le R. d'Angleterre, notre cousine la princesse, le duc de Northumberland, et seigneurs du conseil."

the industry and address of Noailles, the resident ambassador, who, though he would not commit his sovereign by too explicit an avowal of his sentiments, readily offered to the council the aid of France, if foreigners should attempt to disturb the tranquillity of the realm. The hint was sufficient. Northumberland saw that he had nothing to fear, but everything to hope, from the policy of the French monarch.[1]

It was on the evening of the sixth of July that Edward expired at Greenwich. With the view of concealing his death for some days from the knowledge of the public,[2] the guards had been previously doubled in the palace, and all communication intercepted between his chamber and the other apartments. Yet that very night, while the lords sat in deliberation, the secret was communicated to Mary by a note, probably from the earl of Arundel, unfolding the design of the conspirators. She was then at Hoddesdon, in the neighbourhood of London, and, had she hesitated, would by the next morning have been a prisoner in the Tower. Without losing a moment she mounted her horse, and rode with the servants of her household to Kenninghall, in Norfolk.[3]

The council broke up after midnight; and Clinton, the lord admiral, took possession of the Tower, with the royal treasures, the munitions of war, and the prisoners of state. The three next days were employed in making such previous arrangements as were thought necessary for the success of the enterprise. While the death of Edward was yet unknown, the officers of the guards and of the household, the lord mayor, six aldermen, and twelve of the principal citizens, were summoned before the council. All were informed of the recent settlement of the crown, and required to take an oath of allegiance to the new sovereign; the latter were dismissed with an injunction not to betray the secret, and to watch over the tranquillity of the city. On the fourth morning it was determined to publish the important intelligence and the chief of the lords, attended by a numerous escort, rode to Sion House to announce to the lady Jane her succession to the throne of her royal cousin.

Jane has been described to us as a young woman of gentle manners, and superior talents, addicted to the study of the Scriptures and the classics, but fonder of dress than suited the austere notions of the reformed preachers. Of the designs of the duke of Northumberland in her favour, and of the arts by which he had deceived the simplicity of Edward, she knew nothing; nor had she suffered the dark and mysterious predictions of the duchess to make any impression on her mind. Her love of privacy had induced her to solicit, what in the uncertain state of the king's health was readily granted, permission to leave London, and to spend a few days at Chelsea; she was indulging herself in this retirement, when she received by the lady Sydney, her husband's sister, an order from the council to return immediately to Sion House, and to await there the commands of the king. She obeyed; and the next morning was visited by the duke of Northumberland, the marquess of Northampton, and the earls of Arundel, Huntingdon, and Pembroke. At first, the conversation turned on indifferent subjects, but there was in their manner an air of respect, which awakened some uneasiness in her mind, and seemed to

---

[1] Ambassad. de Mess. de Noailles, ii. 45, 50, 53.
[2] See Alford's letter to Cecil, Strype, iv. 349.
[3] Noailles, 56.

explain the hints already given to her by her mother-in-law. Soon afterwards that lady entered, accompanied by the duchess of Suffolk and the marchioness of Northampton; and the duke, addressing the lady Jane, informed her that the king her cousin was dead; that before he expired, he had prayed to God to preserve the realm from the infection of papistry, and the misrule of his sisters Mary and Elizabeth; that, on account of their being bastards, and by act of parliament incapable of the succession, he had resolved to pass them by, and to leave the crown in the right line; and that he had therefore commanded the council to proclaim her, the lady Jane, his lawful heir, and in default of her and her issue, her two sisters, Catherine and Mary. At the words the lords fell on their knees, declared that they took her for their sovereign, and swore that they were ready to shed their blood in support of her right. The reader may easily conceive the agitation of spirits which a communication so important and unlooked for was likely to create in a young woman of timid habits and delicate health. She trembled, uttered a shriek, and sank to the ground. On her recovery she observed to those around her, that she seemed to herself a very unfit person to be a queen; but that, if the right were hers, she trusted God would give her strength to wield the sceptre to his honour and the benefit of the nation.

Such is the account of this transaction given, about a month afterwards, by Jane herself, in a letter from the Tower to Queen Mary.[1] The feelings which she describes are such as we might expect; surprise at the annunciation, grief for the death of her royal cousin, and regret to quit a station in which she had been happy. But modern writers have attributed to her much of which she seems to have been ignorant herself. The beautiful language which they put into her mouth, her forcible reasoning in favour of the claim of Mary, her philosophic contempt of the splendour of royalty, her refusal to accept a crown which was not her right, and her reluctant submission to the commands of her parents, must be considered as the fictions of historians, who, in their zeal to exalt the character of the heroine, seem to have forgotten that she was only sixteen years of age.

About three in the afternoon, the young queen was conducted by water to the Tower, the usual residence of our kings preparatory to their coronation. She made her entry in state. Her train was borne by her mother, the duchess of Suffolk; the lord treasurer presented her with the crown; and her relations saluted her on their knees. At six the same evening, the heralds proclaimed the death of Edward and the succession of Jane; and a printed instrument with her signature was circulated, to acquaint the people with the grounds of her

---

[1] "Le quali cose, tosto chè con infinito dolore dell' animo mio hebbi intese, quanto io restasse fuor di me stordita, e sbattuta, ne lascerò testimoniare à quei Signori, i quali si trovarono presenti, chè soppraggiunta da subita e non aspettata doglia, mi videro in terra cadere, molto dolorosamente piangendo: E dichiarando poi loro l' insofficienza mia, forte mi rammaricai della morte d' un si nobile principe, e insieme mi risolvi a Dio, humilmente pregandolo, e supplicandolo, chè se quello che m'era dato, era dirittamente o legittamamente mio, S.D.M. mi donasse tanta grazia e spirito, ch'io il potesse governare, a gloria sua, e servigio, e utile di questo reame."—From her letter or confession to Mary in August soon after her committal to the Tower. The original in English has probably perished; but we have two different translations of it in Italian, one by Rosso in his "Successi d'Inghilterra dopo la morte di Odoardo sesto," published in Ferrara as early as 1560; and another by Pollini in his Historia Eccl. della Rivoluzion d' Inghilterra, in Roma, 1594.

claim. It alleged, 1. That though the succession, by the thirty-fifth of Henry VIII. stood limited to the ladies Mary and Elizabeth, yet neither of them could take anything under that act, because, by a previous statute of the twenty-eighth of the same reign, which still remained in force, both daughters had been pronounced bastards, and incapable of inheriting the crown; 2. That even, had they been born in lawful wedlock, they could have no claim to the succession after Edward, because being his sisters only by the half-blood, they could not inherit from him according to the ancient laws and customs of the realm; 3. That the fact of their being single women ought to be a bar to their claim, as by their subsequent marriages they might place the sovereign power in the hands of a foreign despot, who would be able to subvert the liberties of the people, and to restore the jurisdiction of the bishop of Rome; 4. That these considerations had moved the late king to limit, by his letters patent, the inheritance of the crown in the first place to the lawful issue of the duchess of Suffolk,[1] her male issue, if any were born to her during his life, otherwise to her daughters and their issue in succession, and after them to the daughter of the late countess of Cumberland, sister to the said duchess, and to her issue, inasmuch as the said ladies were nigh to him of blood, and "naturally born within the realm;" 5. And that therefore the lady Jane, the eldest daughter of the duchess of Suffolk, had now taken upon herself, as belonging to her of right, the government of the kingdoms of England and Ireland, and of all their dependencies.[2] To the arguments contained in this laboured proclamation the people listened in ominous silence. They had so long considered Mary the presumptive heir, that they did not comprehend how her claim could be defeated by any pretensions of a daughter of the house of Suffolk. Not a single voice was heard in approbation; a vintner's boy had the temerity to express his dissent, and the next day paid the forfeit of his folly with the loss of his ears.[3]

The following morning arrived at the Tower a messenger from Mary, the bearer of a letter to the lords, in which, assuming the style and tone of their sovereign, she upbraided them with their neglect to inform her of the death of her brother, hinted her knowledge of their disloyal intention to oppose her right, and commanded them, as they hoped for favour, to proclaim her accession immediately in the metropolis, and as soon as possible, in all other parts of the kingdom.[4]

---

[1] As the duchess of Suffolk was still living, how happened it that the king should overlook her, to leave the crown to her daughter? It evidently entered into the plan of Northumberland to suppress her claims, and probably his argument to Edward was that she had been omitted in his father's will, though her issue had been expressly named. It was differently with respect to the elder branch, the descendants of the queen of Scots. They had been omitted altogether.

[2] Noailles, ii. 62. Burnet, ii. Rec. 239. Somers' Tracts, i. 174. The heads of this instrument are taken out of the will of Edward VI., which is published in Howell's State Trials, i. 754; but the line respecting the jurisdiction of the bishop of Rome was an interpolation. The words, " born within the realm," were added to exclude the Scottish line.

[3] The vintner's boy was nailed to the pillory by the ears, both of which were amputated before he could be released.—Holins. 1065.

[4] The following is her proclamation:—
"Marie, the Quene,
"Knowe ye, all the good subjects of this realme, that yor most noble prince, yor soveraine Lord and King, Edwarde the vjth is upon thursday last being the vjth of July dep'ted this worlde to Godes mercie. And that now the most excellent princes, his sister Marie, by the grace of God ys Quene of E. and Y. and verie owner of the crowne, government and tytle of E. and Y. and all things thereunto belonging, to Godes glory, the honor of the royalme of England, and

This communication caused no change in their counsels, awakened no apprehension in their minds. Mary was a single and defenceless female, unprepared to vindicate her right, without money, and without followers. They had taken every precaution to insure success. The exercise of the royal authority was in their hands; the royal treasures were at their disposal; the guards had sworn obedience; a fleet of twenty armed vessels lay in the river; and a body of troops had been assembled in the Isle of Wight, ready at any moment to execute their orders. Depending on their own resources, contrasted with the apparent helplessness of their adversary, they affected to dread her flight more than her resistance, and returned an answer under the signatures of the archbishop, the chancellor, and twenty-one councillors, requiring her to abandon her false claim, and to submit as a dutiful subject to her lawful and undoubted sovereign.[1]

In a few hours the illusion vanished. The mass of the people knew little of the lady Jane, but all had heard of the ambition of Northumberland. His real object, it was said, was now unmasked. To deprive the late king of his nearest relatives and protectors, he had persuaded Somerset to take the life of the lord admiral, and Edward to take that of Somerset. The royal youth was the next victim. He had been removed by poison to make room for the lady Jane,[2] who, in her turn would be compelled to yield the crown to Northumberland himself. These reports were circulated and believed, and the public voice, wherever it might be expressed with impunity, was unanimous in favour of Mary. The very day on which the answer to her letter had been despatched, brought the alarming intelligence that she was already joined by the earls of Bath and Sussex,[3] and by the eldest sons of the lords Wharton and Mordaunt; that the gentlemen of the neighbouring counties were hastening to her aid with their tenants and dependants; and that in a short time a numerous and formidable army would be embattled under her banners.[4] Northumberland saw the necessity of despatch: but how could he venture to leave the capital where his presence awed the disaffected and secured the cooperation of his colleagues? He

---

all yor comfortes. And her Highness ys not fled thys royalme, ne intendethe to do, as ys most untruly surmised."—Gage's Hengrave, 143.

[1] Fox, iii. 12. Strype, iii. Rec. 3. The emperor was equally persuaded of her inability to contend with the council, and on the 28th of June advised her to offer them a pardon for all past offences, and to consent, if they required it, that they should hold the same offices under her, and that no change should be made in the establishment of religion.—Renard's MSS. folio 6. But when he learned that she meant to fight for her right, he exhorted her to persevere: puisqu'elle s'y est mise si avant, qu'elle perde la crainte, évite de la donner à ceux qui sont de son côté, et qu'elle passe tout outre.—Ibid. fol. 22.

[2] This opinion was so general, that the emperor, Aug. 23, wrote to the queen that she ought to put to death all the conspirators who had any hand in "the death" of the late king.—Renard, apud Griffet, xi. Renard's despatches are in three volumes in the library at Besançon; but the more interesting of those respecting Mary were selected from the third volume and communicated to Griffet, the author of the valuable notes to the best edition of Daniel's History of France. From them Griffet compiled, in a great measure, his "Nouveaux Eclaircissemens sur l'Histoire de Marie Reine d'Angleterre," 12mo. Amst. et Paris, 1766, of which an English translation was published under the title of "New Lights thrown upon the History of Mary, Queen of England," 8vo. London, 1771. The papers employed by Griffet were never replaced; but those which remain bear abundant testimony to his accuracy and fidelity.

[3] Mary granted to the earl of Sussex a licence to wear "his cap, coif, or nightcap, or two of them at his pleasure, in the royal presence, or in the presence of any other person."—Oct. 2, Heylin's Mary, 190.

[4] "Certain noblemen, knights, and gentlemen come to her to mayntayn her title, with also innumerable companies of the common people."—Gage's Hengrave, 143.

proposed to give the command of the forces to the duke of Suffolk, whose affection for his daughter was a pledge of his fidelity, and whose want of military experience might be supplied by the knowledge of his associates. But he could not deceive the secret partisans of Mary, who saw his perplexity, and to liberate themselves from his control, urged him to take the command upon himself. They praised his skill, his valour, and his good fortune; they exaggerated the insufficiency of Suffolk, and the consequences to be apprehended from a defeat; and they prevailed upon Jane, through anxiety for her father, to unite with them in their entreaties to Northumberland. He gave a tardy and reluctant consent. When he took leave of his colleagues he exhorted them to fidelity with an earnestness which betrayed his apprehensions; and, as he rode through the city at the head of the troops, he remarked, in a tone of despondency, to Sir John Gates, "The people crowd to look upon us, but not one exclaims, God speed ye."[1]

From the beginning the duke had mistrusted the fidelity of the citizens: before his departure he requested the aid of the preachers, and exhorted them to appeal from the pulpit to the religious feelings of their hearers. By no one was the task performed with greater zeal than by Ridley, bishop of London, who, on the following Sunday, preached at St. Paul's Cross before the lord mayor, the aldermen, and a numerous assemblage of the people. He maintained that the daughters of Henry VIII. were, by the illegitimacy of their birth, excluded from the succession. He contrasted the opposite characters of the present competitors, the gentleness, the piety, the orthodoxy of the one, with the haughtiness, the foreign connections, and the popish creed of the other. As a proof of Mary's bigotry, he narrated a chivalrous but unsuccessful attempt, which he had made within the last year, to withdraw her from the errors of popery;[2] and in conclusion, he conjured the audience, as they prized the pure light of the gospel, to support the cause of the lady Jane, and to oppose the claim of her idolatrous rival. But the torrent of his eloquence was poured in vain. Among his hearers there were many indifferent to either form of worship. Of the rest, the Protestants had not yet learned that religious belief could affect hereditary right; and the Catholics were confirmed by the bishop's arguments, in their adhesion to the interests of Mary.[3]

That princess, to open a communication with the emperor in Flanders, had unexpectedly left Kenninghall; and, riding forty miles without rest, had reached, on the same evening, the castle of Framlingham. There her hopes were hourly cheered with the most gratifying intelligence. The earl of Essex, the lord Thomas Howard, the Jerninghams, Bedingfelds, Sulyards, Pastons, and most of the neighbouring gentlemen, successively arrived, with their tenants, to fight under her standard.[4] Sir Edward Hastings, Sir Edmund Peckham, and Sir Robert Drury, had levied ten thousand men in the counties of Oxford, Buckingham, Berks, and Middlesex, and purposed to march from Drayton for Westminster and the palace; her more distant friends continued to send her presents

---

[1] Godwin. 106. Stowe, 610, 611.
[2] See Appendix X.
[3] Concionatores, quos bene multos Londini constituit, nihil profecerunt; imo ne quidem egregius ille doctrina vitæque sanctitate vir Ridlæus episcopus æquis auribus auditus est. Utinam vir optimus hac in re lapsus non fuisset.—Godwin, 106. See Stowe, ii. 611; Burnet, 238; Heylin, 184; Holinshed, 1089.
[4] See Appendix Y

of money, and offers of service; Henry Jerningham prevailed on a hostile squadron, of six sail, which had reached the harbour of Yarmouth, to acknowledge her authority; and a timely supply of arms and ammunition from the ships relieved the more urgent wants of her adherents. In a few days Mary was surrounded by more than thirty thousand men, all volunteers in her cause, who refused to receive pay, and served through the sole motive of loyalty.[1]

In this emergency, doubt and distrust seem to have unnerved the mind of Northumberland, who had marched from Cambridge in the direction of Framlingham, accompanied by his son the earl of Warwick, by the marquess of Northampton, the earl of Huntingdon, and the lord Grey. With an army of eight thousand infantry, and two thousand cavalry, inferior, indeed, in number to his opponents, but infinitely superior in military appointments and discipline, he might, by a bold and immediate attack, have dispersed the tumultuary force of the royalists, and have driven Mary across the sea, to the court of her imperial cousin. But he saw, as he advanced, the enthusiasm of the people in her cause; he heard that he had been proclaimed a rebel, and that a price had been fixed on his head;[2] and he feared that Sir Edward Hastings would, in a few days, cut off his communication with the capital. At Bury his heart failed him. He ordered a retreat to Cambridge, and wrote to the council for a numerous and immediate reinforcement. The men perceived the irresolution of their leader; their ignorance of his motives gave birth to the most disheartening reports; and their ranks were hourly thinned by desertion.

In the council there appeared no diminution of zeal, no want of unanimity. It was resolved to send for a body of mercenaries, which had been raised in Picardy, to issue commissions for the levying of troops in the vicinity of the metropolis,[3] and to offer eight crowns per month, besides provisions, to volunteers. But, as such tardy expedients did not meet the urgency of the case, the lords proposed to separate, and hasten to the army, at the head of their respective friends and dependants. Though Suffolk had been instructed to detain them within the walls of the Tower, he either saw not their object, or dared not oppose their pleasure. The next morning the lord treasurer and lord privy seal, the earls of Arundel, Shrewsbury, and Pembroke, Sir Thomas Cheney, and Sir John Mason, left the fortress under the pretence of receiving the French ambassador at Baynard's Castle, a fitter place, it was said, for that purpose than the Tower.[4]

---

[1] Noailles, ii. 94. She, however, gave orders that " where the captains perceived any soldier wanting money, his captain should relieve him, but in such sort, that it appeared not otherwise but to be of his own liberality."—Journal of Council in Haynes, 157.

[2] "Assuring all and everie her said subjects on the word of a rightful queene, that whosoever taketh and bringeth the said duke unto her presence, shall, if he be a nobleman and peer of the realme, have 1,000 pounds in land to him and his heirs; likewise, if he be a knight, 500 pounds lands to him and his heirs, with the honour and advancement to nobilitie; and also, if the same taker and bringer be a gentleman under the degree of a knight, 500 marks land to him and his heirs, and the degree of a knight; and if the said taker and bringer be a yeoman, 100 pounds lands to him and his heirs and the degree of a squire."—From the original in possession of Sir Henry Bedingfield.

[3] Some of them may be seen in Strype, iii. Rec. p. 4; in his Cranmer, App. 165; and in Hearne's Sylloge, ep. 121.

[4] Strype, iv. 349. Yet that very morning they had signed a letter to Lord Rich, thanking him for his services in favour of Jane.—Strype's Cranmer, App. 164. Did they not know that he had already transferred them to Mary?—Haynes, i. 159.

There they were joined by the lord mayor, the recorder, and a deputation of aldermen, who had been summoned by a trusty messenger; and the discussion was opened by the earl of Arundel, who, in a set speech, declaimed against the ambition of Northumberland, and asserted the right of the two daughters of Henry VIII. The moment he had finished, the earl of Pembroke drew his sword, exclaiming, "If the arguments of my lord of Arundel do not persuade you, this sword shall make Mary queen, or I will die in her quarrel." He was answered with shouts of approbation, and Suffolk, who had been sent for, signed with the others the proclamation of Mary. The whole body then rode in procession through the city. At St. Paul's Cross the earl of Pembroke proclaimed the new queen amidst the deafening acclamations of the populace. Te Deum was sung in the cathedral; beer, wine, and money were distributed among the people; and the night was ushered in with bonfires, illuminations, and the accustomed demonstrations of public joy.[1]

While the earl of Arundel and the lord Paget carried the intelligence of this revolution to Framlingham, the earl of Pembroke, with his company of the guard, took possession of the Tower. The next morning the lady Jane departed to Sion House. Her reign had lasted but nine days; and they had been days of anxiety and distress. She had suffered much from her own apprehensions of an unfortunate result, more from the displeasure of her husband, and the imperious humour of his mother.[2] The moment she was gone, the lords, without any distinction of party, united in sending an order to Northumberland to disband his forces, and to acknowledge Mary for his sovereign. But he had already taken the only part which prudence suggested. Sending for the vice-chancellor, Dr. Sands, who, on the preceding Sunday, had preached against the daughters of Henry, he proceeded to the market-place, where, with tears of grief running down his cheeks, he proclaimed the lady Mary, and threw his cap into the air, in token of joy. During the night he was prevented from making his escape by the vigilance of his own men; and on the following morning he was arrested on a charge of high treason, by the earl of Arundel, and conducted, with several of his associates, to the Tower. It required a strong guard to protect the prisoners from the vengeance of the populace.[3]

The lady Elizabeth had taken no

---

[1] Godwin, 107, 108. Stowe, 612. King's MSS. xvii. A. ix. Rosso, 20. Their letter to the queen is in Strype's Cranmer, App. 106.

[2] The quarrel arose from the ambition of Guildford. After a long discussion, Jane consented to give him the crown by act of parliament; but, when she was left to herself, she repented of her facility, and informed him that she would make him a duke, but not king. In his anger he abstained from her company and her bed, and threatened to go back to Sion House; the duchess chided and upbraided her, till she grew so alarmed, as to persuade herself they had given her poison. "Dissi loro, chè se la corona s' aspettava à me, io serei contenta di fare il mio marito Duca, ma non consentirei mai di farlo Rè. La qual mia risoluzione, recò à sua madre (essendole riferto questo mio pensiero) grand' occasione di collora, e di sdegno, dimanierachè adirandosi ella meco molto malamente, è sdegnandosene forte, persuase al suo figliuolo che non dormisse più meco, si come egli fece; affermandomi pure chè non volea in guisa veruna esser duca ma Rè......
...Nel rimanente, io per me non sò quello ch'l consiglio havesse determinato di fare, ma sò ben di certo, chè due volte in questo tempo m'è stato dato il veleno, la prima fù in casa la Duchessa di Nortumberland, e di poi qui in Torre, si come io u' ho ottimi e certissimi testimoni, olirechè, da quel tempo in quà, mi son caduti tutti i peli d'addosso. E tutte queste cose l' ho volute dire, per testimonianza dell' innocenzia mia, e scarico della mia conscienza."—Pollini, p. 357, 358. Rosso, 56.

[3] Stowe, 612. Godwin, 109. The number of prisoners for trial was twenty-seven—the dukes of *Suffolk* and Northumberland; the

part in this contest. To a messenger, indeed, from Northumberland, who offered her a large sum of money, and a valuable grant of lands, as the price of her voluntary renunciation of all right to the succession, she replied, that she had no right to renounce, as long as her elder sister was living. But, if she did not join the lady Jane, she did nothing in aid of the lady Mary. Under the excuse of a real or feigned indisposition, she confined herself to her chamber, that, whichever party proved victorious, she might claim the negative merit of non-resistance. Now, however, the contest was at an end: the new queen approached her capital; and Elizabeth deemed it prudent to court the favour of the conqueror. At the head of a hundred and fifty horse, she met her at Aldgate. They rode together in triumphal procession through the streets, which were lined with the different crafts in their gayest attire. Every eye was directed towards the royal sisters. Those who had seen Henry VIII. and Catherine could discover little in the queen to remind them of the majestic port of her father, or of the beautiful features and graceful carriage of her mother. Her figure was short and small; the lines of care were deeply impressed on her countenance; and her dark piercing eyes struck with awe all those on whom they were fixed. In personal appearance Elizabeth had the advantage. She was in the bloom of youth, about half the age of the queen. Without much pretension to beauty, she could boast of agreeable features, large blue eyes, a tall and portly figure, and of hands, the elegant symmetry of which she was proud to display on every occasion.[1] As they passed, their ears were stunned with the acclamations of the people; when they entered the Tower, they found kneeling on the green, the state prisoners, the duchess of Somerset, the duke of Norfolk, the son of the late marquess of Exeter, and Tunstall and Gardiner, the deprived bishops of Durham and Winchester. The latter pronounced a short congratulatory address. Mary burst into tears, called them *her* prisoners, bade them rise, and having kissed them, gave them their liberty. The same day she ordered a dole to be distributed, of eightpence, to every poor householder in the city.

In the appointment of her official advisers, the new queen was directed by necessity as much as choice. If the lords who, escaping from the Tower, had proclaimed her in the city, expected to retain their former situations, the noblemen and gentlemen who had adhered to her fortunes, when every probability was against

---

marquess of Northampton; the earls of *Huntingdon* and Warwick; the lords *Robert, Henry,* Ambrose, and Guildford Dudley; the lady Jane Dudley; the bishops of Canterbury, *London,* and *Ely;* the lords *Ferrers, Clinton,* and *Cobham;* the judges *Montague* and *Cholmeley;* and *the chancellor of the augmentations;* Andrew Dudley, John Gates, Henry Gates, Thomas Palmer, *Henry Palmer, John Cheek, John York,* knights; and Dr. *Cocks.*—Haynes, 192, 193. When this list was given to the queen, she struck out the names in italics, and reduced the number from twenty-seven to eleven.

[1] They are thus described by the Venetian ambassador, in his official communication to the senate. The queen is donna di statura piccola, di persona magra e delicata, dissimile in tutto al padre et alla madre......... ha gli occhi tanto vivi, che inducano non solo riverentia ma timore. Elisabeth e piu tosto graziosa che bella, di persona grande e ben formata, olivastra in complexione, belli occhi, e sopra tutto bella mano, della quale ne fa professione. The writer was M. Gio. Michele, galantissimo e virtuosissimo gentilhuomo (Ep. Poli, v. App. 349), who, on his return to Venice, compiled an account of England, by order of the senate. It was read in that assembly, May 13, 1537. Mr. Ellis has published a translation from the copy in the British Museum, Nero, B. vii.; but that copy is not so full as that in the Lansdowne MSS. DCCCXL., or one in the possession of Henry Howard of Greystoke Castle, Esq., or another in the Barberin. Library, No. 1,208, from which the quotations are taken.

her, had still more powerful claims on her gratitude. She sought to satisfy both classes, by admitting them into her council; and to these she successively added a few others, among whom the chief were the bishops Gardiner and Tunstall, who, under her father, had been employed in offices of trust, and had discharged them with fidelity and success. The acknowledged abilities of the former soon raised him to the post of prime minister. He first received the custody of the seals, and was soon afterwards appointed chancellor.[1] The next to him, in ability and influence in the council, was the lord Paget.

Though the queen found herself unexpectedly in debt from the policy of Northumberland, who had kept the officers and servants of the crown three years in arrear of their salaries,[2] she issued two proclamations, which drew upon her the blessings of the whole nation. By the first she restored a depreciated currency to its original value, ordered a new coinage of sovereigns and half-sovereigns, angels and half-angels, of fine gold, and of silver groats, half-groats, and pennies of the standard purity; and charged the whole loss and expense to the treasury. By the other she remitted to her people, in gratitude for their attachment to her right, the subsidy of four shillings in the pound on land, and two shillings and eight pence on goods, which had been granted to the crown by the late parliament.[3] As the time of her coronation approached, the queen introduced, within the palace, an innovation highly gratifying to the younger branches of the female nobility, though it foreboded little good to the reformed preachers. Under Edward, their fanaticism had given to the court a sombre and funereal appearance. That they might exclude from it the pomps of the devil, they had strictly forbidden all richness of apparel, and every fashionable amusement. But Mary, who recollected with pleasure the splendid gaieties of her father's reign, appeared publicly in jewels and coloured silks; the ladies, emancipated from restraint, copied her example; and the courtiers, encouraged by the approbation of their sovereign, presumed to dress with a splendour that became their rank in the state.[4] A new impulse was thus communicated to all classes of persons; and considerable sums were expended by the citizens in public and private decorations, preparatory to the coronation. That ceremony was performed after the ancient rite, by Gardiner, bishop of Winchester,[5] and was concluded in

---

[1] Noailles, ii. 123. Gardiner was peculiarly obnoxious to the French ministers, from the uncourteous manner in which, on two occasions, he had executed the harsh and imperious mandates of his master, Henry VIII. Noailles complains that imprisonment had not tamed him.—Ibid.

[2] Noailles, ii. 92. His object had been to attach them to his cause, through the fear of losing their arrears.

[3] Strype, iii. 8, 10. St. 1 Mary, c. xvii. Gage's Hengrave, 153. The sovereign was to pass at thirty, the angel at ten shillings.—Noailles, 141.

[4] Elle a desja osté les *superstitions*, qui estoient par cydevant, que les *femmes* ne portassent dorures ni habillemens de couleur, estant elle mesme et beaucoup de sa compagnie, parées de dorures, et habillées à la Françoise de robes à grandz manches.—Noailles, ii. 104. Elle est l'une des dames du monde, qui prend maintenant sultant de plaisir en habillemens (146). Les millords et jeunes seigneurs portent chausses exquises, soit de thoiles et drapz d'or et broderies, que j'en aye peu veoir en France ne ailleurs (211). Thus also we are assured by Aylmer that, though Henry VIII. had left to his daughter Elizabeth rich clothes and jewels, "he knew it to be true that there never came gold or stone upon her head till her sister forced her to lay off her former soberness, and bear her company in her glittering gayness."

[5] "It was done royally, and such a multitude of people resorted out of all parties of the realme to see the same, that the like had not been seen tofore."—Cont. of Fabyan, 557.

the usual manner, with a magnificent banquet in Westminster Hall.[1] The same day a general pardon was proclaimed, with the exception, by name, of sixty individuals who had been committed to prison, or confined to their own houses, by order of council, for treasonable or seditious offences committed since the queen's accession.

But though Mary was now firmly seated on the throne, she found herself without a friend to whom she could open her mind with freedom and safety. Among the leading members of her council there was not one who had not, in the reigns of her father or her brother, professed himself her enemy; nor did she now dare to trust them with her confidence, till she had assured herself of their fidelity. In this distress she had recourse to the prince who had always proved himself her friend, and who, she persuaded herself, could have no interest in deceiving her. She solicited the advice of the emperor on three very important questions: the punishment of those who had conspired to deprive her of the crown, the choice of her future husband, and the restoration of the ancient worship. It was agreed between them that the correspondence on these subjects should pass through the hands of the imperial ambassador, Simon de Renard, and that he, to elude suspicion, should live in comparative privacy, and very seldom make his appearance at court.

1. To the first question Charles replied, that it was the common interest of sovereigns that rebellion should not go unpunished; but that she ought to blend mercy with justice; and, having inflicted speedy vengeance on the chief of the conspirators, to grant a free and unsolicited pardon to the remainder. In compliance with this advice, Mary had selected out of the list of prisoners seven only for immediate trial; the duke of Northumberland, the contriver and executor of the plot, his son the earl of Warwick, the marquess of Northampton, Sir John Gates, Sir Henry Gates, Sir Andrew Dudley, and Sir Thomas Palmer, his principal counsellors and constant associates. It was in vain that the imperial ministers urged her to include the lady Jane in the number. Were she spared, the queen, they alleged, could never reign in security. The first faction that dared would again set her up as a rival. She had usurped the crown, and policy required that she should pay the forfeit of her presumption. But Mary undertook her defence. She could not, she said, find in her heart or in her conscience to put her unfortunate cousin to death. Jane was not so guilty as the emperor believed. She had not been the accomplice of Northumberland, but merely a puppet in his hands. Neither was she his daughter-in-law; for she had been validly contracted to another person, before she was compelled to marry Guildford Dudley. As for the danger arising from her pretensions, it was but imaginary. Every requisite precaution might be taken, before she was restored to liberty.[2]

For the trial of the three noblemen, the duke of Norfolk had been appointed high steward. When they were brought before their peers, Northumberland submitted to the consideration of the court the following questions: Could that man be guilty of treason who had acted by the authority of the prince and council, and under the warrant of the great seal; or could those persons sit

---

[1] Strype, iii. 36. Stowe, 616. Holings. 1091. In the church Elizabeth carried the crown. She whispered to Noailles, that it was very heavy. "Be patient," he replied, "it will seem lighter when it is on your own head."—Renard apud Griffet, xlii

[2] Renard apud Griffet, xl.

in judgment upon him, who, during the whole proceedings, had been his advisers and accomplices? It was replied, that the great seal of which he spoke was not that of the sovereign, but of an usurper,[1] and that the lords to whom he alluded were able in law to sit as judges, so long as there was no record of attainder against them. In these answers he acquiesced, pleaded guilty, together with his companions, and petitioned the queen that she would commute his punishment into decapitation; that mercy might be extended to his children, who had acted under his direction; that he might have the aid of an able divine to prepare himself for death; and might be allowed to confer with two lords of the council on certain secrets of state which had come to his knowledge while he was prime minister. To these requests Mary assented.[2]

Of the three lords, Northumberland alone, of the four commoners, who also pleaded guilty, Sir John Gates, and Sir Thomas Palmer were selected for execution. The morning before they suffered, they attended and communicated at a solemn mass in the Tower, in presence of several lords, and of the mayor and aldermen. On the scaffold a few words passed between Gates and the duke. Each charged the other with the origin of the conspiracy; but the altercation was conducted with temper, and they ended by reciprocally asking forgiveness. Northumberland, stepping to the rail, addressed the spectators. He acknowledged the justice of his punishment, but denied that he was the first projector of the treason. He called on them to witness that he was in charity with all mankind, that he died in the faith of his fathers, though ambition had induced him to conform in practice to a worship which he condemned in his heart, and that his last prayer was for the return of his countrymen to the Catholic church; for, since their departure from it, England, like Germany, had been a prey to dissensions, tumults, and civil war. Gates and Palmer suffered after the duke, each expressing similar sentiments, and soliciting the prayers of the beholders.[3]

---

[1] It has lately been contended that Northumberland's question referred to the great seal affixed to Edward's new settlement of the succession, but that the judges, to avoid the difficulty of giving a direct answer, purposely mistook it for the great seal of Lady Jane Grey. If this was so, it is marvellous that the duke took no notice of the mistake. In fact, however, he must have been aware that no great seal could be of force in his case, because the statute of the 35th of Henry VIII. c. 1, had made it high treason to do any act for the purpose of disturbing or interrupting the right of any person to the succession according to the provisions of that statute; and Chief Justice Montague had refused to obey Edward's order to him under the great seal to draw a new settlement, unless he should be previously assured of a free pardon the moment that he had drawn it. See before, p. 176.

[2] Stowe, 614. Howell's State Trials, 765. Rosso, 29. Persons (in his Wardword, p. 44) informs us that in consequence of the last request, Gardiner and another counsellor (the informer of Persons) visited him in the Tower. The duke earnestly petitioned for life Gardiner gave him little hope, but promised his services. Returning to court, he entreated the queen to spare the prisoner, and had in a manner obtained her consent; but the opposite party in the cabinet wrote (or rather had written) to the emperor, who by letter persuaded Mary "that it was not safe for her or the state to pardon his life." From Renard's despatches I have no doubt that this account is substantially correct. See also a letter from him to Arundel the night before his execution, in which he asks for life, "yea, the life of a dogge, that he may but lyve and kiss the queen's feet," in Mr. Tierney's interesting "History and Antiquities of the Castle and Town of Arundel," i. 333.

[3] If we may believe Fox (iii. 13), Northumberland was induced to make this profession of his belief by a delusive promise of pardon. He himself asserts the contrary. "I do protest to you, good people, earnestly, even from the bottom of my heart, that this, which I have spoken, is of myself, not being required nor moved thereto of any man, nor for any flattery, nor hope of life. And I take witness of my lord of Worcester here, my ghostly father, that he found me in this mind and opinion when he came to me."—

2. Under the reign of Edward, Mary had spontaneously preferred a single life; but from the moment of her accession to the throne, she made no secret of her intention to marry. Of natives, two only were proposed to her choice, both descended from the house of York; Cardinal Pole, and Courtenay, whom the queen had recently liberated from the Tower. The cardinal she respected for his talents and virtues, his advocacy of her mother's right, and his sufferings in her cause. But his age and infirmities forbade her to think of him for a husband.[1] Courtenay was young and handsome; his royal descent and unmerited imprisonment (for his character was unknown) had made him the favourite of the nation; and his mother, the countess of Exeter, was the individual companion and bedfellow of the queen. Mary at first betrayed a partiality for the young man; she created him earl of Devon; she sought, by different artifices, to keep him near herself and his mother; and she made it her study to fashion his manners, which, during his confinement in the Tower, had been entirely neglected. The courtiers confidently predicted their marriage; and Gardiner promoted it with all the influence of his station. But if Courtenay had made any impression on the heart of the queen, it was speedily effaced by his misconduct. Having once tasted of liberty he resolved to enjoy it without restraint. He frequented the lowest society; he spent much of his time in the company of prostitutes; and he indulged in gratifications disgraceful to his rank, and shocking to the piety and feelings of the queen. It was in vain that she commissioned a gentleman of the court to guide his inexperience; in vain that the French and Venetian ambassadors admonished him of the consequences of his folly; he scorned their advice, refused to speak to his monitor, and pursued his wild career, till he had entirely forfeited the esteem and favour of his sovereign. In public she observed, that it was not for her honour to marry a subject; but to her confidential friends she attributed the cause to the immorality of Courtenay.[2]

The foreign princes, mentioned by the lords of the council, were, the king of Denmark, the prince of Spain, the infant of Portugal, the prince of Piedmont, and the son of the king of the Romans. Mary, who had already asked the advice of the emperor, waited with impatience for his answer. It was obviously the interest of Charles that she should prefer his son Philip. His inveterate enemy, the king of France, was in possession of the young queen of Scots; within two or three years that princess would be married to the dauphin; and in all proba-

---

Stowe, 615. Strype's Cranmer, App. 169. Indeed, he was known, in Edward's reign, to have no other religion than interest, and on one occasion spoke so contumeliously of the new service, that Archbishop Cranmer, in a moment of zeal or passion, challenged him to a duel—ad duellum provocaret.—Parker, Ant. Brit. 341. "He offered to combate with the duke." — Morris apud Strype, 430.

[1] Quant au Cardinal, je ne scay pas qui parle que la royne y eut oppinion; car il n'est ne d'age, ne de sancté convenables à ce qu'elle demande, et qui luy est propre.—Noailles, 207.

[2] Noailles, 111, 112, 147, 218, 220. Ceste Royne est en mauvaise oppinion de luy, pour avoir entendu qu'il faict beaucoup de jeunesses, et mesme d'aller souvent avecques les femmes publiques et de mauvaise vie, et suivre d'aultres compaignies sans regarder la gravité et rang qu'il doibt tenir pour aspirer en si hault lieu.........Mais il est si mal aysé à conduire, qu'il ne veult croire personne, et comme celluy qui a demeuré toute sa vie dans une tour, se voyant maintenant jouyr d'une grande liberté il ne se peult saouller des delices d'icelle, n'ayant aulcune craincte des choses qu'on luy mette devant les yeulx.—Ibid. 219, 320. I have transcribed these passages, because Hume, to account for the rejection of Courtenay, has given us a very romantic statement, for which he could have no better authority than his own imagination.

bility the crown of Scotland would be united to that of France. But if Charles had hitherto envied the good fortune of Henry, accident had now made him amends; the queen of England was a better match than the queen of Scotland; and, if he could persuade Mary to give her hand to Philip, that alliance would confer on him a proud superiority over his rival. He was, however, careful not to commit himself by too hasty an answer, and trusted for a while to the address and influence of Renard. That ambassador was admonished to consider this as the most important but most delicate point in his mission; to bear in mind that the inclination of a woman was more likely to be inflamed than extinguished by opposition; to draw to light, by distant questions and accidental remarks, the secret dispositions of the queen; to throw into his conversation occasional hints of the advantages to be derived from a foreign alliance; and, above all, to commit no act, to drop no word, from which she might infer that he was an enemy to her marriage with Courtenay.[1] Renard obeyed his instructions: he watched with attention the successive steps by which that nobleman sunk in the royal estimation; and soon announced to his sovereign that Courtenay had no longer any hold on the affections of Mary.[2] Charles now ordered him to inform the queen that he approved of the reasons which had induced her to reject her young kinsman, and was sorry that the unambitious piety of Cardinal Pole made him prefer the duties of a clergyman to the highest of worldly distinctions. Still perhaps she had no cause to regret the loss of either: a foreign prince would bring, as a husband, a firmer support to the throne; and, were it that his own age would allow him, he should himself aspire to the honour of her hand. He might, however, solicit in favour of others; nor could he offer to her choice one more dear to himself than his son, the prince of Spain. The advantages of such an union were evident: but let her not be swayed by his authority: she had only to consult her own inclination and judgment, and to communicate the result to him without fear or reserve.[3]

It was soon discovered by the courtiers that Philip had been proposed to the queen, and had not been rejected. The chancellor was the first to remonstrate with his sovereign. He observed to her that her people would more readily submit to the rule of a native than of a foreigner; that the arrogance of the Spaniards had rendered them odious in other nations, and would never be borne by Englishmen; that Philip by his haughty carriage had already earned the dislike of his own subjects; that such an alliance must be followed by perpetual war with the king of France, who would never consent that the Low Countries should be annexed to the English crown; and that the marriage could not be validly celebrated without a dispensation from the pope, whose authority was not yet acknowledged in the kingdom. Gardiner, who spoke the sentiments of the majority of the council, was followed by others of his colleagues; they were op-

---

[1] Car si elle y avoit fantaisie, elle ne layroit, si elle est du naturel des autres femmes, de passer outre, et si se resentiroit à jamais de ce que vous lui en pourriez avoir dit.—Renard's MSS. iii. fol. 38.

[2] Veau par vos lettres qu'elle a si empressement rebouté Cortenay, aux devises entretiens qui passerent entre elle et l'eveque de Wincestre, lequel Cortenay toutefois etoit le plus apparent pour etre du sang royal.—Renard's MSS. iii. fol. 48, Sept. 20. I may observe, as a proof of the emperor's industry, that he wrote all these despatches with his own hand.

[3] Nous ne voudrions choisir autre partie en ce monde que de nous allier nous mêmes avec elle.—Mais au lieu de nous, ne lui saurions mettre en avant personnage, qui nous soit plus cher que notre propre fils.—Renard's MSS. iii. fol. 49. Griffet, xiv.

posed by the duke of Norfolk, the earl of Arundel, and the lord Paget.[1]

On no persons did this intelligence make a deeper impression than on the French and Venetian ambassadors, who deemed it their duty to throw every obstacle in the way of a marriage which would so greatly augment the power of Spain. They secretly gave advice to Courtenay; they promised their influence to create a party in his favour; and they laboured to obtain in the ensuing parliament a declaration against the Spanish match. Noailles went even further. He intrigued with the discontented of every description; and, though it was contrary to the instructions of his sovereign, he endeavoured to propagate a notion, that the rightful heir to the crown was neither Mary, nor Elizabeth, nor Jane, but the young queen of Scotland, Mary Stuart, daughter to the eldest sister of Henry VIII.[2]

3. That attachment to the ancient faith which Mary had shown during the reign of her brother, had not been loosened by the late unsuccessful attempt to identify the cause of rebellion with that of the Reformation. On her accession, she acquainted both the emperor and the king of France with her determination to restore the Catholic worship. Henry applauded her zeal, and offered the aid of his forces, if it were necessary, towards the accomplishment of the work; but Charles advised her to proceed with temper and caution, and to abstain from any public innovation till she had obtained the consent of her parliament. It was in compliance with his wish that she suffered the archbishop to officiate according to the established form at the funeral of her brother in Westminster Abbey; but a solemn dirge and high mass were chanted for him at the same time in the chapel of the Tower, in the presence of the nobility and courtiers, to the number of three hundred persons.[3] She issued no order for the public restoration of the ancient service; but she maintained that she had a right to worship God as she pleased within her own palace; and was highly gratified by the compliance of those who followed her example. The proceedings against the bishops, deprived in the last reign, were revised and reversed in a new court of delegates, held by the royal authority; and Gardiner, Bonner, Tunstall, Heath, and Day recovered the possession of their respective sees. The real object of the queen could not remain a secret; the reformed preachers from the pulpit alarmed the zeal of their hearers; and the Catholic clergy, trusting to the protection of the sovereign, feared not to transgress the existing laws. A riot was occasioned by the unauthorized celebration of mass in a church in the

---

[1] Noailles, i. 214. Renard's MSS. iii. fol. 18. Griffet, xvi. xix. Par votre lettre du 23 nous avons entendu les persuasions dont ont usé les eveques de Wincestre, contreroleur, et autres nommés en votre lettre pour incliuer la volonte de la reine envers Cortenai. Il est apparent que ce doit été un jeu joué par les eveques de Wincester, ayant reparti les argumens entre lui et les autres, pour plus efficacement faire cet office.—Renard's MSS. fol. 70. Most of our historians represent Gardiner as the enemy of Courtenay, and the deviser of the Spanish match. It is, however, evident, from the despatches of both ambassadors, that he was the friend of Courtenay, and the great opponent of the marriage. It must also have been so understood at the time; for Persons, who never saw those despatches, says, "Every child acquainted with that state knoweth or may learn, that B. Gardiner was of the contrary part or faction that favoured young Edward Courtenay, the earl of Devonshire, and would have had him to marry the queen."—Wardword, 46.

[2] Noailles, 145, 157, 161, 164, 168, 194, 211, 221.

[3] Noailles, 108, 129. Griffet, xi. Non se trop haster avec zele—mais qu'elle s'accommode avec toute douceur se conformant aux definitions du parlement, sans rien faire toutefois de sa personne qui soi contre sa conscience, ayant seulement la messe à part en sa chambre—qu'elle attende jusques elle aye opportunité de rassembler parloment.—Renard's MSS. iii. fol. 24.

horse-market. The council reprimanded and imprisoned the priest; and the queen, sending for the lord mayor and aldermen, ordered them to put down all tumultuous assemblies. But the passions of the reformers had been excited; and the very next day the peace of the metropolis was interrupted by another ebullition of religious animosity. Bourne, one of the royal chaplains, had been appointed to preach at St. Paul's Cross. In the course of his sermon he complained of the late innovations, and of the illegal deprivation of the Catholic prelates. "Pull him down," suddenly exclaimed a voice in the crowd. The cry was echoed by several groups of women and children; and a dagger thrown with considerable violence, struck one of the columns of the pulpit. Bourne, alarmed for his life, withdrew into St. Paul's church under the protection of Bradford and Rogers, two of the reformed preachers.

This outrage, evidently preconcerted, injured the cause which it was designed to serve. It furnished Mary with a pretext to forbid, after the example of the two last monarchs, preaching in public without licence. The citizens were made responsible for the conduct of their children and servants; and the lord mayor was told to resign the sword into the hands of the sovereign, if he were unable to maintain the peace of the city.[1] A proclamation followed, in which the queen declared that she could not conceal her religion, which God and the world knew that she had professed from her infancy; but she had no intention to compel any one to embrace it till further order were taken by common consent; and therefore she strictly forbade all persons to excite sedition among the people, or to foment dissension by using the opprobrious terms of heretic or papist.[2]

The reformers now fixed their hopes on the constancy of the lady Elizabeth, the presumptive heir to the throne. They already considered her as the rival of the queen; and it was openly said that it would not be more difficult to transfer the sceptre to her hands, than it had been to place it in those of Mary. On this account it had been proposed by some of the royal advisers, as a measure of precaution, to put Elizabeth under a temporary arrest; but Mary refused her assent, and rather sought to weaken her sister's interest with the reformers, by withdrawing her from the new to the ancient worship. For some time the princess resisted every attempt; but when she learned that her repugnance was thought to arise, not from motives of conscience, but from the persuasions of the factious, she solicited a private audience, threw herself on her knees, and excused her past obstinacy, on the ground that she had never practised any other than the reformed worship, nor ever studied the articles of the ancient faith. Perhaps, if she were furnished with books, and aided by the instructions of divines, she might see her errors, and embrace the religion of her fathers. After this beginning, the reader will not be surprised to learn that her conversion was effected in the short course of a week. Mary now treated her with extraordinary kindness; and Elizabeth, to prove her sincerity, not only accompanied her sister to mass, but opened a chapel in her own house, and wrote to the emperor for leave to purchase, in Flanders, a chalice, cross, and the ornaments usually employed in the celebration of the Catholic worship.[3]

---

[1] Journal of Council in Archæologia, xviii. 173, 174. Haynes, i. 168—170.
[2] Wilk. Con. iv. 86.
[3] Compare the despatches of Noailles, 139, 141, 160, with those of Renard in Griffet, xi. xxiv.

But the Protestant cause was consoled for the defection of Elizabeth by the zeal of the archbishop. Cranmer had hitherto experienced the lenity of the queen. Though he had been the author of her mother's divorce, and one of the last to abandon the conspiracy of Northumberland, he had not been sent to the Tower, but received an order to confine himself to his palace at Lambeth. In this retirement he had leisure to mourn over the failure of his hopes, and to anticipate the abolition of that worship which he had so earnestly laboured to establish. But, to add to his affliction, intelligence was brought to him that the Catholic service had been performed in his church at Canterbury; that by strangers this innovation was supposed to have been made by his order or with his consent; and that a report was circulated of his having offered to celebrate mass before the queen. Cranmer hastened to refute these charges by a public denial; and in a declaration which, while its boldness does honour to his courage, betrays by its asperity the bitterness of his feelings, asserted that the mass was the device and invention of the father of lies, who was even then persecuting Christ, his holy word, and his church; that it was not he, the archbishop, but a false, flattering, lying, and deceitful monk, who had restored the ancient worship at Canterbury; that he had never offered to say mass before the queen, but was willing, with her permission, to show that it contained many horrible blasphemies; and, with the aid of Peter Martyr, to prove that the doctrine and worship established under Edward was the same which had been believed and practised in the first ages of the Christian church.[1] Of this intemperate declaration several copies were dispersed, and publicly read to the people in the streets. The council sent for the archbishop, and "after a long and serious debate committed him to the Tower, as well for the treason committed by him against the queen's highness, as for the aggravating the same his offence by spreading abroad seditious bills, and moving tumults to the disquietness of the present state." A few days afterwards, Latimer, who probably had imitated the conduct of the metropolitan, was also sent to the same prison for "his seditious demeanour."[2]

To Julius III., the Roman pontiff, the accession of Mary had been a subject of triumph. Foreseeing the result, he immediately appointed Cardinal Pole his legate to the queen, the emperor, and the king of France. But Pole hesitated to leave his retirement at Magguzzano, on the margin of the lake of Guarda, without more satisfactory information; and Dandino, the legate at Brussels, despatched to England a gentleman of his suite, Gianfrancesco Commendone, chamberlain to the pontiff. Commendone came from Gravelines to London, in the character of a stranger, whose uncle was lately dead, leaving accounts of importance unsettled in England. For some days he wandered unknown through the streets, carefully noticing whatever he saw or heard; till chance brought him into the company of an old acquaintance of the name of Lee, then a servant in the royal household. Through him Commendone procured more than one interview with Mary, and carried from her the following message to the pope and the cardinal: that it was her most anxious wish to see her kingdom reconciled with the Holy See; that for this purpose she meant to procure the repeal of all laws

---

[1] Strype's Cranmer, 305.

[2] Journal of Council in Archæol. xviii 175. Haynes, i. 183, 184.

trenching on the doctrine or discipline of the Catholic church; that on the other hand she hoped to experience no obstacle on the part of the pontiff, or of her kinsman the papal representative; and that for the success of the undertaking it would be necessary to act with temper and prudence; to respect the prejudices of her subjects; and most carefully to conceal the least trace of any correspondence between her and the court of Rome.[1]

Such was the situation of affairs when Mary met her first parliament.[2] Both peers and commoners, according to the usage of ancient times, accompanied their sovereign to a solemn mass of the Holy Ghost; the chancellor in his speech to the houses, the speaker in his address to the throne, celebrated the piety, the clemency, and the other virtues of their sovereign; and her ears were repeatedly greeted with the loudest expressions of loyalty and attachment. The two objects which at this moment she had principally at heart, were to remove from herself the stain of illegitimacy, and to restore to its former ascendancy the religion of her fathers. To the first she anticipated no objection; the second was an attempt of more doubtful result; not that her subjects, in general, were opposed to the ancient worship, but that they expressed a strong antipathy to the papal jurisdiction. The new service was, indeed, everywhere established; but it had been embraced through compulsion rather than conviction. Men felt for it little of that attachment with which spontaneous proselytes are always inspired. Only four years had elapsed since its introduction; and their former habits, prepossessions, and opinions pleaded in favour of a worship with which they had been familiarized from their infancy. But the supremacy of the pontiff appeared to them in a different light. Its exercise in England had been abolished for thirty years. The existing generation knew no more of the pope, his pretensions, or his authority, than what they had learned from his adversaries. His usurpation and tyranny had been the favourite theme of the preachers, and the re-establishment of his jurisdiction had always been described to them as the worst evil which could befal their country. In addition, it was said and believed, that the restoration of ecclesiastical property was essentially connected with the recognition of the papal authority. If the spoils of the church had been at first confined to a few favourites and purchasers, they were now become, by sales and bequests, divided and subdivided among thousands; and almost every family of opulence in the kingdom had reason to deprecate a measure which, according to the general opinion, would induce the compulsory surrender of the whole, or of a part of its possessions.

By the council it was at first determined to attempt both objects by a most comprehensive bill, which should repeal at once all the acts that had been passed in the two last reigns, affecting either the marriage between the queen's father and mother, or the exercise of religion as it stood in the first year of Henry VIII. By the peers no objection was made; but

---

[1] Pallavicino, ii. 397. Quirini's Collection of Pole's Letters, iv. 111.

[2] Burnet has fallen into two errors, with respect to this parliament: 1st. That Nowel, representative for Loo, in Cornwall, was not allowed to sit, because, being a clergyman, he was *represented* in the convocation, whereas, the reason stated, is, that *he had a voice* in the convocation. — Journals, 27. 2nd. That the lords *altered* the bill of tonnage and poundage. They objected, indeed, to two provisoes; but the Commons, instead of allowing them to be altered, withdrew the old, and introduced a new bill.—Journals 28, 29.

during the progress of the bill through the upper house, it became the general subject of conversation, and was condemned as an insidious attempt to restore the authority of the pope. The ministers felt alarmed at the opposition which was already organized among the Commons; and the queen, coming unexpectedly to the house of Lords, gave the royal assent to three bills (the only bills which had been passed), and prorogued the parliament for the space of three days.[1]

In the succeeding session two new bills were introduced, in the place of the former; one confirming the marriage of Henry and Catherine, the other regulating the national worship. In the first all reference to the papal dispensation was dexterously avoided. It stated that, after the queen's father and mother had lived together in lawful matrimony for the space of twenty years, unfounded scruples and projects of divorce had been suggested to the king by interested individuals, who, to accomplish their design, procured in their favour the seals of foreign universities by bribery, and of the national universities by intrigues and threats; and that Thomas, then newly made archbishop of Canterbury, most ungodlily, and against all rules of equity and conscience, took upon himself to pronounce, in the absence of the queen, a judgment of divorce, which was afterwards, on two occasions, confirmed by parliament; but that, as the said marriage was not prohibited by the law of God, it could not be dissolved by any such authority: wherefore it enacted that all statutes confirmatory of the divorce should be repealed, and the marriage between Henry and Catherine should be adjudged to stand with God's law, and should be reputed of good effect and validity, to all intents and purposes whatsoever. Against this bill, though it was equivalent to a statute of bastardy in respect of Elizabeth, not a voice was raised in either house of parliament.[2]

The next motion was so framed as to elude the objections of those who were hostile to the pretensions of the see of Rome. It had no reference to the alienation of church property; it trenched not on the ecclesiastical supremacy of the crown; it professed to have no other object than to restore religion to that state in which Edward found it on his accession, and to repeal nine acts passed through the influence of a faction during his minority. The opposition was confined to the lower house, in which, on the second reading, the debate continued two days. But, though the friends of the new doctrines are said to have amounted to one-third of the members, the bill passed, apparently without a division.[3] By it was at once razed to the ground that fabric which the ingenuity and perseverance of Archbishop Cranmer had erected in the last reign; the reformed liturgy, which Edward's parliament had attributed to the inspiration of the Holy Ghost, was now pronounced "a new thing, imagined and devised by a few of singular opinions;" the acts estab-

---

[1] Historians have indulged in fanciful conjectures to account for the shortness of the session. The true reason may be discovered in Mary's letter to Cardinal Pole of the 28th of October. Plus difficultatis fit circa auctoritatem sedis apostolicæ quam veræ religionis cultum.........siquidem primus ordo comitiorum existimaverat consultum ut omnia statuta.........abrogarentur .... Cum vero hæc deliberatio secundo ordini comitiorum innotuisset, statim suspicatus est hæc proponi in gratiam pontificis, &o.—Quirini, iv. 119.
[2] Stat. of Realm, iv. 200. Sine scrupulo aut difficultate. Mary to Pole, Nov. 15th, Quirini, iv. 122.
[3] Noailles says, Ce qui a demeuré huict joure en merveilleuse dispute; et n'a sçeu passer ce bill, que la tierce partie de ceulx du tiers estat ne soyent demeurez de contraire opinion.—Noailles, ii. 247. Yet the journals mention no division.—Journals, 29,

lishing the first and second books of common prayer, the new ordinal, and the administration of the sacrament in both kinds, that authorizing the marriages of priests, and legitimating their children, and those abolishing certain festivals and fasts, vesting in the king the appointment of bishops by letters patent, and regulating the exercise of the episcopal jurisdiction, were repealed; and, in lieu thereof, it was enjoined that from the twentieth day of the next month should be revived and practised such forms of divine worship and administration of sacraments, as had been most commonly used in England in the last year of Henry VIII.[1]

By other bills passed in this parliament, all bonds, deeds, and writings, between individuals, bearing date during the short usurpation of the lady Jane, were made as good and effectual in law, as if the name of the rightful sovereign had been expressed; and all treasons created since the twenty-fifth of Edward III., with all new felonies and cases of premunire, introduced since the first of Henry VIII., were abolished; but at the same time the statute of Edward VI. against riotous assemblies was in part revived, and extended to such meetings as should have for their object to change, by force, the existing laws in matters of religion. To these must be added several private bills restoring in blood those persons who had been deprived of their hereditary rights by the iniquitous judgments passed in Henry's reign,[2] and one of severity, attainting the authors and chief abettors of the late conspiracy to exclude the queen from the succession. It was, however, limited to the persons whose condemnation has been already mentioned, and to Thomas, archbishop of Canterbury, Guildford Dudley, "Jane Dudley his wife," and Sir Ambrose Dudley, who had been arraigned and convicted on their own confessions during the sitting of parliament. Mary had no intention that they should suffer; but she hoped that the knowledge of their danger would secure the loyalty of their friends; and, when she signed the pardon of Northampton and Gates, gave orders that the other prisoners should receive every indulgence compatible with their situation.[3]

But that which, during the sitting of the parliament, chiefly interested and agitated the public mind, was the project of marriage between Mary and Philip of Spain. The court was divided into two factions. At the head of the imperialists were the earl of Arundel, the lord Paget, and Rochester, comptroller of the household, all three high in the favour of the queen: they were still opposed by Gardiner, the chancellor, who, though he received but little support from the timidity of his colleagues in the council, was in public seconded by the voices of the more clamorous, if not the more numerous, portion of the people. Protestants and Catholics, postponing their religious animosities, joined in reprobating a measure which would place a foreign and despotic prince on the English throne; and eagerly wished for the arrival of Pole, whom rumour described as an enemy to the Spanish match, and who was believed to possess considerable influence over the royal mind.[4] But their expectations were disappointed by the policy of their adversaries, who

---

[1] Quod non sine contentione, disputatione acri et summo labore fidelium factum est.—Mary to Pole. Quirini, iv. 122.

[2] See Appendix Z.

[3] Stat. iv. 217. Journal of Council, Archæologia, xviii. 176.

[4] Y est il plus demandé que je n'eusse jama's pensé, le desirans mainctenant tant les protestants que catholiques.—Noailles, 271.

predicted to Mary that the presence of a papal legate would prove the signal of a religious war, and at the same time alarmed the emperor with the notion that Pole was in reality a competitor for the hand of their sovereign.[1] The former wrote to the cardinal not to venture nearer than Brussels; the latter commissioned Mendoza to stop him in the heart of Germany. At the instance of that messenger he returned to Dillinghen, on the Danube, where he received an order from the pontiff to suspend the prosecution of his journey till he should receive further instructions.[2]

It was a more difficult task to detect and defeat the intrigues of Noailles, the French ambassador. That minister, urged by his antipathy to the Spanish cause, hesitated not to disobey the commands of his sovereign,[3] and to abuse the privileges of his office. He connected himself with Courtenay, with the leaders of the Protestants, and with the discontented of every description; he admitted them to midnight conferences in his house; he advised them to draw the sword for the protection of their liberties; he raised their hopes with the prospects of aid from France; and he sought by statements, often false, always exaggerated, to draw from Henry himself a public manifestation of his hostility to the intended marriage.[4]

The Commons, at the commencement of the second session, had been induced to vote an address to the queen, in which they prayed her to marry, that she might raise up successors to the throne, but to select her husband not from any foreign family, but from the nobility of her own realm. Noailles, who in his despatches predicted the most beneficial result from this measure, took to himself the whole of the merit.[5] Mary, on the other hand, attributed it to the secret influence of Gardiner, who, having been outnumbered in the cabinet, sought to fortify himself with the aid of the Commons. But the queen had inherited the resolution or obstinacy of her father. Opposition might strengthen, it could not shake her purpose. She declared that she would prove a match for all the cunning of the chancellor;[6] and, sending the very same night for the imperial ambassador, bade him follow her into her private oratory, where, on her knees at the foot of the altar, and before the sacrament, she first recited the hymn Veni Creator Spiritus, and then called God to witness that she pledged her faith to Philip prince of Spain, and while she lived would never take any other man for her husband.[7]

Though this rash and uncalled-for promise was kept a profound secret, the subsequent language of the queen proved to the courtiers that she had taken her final resolution. The young earl of Devon, fallen from his hopes, abandoned himself to the guidance of

---

[1] Noailles, 244. Griffet, xviii.
[2] Pallavicino, ii. 403.
[3] Je vous prie, Mons. de Noailles, comme j'u je vous ay escript, fermer du tout les oreilles à tous ces gens passionez, qui vous mettent partis en avant.—The king to Noailles, Nov. 9th, p. 219. I suspect, however, that this was written merely for the purpose of being shown to the queen, if events rendered it necessary, for the exculpation of Henry; for that prince, on Jan. 26, orders him to do exactly the contrary. Il fauldra conforter soubz main les conducteurs des entreprises que scavez, le plus dextrement que faire se pourra; et s'eslargir plus ouvertment et franchement parler avecques eulx que n'avez encores fait: en maniere qu'ilz mettent la main a l'œuvre (iii. 36).
[4] This is evident from many of his despatches, pp. 228, 302.
[5] Noailles, ii. 233. The emperor also attributed the address to Gardiner, and therefore wrote to Renard, Puisque vous cognoissez les desseigns du chancellier tendre à continuer sa pratique pour Courteney, tant plus est il requis, que soyez soigneux à la contreminer, et lui gagner, si faire se peult, la volonté.—Renard, MSS. iii. fol. 89. [6] Griffet, xxviii. [7] Ibid. xx.

his interested advisers. He was under the strongest obligations to Mary. She had liberated him from the prison to which he had been confined from his infancy by the jealousy of her father and brother; she had restored him to the forfeited honours and property of his family; and she had constantly treated him with distinction above all the nobility at her court. Inexperience may be pleaded in extenuation of his fault; but, if gratitude be a duty, he ought to have been the last person to engage in a conspiracy against his benefactress. Yet he listened to those who called themselves his friends, and urged him to the most criminal attempts. They proposed to commence with the murder of Arundel and Paget, the most powerful among the partisans of Philip. Perhaps if *they* were removed, fear or persuasion might induce Mary to accept the offer of Courtenay. Should she remain obstinate, he might, in defiance of her authority, marry Elizabeth, and repair with her to Devonshire and Cornwall, where the inhabitants were devoted to his family; and he would find the duke of Suffolk, the earl of Pembroke, many other lords, and every naval and military adventurer, ready to join his standard.[1] But the discipline of the Tower was not calculated to impart to the mind that energy of character, that intrepidity in the hour of trial, which becomes a conspirator. Courtenay had issued from his prison timid and cautious; though his ambition might applaud the scheme of his friends, he had not the courage to execute it; and a new plan was devised, that he should take the horses from the royal stables at Greenwich, as he was in the habit of doing for his pleasure, should ride to an appointed place, embark in a vessel lying in the river, and cross the sea to France; that the same night his adherents should assassinate Arundel and Paget, and hasten into Devonshire; and that the earl should rejoin them in that county as soon as circumstances might require.[2] But Noailles, aware that the flight of Courtenay would compromise his sovereign, opposed the project, under pretence that, the moment he left the shores of England, he might bid adieu to the English crown. Other plans were suggested and discussed; but the timidity of the earl checked the eagerness of his advisers; he gladly took hold of some circumstances to conceive new expectations of the royal favour, and prevailed on his friends to suspend their efforts, till they were better apprized of the final determination of Mary.[3]

In the beginning of November the queen had suffered much from a malady to which she was annually subject: after her recovery it was believed that she continued to feign indisposition, for the purpose of postponing the unpleasant task imposed on her by the address of the Commons. But in a few days she sent for the lower house: the speaker read the address; and, when it was expected that the chancellor, according to custom, would answer in her name, she herself replied: that, for their expressions of loyalty, and their desire that the issue of her body might succeed

---

[1] Noailles, ii. 246, 254. L'entreprinze est de vouloir faire espouser audit de Courtenay madame Elizabeth, et l'enlever et emmener au pays de Dampchier (Devonshire et de Cornuailles;………les ducs de Suffolk, comtes de Pembroug et de Combrelant, milord Clynton, et plusieurs des grands seigueurs, seront de ce party.—Id. ii 246. He was mistaken as to all except the duke of Suffolk. [2] Noailles, ii. 258.

[3] Id. 271. On Dec. 1 Noailles informs his court, that though Elizabeth and Courtenay are proper instruments to cause a rising, there is reason to suspect that nothing will be done on account of Courtenay's timidity; who probably will let himself be taken before he will act; comme font ordinairement les Anglois, que ne scavent jamais fuyr leur malheur, ni prevenir le peril do leur vie.—Id. 289.

her on the throne, she sincerely thanked them; but, in as much as they pretended to limit her in the choice of a husband, she thanked them not. The marriages of her predecessors had always been free, nor would she surrender a privilege which they had enjoyed. If it was a subject that interested the Commons, it was one that interested her still more, and she would be careful in her choice, not only to provide for her own happiness, but, which was equally dear to her, for the happiness of her people. This answer was received with applause, though it disappointed the movers of the address.[1]

In the meantime Elizabeth remained at court, watched by the imperialists, and caressed by their opponents; one day terrified by the fear of a prison, and the next day flattered with the prospect of a crown. No pains were spared to create dissension between the royal sisters; to awaken jealousy in the one, alarm and resentment in the other. But Elizabeth explained away the charges against her, and Mary, by her conduct, belied the predictions of her enemies.[2] If she detained her sister at court till the dissolution of the parliament, she treated her with kindness and distinction; and at her departure dismissed her with marks of affection, and a present of two sets of large and valuable pearls.[3]

The emperor, at the suggestion of Paget, had written to six of the lords of the council respecting the marriage of the queen,[4] and Gardiner, convinced at length that to oppose was fruitless, consented to negotiate the treaty on such terms as he deemed requisite to secure the rights and liberties of the nation. The counts of Egmont and Lalain, the lord of Courrieres, and the sieur de Nigry, arrived as ambassadors extraordinary, and were admitted to an audience in presence of the whole court. When they offered to Mary the prince of Spain for her husband, she replied that it became not a female to speak in public on so delicate a subject as her own marriage; they were at liberty to confer with her ministers, who would make known her intentions;

---

[1] Noailles, 269. Griffet, xxviii. Notwithstanding this reply of the queen, Charles was still uneasy on account of the decided opposition of Gardiner. To Renard's account of the address of the Commons, and of the queen's answer, he replies: "Elle a très bien et pertinemment repondu, et nous conferme en bonne espérence. Et puisque vous cognoissez les desseigns du chancellier tendre à continuer ses pratiques pour Cortenay, tant plus est il requis, que soyez soigneux à les contreminer."—A Bruxelles, 21 Nov. Renard's MSS. iii. 89. If additional proof of Gardiner's opposition be desired, it may be found in the despatches of Noailles, who, after the queen had returned her answer to the Commons, writes to his court that, though the cause of Courtenay seems desperate, there still remains a slender hope in the exertions of Gardiner, who is "homme de bien, et qui vouldra avoir quelque regard à l'utilité de ce royaulme, sans se lasser tant aller, comme ont faict les aultres en leurs passions et affections particulieres, et m'a l'on asseuré que en luy seul reste encore quelque petite espérence pour Courtenay."—ii. 260. Again on Dec. 1 he informs his court "que ce chancellier a tenu bien longuement son opinion contraire."—ii. 297. Hence it is plain that Gardiner was an obstinate opponent of the match in the cabinet, and then only sought to make it palatable and useful to the the nation, when he found that it was not in his power to prevent it.

[2] Elizabeth was said to have received nocturnal visits from Noailles, which she convinced Mary to be false.—Noailles, 309. On the other hand, she was told that Mary meant to declare her a bastard by act of parliament; and she was supposed to be in disgrace, because the queen *sometimes* gave the precedence in company to the countess of Lennox and the duchess of Suffolk, the representatives of her aunts the Scottish and French queens.—Noailles, 234, 273.

[3] Ibid. 309.

[4] On 8th of October, Renard informed the emperor that he was on terms of the most infinite confidence with Lord Paget, who advocated with all his power the Spanish match. Charles in his answer enclosed a letter with his own hand to Paget; also added one to Gardiner, others to other lords, and one without address to be delivered by the ambassador according to his direction.—Vol. iii. f. 60.

but this she would have them to bear in mind (fixing at the same time her eyes on the ring on her finger), that her realm was her first husband, and that no consideration should induce her to violate that faith which she had pledged at the time of her coronation.[1]

The terms, which had been already discussed between the chancellor and the resident ambassador, were speedily settled; and it was stipulated that immediately on the marriage Philip and Mary should reciprocally assume the styles and titles of their respective dominions; that he should aid the queen in the government of the realm, saving its laws, rights, privileges, and customs, and preserving to her the full and free disposal of all benefices, offices, lands, revenues, and fruits, which should not be granted to any but native subjects of the realm; that he should settle on her a jointure of 60,000 pounds, secured on landed property in Spain and the Netherlands; that the issue by this marriage should succeed according to law to England, and the territories belonging to the emperor in Burgundy and the Low Countries, and (failing Don Carlos, the son of Philip, and the issue of Don Carlos), to the kingdoms of Spain, Lombardy, and the two Sicilies; and that Philip should promise upon oath to maintain all orders of men in their rights and privileges, to exclude all foreigners from office in the English court; not to carry the queen abroad without her previous request, nor any of her children without the consent of the nobility; not to claim any right to the succession if he should survive his consort; nor to take from the kingdom ships, ammunition, or jewels belonging to the crown; and, lastly, not to engage the nation in the war between his father and the French monarch, but to preserve, as much as in him lay, the peace between England and France.[2]

As soon as the treaty was signed, the chancellor explained the articles to the lord mayor and aldermen, and displayed in an eloquent discourse, the many and valuable benefits which he anticipated from an union between their sovereign and a prince, the apparent heir to so many rich and powerful territories. The death of the queen without issue prevented the accomplishment of his predictions; but he deserves praise for the solicitude with which he guarded the liberties of the nation against the possible attempts of a foreign prince on the throne, and to his honour it may be remarked, that, when Elizabeth thought of marrying the duke of Anjou, she ordered her ministers to take this treaty negotiated by Gardiner for the model of their own.

The official annunciation of the marriage provoked its opponents to speak and act with greater freedom. They circulated the most incredible tales, and employed every artifice to kindle and inflame the public discontent. One day it was reported that Edward was still alive; the next, that an army of eight thousand imperialists was coming to take possession of the ports, the Tower, and the fleet; the private character of Philip, and the national character of the Spaniards, were loaded with the imputation of every vice which could disgrace a prince or a people; of Mary herself it was said, that at her accession she had promised to make no change in religion, and to marry no foreigner, and that now, as she had broken her faith, she had forfeited her right to the crown. Among the leading conspirators some advised an immediate rising: the more prudent objected the severity of the weather,

---

[1] Griffet, xxx.

[2] Rym xv. 377—381.

the impassable state of the roads, and the difficulty of collecting their followers, or of acting in concert in the midst of winter. They finally determined to wait for the arrival of Philip, who was expected in the spring; at the first news of his approach to arm and oppose his landing; to marry Courtenay to the lady Elizabeth; to place them under the protection of the natives of Devonshire, and to proclaim them king and queen of England. Of any previous affection between the parties there appears no evidence; but Elizabeth had been taught that this marriage was her only resource against the suspicions of Mary and the malice of Philip, and the disappointment of Courtenay induced him to consent to a measure which would bring the crown once more within his grasp. Noailles now flattered himself that he should infallibly reap the fruit of his intrigues, if he could only keep for a few days the weak and vacillating mind of the earl firm to his engagements.[1] The representations of the ambassador so wrought on the king of France, that he authorized him to give to the conspirators hope of assistance, sent him the paltry sum of five thousand crowns for the relief of the more needy, and ordered the governors of his ports, and the officers of his navy, to furnish such aid and countenance as might not be deemed an open infraction of the peace between the two countries.[2]

The council, however, was not inattentive to the intrigues of the ambassador, or the designs of the factious. Paget had sent a messenger to admonish Elizabeth of her duty to the queen,[3] and Gardiner, in a private conference with Courtenay, extracted the whole secret from his fears or simplicity.[4] The next day the conspirators learned that they had been betrayed; yet, surprised and unprepared as they were, they resolved to bid defiance to the royal authority, and Thomas, brother to the duke of Suffolk, exclaimed that he would put himself in the place of Courtenay, and stake his head against the crown.[5] They immediately departed, the duke to arm his tenants in Warwickshire, Sir James Croft to raise the borderers of Wales, and Sir Thomas Wyat to put himself at the head of the discontented in Kent; Courtenay remained near the queen, making a parade of his loyalty, but mistrusted and de-

---

[1] Noailles, iii. 16, 17, 18, 22, 23. Ladicte dame Elizabeth est en peyne d'estre de si pres esclainée; ce qui n'est faict sans quelque raison; car je vous puis asseurer, sire, qu'elle desire fort do se mettre hors de tutelle; et a ce que j'entends, il ne tiendra que au milord de Courtenay qu'il ne l'epouse, et qu'elle ne le suive jusques au pays de Dampchier (Devonshire).........ou ils seroient pour avoir une bonne part a ceste couronne ....Mais le malheur est tel que ledict de Courtenay est en si grand craincte qu'il n'ose rien entreprendre. Je ne veois moyen qui soit pour l'empeschier sinon la faulte de cueur (ii. 310).

[2] Noailles, iii. 36. This was in consequence of information carried by La Marque, a special messenger, on Jan. 15, who was instructed to show that the object of the conspirators was to place Elizabeth and Courtenay on the throne; for which purpose they solicited supplies of money and arms from France. "Ils deliberent d'eslever pour leur roy et royne milord de Courtenay et madame Elizabeth. Toutesfoyes les principaux autheurs et conducteurs de cette enterprinze craignent avoir grant faulte d'armes, artilherye, munytions, et argent, et suplyent fort humblement le roy de faire qu'il y s'interesse."—Noailles, iii. 23. In the printed copies the latter part is omitted. It occurs in the MS. i. 273.

[3] It was occasioned by information given by the officers of her household, that a stranger, calling himself a pastor of the French church, had, during the last month, had several conferences with her. It was suspected that he was an agent of the disaffected; and a motion was made to confine the princess for greater security. But the queen would not listen to it.—Griffet, xxv.

[4] Noailles, iii. 31, 43.

[5] Qu'il est deliberé de tenir son lieu, qu'il fault qu'il soit roy ou pendu.—Noailles, iii. 48. As late as January 26, Noailles writes: Toutes choses, graces a Dieu, sont en bon chemin : et beintost j'espere que vous, sire, en aurez d'aultres nouvelles (iii. 45).

spised.¹ Elizabeth had repaired to her house at Ashridge: but Ashridge was thought to be too near to the capital, and Sir James Croft begged of her to retire to the castle of Dunnington. The very next day a letter to her from Wyat recommending a removal to the same place, was intercepted by the government; and she immediately received from Mary an order or invitation in the most friendly terms to come to the palace of St. James's, where she would be right welcome, and in much greater security than at Ashridge or Dunnington; a very intelligible hint that her connection with the insurgents had been discovered.² She resolved to do neither; and alleging as an excuse the state of her health, which rendered it dangerous to travel, ordered her servants to fortify the house and solicit the aid of her friends.³

In calculating the probability of success, the conspirators had been misled by the late revolution. With the exception of the duke of Suffolk and his brothers, they reckoned among them no individual of illustrious name or extensive influence; but they had persuaded themselves that the nation unanimously condemned the Spanish match, and that as public opinion had recently driven Jane, so it would now, with equal facility, drive Mary from the throne.⁴ The experience of a few days dispelled the illusion. 1. The men of Devonshire, on whose attachment to the house of Courtenay so much reliance had been placed, were the first to undeceive the insurgents. Sir Peter Carew, with Gibbs and Champernham, the appointed leaders, having waited in vain for the arrival of the recreant earl, assembled the citizens of Exeter, and proposed to them to sign an address to the queen. It stated that the object of the Spaniards, in coming to England, was to oppress the natives, to live at free quarters, and to violate the honour of females; that every Englishman was ready to sacrifice his life before he would submit to such tyranny; and that they had, therefore, taken up arms to resist the landing of any foreigners who should approach the western coast. But the

---

¹ .... Principalement pour ce qui par les lettres de l'ambassadeur de France (some had been intercepted): l'on s'apperceu comme toute la rebellion se faisoit en faveur de Cortenai, aucteur d'icelle, et que Elizabeth faisoit gens de guerre de son coustel.—Renard's MSS. iii. fol. 287, 289.

² J'ai conseillé a la dit dame pour incontinant envoyer apres Elizabeth pour la saisir, car je craine qu'elle se retire.—Renard's MSS. iii. fol. 288.

³ At the departure of the conspirators, Elizabeth left her residence for Ashridge, thirty miles further off.—Noailles, iii. 44. Here Croft exhorted her to go on to Dunnington.—Fox, iii. 794. Wyat's intercepted letter to the same effect was acknowledged by him at his trial.—Howell's State Trials, i. 863. Mary's letter to recall her to London is in Strype, iii. 83, and Hearne, 154. That Elizabeth fortified her house at Ashridge, and assembled armed men, is stated by Noailles, January 26,—ou, comme on dict, se faict desja assemblée de gens à sa devotion (iii. 44); and by Renard, in his letter to the emperor: Elizabeth faisoit gens de guerre—elle se fortifie en sa maison, ou elle est malade.—Renard's MSS. iii. fol. 287, 189. She was afterwards examined respecting her reasons for wishing to go to Dunnington; at first she affected not to know that she had such a house, or that she had ever spoken with any one on the subject; but when Sir James Croft was produced before her, she said: "I do remember that Master Hobby and mine officers, and you, Sir James, had such talk: but what is that to the purpose, but that I may go to mine own houses at all times?" Sir James, after expressing his sorrow to be a witness against her, falling on his knees, said, "I take God to record, before all your honours, I do not know any thing of that crime that you have laid to my charge."—Fox, iii. 794. And yet, Noailles, in his despatch of January 23, reckons him among the chiefs, "les intrepreneurs," who were not dispirited, though their secret had been betrayed.—Noailles, iii. 31. The reader must excuse the length and frequency of these notes. They are necessary to support a narrative, which might otherwise be attributed to the imagination or the partiality of the writer.

⁴ "The cause of this insurrection, as they boaste in all these places, is the Quene's mariage with the prince of Spaine." —Earl of Arundel to Lord Shrewsbury, Jan. 27.

people showed no disposition to comply; and, on the arrival of the earl of Bedford, a few of the conspirators were apprehended, the rest sought an asylum in France. 2. Though Sir James Croft reached his estates on the borders of Wales, he was closely followed, and, before he could raise his tenants, was made prisoner in his bed. 3. The duke of Suffolk was equally unfortunate. Of his disaffection no suspicion had been entertained. Instead of suffering with Northumberland on the scaffold, he had been permitted, after a detention of only three days in the Tower, to retire to his own house: the clemency of the queen had preserved him from the forfeiture of his property and honours; his duchess had been received at court with a distinction which excited the jealousy of Elizabeth; and Suffolk himself had given to Mary repeated assurances of his attachment to her person, and of his approbation of her marriage. But, under these appearances, he concealed far different sentiments. A precisian in point of religion, a disciple of the most stern and uncompromising among the reformed teachers, he deemed it a duty to risk his life, and the fortune of his family, in the support of the new doctrines. With his brothers, the lords John and Thomas Grey, and fifty followers, he left Shene for his estates in Warwickshire. To me, it seems uncertain whether he meant, with the other conspirators, to set up the lady Elizabeth as the competitor of Mary, or to revive the claim of his daughter, the lady Jane.[1] In the towns through which he passed he called on the inhabitants to rise, like their brethren in the south, and to arm in defence of their liberties, which had been betrayed to the Spaniards. They listened with apathy to his eloquence, and refused the money which he scattered among them: the earl of Huntingdon, once his fellow-prisoner in the Tower, pursued him, by command of the queen; and a trifling skirmish in the neighbourhood of Coventry convinced him that he was no match for the forces of his adversary. He bade his followers reserve themselves for a more favourable opportunity, and trusted himself to the fidelity of a tenant, of the name of Underwood, who concealed him within a hollow tree, and then, through the fear of punishment, or the hope of reward, betrayed him to his pursuers. In less than a fortnight from his departure, he was an inmate of the Tower. Of his brothers, John was already there, and Thomas joined him soon afterwards.[2]

It was in Kent, only, that the insurrection assumed a formidable appearance under the direction of Sir Thomas Wyat. If we may believe his own assertion, he ought not to be charged with the origin of the conspiracy. It was formed without his knowledge, and was first communicated to him by the earl of Devon; but he engaged in it with cheerfulness, under the persuasion that the marriage of the queen with Philip would be followed by the death of the lady Elizabeth, and by the subversion of the national liberties. By the apostasy of Courtenay, he became one of the principals in the insurrection; and while his associates, by their presumption and weakness, proved themselves unequal to the attempt, he excited the applause of his very adversaries, by the secrecy and address with which he organized the rising, and by the spirit and perseverance with which

---

[1] Noailles describes his brother as a partisan of the lady Elizabeth (iii. 48); yet Rosso (44, 52), Thuanus (i. 449), Stowe (622), and Heylin (165—263), assert that the duke proclaimed the lady Jane at different places on the road.

[2] Griffet, xxxii. Lodge, i. 187. Rosso, 46 Stowe, 618. Holins. 1094, 1095.

he conducted the enterprise.[1] The moment he drew the sword, fifteen hundred armed men assembled around him; while five thousand others remained at their homes, ready, at the first toll of the alarum-bell, to crowd to his standard. He fixed his head-quarters in the old and ruinous castle of Rochester; a squadron of five sail, in the Thames, under his secret associate Winter, supplied him with cannon and ammunition; and batteries were erected to command the passage of the bridge, and the opposite bank of the river. Yet fortune did not appear to favour his first attempts. Sir Robert Southwell dispersed a party of insurgents under Knevet; the lord Abergavenny defeated a large reinforcement led by Isley, another of the conspirators; and the citizens of Canterbury rejected his entreaties and derided his threats. It required all his address to keep his followers together. Though he boasted of the succours which he daily expected from France, though he circulated reports of successful risings in other parts of the country, many of the insurgents began to waver; several sent to the council offers to return to their duty, on condition of pardon; and there is reason to believe that the main force under Wyat would have dissolved of itself, had it been suffered to remain a few days longer in a state of inactivity.[2]

But the duke of Norfolk had already marched from London, with a detachment of guards, under the command of Sir Henry Jerningham. He was immediately followed by five hundred Londoners, led by Captain Bret, and was afterwards joined by the sheriff of Kent with the bands of the county. This force was far inferior in number to the enemy; and, what was of more disastrous consequence, some of its leaders were in secret league with Wyat. The duke, having in vain made an offer of pardon, ordered the bridge to be forced. The troops were already in motion, when Bret, who led the van, halted his column, and raising his sword, exclaimed, "Masters, we are going to fight in an unholy quarrel against our friends and countrymen, who seek only to preserve us from the dominion of foreigners. Wherefore I think that no English heart should oppose them, and am resolved for my own part to shed my blood in the cause of this worthy captain, Master Wyat." This address was seconded by Brian Fitzwilliam; shouts of "a Wyat! a Wyat!" burst from the ranks; and the Londoners, instead of advancing against the rebels, faced about to oppose the royalists.[3] At that moment Wyat himself joined them at the head of his cavalry; and the duke, with his principal officers, apprehending a general defection, fled towards Gravesend. Seven pieces of artillery fell into the hands of the insurgents; their ranks were recruited from the deserters; and the whole body, confident of victory, began their march in the direction of London.[4]

This unexpected result revealed to the queen the alarming secret that the conspiracy had pushed its branches into the very heart of the metropolis. Every precaution was immediately taken for the security of the court,

---

[1] Howell's State Trials, i. 863. Noailles calls Wyat, ung gentilhomme le plus vaillant, et asseuré de quoy j'aye jamais ony parler (iii. 59).

[2] Noailles, iii. 46, 47. Lodge, i. 187. Cont. of Fabyan, 558. Holins. 1093, 1095.

[3] Noailles, the day before the event, informed his sovereign of the intended desertion of the officers of the Londoners. De ceux la mesme, selon que le bruict en court, les principaulx capituines des gens de pied se tourneront vers icelles, quand ce viendra au besoign (iii. 47).

[4] Rosso says that the duke fell into the hands of Wyat, who behaved to him with respect, and told him that he was at liberty to return to the queen, and inform her that the rising was not against her, but against the tyranny of the Spaniards (p. 47).

the Tower, and the city; the bridges for fifteen miles were broken down, and the boats secured on the opposite bank of the river; the neighbouring peers received orders to raise their tenantry, and hasten to the protection of the royal person; and a reward of one hundred pounds per annum in land was offered for the apprehension of Wyat. That chieftain, with fifteen thousand men under his command, had marched through Dartford to Greenwich and Deptford, when a message from the council, inquiring into the extent of his demands, betrayed their diffidence, and added to his presumption. In the court and the council-room, nothing was to be heard but expressions of mistrust and apprehension; some blamed the precipitancy of Gardiner in the change of religion; some the interested policy of the advisers of the Spanish match; and the imperial ambassadors, with the exception of Renard, fearing for their lives, escaped in a merchant-vessel lying in the river.[1] The queen alone appeared firm and collected; she betrayed no symptom of fear, no doubt of the result; she ordered her ministers to provide the means of defence, and undertook to fix, by her confidence and address, the wavering loyalty of the Londoners.[2] The lord mayor had called an extraordinary meeting of the citizens; and, at three in the afternoon, Mary, with the sceptre in her hand, and accompanied by her ladies and officers of state, entered the Guildhall. She was received with every demonstration of respect, and, in a firm and dignified tone, complained of the disobedience and insolence of the men of Kent. At first the leaders had condemned her intended marriage with the prince of Spain; now they had betrayed their real design. They demanded the custody of her person, the appointment of her council, and the command of the Tower. Their object was to obtain the exercise of the royal authority, and to abolish the national worship. But she was convinced that her people loved her too well to surrender her into the hands of rebels. "As for this marriage," she continued, "ye shall understand that I enterprised not the doing thereof, without the advice of all our privy council; nor am I, I assure ye, so bent to my own will, or so affectionate, that for my own pleasure I would choose where I lust, or needs must have a husband. I have hitherto lived a maid; and doubt nothing, but with God's grace I am able to live so still. Certainly, did I think that this marriage were to the hurt of you my subjects, or the impeachment of my royal estate, I would never consent thereunto. And, I promise you, on the word of a queen, that, if it shall not appear to the Lords and Commons in parliament to be for the benefit of the whole realm, I will never marry while I live. Wherefore, stand fast against these rebels, your enemies and mine; fear them not, for I assure ye, I fear them nothing at all; and I will leave with you my Lord Howard and my lord admiral, who will be assistant with the mayor for your defence." With these words she departed; the hall rang with acclamations; and by the next morning more than twenty thousand men had enrolled their names for the protection of the city.[3]

The next day Wyat entered South-

---

[1] Noailles, iii. 53. Griffet, xxx. iii.
[2] So says Renard (ibid.) and a writer inter Poli Epis. Tu, cæteris tam repentino tuo periculo perturbatis, animo ipsa minime fracta ac debilitata es, sed ita te gessisti, &c. (tom. v. App. 382). Noailles, on the contrary, says: Jo me deliberay en cape de veoir de quel visaige elle et sa compaignie y alloient, que je cogneus estre aussy triste et desplorée qu'il se peult penser (iii. 51)
[3] Holins. 1096. Noailles, iii. 52, 66. Fox, iii. 25. She spoke with so much ease, that Fox adds, "she seemed to have perfectly conned it without book."—Ibid.

wark. But his followers had dwindled to seven thousand men, and were hourly diminishing. No succours had arrived from France; no insurrection had burst forth in any other county; and the royal army was daily strengthened by reinforcements. The batteries erected on the walls of the Tower compelled him to leave Southwark;[1] but he had by this time arranged a plan with some of the reformers in the city to surprise Ludgate an hour before sunrise; and for that purpose directed his march towards Kingston. Thirty feet of the wooden bridge had been destroyed; but he swam, or prevailed on two seamen to swim, across the river, and, having procured a boat from the opposite bank, laboured with a few associates at the repairs, while his men refreshed themselves in the town. At eleven at night the insurgents passed the bridge; at Brentford they drove in the advanced post of the royalists; but an hour was lost in repairing the carriage of a cannon, and, as it became too late for Wyat to keep his appointment at Ludgate, the chief of his advisers abandoned him in despair. Among these were Poinet, the Protestant bishop of Winchester, who now hastened to the continent; and Sir George Harper, who rode to St. James's, and announced the approach and expectations of Wyat. He arrived about two hours after midnight. The palace was instantly filled with alarm; the boldness of the attempt gave birth to reports of treason in the city and the court; and the ministers on their knees, particularly the chancellor, conjured the queen to provide for her own safety, by retiring into the Tower. But Mary scorned the timidity of her advisers: from the earl of Pembroke and Lord Clinton she received assurances that they would do their duty; and in return she announced her fixed determination to remain at her post. In a council of war it was decided to place a strong force at Ludgate, to permit the advance of Wyat, and then to press on him from every quarter, and to inclose him like a wild beast in the toils.[2]

At four in the morning the drum beat to arms; and in a few hours the royalists under Pembroke and Clinton amounted to ten thousand infantry and fifteen hundred cavalry. The hill opposite St. James's was occupied with a battery of cannon and a strong squadron of horse; lower down, and nearer to Charing Cross, were posted two divisions of infantry; and several smaller parties were detached to different points in the vicinity. About nine, Wyat reached Hyde Park Corner. Many of his followers, who heard of the queen's proclamation of pardon, had slunk away in the darkness of the night; the rest were appalled at the sight of the formidable array before their eyes. But their leader saw that to recede must be his ruin; he still relied on the co-operation of the conspirators and reformers in the city; and after a short cannonade, seizing a standard, rushed forward to charge the cavalry. They opened; allowed three or four hundred men to pass; and, closing, cut

---

[1] Here his followers had pillaged the house of Gardiner, and destroyed the books in his library, "so that a man might have gone up to the knees in the leaves of books, cut out and thrown under foot."—Stowe, 619.

[2] Griffet, xxxv. Cum tui te hortando et obsecrando urgere non desisterent, ut in arcem te reciperes, ne tum quidem ullius timoris signum dedisti.—Pol. Ep. tom. v. App. 332. "It was more than marvel to see that day the invincible heart and constancy of the queen."—Holins. 1096. Renard says that she showed, tel cueur qu'elle dit ne se vouloir retirer, si le comte de Pembroke et Clinton vouloient faire leur devoir, et incontenent envoya devers eux, qui la suppliarent ne bouger.—Renard's MSS. iii. 287. Rosso adds that she had a guard of one hundred and fifty men, and beheld the charge made by Pembroke at the distance of musket-shot.—Rosso, 50.

off the communication between them and the main body. The insurgents, separated from their leader, did not long sustain the unequal contest; about one hundred were killed, great numbers wounded, and four hundred made prisoners. Wyat paid no attention to the battle which raged behind his back. Intent on his purpose, he hastened through Piccadilly, insulted the gates of the palace, and proceeded towards the city. No molestation was offered by the armed bands stationed on each side of the street. At Ludgate he knocked, and demanded admittance, "for the queen had granted all his petitions."—"Avaunt, traitor!" exclaimed from the gallery the lord William Howard, "thou shalt have no entrance here." Disappointed and confounded, he retraced his steps, till he came opposite the inn called the Bel Savage. There he halted a few minutes. To the spectators he seemed absorbed in thought; but was quickly aroused by the shouts of the combatants, and with forty companions continued to fight his way back, till he reached Temple Bar. He found it occupied by a strong detachment of horse; whatever way he turned, fresh bodies of royalists poured upon him; and Norroy king-at-arms advancing, exhorted him to spare the blood of his friends, and to yield himself a prisoner. After a moment's pause, he threw away his sword, and surrendered to Sir Maurice Berkeley, who carried him first to the court, and thence to the Tower. There, in the course of a few hours, he was rejoined by the chief of the surviving conspirators. The nobility and gentry crowded to St. James's to offer their congratulations to the queen, who thanked them in warm terms for their loyalty and courage. Two were excepted, Courtenay and the young earl of Worcester; who, on the first advance of the enemy, through timidity or disaffection, had turned the heads of their horses and fled, exclaiming that all was lost.[1]

At the termination of the former conspiracy, the queen had permitted but three persons to be put to death, —an instance of clemency, considering all the circumstances, not perhaps to be paralleled in the history of those ages. But the policy of her conduct had been severely arraigned both by the emperor and some of her own counsellors. Impunity, they argued, encourages the factious to a repetition of their offence; men ought to be taught by the punishment of the guilty, that if they presume to brave the authority of the sovereign, it must be at the peril of their lives and fortunes. Mary now began to admit the truth of these maxims; she condemned her former lenity as the cause of the recent insurrection,[2] and while her mind was still agitated with the remembrance of her danger, was induced to sign, on the morrow of the action at Temple Bar, a warrant for the execution of "Guilford Dudley and his wife," at the expiration of three days. On the fatal morning the queen sent them permission to take a last farewell of each other; but Jane refused the indulgence, saying, that in a few hours they should meet in heaven. From

---

[1] Stowe, 620—622. Strype, iii. 89. Noailles, iii. 59, 64—69. Courtenay et le compte d'Orcestre pour leur premiere guerre se retirarent arriere contre la cour, sans coup frapper, et dirent que tout etoit perdu, que la victoire étoit aux enemys, qu'a été singuliérement noté, et confirme ce que l'ambassadeur de France ecrivoit, que l'emprinse se faisoit pour lui.........Il (Courtenay) montra ce qu'il avoit dans le cueur, dont ladite dame est fort irritée.—Renard's MSS. iii. 289.

[2] Ledit Thomas, le second fils dudit duc de Suffolk, étant prisonnier, a ecris lettre à ladite dame pour misericorde : mais elle est déterminée de passer ses affaires par la justice requise, puis qu'ils ont mesusé et abusé de sa clemence et misericorde, et de incontinent leur faira trancher la tet .— Ren: MSS. 289.

the window of her cell she saw her husband led to execution, and beheld his bleeding corpse brought back to the chapel. *He* had been beheaded on Tower Hill, in sight of an immense multitude; *she*, on account of her royal descent, was spared the ignominy of a public execution. With a firm step and cheerful countenance she mounted the scaffold, which had been erected on the green within the Tower, and acknowledged in a few words to the spectators her crime in having consented to the treason of Northumberland, though she was not one of the original conspirators. "That device," she said, "was never of my seeking, but by the counsel of those who appeared to have better understanding of such things than I. As to the procurement or desire of such dignity by me, I wash my hands thereof before God and all you Christian people this day." Here she wrung her hands, then having expressed her confidence of obtaining mercy through the blood of Christ, requested the spectators to assist her in that trial with their prayers, repeated a psalm with Feckenham, formerly abbot of Westminster, and laid her head upon the block. At one stroke it was severed from the body.[1] Her life had before been spared as a pledge for the loyalty of the house of Suffolk. That pledge was indeed forfeited by the rebellion of the duke, but it would have been to the honour of Mary if she had overlooked the provocation, and refused to visit on the daughter the guilt of the father. Her youth ought to have pleaded most powerfully in her favour; and, if it were feared that she would again be set up by the factious as a competitor with her sovereign, the danger might certainly have been removed by some expedient less cruel than the infliction of death.

The chief of the conspirators had been conveyed to the Tower, to abide their trials; against the common men who had been taken in the field, it was determined to proceed by martial law. About fifty of those who had deserted with Bret were hanged in different parts of the metropolis; half a dozen suffered in Kent; and the remainder, amounting to four hundred, were led to the palace with halters round their necks. Mary appeared at a balcony, pronounced their pardon, and bade them return in peace to their homes.[2]

Most of the prisoners in the Tower on the expression of their sorrow obtained their discharge. Of six who were brought to the bar, Sir Nicholas Throckmorton alone pleaded his cause with success. There can be little doubt that he was deeply engaged in the conspiracy; but he claimed the benefit of the recent statute abolishing all treasons created since the reign of Edward III.; disputed every point with the counsel and the bench, and contended that no overt act of treason had been proved against him. He was acquitted by the jury; but the judges, on the ground that the verdict was contrary to law, remanded him to the Tower, from which he was not discharged till the next year. On the same account the jurors were called before the Star Chamber, where some made their submission; the others were fined and imprisoned.[3]

---

[1] Loseley MSS. 122. Fox, iii. 29. Holins. 1099. Noailles, iii. 125. Fox has published several letters said to be the production of this unfortunate lady. They breathe a contempt of death, sublime sentiments of piety, and a profound hatred of the ancient creed, expressed in the most bitter language against its professors. It is, however, difficult to believe them the unaided composition of a young woman of seventeen.

[2] Noailles and Renard represent the sufferers as more numerous; but our own writers, who could not be mistaken, agree in the number mentioned in the text.

[3] We have an elaborate and copious report of this remarkable trial. The author

Of the five conspirators who had received judgment, Croft obtained a pardon. 1. The duke of Suffolk fell unpitied. His ingratitude to the queen, his disregard of his daughter's safety, and his meanness in seeking to purchase forgiveness by the accusation of others, had sharpened the public indignation against him. 2. Suffolk was followed to the scaffold by Wyat, the chief support of the insurrection; but his weak and wavering conduct in the Tower provoked a suspicion that he had little claim to that firmness of mind for which, by his daring in the field, he had obtained credit. 3. The next victim was the lord Thomas Grey,[1] a nobleman of venturous spirit and towering ambition, who by his unbounded influence over his brother, the duke, was believed to have drawn him into this unfortunate enterprise. The last who suffered was William Thomas, private secretary to the late king. Discontent and fanaticism had urged him to the most daring attempts; he was convicted of a design to murder the queen; and, though he stabbed himself in his prison, expired on the scaffold. These executions have induced some writers to charge Mary with unnecessary cruelty: perhaps those who compare her with her contemporaries in similar circumstances will hesitate to subscribe to that opinion. If, on this occasion, sixty of the insurgents were sacrificed to her justice or resentment, we shall find in the history of the next reign that, after a rebellion of a less formidable aspect, some hundreds of victims were required to appease the offended majesty of her sister.[2]

That princess was still at Ashridge, where we left her a fortnight ago, labouring, or pretending to labour, under some severe indisposition. But in that short space much had come to light which tended to implicate her in the conspiracy;[3] and it was believed that her refusal to join the queen in

---

is unknown: but it is an impeachment of his credit that he was a warm partisan of Throckmorton, or of the cause which Throckmorton supported. This is plain from his anxiety to exhibit the answers and speeches of the prisoner in the most favourable light, whilst the pleadings of his opponents and the remarks of the judges are often hastily slurred over, or perhaps wilfully suppressed. The punishment of the jury must not be considered as a solitary instance. "The fact is," says Mr. Jardine (Criminal Trials, i. 114), "that the judges had for centuries before exercised a similar authority, though not without some murmuring against it, and it was not till more than a century afterwards that, in the reign of Charles II. (1670), a solemn decision was pronounced against its legality."

[1] The lord John was also condemned, but pardoned and discharged by order of the queen.

[2] If we look at the conduct of government after the rebellions of 1715 and 1745, we shall not find that the praise of superior lenity is due to more modern times.

[3] When prisoners, to save their own lives, accuse others, their depositions are not, separately, more worthy of credit than the contrary assertions of the accused. On both sides there is the same motive for falsehood. But in the present case the charge against Elizabeth and Courtenay is confirmed by the despatches of Noailles, written in the months of December and January, immediately preceding the rebellion. It has, indeed, been said that Wyat, at his death, declared both the prisoners innocent. But a little reflection will show that nothing can be deduced from the words and conduct of Wyat. 1. He visited Courtenay, and remained with him half an hour in his cell. If we believe the sheriffs, he asked Courtenay's pardon for having accused him: if we believe Lord Chandois, who was also present, he exhorted him to confess his offence. It is plain that, from such contradictory statements nothing certain can be elicited. 2. It was rumoured, that on the scaffold he pronounced both the prisoners innocent. This was reported by Noailles to his court; but two persons who had propagated the same story in the city were put in the pillory, for spreading false intelligence.—His words are said to have been: "Where it is noised abroad that I should accuse the lady Elizabeth, and the lord Courtenay, it is not so, good people; for I assure you neither they, nor any other now yonder, in hold, was privy of my rising before I began, as I have declared no less to the queen's council: and that is most true." It may certainly be true; for he rose unexpectedly, six weeks before the time originally fixed upon. But Dr. Weston immediately said, "Mark this, my masters,

the capital proceeded more from consciousness of guilt than infirmity of body. The council resolved to enforce submission; but Mary insisted that, at the same time, due consideration should be paid to her health and her rank. A very kind invitation was written to her by the queen,[1] and a nobleman in high favour with the princess, the lord William Howard, lord admiral, was commissioned with two colleagues, Hastings and Cornwallis, members of the council, to bring her to the court. They were instructed to take with them two of the queen's physicians, to ascertain her ability to travel, and also the queen's litter for her greater convenience on the road. It was with the utmost reluctance that Elizabeth yielded. The physicians assured her that there was no danger; the commissioners proposed to divide the road into five short stages of about six miles each, by which she might proceed from one gentleman's house to another, and perform the mighty journey of thirty miles in the course of six days.[2] This arrangement, however, did not take place: a respite of another week was granted; and she at last reached London in great state, "preceded by one hundred velvet coats, and followed by one hundred more in scarlet and silver." At Aldgate the litter was thrown open by her order. Her features, pale and emaciated, showed how severely she had suffered from bodily disease or mental anxiety. She was dressed entirely in white, and met with an air of haughtiness and defiance the rude gaze of the populace.

On her arrival she asked in vain for an interview with the queen, and was immediately conducted to apartments provided for her in a quarter of the palace out of which there was no egress but through a passage occupied by the guard. Of her numerous suite there remained to wait upon her two of her gentlemen, six ladies, and two servants: the rest were lodged in the city.[3]

It now became a most perplexing question, in what manner to proceed with respect to Elizabeth and Courtenay. Of their participation in the treason of the insurgents there could hardly exist a doubt. Additions were daily made to the great mass of evidence against them by the disclosures and confessions of the prisoners; besides which, the council had intercepted three despatches of Noailles, the fomenter, if not the originator, of the conspiracy,[4] and had derived from them detailed accounts of the plans and resources of the leaders: they held, moreover, two notes from Wyat to the princess; one advising her to remove to Donnington, and another announcing to her his triumphant entry into Southwark: they were also in possession of a document of more questionable authenticity,— a letter purporting to have been written by Elizabeth herself to the king of France. Mary, however, grew weary of being the gaoler of her sister. She proposed to the council that some one of the lords should take charge of her in a private house in the country. But no man was willing to incur the responsibility; and an order was made for her committal to the Tower.

---

that that which he hath shown to the council of them in writing, is true." Wyat made no reply. Was not this silence equivalent to an acknowledgment?—See Stowe, 624.

[1] Strype, iii. 130; reprint of 1816.
[2] We owe the knowledge of these minute particulars to the researches of Mr. Tytler (ii. 420). They are interesting, because they show how little credit is due to the tragic description of the same event in Fox, 792.

[3] Noailles, 88, 100. Renard, March 22. Fox, 792. Strype, iii. 150.

[4] Dated 26th, 28th, and 30th of January. They were written in cipher, the key to which Noailles thought would not be discovered.—Noailles, p. 91, 133, 134. He was, however, mistaken. Renard's MSS. iii. 286.

She received the intelligence with dismay, and most earnestly solicited permission to speak to, or if that could not be, to write to, the queen. The last was granted; and in the letter said to have been written on that occasion, she maintained with oaths and imprecations that she had never received any letter from Wyat, never written a single line to the French king, never consented to any project that could endanger the life or crown of her sister.[1] It was a Saturday, and the barge was in readiness to convey her to the Tower. But she continued writing till the tide would no longer serve, and by that ingenious artifice procured a respite till the following Monday.[2]

In the Tower Elizabeth abandoned herself to the most gloomy anticipations; she was saved from the danger by the abilities and good offices of one whom it has been the fashion to describe as her bitterest enemy. For several weeks Renard, the imperial ambassador, laboured incessantly to extort the queen's consent, that the princess should be condemned and sent to the scaffold. She was a competitor for the crown; she had accepted the offer of the rebels, and ought to suffer the penalty of her treason. To spare her was to prepare the way for another insurrection in her favour; as long as she lived, Mary could never sit on the throne in security; nor could the prince of Spain venture to set his foot on English ground without danger to his person. If these representations, made in the name of the emperor, produced no effect, the ambassador was aware that the failure arose from the influence of Gardiner over the mind of the queen. No reasoning, no remonstrances, could divert the English minister from his purpose. He amused the ambassador with fair words, and feigned to be of his opinion.[3] But certain accustomed forms must be observed, and care be taken that the proceedings should be conducted according to law and precedent; a task which he would take upon himself without delay. He began with the charge against Courtenay. The preliminary examinations were made, and the law officers of the crown gave an opinion that the evidence against him was sufficient to insure his conviction of the crime of high treason. But here Gardiner unaccountably paused; and Courtenay, instead of being brought to trial, was suffered to remain a quiet prisoner in the Tower. With respect to the princess Elizabeth, the same

---

[1] "To this present hower," she says, " I protest afore God (who shal juge my truethe, whatsoever malice shal devise) that I never practised, conciled, nor consented to any thinge, that might be prejudicial to your parson any way, or dangerous to the state by any mene. As for the traitor Wyat, he might paraventur writ me a lettar: but on my faithe I never received any from him, and as for the copie of my lettar sent to the French kinge, I pray God confound me eternally, if ever I sent him word, message, token, or lettar by any menes;—and to this my trueth I wil stand in to my dethe."—Neve on Philips, App. No. II. Ellis, 2nd series, ii. 259.

[2] Renard, March 22.

[3] In the beginning of April, during a conference between Renard and Gardiner, in the presence of the queen, Gardiner is stated by the ambassador to have owned that "as long as Elizabeth was alive there was no hope that the kingdom could be tranquil;" and to have said afterwards, that " if everybody went as roundly to work in providing the necessary remedies as he did, things would go on better."—Tyt. ii. 365. It is a pity that this interesting letter has not been published, as well as others of much less interest. From the two short extracts copied above, it has been inferred that Gardiner really thirsted for the blood of Elizabeth. But no such inference can be fairly deduced from them; nor does the first of the two prove any thing more than that the wily statesman was willing to appear of the same opinion with the emperor. Of his real intention with respect to the princess we may judge from the fact that he continued after this conference to shield her, as he had done before, from the repeated attempts of the ambassador to have her brought to trial, and put to death.

answer was always returned to the inquiries of Renard, that the queen had not yet made up her mind, but waited till more decisive proof might be obtained. Mary called for the first of the intercepted despatches of Noailles, the document said to contain the damning proof of her connection with the rebels, but it was not forthcoming. The chancellor could not deny that it had originally been in his possession; but now, after a long search, it could nowhere be found.[1] Was it not that he had determined to suppress it? Were not the queen and her minister acting in concert? For otherwise it is difficult to understand how she could have passed over in silence a matter so likely to provoke suspicion. Thus the time passed on till the dissolution of parliament. The Whitsuntide holidays followed; and the queen repaired to her palace at Richmond, whence she sent an order to Elizabeth to come from the Tower by water, and join the court. A few days later the princess was sent forward to Woodstock, which had been selected for her residence, and where she remained till the beginning of the next year, under the care and superintendence of Sir Henry Bedingfeld.[2] Courtenay was also liberated, and conducted to Fotheringay Castle by Sir Thomas Tresham.

Another subject of discussion was the conduct to be observed in relation to Noailles, whose clandestine intrigues with the conspirators had been by them betrayed to the council. Renard maintained to the queen, that by fomenting a rebellion within the realm, he had forfeited the privilege of an ambassador; that he ought to be sent out of England, or put under arrest, till the pleasure of his sovereign was known; and that the king of France should be informed, that, if the culprit had been treated with so much lenity, it was not through any doubt of his guilt, but through respect for him, whose representative he had been. But to the majority of the council this measure appeared too bold and hazardous. It might lead to a war, which it was their object to avoid; and they determined to connive at his past, and to watch his subsequent conduct. Mary, however, who knew the secret enmity of the man, could ill disguise her feelings; and on more than one occasion answered him with an asperity of language, of the real cause of which he appears not to have been aware.[3] The Venetian ambassador, who had seconded the attempts of Noailles, was recalled by the senate.

The rebellion had suspended, for a few weeks, the proceedings relative to the queen's marriage; but in the beginning of March the count Egmont returned from Brussels with the ratification of the treaty on the part of the emperor. On an appointed day the lords of the council accompanied Mary to her private oratory; and the count was introduced by the lord admiral and the earl of Pembroke. The queen, having knelt before the altar, said that she took this solemn occasion to express her mind in their presence, and to call on God to witness the truth of her words. She had not determined to marry through dislike of celibacy, nor had she chosen the prince of Spain through respect of kindred. In the one and the other, her chief object had been to promote

---

[1] Il a confesse l'avoir heu, et recen, mais il ne scavoit ou il l'avoit mis.—Renard, 1 Mai.

[2] Elizabeth, after her liberation, familiarly called Bedingfeld "her jailor." His conduct has been vindicated from the slander of Fox, by Warton (Life of Sir T. Pope, 75) and Miss Aikin in her Court of Queen Elizabeth. It appears from the family papers that Bedingfeld considered himself in favour with Elizabeth, and frequently repaired to her court to pay his respects to her after she became queen.

[3] Griffet, xxxviii.

the honour of her crown, and to secure the tranquillity of her realm. To her people she had pledged her faith on the day of her coronation; it was her firm resolve to redeem that pledge; nor would she ever permit affection for her husband to seduce her from the performance of this, the first, the most sacred of her duties. After this address she exchanged the ratification of the treaty with the ambassador: he espoused her in the name of the prince of Spain; and she put on her finger a valuable ring, sent by the emperor as a present from his son.[1]

The parliament had been summoned to meet at Oxford, but was transferred to Westminster, apparently at the request of the citizens.[2] The chief object of the queen was to silence the arguments of the insurgents by the authority of the legislature. 1. The cause of the lady Jane had been espoused by many of the reformed preachers. They had then no objection to a female sovereign. But the failure of their hopes had removed the veil from their eyes; and the more violent had now discovered that the government of a woman was prohibited by the word of God. In the Old Testament it had been ordered to take the king from 'the midst of the "brethren," an expression which, they contended, must exclude all females; and in the New we are taught that the man is the head of the woman; whence they inferred, that no woman ought to possess the supreme authority over men.[3] In confirmation of their doctrine they appealed to the statutes of the realm. What authority did they give to queens? It was to kings, and to kings alone, that they assigned the royal prerogatives, and the punishment of offences against the crown. In opposition to this dangerous notion, it was now declared, without a dissentient voice in either house, that by the ancient law of the land, whatever person, male or female, is invested with the kingly office, he or she ought to possess and exercise, in their full extent, all the pre-eminence, jurisdiction, and powers, belonging to the crown.[4] 2. To prove the policy of the intended marriage with Philip against the reasoning of its adversaries, the members were requested to cast their eyes on the situation of the neighbouring nations. France and Scotland were the natural enemies of England. Hitherto they had been connected only by treaties; but now the young queen of Scotland was contracted to the dauphin of France. Where was England to find a counterpoise but in the marriage of the queen to Philip of Spain? Let the issue of Mary Stuart inherit the two crowns of France and Scotland. By this marriage, the issue of the English queen would inherit England with the Netherlands; and that country, in the estimation of every reasonable man, would prove a more valuable acquisition to the English crown, than Scotland could ever prove to that of France.[5] But, it was objected, would not this marriage place the liberties of the nation at the mercy of a foreign despot? Undoubtedly not. Let them examine the articles of the treaty. They had been drawn after long and mature deliberation; they contained every security which the most ingenious could devise, or the

---

[1] Griffet, xxxix.
[2] It has been said, but groundlessly, that the queen had dissolved the last parliament on account of the refractory spirit of the Commons. Mary, in her letter to Pole, of Nov. 15, 1553, informs him of her intention to dissolve it, because the session could not be prolonged at that time, and to call another in the course of three months.—Ep. Poli, iv. 119.
[3] Strype, iii. 11. [4] Stat. iv. 222.
[5] See a state paper in Noailles, iii. 109, 118. Also his account of Gardiner's speech, iii. 152.

most timorous could desire; they excluded all foreigners from office; they placed the honour, the franchises, and the rights of the natives beyond danger or controversy. Satisfied by this reasoning, both houses unanimously concurred in an act, confirming the treaty of marriage, and declaring that the queen, after its solemnization, should continue to enjoy and exercise the sovereignty as sole queen, without any right or claim to be given unto Philip as tenant by courtesy, or by any other manner.[1] Mary, having thus obtained her chief object, dissolved the parliament in person, with an address, which was repeatedly interrupted by the acclamations of the audience. Both Lords and Commons assured her that the prince of Spain, on his arrival would receive a most hearty welcome from a dutiful and affectionate people.[2]

Still the king of France indulged a hope that some favourable incident might occur to interrupt the marriage. He not only opened an asylum for the English rebels who had fled from justice, but encouraged them to fit out vessels for the purpose of cruising against the subjects of Charles; and he ordered his ambassador in England to persist in his intrigues, and to keep alive, by his promises, the hopes of th factious.[3] That minister had several warm altercations with Mary. He complained, in a haughty tone, that his despatches had been intercepted; she, that her rebellious subjects were countenanced and protected by his master. He, to intimidate, hinted that at the death of Edward all the treaties between the two crowns had expired; she, for the same purpose, required an explanation of his meaning, that she might take measures for her own security. In the mean time he saw the preparations for the marriage proceeding with activity; and to console his chagrin, employed his time in collecting unfounded tales for the information of his sovereign, exaggerating the discontent of the nation, and describing with a sarcastic levity, the impatience of the old woman longing for the presence of her young husband.[4] To his sorrow, that husband in a short time arrived. He had

---

[1] Stat. iv. 222—226. According to Noailles, Gardiner, in his speech, had suggested that, as the queen and her sister Elizabeth only remained of the descendants of Henry VIII., Mary, like her father, ought to have the power of regulating the succession after her death.—Noailles, iii. 153. If it was so, the subject was not followed up. There is no mention of any such motion in the journals.

[2] Griffet, xlvii. Que me met en entiere confidence que votre venue par deca sera seuro et aygreable.—Mary to Philip, Apr. 24th, apud Hearne, Sylloge, ep. 156.

[3] One of their contrivances deserves to be mentioned. The most extraordinary sounds were heard to issue from a wall in Aldersgate Street, intermixed with words of obscure meaning, which were immediately interpreted to the crowd by persons in the secret. The voice was believed to be superhuman, the voice of the Holy Ghost warning a wicked and incredulous generation. The imposture was carried on in the following manner. A man in the crowd called out, "God save the queen;" the voice was silent. Then another would exclaim, "God save the princess." Amen, in a loud shrill voice would appear to issue from the wall. Others followed, propounding questions respecting the prince of Spain, the Spanish match, the mass, and the several practices in the Catholic worship; to all which, answers were returned from the wall in abusive and seditious language. On the second or third day, the crowd attracted by this wonder was calculated at between fifteen and twenty thousand persons (Mar. 14), but the lord admiral, at the head of the guards, cleared the street, and the lord mayor followed, accompanied by two hundred workmen, who immediately began to demolish the wall. They had not proceeded far, when the spirit, assuming a bodily form, crept out of a secret recess; and was found to be a young woman of eighteen, by name Elizabeth Crofts. She was made to confess the imposture publicly at St. Paul's Cross, and to name her accomplices.—Renard, March 14 Strype, iii. 99, 136. Stowe, 624. Holins. 1117.

[4] Noailles, iii. 195, 211, 240, 251. The geographical blunders of this minister are often amusing. On two occasions he informs his court that the queen is going to

sailed from Corunna, and in seven days came within sight of Southampton, escorted by the combined fleets of England, the Netherlands, and Spain. The morning after his arrival, the lords of the council, with a numerous retinue, proceeded to the fleet, and Philip, accompanied by the dukes of Alva and Medina Celi, the admiral of Castile, and Don Ruy Gomez, his governor, entered the royal yacht, where he was received by the duke of Norfolk and the earls of Arundel, Shrewsbury, and Derby. He had already sworn to the articles of the treaty, in presence of the lords Bedford and Fitzwalter, the English ambassadors: he now took an oath before the council, to observe the laws, customs, and liberties of the realm. The moment he set his foot on the beach, he was invested with the insignia of the order of the Garter; and instantly a royal salute was fired by the batteries and the ships in the harbour. The queen had sent him a Spanish genet, richly caparisoned; and, as he rode first to the church, and thence to his lodging, the people crowded around him to see the husband of their sovereign. His youth, the grace of his person,[1] the pleasure displayed in his countenance, charmed the spectators: they saluted him with cries of "God save your grace;" and he, turning on either side, expressed his thankfulness for their congratulations. Before he dismissed the English lords, he addressed them in a Latin speech. It was not, he said, want of men or of money, that had drawn him from his own country. But God had called him to marry their virtuous sovereign, and he was come to live among them, not as a foreigner, but as a native Englishman. He received with pleasure their assurances of faith and loyalty; and promised, in return, that they should always find him a grateful, affable, and affectionate prince. Then turning to the Spanish lords, he expressed a wish that, while they remained in England, they would conform to the customs of England; and to give the example, drank farewell to the company in a tankard of ale, a beverage which he then tasted for the first time.[2]

Philip before he left Southampton, ordered his fleet to sail to Flanders, and sent to the queen a present of jewels, valued at one hundred thousand crowns. On the festival of St. James, the patron saint of Spain, the marriage was celebrated in the cathedral church at Winchester, before crowds of noblemen collected from every part of Christendom, and with a magnificence which has seldom been surpassed.[3] Immediately before the ceremony, Figueroa, an imperial counsellor, presented to Gardiner, the officiating prelate, two instruments, from which he said it would appear that his sovereign, thinking it beneath the dignity of so great a queen to marry one who was not a king, had resigned to his son the crown of Naples with the duchy of Milan. The bishop before he proceeded to the marriage ceremony, read aloud these cessions and the articles of the treaty. After the mass, the king and queen left the church, under a canopy, walking hand in hand, Mary on the right and Philip on the left, with two naked swords borne before them. They dined in public, in the episcopal palace; and several days were devoted

---

reside at York, because York is situated in the neighbourhood of Bristol, where the prince of Spain intends to land.—iii. 96.

[1] "He is so well proportioned of bodi, arme, legge, and every othere limme to the same, as nature cannot worke a more perfect paterne."—Elder apud Andrews, i. 20.

[2] Noailles, iii. 284. Contin. of Fabyan, 561. Pollini, 362. Rosso, 59.

[3] See a description of the whole ceremony in Rosso, p. 61.

to feasting and rejoicings. From Winchester the royal pair proceeded, by slow journeys, to Windsor and the metropolis. The city had been beautified at considerable expense, and the most splendid pageants had been devised to welcome their arrival. If external appearances could be taken for proofs of internal feeling, the king and queen might justly flatter themselves that they reigned in the hearts and affections of their subjects.

The facility with which Mary had effected her marriage showed how much the failure of the insurrection had added to the power of her government; and she immediately resolved to attempt that which she had long considered an indispensable duty, the restoration of the religious polity of the kingdom to that state in which it existed at the time of her birth. The reader will recollect that in her first parliament she had prudently confined her efforts to the public re-establishment of the ancient form of worship. The statute was carried into execution on the appointed day, almost without opposition; the married clergy, according to the provisions of the canon law, were removed from their benefices;[2] and Gardiner, with the secret approbation of the pontiff, had consecrated Catholic prelates to supersede the few Protestant bishops who remained in possession of their sees.[3] Thus one-half of the measure had been already accomplished; the other, the recognition of the papal supremacy, a more hazardous task, was intrusted to the care and dexterity of the chancellor. There were two classes of men from whom he had to fear opposition; those who felt conscientious objections to the authority of the pontiff, and those who were hostile to it from motives of interest. The former were not formidable either by their number or their influence; for the frequent changes of religious belief had generated in the higher classes an indifference to religious truth. Their former notions had been unsettled; and no others had been firmly planted in their place. Unable or unwilling to compare the conflicting arguments of polemics, they floated on a sea of uncertainty, ready at all times to attach themselves to any form of religion which suited their convenience or interest.[4] But the second class comprised almost every opulent family in the kingdom. They had all shared the plunder of the church: they would never consent to the restoration of that jurisdiction which might call in question their right to

---

[1] No one but the bishop dined at the same table with the king and queen. On one side was placed a cupboard, containing, for show, ninety-six large vases of gold and silver. As soon as dinner was over, the tables were removed; and the rest of the day was spent in dancing.—Pollini, 373. Cabrera, 20. Rosso, 70.

[2] The canon law had been restored to its former authority by the repeal of the nine statutes in the last parliament. The clergymen who were removed might, by conforming, recover their benefices.—If we may judge of other dioceses from that of Canterbury, the number of married was to that of unmarried clergymen as one to five.—Harmer, 138.

[3] They were seven: Holgate of York, Taylor of Lincoln, Hooper of Worcester, Harley of Hereford, Ferrar of St. David's, Bush of Bristol, and Bird of Chester. Some of them had married; some had been consecrated according to the new ordinal, which was held to be insufficient; and all had accepted their bishoprics to hold them at the pleasure of the crown, with the clause, quam diu bene se gesserint. On one, or other, or all of these grounds, they were deprived.—Rym. xv. 370, 371.

[4] This is the character of the English gentry and nobility at this period, as it is drawn by Renard, Noailles, and the Venetian ambassador, in their despatches. The latter represents them as without any other religion than interest, and ready at the call of the sovereign to embrace Judaism or Mohammedanism. Il medesimo fariano della Macometana, ore della Judæa, purche il re mostrassi di credere e volere cosi, e accommodariansi a tutto, ma a quella piu facilmente della quale ne sperassero over maggior licentia e libertà di vivere o vera qualche utilità.—MSS. Barber. 1208.

their present possessions. Hence Gardiner saw that it was necessary, in the first place, to free them from apprehension, and, for that purpose, to procure from the pontiff a bull confirming all past alienation of the property of the church.

This subject had from the commencement been urged on the consideration of the court of Rome. At first Pole, the legate, had been authorized "to treat, compound, and dispense," with the holders of ecclesiastical property, as to the rents and profits which they had hitherto received; afterwards, this power was extended from rents and profits, to lands, tenements, and tithes. But Gardiner was not satisfied.[1] He knew it to be the opinion of Pole that all the property belonging to the parochial livings ought to be restored; and he feared that the words "to treat, compound, and dispense," might furnish the cardinal with a pretext to call individuals before his tribunal. The imperial court entered into the views of the English minister; and it was determined to detain the cardinal in Flanders,[2] while Manriquez explained the difficulty to the pontiff, in the name of Philip and Mary. Julius, having consulted his canonists and divines, assured the envoy that the wishes of the king and queen should be gratified, and shortly afterwards signed a bull, empowering the legate to give, alienate, and transfer to the present possessors all property, moveable or immoveable, which had been torn from the church during the reigns of Henry VIII. and Edward VI.[3]

The parliament had been convoked for the middle of November. Mary no longer regarded the murmurs of the discontented; she was assured of the concurrence of the Peers; and, to lessen the chance of opposition in the Commons, had ordered the sheriffs to recommend to the electors those candidates who were distinguished by their attachment to the ancient faith.[4] The procession was opened by the commoners; the peers and prelates followed; and next came Philip and Mary, in robes of purple, the king on horseback, attended by the lords of his household, the queen in a litter, followed by the ladies of her establishment. The chancellor, having taken his place in front of the throne, addressed the two houses. The queen's first parliament, he said, had re-established the ancient worship, her second had confirmed the articles of her marriage; and their majesties expected that the third, in preference to every other object, would accomplish the reunion of the realm with the universal church. As a preliminary step, a bill was introduced to repeal the attainder of Cardinal Pole. It was passed with the greatest expedition, and the next day the king and queen attended in person to give to it the royal assent.[5]

The lord Paget, and Sir Edward

---

[1] Burnet, iii. Rec. 222.

[2] The cardinal had been allowed to go to Brussels, and thence to Paris, to offer the papal mediation in the war between the emperor and the king of France. While he was there, a letter was written to Mary by some one in his suite, dissuading her from the marriage with Philip. Charles attributed it to the cardinal, and from that moment treated him with neglect.

[3] There is a letter from Cardinal Morone to Pole, informing him that all who had been consulted were of opinion that in this particular case the alienation was lawful, and hoping that there would now be an end of his scruples; in lei sara cessato tutto lo scrupolo che aveva.—Quirini, iv. 170. The clause, "to give, aliene, and transfer," had been devised by Gardiner, as the most likely to tranquillize the present possessors, and to secure them against subsequent claims.—Pallavicino, ii. 411.

[4] It was customary for the ministers to send such instructions. It was done in Edward's reign (Lansdowne MSS. iii. 19); and also in Elizabeth's (Strype, i. 32. Clarendon Papers, 02).

[5] Journals of Lords, 467; Commons, 37, 39. Ep. Poli, iv. App. 289. Strype, iii. 155.

Hastings, with Sir William Cecil, and a numerous train of gentlemen, had already reached Brussels to conduct the legate to England.[1] At Dover he was received by the lord Montague and the bishop of Ely; and, as he advanced, his retinue was swelled by the accession of the country gentlemen, till it amounted to eighteen hundred horse. He entered his barge at Gravesend, where he was presented, by the earl of Shrewsbury and the bishop of Durham, with a copy of the act repealing his attainder; and fixing his cross, the emblem of his dignity, in the prow, he proceeded by water to Westminster. The chancellor received him on his landing, the king at the gate of the palace, and the queen at the head of the staircase. After a short conversation, he retired to the archiepiscopal palace at Lambeth, which had been prepared for his residence.[2]

In consequence of a royal message, the Lords and Commons repaired to the court; and, after a few words from the chancellor, Pole, in a long harangue, returned them thanks for the act which they had passed in his favour, exhorted them to repeal, in like manner, all the statutes enacted in derogation of the papal authority, and assured them of every facility on his part to effect the reunion of the church of England with that of Rome.[3] The chancellor, having first taken the orders of the king and queen, replied, that the two houses would deliberate apart, and signify their determination on the following morning.

The motion for the reunion was carried almost by acclamation. In the Lords every voice was raised in its favour; in the Commons, out of three hundred members, two only demurred, and these desisted from their opposition the next day.[4] It was determined to present a petition in the name of both houses to the king and queen, stating, that they look back with sorrow and regret on the defection of the realm from the communion of the Apostolic See; that they were ready to repeal, as far as in them lay, every statute which had either caused or supported that defection; and that they hoped, through the mediation of their majesties, to be absolved from all ecclesiastical censures, and to be received into the bosom of the universal church.

On the following day, the feast of St. Andrew, the queen took her seat on the throne. The king was placed on her left hand, the legate, but at greater distance, on her right. The chancellor read the petition to their majesties; they spoke to the cardinal; and he, after a speech of some duration, absolved "all those present, and the whole nation, and the dominions

---

[1] Pole, ignorant of the proceedings at Rome, had written a most urgent letter to Philip, who sent Renard to explain the objections to his admission as legate without sufficient powers. Pole replied, that in addition to his former powers, he had another bull from the pope, promising, in verbo pontificis, to ratify whatever concessions he might think proper to make. Renard lamented that this was not previously known. Immediately on the return of Renard, Pole was desired to prepare for his journey.—Pallavicino, ii. 411, ex registro Poli.

[2] Strype, iii. 157. Ep. Poli, v. App. 291, 307, 310. A writ authorizing him to exercise his powers had been signed on the 10th of November.—Strype, ibid.

[3] Burnet tells us, that the queen was so much affected, that she mistook her emotion for the "quickening of a child in her belly" (ii. 292). The fact took place four days before. She sent Lord Montague to inform the legate, che infino allora ella non havea voluta confessare apertamente d' esser gravida; ma que nella *giunta* de sua S. R. s' havea sentito muover la creatura nel ventre, e pero non lo poteva più negare. On the 27th, it was publicly announced by a circular from the council.—Fox, iii. 88. Noailles, iv. 23.

[4] Sir Ralph Bagnal (Strype, iii. 204) had refused to vote; the other grounded his objection on the oath of supremacy which he had taken.—Ep. Poli, v. App. 314.

thereof, from all heresy and schism, and all judgments, censures, and penalties for that cause incurred; and restored them to the communion of holy church, in the name of the Father, Son, and Holy Ghost." "Amen," resounded from every part of the hall; and the members, rising from their knees, followed the king and queen into the chapel, where Te Deum was chanted in thanksgiving for the event.[1] The next Sunday the legate, at the invitation of the citizens, made his public entry into the metropolis; and Gardiner preached at St. Paul's Cross the celebrated sermon, in which he lamented in bitter terms his conduct under Henry VIII., and exhorted all, who had fallen through his means, or in his company, to rise with him, and seek the unity of the Catholic church.[2]

To proceed with this great work, the two houses and the convocation simultaneously presented separate petitions to the throne. That from the Lords and Commons requested their majesties to obtain from the legate all those dispensations and indulgences which the innovations made during the schism had rendered necessary, and particularly such as might secure the property of the church to the present possessors without scruple of conscience, or impeachment from the ecclesiastical courts. The other, from the clergy, stated their resignation of all right to those possessions of which the church had been deprived; and their readiness to acquiesce in every arrangement to be made by the legato. His decree was soon afterwards published: 1. That all cathedral churches, hospitals, and schools founded during the schism, should be preserved; 2. That all persons, who had contracted marriage within the prohibited degrees without dispensation, should remain married; 3. That all judicial processes, made before the ordinaries, or in appeal before delegates, should be held valid; and 4. That the possessors of church property should not, either now or hereafter, be molested, under pretence of any canons of councils, decrees of popes, or censures of the church; for which purpose, in virtue of the authority vested in him, he took from all spiritual courts and judges the cognizance of these matters, and pronounced, beforehand, all such processes and judgments invalid and of no effect.[3]

In the mean time a joint committee of Lords and Commons had been actively employed in framing a most important and comprehensive bill, which deserves the attention of the

---

[1] Poli Ep. v. App. 315—318. Fox, 91. Journal of Commons, 38.

[2] This sermon is noticed by Fox, iii. 92. A Latin translation of it may be seen inter Ep. Poli, v. 293, 300. Gardiner asserts, that Henry VIII., during the rebellion in 1536, entertained serious thoughts of seeking a reconciliation with the pontiff; and that in 1541, he employed him and Knyvett, during the diet at Ratisbon, to solicit secretly the mediation of the emperor for that purpose. They were, however, discovered, and Gardiner was accused of holding communication with Contarini, the papal legate. Henry was careful to hush up the matter. See some account of it in Fox, who knew not of Gardiner's commission, Fox, iii. 448, 449.

[3] The next year, on the 14th of July, Paul IV. published a bull, condemning and revoking, in general terms, the alienations of church property to secular uses.—Burnet, iii. Rec. 3. This bull, however, did not regard the late proceedings in England, for egli dichiara di parlare di quelle alienazioni, che si erano fatte senza le dovute solennità.—Becchetti, Istoria, x. 197. But, to prevent doubts on the subject, Pole obtained from him a bull expressly excepting the church property in England from the operation of the second bull, qua hujus regni bona ecclesiastica ab ejus sanctitutis revocatione nominatim excipiuntur (Poli Ep. v. 42, Sept. 16, 1555); and also "confirming his doings respecting assurance of abbey lands, &c."—Journal of Commons, 42. It was read to both houses at the opening of parliament on the 23rd of October. Besides this, the cardinal obtained from him a breve declaratorium ejus bullæ, qua bonorum ecclesiasticorum alienationes rescinduntur, et confirmatorium eorum, quæ majestatibus vestris remisi.—Poli Ep. v. 85.

reader, from the accuracy with which it distinguishes between the civil and ecclesiastical jurisdictions, and the care with which it guards against any encroachment on the part of the latter. It first repeals several statutes by name, and then, in general, all clauses, sentences, and articles in every other act of parliament made since the twentieth of Henry VIII. against the supreme authority of the pope's holiness or see apostolic.[1] It next recites the two petitions, and the dispensation of the legate; and enacts, that every article in that dispensation shall be reputed good and effectual in law, and may be alleged and pleaded in all courts spiritual and temporal. It then proceeds to state, that, though the legate hath by his decree taken away all matter of impeachment, trouble, or danger to the holders of church property, from any canon, or decree of ecclesiastical judge or council; yet, because the title of lands and hereditaments in this realm is grounded on the laws and customs of the same, and to be tried and judged in no other courts than those of their majesties, it is therefore enacted, by authority of parliament, that all such possessors of church property shall hold the same in manner and form as they would have done had this act never been made; and, that any person who shall molest such possessors by process out of any ecclesiastical court, either within or without the realm, shall incur the penalty of premunire. Next it provides, that all papal bulls, dispensations, and privileges, not containing matter prejudicial to the royal authority, or to the laws of the realm, may be put in execution, used, and alleged in all courts whatsoever; and concludes by declaring, that nothing in this act shall be explained to impair any authority or prerogative belonging to the crown in the twentieth year of Henry VIII.; that the pope shall have and enjoy, without diminution or enlargement, the same authority and jurisdiction which he might then have lawfully exercised; and that the jurisdiction of the bishops shall be restored to that state in which it existed at the same period. In the Lords, the bill was read thrice in two days; in the Commons, it was passed after a sharp debate on the third reading.[2] Thus was re-established in England the whole system of religious polity which had prevailed for so many centuries before Henry VIII.

The French ambassador had persuaded himself that the great object of the emperor was to employ the resources of England against his adversary the king of France; and that the fondness of Mary for her husband would induce her to gratify all his wishes, let them be ever so illegal or unjust. On this account, he con-

---

[1] Most readers have very confused and incorrect notions of the jurisdiction which the pontiff, in virtue of his supremacy, claimed to exercise within the realm. From this act, and the statutes which it repeals, it follows, that that jurisdiction was comprised under the following heads: 1. He was acknowledged as chief bishop of the Christian church, with authority to reform and redress heresies, errors, and abuses within the same. 2. To him belonged the institution or confirmation of bishops elect. 3. He could grant to clergymen licenses of non-residence, and permission to hold more than one benefice, with cure of souls. 4. He dispensed with the canonical impediments of matrimony; and, 5. He received appeals from the spiritual courts.

[2] Stat. iv. 246—254. From the Journals it appears that the subject of discussion was not so much the substance of the bill, as some of its provisions involving particular interests. In the Lords, Bonner, bishop of London, voted against it; the Commons added two provisions respecting lands to be hereafter given to the church, and the recovery of those already taken from it; and requested the erasure of nineteen lines regarding the bishop of London and the lord Wentworth. The Lords agreed, and the chancellor cut out the nineteen lines with a knife; yet the lord Montague, and the bishops of London, and Lichfield and Coventry, voted against the bill in its amended shape.—Journals, 481.

tinued to intrigue with the factious; he warned them that England would soon become a province under the despotic government of Spain; he exhorted them to be on the watch, to oppose every measure dictated by Philip, and to preserve, at every personal risk, their liberties for their children, and the succession to the crown for the true heir. In his despatches to his court, he described the discontent of the nation as wound up to the highest pitch; the embers of revolt, he said, were still alive; in a few months, perhaps a few weeks, the flame would burst forth with redoubled violence.[1] But he mistook his wishes for realities; his information frequently proved erroneous; and his predictions were belied by the event. In the present parliament, he assured his sovereign, that, in pursuance of the emperor's plan, the queen would ask for a matrimonial crown for her husband, would place the whole power of the executive government in his hands, and would seek to have him declared presumptive heir to the crown. What projects she might have formed, we know not; but it would be rash to judge of her intentions from the malicious conjectures of Noailles; and the fact is, that no such measures as he describes were ever proposed. The two houses, however, joined in a petition to Philip that, "if it should happen to the queen otherwise than well, in the time of her travail, he would take upon himself the government of the realm during the minority of her majesty's issue, with the rule, order, education, and government of the said issue." The king signified his assent; and an act passed, intrusting to him the government, till the child, if a female, were fifteen, if a male, eighteen years old; making it high treason to imagine or compass his death, or attempt to remove him from the said government and guardianship; and binding him, in the execution of his office, to all the conditions and restrictions which were contained in the original treaty of marriage.[2]

The dissolution of the parliament was followed by an unexpected act of grace. The lord chancellor, accompanied by several members of the council, proceeded to the Tower, called before him the state prisoners, still confined on account of the attempts of Northumberland and Wyat, and informed them that the king and queen had, at the intercession of the emperor, ordered them to be discharged.[3] The same favour was extended to Elizabeth and Courtenay. The earl, having paid his respects to Philip and Mary, received a permis-

---

[1] Noailles, iii. 318; iv. 27, 62, 76, 153. This ambassador found that he had failed in the object of his mission, in his intrigues with the discontented, and in the predictions with which he had amused his court. After this, his chagrin, and his hatred of the queen and her advisers, betray themselves in almost every page of his despatches, and detract much from the credit which might otherwise be given to his representations.

[2] Noailles, iv. 137. Stat. of Realm, iv. 255. An unusual circumstance occurred about the close of the session. It was customary for both houses to adjourn at Christmas over the holidays; and several members had sent for their servants and horses to visit their families during the recess. But on the 22nd of December orders were issued, that neither Lords nor Commons should depart before the end of the parliament. The two houses continued to sit, but thirty-seven members of the lower absented themselves, in opposition to the royal command. A bill for the punishment of such knights and burgesses as should neglect their duty passed the Commons; but the day after it had been read the first time in the Lords, the parliament was dissolved. Griffith, however, the attorney-general, indicted the offenders in the King's Bench. Six submitted, the rest traversed, and the matter was suffered to die away. Lord Coke represents them as seceding on account of their attachment to the reformed church.—See Cobbett's Parliamentary History, i. 625, and the Journals, p. 41.

[3] They were Holgate, archbishop of York, Ambrose, Robert, Henry, and Andrew Dudley, sons to the late duke of Northumberland, James Croft, Nicholas Throckmorton, &c.

sion, equivalent to a command, to travel for his improvement; and having remained for some time in the imperial court at Brussels, proceeded to Italy, with recommendatory letters from Philip to the princes of that country. It was reported that the queen proposed at the same time to send Elizabeth to Spain, that she might reside in some convent, but was dissuaded by the policy of her husband, who, as he had married to secure the aid of England in defence of his dominions in the Netherlands, against the ambitious designs of the French monarch, now brought forward his wife's sister as presumptive heir to the crown, in opposition to Mary of Scotland, about to be married to the dauphin of France. On the departure of Courtenay, Elizabeth reappeared at court. By the king and queen she was treated with kindness and distinction; and, after a visit of some months, returned to her own house in the country.[1] Philip made her a present of a diamond valued at four thousand ducats; to Mary he had given another valued at eight thousand.[2]

In consequence of the act restoring the exercise of the papal authority in England, the viscount Montague, the bishop of Ely, and Sir Edward Carne had been appointed ambassadors to the Roman see. But they had not proceeded far on their journey when Julius died. In the preceding conclave the cardinal Farnese had employed his influence to raise Pole to the papacy; he had even obtained one evening the requisite number of votes: but the English cardinal, irresolute and unambitious, bade him wait till the following morning, and on that morning another candidate was proposed and chosen. On the present vacancy Farnese espoused again the interests of his friend: he procured from the French king letters in favour of Pole; and hastened with these documents from Avignon to Rome. Before his arrival, at the very opening of the conclave, Cervini was unanimously elected,—a prelate whose acknowledged merit awakened the most flattering expectations. But the new pontiff, who had taken the name of Marcellus II., died within one-and-twenty days; and the friends of Pole laboured a third time to honour him with the tiara. Philip and Mary and Gardiner employed letters and messengers: the French king, though it was suspected that he secretly gave his interest to the cardinal of Ferrara, promised his best services; and Farnese, without waiting for new credentials, exhibited the letters which he had brought to the last conclave. But the cardinals, as well in the imperial as in the French interest, refused their voices; the former believing from past events that Pole was in secret an object of suspicion to their sovereign, the latter alleging that they could not vote without new instructions in his favour. Had he been present, he might have obtained the requisite majority of suffrages; in his absence Caraffa was chosen, and took the name of Paul IV. On the very day of the coronation of this pontiff, the English ambassadors reached Rome. Pole had foreseen that the new title of king and queen of Ireland, assumed by Philip and Mary, in imitation of Henry and Edward, might create some difficulty, and had therefore requested that Ireland might be declared a kingdom before the arrival of the ambassadors.[3] But the death of Julius, succeeded by that of Marcellus, had prevented those pontiffs from complying with his advice; and the first act of the new pope, after his

---

[1] See the reports of Michele and Soriano to the Venetian Senate; also Cabrera, 28.
[2] Fenclar's Despatches, iii 324.
[3] Poli Ep. l. v. ep. 5.

coronation, was to publish a bull, by which, at the petition of Philip and Mary, he raised the lordship of Ireland to the dignity of a kingdom.[1] Till this had been done, the ambassadors waited without the city; three days later they were publicly introduced. They acknowledged the pontiff as head of the universal church, presented to him a copy of the act by which his authority had been re-established, and solicited him to ratify the absolution pronounced by the legate, and to confirm the bishoprics erected during the schism. Paul received them with kindness, and granted their requests. Lord Montague and the bishop of Ely were dismissed with the usual presents; Carne remained as resident ambassador.[2]

---

[1] See the bull in Bsovius, Ann. Eccl. tom. xx. p. 301; and the extract from Act. Consistorial. inter Poli Ep. v. 136. It was sealed with lead; but Pole was careful to procure a second copy sealed with gold. (Ibid. 42. Such was the custom. Thus the bull giving to Henry VIII. the title of Defender of the Faith has a gold seal to it). As the natives of Ireland had maintained that the kings of England originally held Ireland by the donation of Adrian IV., and had lost it by their defection from the communion of Rome, the council delivered the second bull to Dr. Carey, the new archbishop of Dublin, with orders that it should be deposited in the treasury, after copies had been made, and circulated throughout the island. — Extract from Council Book, Archæol. xviii. 183.

[2] The ambassadors had acted under the authority originally given to them, to negotiate with the late pontiff; but after the departure of Lord Montague other credentials arrived, by which they were deputed ambassadors to the new pope. The bishop and Carne, in consequence, went through the former ceremonial a second time, but in a private consistory, on June 21. See Paul's letter to the king and queen, Poli, Ep. v. 136—139. A very erroneous statement of the whole transaction has been copied from Fra Paolo by most of our historians: the above is taken from the original documents furnished by Pole's letters.

CHAPTER VI.

PERSECUTION OF THE REFORMERS—SUFFERINGS OF RIDLEY AND LATIMER—RECANTATIONS AND DEATH OF CRANMER—DURATION AND SEVERITY OF THE PERSECUTION—DEPARTURE OF PHILIP—DEATH OF GARDINER—SURRENDER BY THE CROWN OF TENTHS AND FIRSTFRUITS—TREASONABLE ATTEMPTS—WAR WITH FRANCE AND SCOTLAND—VICTORY AT ST. QUINTIN—LOSS OF CALAIS—DEATH AND CHARACTER OF THE QUEEN.

It was the lot of Mary to live in an age of religious intolerance, when to punish the professors of erroneous doctrine was inculcated as a duty, no less by those who rejected, than by those who asserted the papal authority.[1] It might perhaps have been expected that the reformers, from their sufferings under Henry VIII., would have learned to respect the rights of conscience. Experience proved the contrary. They had no sooner obtained the ascendancy during the short reign of Edward, than they displayed the same persecuting spirit which they had formerly condemned, burning the Anabaptist, and preparing to burn the Catholic at the stake, for no other crime than adherence to religious opinion. The former, by the existing law, was already liable to the penalty of death; the latter enjoyed a precarious respite, because his belief had

---

[1] This is equally true of the foreign religionists —See Calvin, de supplicio Serveti; Beza, de Hæreticis a civili magistratu puniendis; and Melancthon, in locis Com. c. xxxii. de Ecclesia.

not yet been pronounced heretical by any acknowledged authority. But the zeal of Archbishop Cranmer observed and supplied this deficiency; and in the code of ecclesiastical discipline which he compiled for the government of the reformed church, he was careful to class the distinguishing doctrines of the ancient worship with those more recently promulgated by Muncer and Socinus. By the new canon law of the metropolitan, to believe in transubstantiation, to admit the papal supremacy, and to deny justification by faith only, were severally made heresy; and it was ordained that individuals accused of holding heretical opinions should be arraigned before the spiritual courts, should be excommunicated on conviction; and after a respite of sixteen days should, if they continued obstinate, be delivered to the civil magistrate, to suffer the punishment provided by law. Fortunately for the professors of the ancient faith, Edward died before this code had obtained the sanction of the legislature: by the accession of Mary the power of the sword passed from the hands of one religious party to those of the other; and within a short time Cranmer and his associates perished in the flames which they had prepared to kindle for the destruction of their opponents.

With whom the persecution under Mary originated is a matter of uncertainty. By the reformed writers the infamy of the measure is usually allotted to Gardiner, more, as far as I can judge, from conjecture and prejudice than from real information. The charge is not supported by any authentic document; it is weakened by the general tenour of the chancellor's conduct.[2] All that we know with certainty is, that after the queen's

---

[1] Ad extremum ad civilem magistratum ablegatur *puniendus*.—Reform. leg. cont. Hæret. c. 3. To elude the inference which may be drawn from this passage, it has been ingeniously remarked, that " there is a wide interval between the *infliction of punishment* and the *privation of life*."—Mackintosh, ii. 318, not. But, 1. even then, this passage establishes the principle of religious persecution, that it is the duty of the civil magistrate to inflict punishment on heretics condemned by ecclesiastical authority. 2. There cannot be a doubt that the punishment here contemplated is the *privation of life*. Such was the meaning of the words in the legal phraseology of the age. For this we have the testimony of Cranmer himself, who must be the best interpreter of his own language. When he condemned Anne Bocher to be delivered to the civil magistrate, and officially informed Edward that she was to be *deservedly punished* (condigna animadversione plectendam.—Wilk. Con. iv. 44), what was the punishment which he prevailed on the reluctant prince to inflict? Death by burning. When he pronounced the same sentence on Van Parris, and gave similar information to the king (animadversione vestra regia *puniendum*—Ibid. iv. 45), what did the word *puniendum* import? Death by burning. Again, it has been remarked that in a MS. copy which belonged to the archbishop (Harl. MSS. 426), after " puniendus" is added, in the hand, as is thought, of Peter Martyr, vel ut in perpetuum pellatur exilium, vel ad æternas carceris deprimatur tenebras (Todd, ii. 334). But it is plain that, on revision, this suggestion was abandoned; for it was omitted in "the later and more perfect draft of these laws, as they were completed and finished in King Edward's reign, and were published by Archbishop Parker in 1571."—Strype, 134.

[2] The only instance in which Gardiner was known to take any part in the persecution will be mentioned later, and then he acted in virtue of his office as chancellor. When at a later period Sir Francis Hastings applied to him the epithet "bloody," Persons indignantly answered:—" Verely I beleeve that if a man should ask any good-natured Protestant that lived in Queen Maries tyme, and had both wit to judge and indifferency to speake the truthe without passion, he will confesse that no one great man in that government was further off from blood and bloodiness, or from crueltie and revenge, than Bishop Gardiner, who was known to be a most tender-harted and myld man in that behalf; in so much that it was sometymes, and by some great personages, objected to him for no small fault, to be ever full of compassion in the office and charge that he bare: yea, to him especially it was imputed, that none of the greatest and most knowen Protestantes in Queen Maries reigne, were ever called to accompt, or put to trooble for religion."—Ward-worde, p. 42. I add the following testimony of Ascham:—" Noe bishop in Quene Marye's days wold have dealt soe with me, for such estimac'on in those even the learnedst and wisest men (as Gar-

marriage this question was frequently debated by the lords of the council; and that their final resolution was not communicated to her before the beginning of November. Mary returned the following answer in writing: "Touching the punishment of heretics, we thinketh it ought to be done without rashness, not leaving in the mean time to do justice to such as, by learning, would seem to deceive the simple; and the rest so to be used, that the people might well perceive them not to be condemned without just occasion; by which they shall both understand the truth, and beware not to do the like. And especially within London, I would wish none to be burnt without some of the council's presence, and both there and everywhere good sermons at the same time."[1]

Though it had been held in the last reign that by the common law of the land heresy was a crime punishable with death, it was deemed advisable to revive the three statutes which had formerly been enacted to suppress the doctrines of the Lollards.[2] An act for this purpose was brought into the Commons in the beginning of the next year: every voice was in its favour; and in the course of four days it had passed the two houses. The reformed preachers were alarmed. The most eminent among them had long since been committed to prison; some as the accomplices of Northumberland, or Suffolk, or Wyat, others for having presumed to preach without licence, and several on charges of disorderly or seditious conduct. To ward off the impending danger, they composed and forwarded petitions, including their confession of faith, both to the king and queen, and to the lords and commons assembled in parliament. In these instruments they declare, that the canonical books of the Old, and all the books of the New Testament, are the true word of God; that the Catholic church ought to be heard, as being the spouse of Christ; and that those who refuse to hear her "obeying the word of her husband," are heretics and schismatics. They profess to believe all the articles of doctrine "set forth in the symbols of the councils of Nice, of Constantinople, of Ephesus, of Chalcedon, and of the first and fourth of Toledo; and in the creeds of the apostles, of Athanasius, of Irenæus, of Tertullian, and of Damasus; so that whosoever doth not believe generally and particularly the doctrine of those symbols, they hold him to err from the truth." They reject free-will, merits, works of supererogation, confession and satisfaction, the invocation of the saints, and the use in the liturgy of an unknown tongue. They admit two sacraments,—baptism, and the Lord's supper; but disallow transubstantiation, communion under one kind, the sacrifice of the mass, and the inhibition of marriage to the clergy. They offer to prove the truth

---

diner, Heath, and Cardinal Poole) made of my poore service, that although they knew perfectly that in religion by open writing and privy talke I was contrary unto them, yett that, when Sir Francis Inglefield by name did note me specially at the councell board, Gardiner would not suffer me to be called thither, nor touched elsewhere, saying such words of me as in a letter, though letters cannot blushe, yet should I blushe, to write therein to your lo'pp—Winchester's good will stood not in speakeing fare, and wishing well, but he did indeed that for me, whereby my wife and children shall live the better when I am gone."—Roger Ascham to Lord Leicester, in Whitaker's History of Richmondshire, p. 286. See also other instances of Gardiner's moderation in Fuller, l. viii. p. 17; and Strype's Life of Sir Thos. Smith, p. 48, edit. 1820.

[1] The date of this paper, which disproves the pretended dispute between Gardiner and Pole in Hume, c. xxxvii., is evident from its mentioning those who "have to talk with my lord cardinal at his first coming." It is in Collier, ii. 371. Of course Pole had not yet arrived to hold the language attributed to him by the historian.

[2] See this History, vol. iii. p. 234, 318 Stat. iv. 241.

of their belief by public disputation; and are willing to submit to the worst of punishments, if they do not show that the doctrine of the church, the homilies, and the service set forth by King Edward, are most agreeable to the articles of Christian faith. Lastly, they warn all men against sedition and rebellion, and exhort them to obey the queen in all matters which are not contrary to the obedience due to God, and to suffer patiently as the will and pleasure of the higher powers shall adjudge.[1]

While the ministers in prison sought to mollify their sovereign by this dutiful address, their brethren at liberty provoked chastisement by the intemperance of their zeal. On the eve of the new year, Ross, a celebrated preacher, collected a congregation towards midnight; administered the communion, and openly prayed that God would either convert the heart of the queen, or take her out of this world. He was surprised in the fact, and imprisoned with his disciples; and the parliament hastened to make it treason to have prayed since the commencement of the session, or to pray hereafter, for the queen's death. It was, however, provided that all who had been already committed for this offence might recover their liberty, by making a humble protestation of sorrow, and a promise of amendment.[2]

The new year opened to the reformed preachers with a lowering aspect: before the close of the month the storm burst on their heads. On the twenty-second of January, the chancellor called before him the chief of the prisoners, apprized them of the statutes enacted in the last parliament, and put them in mind of the punishment which awaited their disobedience. In a few days the court was opened. Gardiner presided, and was attended by thirteen other bishops, and a crowd of lords and knights. Six prisoners were called before them; of whom one pretended to recant; another petitioned for time; and the other four, Hooper, the deprived bishop of Gloucester, Rogers, a prebendary of St. Paul's, Saunders, rector of Allhallows, in London, and Taylor, rector of Hadley, in Suffolk, replied, that their consciences forbade them to subscribe to the doctrines now established by law, and that the works of Gardiner himself had taught them to reject the authority of the bishop of Rome. A delay of twenty-four hours was offered them: on their second refusal they were excommunicated; and excommunication was followed by the delivery of the recusants to the civil power. Rogers was the first victim. He perished at the stake in Smithfield; Saunders underwent a similar fate at Coventry, Hooper at Gloucester, and Taylor at Hadley. An equal constancy was displayed by all: and, though pardon was offered them to the last moment, they scorned to purchase the continuance of life by feigning an assent to doctrines which they did not believe. They were the protomartyrs of the reformed church of England.

To give solemnity to these, the first prosecutions under the revived statutes, they had been conducted before the lord chancellor. But whether it was, that Gardiner disapproved of the measure, or that he was called away by more important duties, he never afterwards took his seat on the bench, but transferred the ungracious office, in the metropolis, to Bonner, bishop of London. That prelate, accompanied by the lord mayor and sheriffs, and several members of the council, excommunicated six other prisoners, and delivered them to the civil power.

---

[1] Strype, iii. Rec. 42. Fox, iii. 97.   [2] Stat. of Realm. iv. 254.

But the next day, Alphonso di Castro, a Spanish friar, confessor to Philip, preached before the court, and, to the astonishment of his hearers, condemned these proceedings in the most pointed manner. He pronounced them contrary, not only to the spirit, but to the text of the gospel: it was not by severity, but by mildness, that men were to be brought into the fold of Christ; and it was the duty of the bishops, not to seek the death, but to instruct the ignorance, of their misguided brethren. Men were at a loss to account for this discourse, whether it were spontaneous on the part of the friar, or had been suggested to him by the policy of Philip, or by the humanity of the cardinal, or by the repugnance of the prelates. It made, however, a deep impression; the execution of the prisoners was suspended; the question was again debated in the council, and five weeks elapsed before the advocates of severity could obtain permission to rekindle the fires of Smithfield.[1]

It is not improbable that the revival of the persecution was provoked by the excesses which were, at this time, committed by the fanaticism of some among the gospellers,[2] and by the detection of a new conspiracy which had been organized in the counties of Cambridge, Suffolk, and Norfolk. As soon as the ringleaders were arrested and committed to the Tower, the magistrates received instructions to watch over the public peace in their respective districts; to apprehend the propagators of seditious reports, the preachers of erroneous doctrine, the procurers of secret meetings, and those vagabonds who had no visible means of subsistence; to try, by virtue of a commission of oyer and terminer, the prisoners charged with murder, felony, and other civil offences; and, with respect to those accused of heresy, to reform them by admonition, but, if they continued obstinate, to send them before the ordinary, that "they might by charitable instruction, be removed from their naughty opinions, or be ordered according to the laws provided in that behalf."[3] In obedience to this circular, several of the preachers, with the most zealous of their disciples, were apprehended, and transmitted to the bishops, who, in general, declined the odious task of proceeding against them, on some occasions refusing, under different pretexts, to receive the prisoners, on others, suffering the charge to lie unheard until it was forgotten. This reluctance of the prelates was remarked by the lord treasurer, the marquess of Winchester, who complained to the council, and procured a reprimand to be sent to Bonner, stating that the king and queen marvelled at his want of zeal and diligence, and requiring him to proceed according to law, for the advancement of God's glory, and the better preservation of the peace of the realm.[4]

---

[1] Strype, iii. 209.
[2] See examples in Strype, 210, 212.
[3] Strype, iii. 213, 214. Burnet, ii. Rec. 283. Burnet tells us, ii. 347, and Hume gravely repeats the information, c. xxxvii., that this was an attempt to introduce the Spanish inquisition. The difference was immense. The magistrates were here commanded to send spiritual offenders before the ordinary: it was the leading feature in the inquisition, that it took the cognizance of spiritual offences from the ordinary. In effect, the inquisition was not introduced into England before the reign of Elizabeth, when the High Commission court was established on similar principles, and, in a short time, obtained and exercised the same powers as the Spanish inquisition.—See those powers in Rymer, xvi. 291—297, 546—551.
[4] Fox, iii. 208. Strype, iii. 217. Burnet, ii. Rec. 285. From this reprimand, I have been inclined to doubt whether Bonner really deserved all the odium which has been heaped upon him. It certainly fell to his lot, as bishop of London, to condemn a great number of the gospellers; but I can find no proof that he was a persecutor from choice, or went in search of victims. They were sent to him by the council, or by com-

The prelates no longer hesitated; and of the prisoners sent before them by the magistrates, many recanted, but many also refused to listen to their exhortations, and defied their authority. Conviction followed conviction; and the fate of one victim served only to encourage others to imitate his constancy. To describe the sufferings of each individual would fatigue the patience, and torture the feelings of the reader; I shall therefore content myself with laying before him the last moments of Cranmer, Ridley, and Latimer, the most distinguished among the English reformers. During the preceding reign they had concurred in sending the Anabaptists to the stake: in the present they were compelled to suffer the same punishment which they had so recently inflicted.

The history of the archbishop has been sufficiently detailed in the preceding pages. Ridley was born at Wilmontswick in Tynedale, had studied at Cambridge, Paris, and Louvain, and, on his return to England, obtained preferment in the church by the favour of Cranmer. During the reign of Henry he imitated his patron, by conforming to the theological caprice of the monarch; but on the accession of Edward he openly avowed his sentiments, and gave his valuable aid to the metropolitan. His services were rewarded with the bishopric of Rochester, and, on the deprivation of Bonner, with that of London; and as, under Henry, he had been employed to examine and detect sacramentaries, so, under the son of Henry, he sat in judgment at the condemnation of heretics.[1] In learning he was acknowledged superior to the other reformed prelates; and his refusal to avail himself of the permission to marry, though he condemned not the marriages of others, added to his reputation. Unfortunately his zeal for the new doctrines led him to support the treasonable projects of Northumberland; and his celebrated sermon against the claims of Mary and Elizabeth furnished sufficent ground for his committal to the Tower. There he had the weakness to betray his conscience by conforming to the ancient worship; but his apostasy was severely lashed by the pen of Bradford; and Ridley, by his speedy repentance and subsequent resolution, consoled and edified his afflicted brethren.[2]

Latimer, at the commencement of his career, displayed little of that strength of mind, or that stubbornness of opinion, which we expect to find in the man who aspires to the palm of martyrdom. He first attracted notice by the violence of his declamations against Melancthon and the German reformers; then professed himself their disciple and advocate; and ended by publicly renouncing their doctrine, at the command of Cardinal Wolsey. Two years had not elapsed, before he was accused of

---

missioners appointed by the council (Fox, iii. 208, 210, 223, 317, 328, 344, 522, 589, 660, 723. Strype, iii. 239, 240); and as the law stood, he could not refuse to proceed, and deliver them over to the civil power. He was, however, careful in the proceedings to exact from the prisoners, and to put on record, the names of the persons by whom, and a statement of the reasons for which, they had been sent before him.—Fox, iii. 514, 593. Several of the letters from the council show that he stood in need of a stimulus to goad him to the execution of this unwelcome office; and he complained much that he was compelled to try prisoners who were not of his own diocese. "I am," said he to Philpot, "right sorry for your trouble; neither would I you should think that I am the cause thereof. I marvel that other men will trouble me with their matters, but I must be obedient to my betters. And I fear men speak of me otherwise than I deserve."—Fox, iii. 462. Of the council, the most active in these prosecutions, either from choice or from duty, was the marquess of Winchester.—See Fox, iii. 203, 208, 317.

[1] State Papers, i. 843. Wilk. Con. iv. 45.
[2] "He never after polluted himself with that filthy dregs of anti-christian service."—Fox, iii. 836.

reasserting what he had abjured. The archbishop excommunicated him for contumacy; and a tardy and reluctant abjuration saved him from the stake. Again he relapsed; but appealed from the bishops to the king. Henry rejected the appeal; and Latimer on his knees acknowledged his error, craved pardon of the convocation, and promised amendment.[1] He had, however, powerful friends at court,—Butts the king's physician, Cromwell the vicar-general, and Anne Boleyn the queen consort. By the last he was retained as chaplain. Henry heard him preach; and, delighted with the coarseness of his invectives against the papal authority, gave him the bishopric of Worcester. In this situation he was cautious not to offend by too open an avowal of his opinions; but the debate on the Six Articles put his orthodoxy to the test; and with Cranmer he ventured to oppose the doctrine, but had not the good fortune with Cranmer to lull the suspicion, of the royal theologian. Henry was, however, satisfied with his resignation of the bishopric, and suffered him still to officiate as vicar of St. Bride's. Yet there he contrived to involve himself in new difficulties. He was brought with Crome and other gospellers before the royal commissioners. *They* boldly avowed their belief, and perished for it at the stake; *he* disguised his under evasive and ambiguous language; which, though it deceived no one, saved him from the fate of his colleagues.[2] He was permitted to languish in prison, till the death of the king and the accession of Edward restored him to liberty and recalled him to court. As preacher to the infant monarch, he lashed with apparent indifference the vices of all classes of men; inveighed with intrepidity against the abuses which already disfigured the new church and painted in the most hideous or most ludicrous colours the practices of the ancient worship. His eloquence was bold and vehement, but poured forth in coarse and sarcastic language, and seasoned with quaint conceits, low jests, and buffoonery. Such, however, as it was, it gratified the taste of his hearers; and the very boys in the streets, as he proceeded to preach, would follow at his heels, exclaiming, "Have at them, Father Latimer, have at them." But it was his misfortune, as it was that of Ridley, to abandon, on some occasions, theological for political subjects. During the reign of Edward, he treated in the pulpit the delicate question of the succession, and pronounced it better that God should take away the ladies Mary and Elizabeth, than that, by marrying foreign princes, they should endanger the existence of the reformed church. The same zeal probably urged him to similar imprudence in the beginning of Mary's reign, when he was imprisoned, by order of the council, on a charge of sedition.[3]

From the Tower Cranmer, Ridley, and Latimer, after the insurrection of Wyat, were conducted to Oxford, and ordered to confer on controverted points with the deputies of the convocation and of the two universities. The disputation was held in public on three successive days. Cranmer was severely pressed with passages from the fathers; Ridley maintained his former reputation; and Latimer excused himself, on the plea of old age, of disuse of the Latin tongue and of weakness of memory. In conclusion, Weston the moderator decided in favour of his own church:

---

[1] Fox, iii. 379, 383. Wilk. Conc. iii. 748, 749.
[2] See State Papers in the reign of Henry VIII., i. p. 848, 849, 850.
[3] Strype, iii. 131. Fox, iii. 385.

and the hall resounded with cries of "vincit veritas;" but the prisoners wrote in their own vindication to the queen, maintaining that they had been silenced by the noise, not by the arguments of their opponents.[1] Two days later they were again called before Weston; and, on their refusal to conform to the established church, were pronounced obstinate heretics. From that moment they lived in daily expectation of the fate which awaited them; but eighteen months were suffered to elapse before Brookes, bishop of Gloucester, as papal sub-delegate, and Martin and Story as royal commissioners, arrived at Oxford, and summoned the archbishop before them.[2] The provisions of the canon law were scrupulously observed; Cranmer had been served, as a matter of form, with a citation to answer before the pontiff in the course of eighty days,—a distinction which he owed to his office of archbishop; his companions having appeared twice before the bishops of Lincoln, Gloucester, and Bristol, as commissioners of the legate, and twice refused to renounce their opinions, were degraded from the priesthood, and delivered to the secular power. It was in vain that Soto, an eminent Spanish divine, laboured to shake their resolution. Latimer refused to see him; Ridley was not convinced by his reasoning.[3] At the stake, to shorten their sufferings, bags of gunpowder were suspended from their necks. Latimer expired almost the moment that the fire was kindled; but Ridley was doomed to suffer the most excruciating torments. To hasten his death, his brother-in-law had almost covered him with fagots; but the pressure checked the progress of the flames; and the lower extremities of the victim were consumed, while the more vital parts remained untouched. One of the bystanders, hearing him repeatedly exclaim, that "he could not burn," opened the pile, and an explosion of gunpowder almost immediately extinguished his life. It is said that the spectators were reconciled to these horrors, by the knowledge that every attempt had been previously made to save the victims from the stake;[4] the constancy with which they suffered consoled the sorrow, and animated the zeal, of their disciples.

From the window of his cell the archbishop had seen his two friends led to execution. At the sight his resolution began to waver; and he let fall some hints of a willingness to relent, and of a desire to confer with the legate.[5] But in a short time he recovered the tranquillity of his mind, and addressed, in defence of his doctrine, a long letter to the queen, which at her request was answered by Cardinal Pole.[6] At Rome, on the expiration of the

---

[1] Cranmer, in his letter to the council, says: "I never knewe nor heard of a more confused disputation in all my life. For albeit there was one appoynted to dispute agaynste me, yet every man spake hys mynde, and brought forth what hym liked without order, and such hast was made, that no answer could be suffered to be given."—Letters of Martyrs in Eman. Coll. No. 60, let. 3. This is an exact counterpart to the complaints of the Catholics respecting similar disputations in the time of Edward.

[2] From the proceedings it appears that Cranmer had been arraigned for high treason, had pleaded guilty, and had received judgment. He said he had confessed more than was true.—Fox apud Wordsworth, iii. 533.

[3] Alter ne loqui quidem cum eo voluit: cum altero est locutus, sed nihil profecit.—Pole to Philip, v. 47.

[4] De illis supplicium est sumptum, non illibenter, ut ferunt, spectante populo, cum cognitum fuisset nihil esse prætermissum, quod ad eorum salutem pertineret.—Ibid.

[5] Is non ita se pertinacem ostendit, aitque se cupere mecum loqui.—Ibid. Magnam spem initio dederat, eique veniam Polus ab ipsa regina impetraverat.—Dudith, inter Ep. Poli, i. 143.

[6] The letter and answer may be seen in Fox, iii. 563; Strype's Cranmer, App. 206; Le Grand, i. 289.

eighty days, the royal proctors demanded judgment; and Paul, in a private consistory, pronounced the usual sentence.[1] The intelligence of this proceeding awakened the terrors of the archbishop. He had not the fortitude to look death in the face. To save his life he feigned himself a convert to the established creed, openly condemned his past delinquency, and, stifling the remorse of his conscience, in seven successive instruments abjured the faith which he had taught, and approved of that which he had opposed. He first presented his submission to the council; and, as that submission was expressed in ambiguous language, replaced it by another in more ample form. When the bishops of London and Ely arrived to perform the ceremony of his degradation, he appealed from the judgment of the pope to a general council; but, before the prelates left Oxford, he sent them two other papers; by the first of which he submitted to all the statutes of the realm respecting the supremacy and other subjects, promised to live in quietness and obedience to the royal authority, and submitted his book on the sacrament to the judgment of the church and of the next general council; in the second he professed to believe on all points, and particularly respecting the sacraments, as the Catholic church then did believe, and always had believed from the beginning.[2] To Ridley and Latimer life had been offered, on condition that they should recant; but when the question was put, whether the same favour might be granted to Cranmer, it was decided by the council in the negative. His political offences, it was said, might be overlooked; but he had been the cause of the schism in the reign of Henry, and the author of the change of religion in the reign of Edward; and such offences required that he should suffer for "ensample's sake."[3] The writ was directed to the mayor or bailiffs of Oxford, the day of execution was fixed; still he cherished a hope of pardon; and in a fifth recantation, as full and explicit as the most zealous of his adversaries could wish, declared that he was not actuated by fear or favour, but that he abjured the erroneous doctrines which he had formally maintained, for the discharge of his own conscience, and the instruction of others.[4] This paper was accompanied with a letter to Cardinal Pole, in which he begged a respite during a few days, that he might have leisure to give to the world a more convincing proof of his repentance, and might do away, before his death, the scandal given by his past conduct.[5] This prayer was cheerfully granted by the queen; and Cranmer in a sixth confession acknowledged that he had been a greater persecutor of the church than Paul, and wished that like Paul he might be able to make

---

[1] Ex actis consistor. apud Quirini, v. 140. Fox, iii. 536. Much confusion has arisen from erroneous dates in Fox, iii. 544. The citation was served on Wednesday, the 11th of September. The eighty days expired on the 29th of November.

[2] The submissions are in Strype, iii. 233, 234; the appeal in Fox, iii. 556.

[3] Strype's Cranmer, 385.

[4] This recantation is in Fox, iii. 559.

[5] Il envoya prier M. le cardinal Polus de differer pour quelques jours son execution, esperant que Dieu l'inspireroit cependant: de quoi ceste royne et susdit cardinal furent fort ayses, estimans que par l'exemple de sa repentance publique la religion en sera plus fortifiée en ce royaulme: ayant depuis faict une confession publicque et amende honorable et volontaire.—Noailles, v. 319. In the council-book we meet with two entries, one of March 13, the other of March 16, by which the printers Rydall and Copeland are ordered to give up the printed copies of Cranmer's recantation to Cawoode, the queen's printer, that they may be burnt. These orders, from the dates, appear to refer to the fifth recantntion. Perhaps Rydall and Copeland had invaded the privilege of the queen's printer.

amends. He could not rebuild what he had destroyed; but, as the penitent thief on the cross, by the testimony of his lips, obtained mercy, so he (Cranmer) trusted that, by this offering of his lips, he should move the clemency of the Almighty. He was unworthy of favour, and worthy not only of temporal but of eternal punishment. He had offended against King Henry and Queen Catherine: he was the cause and author of the divorce, and, in consequence, also of the evils which resulted from it. He had blasphemed against the sacrament, had sinned against Heaven, and had deprived men of the benefits to be derived from the eucharist. In conclusion, he conjured the pope to forgive his offences against the Apostolic See, the king and queen to pardon his transgressions against them, the whole realm, the universal church, to take pity of his wretched soul and God to look on him with mercy at the hour of his death.[1] He had undoubtedly flattered himself that this humble tone, these expressions of remorse, these cries for mercy, would move the heart of the queen. She, indeed, little suspecting the dissimulation which had dictated them, rejoiced at the conversion of the sinner; but she had also persuaded herself, or been persuaded by others, that public justice would not allow her to save him from the punishment to which he had been condemned.

At length the fatal morning arrived; at an early hour Garcina, a Spanish friar, who had frequently visited the prisoner since his condemnation, came, not to announce a pardon, but to comfort and prepare him for the last trial. Entertaining no suspicion of his sincerity, Garcina submitted to his consideration a paper, which he advised him to read at the stake, as a public testimony of his repentance. It consisted of five parts: a request that the spectators would pray with him; a form of prayer for himself; an exhortation to others to lead a virtuous life; a direction to declare the queen's right to the crown; and a confession of faith, with a retractation of the doctrine in his book on the eucharist. Cranmer, having dissembled so long, did not hesitate to carry on the deception. He transcribed and signed the paper; and, giving one copy to the Spaniard, retained the other for his own use. But when the friar was gone, he appears to have made a second copy, in which, entirely omitting the fourth article, the declaration of the queen's right, he substituted, in lieu of the confession contained in the fifth, a disavowal of the six retractations which he had already made.[2] Of his motives we can judge only from his conduct. Probably he now considered himself doubly armed. If a pardon were announced, he might take the benefit of it, and read the original paper; if not, by reading the copy he would disappoint the expectations of his

---

[1] See it in Strype, iii. 235.

[2] Compare Fox, iii. 559, with Strype, iii. 236. To extenuate the fall of Cranmer, his friends have said that either these recantations are forgeries, or that he was seduced to make them by the artful promises of persons sent from the court for that purpose. But this pretence is refuted by his last speech, and gives the lie to his own solemn declaration; for, instead of making any such apology for himself, he owns that his confessions proceeded from a wish to save his life. "I renounce and refuse them, as things written with my hand, contrary to the truth which I thought in my heart; and written for fear of death, and to save my life, *if it might be;* and that is, all such bills and papers as I have written or signed with my hand since my degradation, wherein I have written many things untrue."......... "Always hitherto I have been a hater of falsehood and a lover of simplicity, and never before this time have I dissembled." These words certainly amount to an acknowledgment that he had written such recantations, though no promise of life had been made to him; indeed, it is evident from Noailles, v. 319, that he did not openly ask for mercy, though he hoped to obtain it.

adversaries, and repair the scandal which he had given to his brethren. At the appointed hour the procession set forward, and, on account of the rain, halted at the church of St. Mary, where the sermon was preached by Dr. Cole. Cranmer stood on a platform opposite the pulpit, appearing, as a spectator writes, "the very image of sorrow." His face was bathed in tears; his eyes were sometimes raised to heaven, sometimes fixed through shame on the earth. At the conclusion of the sermon he began to read his paper, and was heard with profound silence till he came to the fifth article. But when he recalled all his former recantations, rejected the papal authority, and confirmed the doctrine contained in his book, he was interrupted by the murmurs and agitation of the audience. The lord Williams called to him to "remember himself, and play the Christian." "I do," replied Cranmer; "it is now too late to dissemble. I must now speak the truth." As soon as order could be restored, he was conducted to the stake, declaring that he had never changed his belief; that his recantations had been wrung from him by the hope of life; and that, "as his hand had offended by writing contrary to his heart, it should be the first to receive its punishment." When the fire was kindled, to the surprise of the spectators, he thrust his hand into the flame, exclaiming, "This hath offended." His sufferings were short; the flames rapidly ascended above his head, and he expired in a few moments. The Catholics consoled their disappointment by invectives against his insincerity and falsehood; the Protestants defended his memory by maintaining that his constancy at the stake had atoned for his apostasy in the prison.[1]

Historians are divided with respect to the part which Pole acted during these horrors. Most are willing to acquit him entirely; a few, judging from the influence which he was supposed to possess, have allotted to him a considerable share of the blame. In a confidential letter to the cardinal of Augsburg he has unfolded to us his own sentiments without reserve. He will not, he says, deny that there may be men, so addicted to the most pernicious errors themselves, and so apt to seduce others, that they may justly be put to death, in the same manner as we amputate a limb to preserve the whole body. But this is an extreme case; and, even when it happens, every gentler remedy should be applied before such punishment is inflicted. In general, lenity is to be preferred to severity; and the bishops should remember that they are fathers as well as judges, and ought to show the tenderness of parents, even when they are compelled to punish. This has always been his opinion; it was that of his colleagues who presided with him at the council of Trent, and also of the prelates who composed that assembly.[2] His conduct in England was conformable to these professions. On the deprivation of Cranmer, he

---

[1] See a most interesting narrative by an eye-witness, in Strype's Cranmer, 384. The seven recantations of Cranmer were published by Cawoode, with Bonner's approbation, under the title of "All the submyssions and recantations of Thomas Cranmer, late archebyshop of Canterburye, truly set forth in Latyn and English, agreeable to the originalles, wrytten and subscribed with his own hand." It has been pretended that the seventh of these is a forgery, because it is contrary to his declaration at his death; but the same reason would prove that they were all forgeries, for he then revoked them all. But that he actually wrote and subscribed a seventh, is evident from Fox (Acts and Mon. 559), and, as he gave a copy so subscribed to Garcina, why should we doubt that it was that which was published as such?

[2] Poli Epist. iv. 156. See also in Fox, iii. 659, Bonner's letter to him of December 26, 1556, which shows that the cardinal disapproved of some of Bonner's proceedings against the reformers.

was appointed archbishop; and his consecration took place on the day after the death of his predecessor.[1] From that moment the persecution ceased in the diocese of Canterbury. Pole found sufficient exercise for his zeal in reforming the clergy, repairing the churches, and re-establishing the ancient discipline. His severity was exercised against the dead rather than the living; and his delegates, when they visited the universities in his name, ordered the bones of Bucer and Fagius, two foreign divines, who had taught the new doctrines at Cambridge, to be taken up and burnt. But his moderation displeased the more zealous; they called in question his orthodoxy; and, in the last year of his life (perhaps to refute the calumny), he issued a commission for the prosecution of heretics within his diocese. Five persons were condemned; four months afterwards they suffered, but at a time when the cardinal lay on his death-bed, and was probably ignorant of their fate.[2]

It had at first been hoped that a few of these barbarous exhibitions would silence the voices of the preachers, and check the diffusion of their doctrines. In general they produced conformity to the established worship; but they also encouraged hypocrisy and perjury. It cannot be doubted that among the higher classes there were some who retained an attachment to the doctrines which they professed under Edward, and to which they afterwards returned under Elizabeth. Yet it will be useless to seek among the names of the sufferers for a single individual of rank, opulence, or importance.[3] All of this description embraced, or pretended to embrace, the ancient creed; the victims of persecution, who dared to avow their real sentiments, were found only in the lower walks of life. Of the reformed clergy a few suffered; some, who were already in prison, and some whose zeal prompted them to brave the authority of the law. Others, who aspired not to the crown of martyrdom, preferred to seek an asylum in foreign climes. The Lutheran Protestants refused to receive them, because they were heretics, rejecting the corporeal presence in the sacrament;[4] but they met with a cordial welcome from the disciples of Calvin and Zwinglius, and obtained permission to open churches in Strasburg, Frankfort, Basle, Geneva, Arau, and Zurich. Soon, however, the demon of discord interrupted the harmony of the exiles. Each followed his own judgment; some retained with pertinacity the book of Common Prayer and the articles of religion published under Edward; others, deriving new lights from the society of foreign religionists, demanded a form of service less defiled with superstition; and with this view adopted in their full extent the rigid principles of the Genevan theo-

---

[1] It has been said that Pole hastened the death of Cranmer, that he might get possession of the archbishopric. But the life of Cranmer, after his deprivation, could be no obstacle. The fact is, that Pole procured several respites for Cranmer, and thus prolonged his life.—Noailles, v. 319. Dudith, inter Ep. Poli, i. 43.

[2] Wilk. Con. iv. 173, 174. Fox, iii. 750. It is a mistake to suppose that inquisitors of heretical pravity were appointed by Pole in the convocation of 1558.—See Wilkins, iv. 156.

[3] Perhaps I should except Sir John Cheke, preceptor to the late king, and to many of the nobility. Yet I suspect that his incarceration was for some other cause than religion, as he was apprehended and brought from the Low Countries in company with Sir Peter Carew. However, Feckenham, dean of St. Paul's, prevailed on him to conform; and, to show his sincerity, he persuaded, after several discussions, twenty-eight other prisoners to follow his example, and sat on the bench at the trial of some others. He died the next year, if we may believe the reformed writers, of remorse for his apostasy.—See Strype, iii. 315, Rec. 186—189; and a letter from Priuli inter Ep. Poli. v. 346.

[4] Vociferantem martyres Anglicos esse martyres diaboli.—Melancthon apud Heylin, 250. Pet. Martyr, ibid.

logy. Dissension, reproaches, and schisms divided the petty churches abroad, and from them extended to the reformed ministers at home The very prisons became theatres of controversy; force was occasionally required to restrain the passions of the contending parties; and the men who lived in the daily expectation of being summoned to the stake for their denial of the ancient creed, found leisure to condemn and revile each other for difference of opinion respecting the use of habits and ceremonies, and the abstruse mysteries of grace and predestination.[1]

The persecution continued till the death of Mary. Sometimes milder counsels seemed to prevail; and on one occasion all the prisoners were discharged on the easy condition of taking an oath to be true to God and the queen.[2] But these intervals were short, and, after some suspense, the spirit of intolerance was sure to resume the ascendancy. Then new commissions were issued by the crown.[3] The magistrates were careful to fulfil their instructions: and the council urged the bishops "to reclaim the prisoners, or to deal with them according to law." The reformed writers have described, in glowing colours, the sufferings, and sought to multiply the number, of the victims; while the Catholics have maintained that the reader should distrust the exaggerations of men heated with enthusiasm and exasperated by oppression; and that from the catalogue of the martyrs should be expunged the names of all who were condemned as felons or traitors, or who died peaceably in their beds, or who survived the publication of their martyrdom, or who would for their heterodoxy have been sent to the stake by the reformed prelates themselves, had they been in possession of the power.[4] Yet these deductions will take but little from the infamy of the measure. After every allowance, it will be found that, in the space of four years, almost two hundred persons perished in the flames for religious opinion; a number, at the contemplation of which the mind is struck with horror, and learns to bless the legislation of a more tolerant age, in which dissent from established forms, though in some countries still punished with civil disabilities, is nowhere liable to the penalties of death.

If anything could be urged in extenuation of these cruelties, it must have been the provocation given by the reformers. The succession of a Catholic sovereign had deprived them of office and power; had suppressed the English service, the idol of their affections; and had re-established the ancient worship, which they deemed antichristian and idolatrous. Disappointment embittered their zeal; and enthusiasm sanctified their intemperance. They heaped on the queen, her bishops, and her religion, every indecent and irritating epithet which language could supply. Her clergy could not exercise their functions without danger to their lives; a dagger was thrown at one priest in the pulpit; a gun was discharged at another; and several wounds were inflicted on a third, while he administered the communion in his church. The chief supporters of the treason of Northumberland, the most active among the adherents of Wyat, professed the reformed creed; an impostor was suborned to personate Edward VI.;[5] some congregations prayed for the death of the queen; tracts

---

[1] Phœnix, ii. 44.
[2] Strype, iii. 307. Fox, iii. 660.
[3] See similar commissions under Edward,
Rymer, xv. 181—183, 250—252. Many were also issued under Elizabeth.
[4] See the second part of Appendix, A A.
[5] His name was Fetherstone. For the

filled with libellous and treasonable matter were transmitted from the exiles in Germany;[1] and successive insurrections were planned by the fugitives in France. It is not improbable that such excesses would have considerable influence with statesmen, who might deem it expedient to suppress sedition by prosecution for heresy; but I am inclined to believe that the queen herself was not actuated so much by motives of policy as of conscience; that she had imbibed the same intolerant opinion, which Cranmer and Ridley laboured to instil into the young mind of Edward: "that, as Moses ordered blasphemers to be put to death, so it was the duty of a Christian prince, and more so of one who bore the title of Defender of the Faith, to eradicate the cockle from the field of God's church, to cut out the gangrene, that it might not spread to the sounder parts."[2] In this principle both parties seem to have agreed; the only difference between them regarded its application, as often as it affected themselves.

But it is now time to turn from these cruelties to the affairs of state. The French ambassador, when he congratulated Philip on the marriage, had been ordered to express an ardent wish for the continuation of the amity between England and France; and the new king, aware of the declaration of Henry, that he had no league but that of friendship with Mary, coldly replied, that he should never think of drawing the nation into a war, as long as it was for its interest to preserve peace. This ambiguous answer alarmed the French cabinet: it was expected that England would in a short time make common cause with Spain and the Netherlands against France; and Noailles was informed that his sovereign had no objection to a negotiation for a general peace, provided the first motion did not appear to originate from him. Mary offered her mediation: Pole and Gardiner solicited the concurrence of Charles and Henry; and the two monarchs, after much hesitation, gave their consent. But pride, or policy, induced them to affect an indifference which they did not feel. Many weeks passed in useless attempts by each to draw from the other some intimation of the terms to which he would consent; and as many more were lost in deciding on the persons of the negotiators, because etiquette required that all employed by the one should be of equal rank with those employed by his opponent. At length the congress opened at Marque, within the English pale; where the cardinal, Gardiner, Arundel, and Paget, appeared as the representatives of Mary, the mediating sovereign. It was soon found that a treaty was impracticable: Charles would not abandon the interests of his ally Philibert duke of

---

first offence he was publicly whipped; for the repetition of it was executed as a traitor.—Stowe, 626, 628. Noailles says falsely, that he was torn to pieces by four horses, as traitors were sometimes in France (v. 318).

[1] If scurrility and calumny form the merit of a libel, it will be difficult to find anything to rival these publications. The reader will meet with some samples in Strype, iii. 251, 252, 328, 388, 410, 460.

[2] Thus Edward was made to say, Etsi regibus quidem omnibus.........nobis tamen qui fidei defensor peculiari quodam titulo vocitamur, maximæ præ cæteris curæ esse debet, to eradicate the cockle, &c.—Rym. xv. 182, 250. To the same purpose Elizabeth, in a commission for the burning of heretics, to Sir Nicholas Bacon, says, "they have been justly declared heretics, and therefore, as corrupt members to be cut off from the rest of the flock of Christ, lest they should corrupt others professing the true Christian faith,.........we, therefore, according to regal function and office, minding the execution of justice in this behalf, require you to award and make out our writ of execution," &c.........—Rymer, xv. 740. And again, Nos igitur ut zelator justitiæ et fidei Catholicæ defensor, volentesque......... hujusmodi hæreses et errores ubique (quantum in nobis est) eradicare et extirpare, ac hæreticos sic convictos animadversione condigna puniri, &c.—Id. xv. 741.

Savoy, and Henry would not restore the dominions of that prince, unless he were to receive Milan from the emperor. Yet the necessities of the belligerent powers imperiously required a cessation of war; and the English ministers, at the conclusion of the congress, returned with the persuasion, that, notwithstanding the insuperable objections to a peace, it would not be difficult to conclude a truce for several years; which was accordingly accomplished a few months afterwards.[1]

From the moment of his arrival in England, Philip had sought to ingratiate himself with the natives. He had conformed to the national customs, and appeared to be delighted with the national amusements. He endeavoured to attach the leading men to his interest, by the distribution among them of pensions from his own purse, under the decent pretence of rewarding the services rendered to his wife during the insurrection; and, throwing aside the hauteur and reserve of the Spanish character, he became courteous and affable, granting access to every suitor, even to those in the humblest condition of life, and dismissing all with answers, expressive of his sympathy, if not promissory of his support. In the government of the realm he appeared not to take any active part; and, when favours were conferred, was careful to attribute them to the bounty of the queen, claiming for himself no other merit than that of a well-wisher and intercessor. But he laboured in vain. The antipathy of the English was not to be subdued; personally, indeed, he was always treated with respect, but his attendants met with daily insults and injuries; and when, in answer to their complaints, he referred them to the courts of law for redress, they replied that justice was not to be obtained against the natives, through the dilatory form of the proceedings, and the undisguised partiality of the judges.[2]

Under these circumstances the king grew weary of his stay in England, and his secret wishes were aided by letters from his father, who, exhausted with disease and the cares of government, earnestly entreated him to return; but the queen, believing herself in a state to give him an heir to his dominions, extorted from him a promise not to leave her till after her expected delivery. The delusion was not confined to herself and Philip; even the females of her family and her medical attendants entertained the same opinion. Preparations were made; public prayers were ordered for her safety, and that of her child; her physicians were kept in daily attendance; ambassadors were named to announce the important intelligence to foreign courts; and even letters were written beforehand, with blank spaces which might afterwards be filled up with the sex of the child and the date of the birth.[3] Week after week passed away; still Mary's expectations were disappointed; and it was generally believed that she was in the same situation with the lady Ambrose Dudley, who very recently had mistaken for pregnancy a state of disease. But the midwife, contrary to her own conviction, thought proper to encourage the hopes of the king and queen; and, on a supposition of miscalculation of time, two more months were suffered to elapse before the delusion was removed.[4] Some-

---

[1] See the despatches of Noailles through the whole of vol. iv.
[2] MS. Report of Soriano to the Venetian Senate.
[3] Those addressed to the emperor, the kings of France, Hungary, Bohemia, to several queens, and to the Doge of Venice, are still in the State Paper Office.—See Transcripts for the New Rymer, 353, 354.
[4] The queen yielded again to this delusion

times it was rumoured that Mary had died in childbed; sometimes that she had been delivered of a son; her enemies indulged in sarcasms, epigrams, and lampoons; and the public mind was kept in a constant state of suspense and expectation. At last, the royal pair, relinquishing all hope, proceeded in state from Hampton Court through London to Greenwich; whence Philip, after a short stay, departed for Flanders. He left the queen with every demonstration of attachment, and recommended her in strong terms to the care of Cardinal Pole.[1]

Mary consoled her grief for the bsence of her husband by devoting the more early part of each day to practices of charity and devotion, and the afternoon to affairs of state, to which she gave such attention as in a short time injured her health. The king, though occupied by the war with France, continued to exercise considerable influence in the government of the kingdom. He maintained a continual correspondence with the ministers; and no appointment was made, no measure was carried into execution, without his previous knowledge and consent.[2] Before his departure he had reluctantly acquiesced in the wish of the queen, who, considering the impoverished state of the church, judged it her duty to restore to it such ecclesiastical property as during the late reigns had been vested in the crown. She had renounced the supremacy, could she retain the wealth which resulted from the assumption of that authority? She saw the clergy suffering under the pressure of want, was she not bound to furnish relief out of that portion of their property which still remained in her hands? Her ministers objected the amount of her debts, the poverty of the exchequer, and the necessity of supporting the dignity of the crown: but she replied, that "she set more by the salvation of her soul than by ten such crowns." On the opening of the parliament, to relieve the apprehensions of the other possessors of church property, a papal bull was read, confirming the grant already made by the legate, and, for greater security, excepting it from the operation of another bull recently issued; after which Gardiner explained to the two houses the wants of the clergy and of the crown, and the solicitude of the queen to make adequate provision for both. He spoke that day and the next, with an ability and eloquence that excited universal applause.[3] But the exertion was too great for his debilitated frame. His health had long been on the decline; at his return from the house on the second day, he repaired to his chamber; and, having lingered three weeks, expired. His death was a subject of deep regret to Mary, who lost in him a most able, faithful, and zealous servant; but it was hailed with joy by the French ambassador,

in the beginning of 1558, and Philip wrote to her on Jan. 21, that the announcement of her pregnancy was "the best news which he had received in alleviation of his grief for the loss of Calais."—See Apuntamientos para la Historia del Roy Don Felipe II., por Den Tomas Gonzalez, p. 4. The documents quoted in that work are at Simancas.

[1] Noailles, iv. 331, 334; v. 12, 50, 77, 83, 99, 126. Michele's Memoir to the Senate, MSS. Barberini, 1208. The cabinet, after his departure, consisted of the cardinal, whenever he could and would attend (for he objected to meddle in temporal matters), the chancellor and treasurer, the earls of Arundel and Pembroke, the bishop of Ely and Lord Paget, Rochester, and Petre, the secretary.—See the instrument of appointment in Burnet, iii. Rec. 256.

[2] Poli Ep. v. 41, 44.

[3] His duobus diebus ita mihi visus est non modo seipsum iis rebus superasse, quibus cæteros superare solet, ingenio, eloquentia, prudentia, pietate, sed etiam ipsas sui corporis vires.—Pole to Philip, v. 46. From this and similar passages in the letters of Pole, I cannot believe that that jealousy existed between him and Gardiner, which it has pleased some historians to suppose.

the factious, and the reformers, who considered him as the chief support of her government.[1] During his illness he edified all around him by his piety and resignation, often observing, "I have sinned with Peter, but have not yet learned to weep bitterly with Peter."[2] By his will he bequeathed all his property to his royal mistress, with a request that she would pay his debts, and provide for his servants. It proved but an inconsiderable sum, though his enemies had accused him of having amassed between thirty and forty thousand pounds.[3]

The indisposition of the chancellor did not prevent the ministers from introducing a bill for a subsidy into the lower house. It was the first aid that Mary had asked of her subjects; but Noailles immediately began his intrigues, and procured four of the best speakers among the Commons to oppose it in every stage. It had been proposed to grant two fifteenths, with a subsidy of four shillings in the pound; but, whether it were owing to the hirelings of Noailles, or to the policy of the ministers, who demanded more than they meant to accept, Mary, by message, declined the two fifteenths, and was content with a subsidy of less amount than had been originally proposed.[4]

The death of Gardiner interrupted the plans of the council. That minister had undertaken to procure the consent of parliament to the queen's plan of restoring the church property vested in the crown: now Mary herself assumed his office, and, sending for a deputation from each house, explained her wish, and the reasons on which it was grounded. In the Lords, the bill passed with only two dissentient voices; in the Commons it had to encounter considerable opposition, but was carried by a majority of 193 to 126. By it the tenths and first-fruits, the rectories, benefices appropriate, glebe-lands, and tithes annexed to the crown, since the twentieth of Henry VIII., producing a yearly revenue of about sixty thousand pounds, were resigned by the queen, and placed at the disposal of the cardinal, for the augmentation of small livings, the support of preachers, and the furnishing of exhibitions to scholars in the universities; but subject, at the same time, to all the pensions and corrodies with which they had been previously encumbered.[5] In consequence of this cession, Pole ordered that the

---

[1] See Appendix, AA.
[2] "He desired that the Passion of our Saviour might be redde unto him, and when they came to the denial of St. Peter, he bid them stay there, for (saythe he) negavi cum Petro, exivi cum Petro, sed nondum flevi amare cum Petro."—Wardword, 48. Speaking of Gardiner's sickness, Pole writes thus: Dicam quasi simul cum eo religio et justitia laborarent, sic ab eo tempore, quo is ægrotare cœpit, utrumque in hoc regno esse infirmatam, rursusque impietatem et injustitiam vires colligere cœpisse.—Poli Ep. v. 52. I give this quotation, because it has been brought as a plain proof that Gardiner was the very soul of the persecution!—Soames, iv. 382.   [3] Ibid. 206.
[4] The subsidy was of two shillings in the pound on lands, eight pence on goods to ten pounds, twelve pence to twenty pounds, and sixteen pence above twenty (Stat. iv. 301); but those who paid for lands were not rated for their personalties. Lord Talbot tells his father, that "the common housse wold have graunted hurr ii fyftenes," but that she, "of hurr lyberalyte, refusyd it, and said, sho wold not take no more of them at that tyme."—Lodge, i. 207. "She gave thanks for the two fifteenths, and was contented to refuse them."—Journal of Commons, p. 43. "We have forborne to ask any fifteenths."—The queen to the earl of Bath, in Mr. Gage's elegant "History and Antiquities of Hengrave," p. 154. Yet Noailles asserts that the fifteenths were refused by parliament, and takes to himself the merit of the refusal (v. 155, 190, 252). I often suspect that this ambassador deceived his master intentionally.
[5] Stat. iv. 275. Pole, v. 46, 51, 53, 56. Some writers have said that the queen sought to procure an act, compelling the restoration of church property, in whatever hands it might be. The contrary is evident from the whole tenour of Pole's correspondence

exaction of the first-fruits should immediately cease; that livings of twenty marks and under should be relieved from the annual payment of tenths; that livings of a greater value should, for the present, contribute only one twentieth toward the charges with which the clergy were burdened; and that the patronage of the rectories and vicarages, previously vested in the crown, should revert to the bishops of the respective dioceses, who, in return, should contribute proportionably to a present of seven thousand pounds to be made to the king and queen.[1]

About the same time, that the monastic bodies might not complain of neglect, Mary re-established the Grey Friars at Greenwich, the Carthusians at Sheen, and the Brigittins at Sion; three houses, the former inhabitants of which had provoked the vengeance of Henry, by their conscientious opposition to his innovations. The dean and prebendaries of Westminster retired on pensions, and yielded their places to a colony of twenty-eight Benedictine monks, all of them beneficed clergymen, who had quitted their livings, to embrace the monastic institute.[2] In addition, the house of the Knights of St. John arose from its ruins, and the dignity of lord prior was conferred on Sir Thomas Tresham. But these renewed establishments fell again on the queen's demise; her hospital at the Savoy was alone suffered to remain. She had endowed it with abbey lands; and the ladies of the court, at her recommendation or command, had furnished it with necessaries.

While Gardiner lived, his vigilance had checked the intrigues of the factious: his death emboldened them to renew their machinations against the government. Secret meetings were now held; defamatory libels on the king and queen, printed on the continent, were found scattered in the streets, in the palace, and in both houses of parliament; and reports were circulated that Mary, hopeless of issue to succeed her, had determined to settle the crown on her husband after her decease. If we may believe her counsellors, there was no foundation for these rumours; she had never hinted any such design; nor, if she had, would she have found a man to second it.[3] But it was for the interest of the French monarch that the falsehood should be believed; and Noailles made every effort to support its credit. Under the auspices of that intriguing minister, and by the agency of Freitville, a French refugee, a new conspiracy was formed, which had for its object to depose Mary, and to raise Elizabeth to the throne. The conduct of the enterprise was intrusted to Sir Henry Dudley, a relation and partisan of the attainted duke of Northumberland, whose services had been purchased by the French king with the grant of a considerable pension. The connections of Dudley with the chiefs of the gospellers and of the discontented in the southern counties, furnished well-grounded hopes

---

[1] Wilk. Con. 153, 175, 177. Noailles says that several bills proposed by the court were rejected (v. 252); yet only one of them is mentioned in the journals of either house, "against such as had departed the realm without leave, or should contemptuously make their abode there." It was unanimously passed by the Lords, but was lost on a division in the Commons.—Journals, 46. I may add, that Burnet (ii. 322) represents Story as opposing, in this parliament, "licenses" from Rome. The journals show that the "licenses" were monopolies, granted by the queen, her father, and her brother.—Journals of Commons, p. 41.

[2] Feckenham was again appointed abbot, but only for three years; for the cardinal disapproved of the ancient custom of abbots for life; and had sent to Italy for two monks, who might establish in England the discipline observed in the more rigid communities abroad.—Priuli to Beccatello, in Pole's Ep. v. App. 347.

[3] Noailles, v. 174, 242, 365.

of success; assurances had been obtained of the willing co-operation of Elizabeth and her friends; and the French cabinet had engaged to convey to England, at the shortest warning, the earl of Devon, then on his road from Brussels to Italy. To arrange the minor details, and to procure the necessary supplies, Dudley, in disguise, sailed to the coast of Normandy, and was followed by three more of the conspirators; but they arrived at a most inauspicious moment, just when the king had, in opposition to the remonstrances of his minister Montmorency, concluded a truce for five years with Philip. Henry was embarrassed by their presence. Ashamed to appear as an accomplice in a conspiracy against a prince with whom he was now on terms of amity, he ordered Dudley and his companions to keep themselves concealed, and advised their associates in England, particularly the lady Elizabeth, to suspend, for some time, the projected insurrection. Events, he observed, would follow more favourable to the success of the enterprise; at present it was their best policy to remain quiet, and to elude suspicion by assuming the mask of loyalty.[1]

But dilatory counsels accorded not with the desperate circumstances of Kingston, Throckmorton, Udal, Staunton, and the other conspirators; who, rejecting the advice of their French ally, determined to carry into immediate execution the first part of the original plot. To excite or foment the public discontent, they had reported that Philip devoted to Spanish purposes the revenue of the English crown; though at the same time they knew that, on different occasions, he had brought an immense mass of treasure into the kingdom,[2] of which one portion had been distributed in presents, another had served to defray the expenses of the marriage, and the remainder, amounting to fifty thousand pounds, was still lodged in the Exchequer. A plan was devised to surprise the guard, and to obtain possession of this money; but one of the conspirators proved a traitor to his fellows; of the others, several apprehended by his means paid the forfeit of their lives, and many sought and obtained an asylum in France. The lord Clinton, who had been commissioned to congratulate Henry on the conclusion of the truce, immediately demanded the fugitives, as "traitors, heretics, and outlaws." Mary had recently gratified the king in a similar request; he could not, in decency, return a refusal, but replied, that he knew nothing of the persons in question; if they had been received in France, it must have been through respect to the queen, whose subjects they had stated themselves to be; all that he could do was to make inquiry, and to order that the moment they were discovered they should be delivered to the resident ambassador. With this illusory answer Lord Clinton returned.[3]

---

[1] Noailles, 232, 234, 254, 255, 256, 262, 263, 302. That the lady Elizabeth was concerned in it, seems placed beyond dispute by the following passage in the instructions to Noailles, after the conclusion of the truce: Et surtout eviter que madame Elizabeth ne se remue en sorte du monde pour entreprendre ce que m'escrivez ; car se seroit tout gaster, et perdre le fruict qu'ilz peulvent attendre de leurs desseings, qu'il est besoign traicter et mesner à la longue.—Ibid. 299.

[2] On one occasion, twenty-seven chests of bullion, each above a yard long, were conveyed to the Tower in twenty carts; on another ninety-nine horses and two carts were employed for a similar purpose.— Stowe, 626. Heylin, 209. Persons assure us that Philip defrayed all the expenses of the combined fleet which escorted him to England, and of the festivities in honour of the marriage.—Wardword, 108. And the Venetian ambassador informs the senate, that the report of his spending the money of the nation was false; he had spent immense sums of his own.—Barber. MSS. No. 1208.

[3] Stowe, 629. Noailles, 313, 327, 347, 353. The object of the French king was d'entra-

Among the prisoners apprehended in England were Peckham and Werne, two officers in the household of Elizabeth, from whose confessions much was elicited to implicate the princess herself. She was rescued from danger by the interposition of Philip, who, despairing of issue by his wife, foresaw that, if Elizabeth were removed out of the way, the English crown, at the decease of Mary, would be claimed by the young queen of Scots, the wife of the dauphin of France. It was for his interest to prevent a succession which would add so considerably to the power of his rival, and for that purpose to preserve the life of the only person who, with any probability of success, could oppose the claim of the Scottish queen. By his orders the inquiry was dropped, and Mary, sending to her sister a ring in token of her affection, professed to believe that Elizabeth was innocent, and that her officers had presumed to make use of her name without her authority. They were executed as traitors; and the princess gladly accepted, in their place, Sir Thomas Pope and Robert Gage, at the recommendation of the council.[1]

Many weeks did not elapse before the exiles in France made a new attempt to excite an insurrection. There was among them a young man, of the name of Cleobury, whose features bore a strong resemblance to those of the earl of Devon. Having been instructed in the character which he had undertaken to act, he was landed on the coast of Sussex, assumed the name of the earl, spoke of the princess as privy to his design, and took the opportunity to proclaim in the church of Yaxely, "the lady Elizabeth queen, and her beloved bed-fellow, Lord Edward Courtenay, king." There was supposed to exist a kind of magic in the name of Courtenay; but the result dissipated the illusion. The people, as soon as they had recovered from their surprise, pursued and apprehended Cleobury, who suffered, at Bury, the penalty of his treason.[2] Two months later the real earl of Devon died of an ague in Padua.

Though Cleobury had employed the name of Elizabeth, we have no reason to charge her with participation in the imposture. The council pretended at least to believe her innocent; and she herself, in a letter to Mary, expressed her detestation of all such attempts, wishing that "there were good surgeons for making anatomies of hearts; then, whatsoever others should subject by malice, the queen would be sure of by knowledge; and the more such misty clouds should offuscate the clear light of her truth, the more her tried thoughts would glister to the dimming of their hidden malice."[3] Agitated, however, by her fears, whether they arose from the consciousness of guilt or from the prospect of future danger, she resolved to seek an asylum in France, of which she had formerly received an offer from Henry through the hands of Noailles.[4] With the motives of the king we are not acquainted. He may have wished to create additional embarrassment to Mary, perhaps to have in his power the only rival of his daughter-in-law, the

---

tenir Duddelay doulcement et secrettement, pour s'en servir, s'il en est de besoign, lui donnant moyen d'entretenir aussy par delà les intelligences.—Ibid. 310.

[1] MS. Life of the Duchess of Feria, 154. Strype, 297, 298. Philopater, Resp. ad edictum, p. 70.

[2] See a letter from the privy council to the earl of Bath, with a passage from the Harl. MS. 537, in Gage's Hengrave, 158.

[3] Stowe, 628. The letters are in Burnet, ii. Rec. 314; Strype, iii. 335, 339. In the correspondence of Noailles with his sovereign, to encourage these conspirators is elegantly termed, keeping la puce à l'oreille de la royne.—Noailles, 309, 329.

[4] Camden, Apparat. 20.

queen of Scotland. But Noailles was gone; and his brother and successor, the bishop of Acqs, appears to have received no instructions on the subject. When the countess of Sussex waited on him in disguise, and inquired whether he possessed the means of transporting the princess in safety to France, he expressed the strongest disapprobation of the project, and advised Elizabeth to learn wisdom from the conduct of her sister. Had Mary, after the death of Edward, listened to those who wished her to take refuge with the emperor in Flanders, she would still have remained in exile. If Elizabeth hoped to ascend the throne, she must never leave the shores of England. The countess returned with a similar message, and received again the same advice. A few years later the ambassador boasted that Elizabeth was indebted to him for her crown.[1]

Had the princess been willing to marry, she might easily have extricated herself from these embarrassments; but from policy or inclination she obstinately rejected every proposal. As presumptive heir to the crown, she was sought by different princes; and, as her sincerity in the profession of the ancient faith was generally questioned, men were eager to see her united, the Catholics to a Catholic, the Protestants to a Protestant husband. Her suitors professing the reformed doctrines were the king of Denmark for his son, and the king of Sweden for himself. The envoy of the latter reached her house in disguise; but he was refused admission, and referred to the queen, to whom Elizabeth averred that she had never heard the name of his master before, and hoped never to hear it again; adding, that as, in the reign of Edward, she had refused several offers, so she persisted in the same resolution of continuing, with her sister's good pleasure, a single woman. The Catholic suitor was Philibert, duke of Savoy, whose claim was strenuously supported by Philip, through gratitude, as he pretended, to a prince who had lost his hereditary dominions in consequence of his adherence to the interests of Spain; but through a more selfish motive, if we may believe politicians, a desire to preserve after the death of Mary the existing alliance between the English and Spanish crowns. In despair of issue by the queen, what could he do better than give to Elizabeth, the heir apparent, his personal friend for a husband? He met, however, with an obstinate, and probably unexpected, opponent in his wife; and, aware of her piety, sought to remove her objection by the authority of his confessor, and of other divines, who are said to have represented the proposed marriage as the only probable means of securing the permanence of the Catholic worship after her death. Overcome rather than convinced, Mary signified her assent; but revoked it the next day, alleging that it was essential to marriage that it should be free, and that her conscience forbade her to compel her sister to wed the man of whom she disapproved.[2] From that period, the princess resided, apparently at liberty, but in reality under the eyes of watchful guardians, in her house at Hatfield, and occasionally at court. Her friends complained that her allowance did not enable her to keep up the dignity

---

[1] See his letter of December 2, 1570, to Du Haillant in Noailles, i. 334.

[2] MS. reports of Michele and Soriano. Camden, 20. Burnet, ii. Rec. 325. Strype, iii, 317, 318, Rec. 189. The Spaniards attributed her refusal to her dislike of Elizabeth, and the advice of Cardinal Pole, whom they hated because he constantly opposed their attempts to make Philip "absoluto lord; per far il re signor absoluto." Hence Grandvelt said to Soriano that the cardinal was "no statesman, nor fit either to advise or govern."—Soriano, ibid.

of second person in the realm. But it would have been folly in the queen to have supplied Elizabeth with the means of multiplying her adherents; and she was, at the same time, anxious to reduce the enormous debt of the crown. With this view she had adopted a severe system of retrenchment in her own household; it could not be expected that she should encourage expense in the household of her sister.

But whatever were the mental sufferings of Elizabeth, they bore no proportion to those of Mary. 1. The queen was perfectly aware that her popularity, which at first had seated her on the throne, had long been on the decline. She had incurred the hatred of the merchants and country gentlemen by the loans of money which her poverty had compelled her to require; her economy, laudable as it was in her circumstances, had earned for her the reproach of parsimony from some, and of ingratitude from others; the enemies of her marriage continued to predict danger to the liberties of England from the influence of her Spanish husband; the Protestants, irritated by persecution, ardently wished for another sovereign; the most malicious reports, the most treasonable libels, even hints of assassination, were circulated; and men were found to misrepresent to the public all her actions, as proceeding from interested or anti-national motives. 2. She began to fear for the permanency of that religious worship which it had been the first wish of her heart to re-establish. She saw, that the fires of Smithfield had not subdued the obstinacy of the dissenters from the established creed; she knew that in the higher classes few had any other religion than their own interest or convenience; and she had reason to suspect that the presumptive heir to the crown, though she had long professed herself a Catholic, still cherished in her breast those principles which she had imbibed in early youth. 3. On Elizabeth herself she could not look without solicitude. It was natural that the wrongs which Catherine of Arragon had suffered from the ascendancy of Anne Boleyn should beget a feeling of hostility between their respective daughters. But the participation of Elizabeth in the first insurrection had widened the breach; and the frequent use made of her name by every subsequent conspirator served to confirm the suspicions of one sister and to multiply the apprehensions of the other. In the eye of Mary, Elizabeth was a bastard and a rival; in that of Elizabeth, Mary was a jealous and vindictive sovereign. To free her mind of this burden, the queen had lately thought of declaring her by act of parliament illegitimate and incapable of the succession; but the king would consent to no measure which, by weakening the claim of Elizabeth, might strengthen that of the dauphiness to the crown.[1] Mary acquiesced in the will of her husband; and from that time, whenever Elizabeth came to court, treated her in private with kindness, and in public with distinction. Yet it was thought that there was in this more of show than of reality; and that doubt and fear, jealousy and resentment, still lurked within her bosom. Lastly, the absence of her husband was a source of daily disquietude. If

---

[1] Nel tempo della gravidanza della regina, chè fu fatta venire in corte, seppe cosi ben providere et mettersi in gratia della natione Spagnuola, et particolarmente del Re, chè da niuno poi e stata piu favorita chè da lui; il quale non solo non vello permettere, ma si oppose et impedi, chè non fosse, come volea la regina, per atto di parliamento directata et declarata bastarda, et consequentemente inhabile alla successione.—Lansdowne MS. No. 840, D.

she loved him, Philip had deserved it by his kindness and attention. To be deprived of his society was of itself a heavy affliction; but it was most severely felt when she stood in need of advice and support.[1] Gardiner, whose very name had awed the factious, was no more. His place had, indeed, been supplied by Heath, archbishop of York, a learned and upright prelate; but, though he might equal his predecessor in abilities and zeal, he was less known, and therefore less formidable, to the adversaries of the government. It is not surprising, that, in such circumstances, the queen should wish for the presence and protection of her husband. She importuned him by long and repeated letters; she sent the lord Paget to urge him to return without delay. But Philip, to whom his father had resigned all his dominions in Spain, Italy, and the Netherlands, was overwhelmed with business of more importance to him than the tranquillity of his wife or of her government; and, to pacify her mind, he made her frequent promises, the fulfilment of which it was always in his power to elude. He had lately seen with alarm the elevation to the pontifical dignity of the cardinal Caraffa, by birth a Neapolitan, who had always distinguished himself by his opposition to the Spanish ascendancy in his native country, and on that account had suffered occasional affronts from the resentment of Ferdinand and Charles. The symptoms of dissension soon appeared. Philip suspected a design against his kingdom of Naples; and the new pontiff supported with menaces what he deemed the rights of the Holy See. The negotiations between the two powers, their mutual complaints and recriminations, are subjects foreign from this history; but the result was a strong suspicion in the mind of Paul, that the Spaniards sought to remove him from the popedom, and a resolution on his part to place himself under the protection of France. It chanced that about midsummer, in the year 1556, despatches were intercepted at Terracina, from Garcilasso della Vega, the Spanish agent in Rome, to the duke of Alva, the viceroy of Naples, describing the defenceless state of the papal territory, and the ease with which it might be conquered, before an army could be raised for its defence. The suspicion of the pontiff was now confirmed: he ordered the chiefs of the Spanish faction in Rome to be arrested as traitors; and instructed his officers to proceed against Philip for a breach of the feudal tenure by which he held the kingdom of Naples. But the viceroy advanced with a powerful army as far as Tivoli; Paul, to save his capital, submitted to solicit an armistice; and the war would have been terminated without bloodshed had not the duke of Guise, at the head of a French army, hastened into Italy. Henry had secretly concluded a league with the pope soon after his accession to the pontificate; he violated that treaty by consenting to the truce with Philip for five years; and now he broke the truce, in the hope of humbling the pride of the Spanish monarch, by placing a French prince on the throne of Naples, and investing another with the ducal coronet of Milan.[2]

It seems that, in the estimation of this prince, every breach of treaty,

---

[1] All these particulars respecting Elizabeth, and the troubles of Mary, are taken from the interesting memoir of Michele, the Venetian ambassador. — Lansdowne MSS. 840, B. fol. 155, 157, 160. Noailles represents her as afflicted with jealousy; but this writer declares the contrary.

[2] See these particulars, drawn from the original documents by Pallavicino, ii. 436—476. The complaints of the duke of Alva, and the recrimination of the college of cardinals, are in the Lettere de' Principi, i. 190.

every departure from honesty, might be justified on the plea of expediency.[1] He had no real cause of resentment against Mary; and yet, from the commencement of her reign, he had acted the part of a bitter enemy. His object had been, first to prevent the marriage of the queen with Philip, and then to disable her from lending aid to her husband. With these views he had, under the mask of friendship, fomented the discontent of her subjects, had encouraged them to rise in arms against her, and had offered an asylum and furnished pensions to her rebels. Having determined to renew the war with Philip, he called on Dudley and his associates to resume their treasonable practices against Mary. In Calais, and the territory belonging to Calais, were certain families of reformers, whose resentment had been kindled by the persecution of their brethren. With these the chiefs of the fugitives opened a clandestine correspondence; and a plan was arranged for the delivery of Hammes and Guisnes, two important fortresses, into the hands of the French.[2] But the enterprise, to the mortification of Henry, was defeated by the communications of a spy in the pay of the English government, who wormed himself into the confidence, and betrayed the secrets, of the conspirators. Within a few days a different attempt was made by another of the exiles, Thomas Stafford, second son to Lord Stafford, and grandson to the last duke of Buckingham. With a small force of Englishmen, Scots, and Frenchmen, he sailed from Dieppe, surprised the old castle of Scarborough, and immediately published a proclamation, as protector and governor of the realm. He was come, "not to work to his own advancement, touching the possession of the crown," but to deliver his countrymen from the tyranny of strangers, and "to defeat the most devilish devices of Mary, unrightful and unworthy queen," who had forfeited her claim to the sceptre by her marriage to a Spaniard, who lavished all the treasures of the realm upon Spaniards, and who had resolved to deliver the twelve strongest fortresses in the kingdom to twelve thousand Spaniards. He had determined to die bravely in the field, rather than see the slavery of his country; and he called on all Englishmen, animated with similar sentiments, to join the standard of independence, and to fight for the preservation of their lives, lands, wives, children, and treasures, from the possession of Spaniards. But his hopes were quickly extinguished. Not a man obeyed the proclamation. Wotton, the English ambassador, had apprized the queen of his design; and on the fourth day, before any aid could arrive from France, the earl of Westmoreland appeared with a considerable force, when Stafford, unable to defend the ruins of the castle, surrendered at discretion.[3] The failure of these repeated attempts ought to have undeceived the French monarch. Noailles and the exiles had persuaded him that dis-

---

[1] It is amusing to observe that, while Noailles perpetually accuses Englishmen of habits of falsehood, he is continually practising it himself, sometimes of choice, sometimes by order of his sovereign. Thus, with respect to the league with the pope, he was instructed to keep it secret, couvrant, niant, cachant, et desniant ladicte intelligence avecques sadite sainctete.—Noailles, v. 199.

[2] The information given by the spy, is in Strype, iii. 358.

[3] Stafford's proclamation, and the queen's answer, are in Strype, iii. Rec. 259—262; Godwin, 129; Heylin, 243. The pretence that this plot was got up by Wotton, the English ambassador in France, in order to provoke the queen to war, is improbable in itself, and must appear incredible to those who have read, in the letters of Noailles, his notices of the important, though hazardous enterprises designed by the exiles.—Noailles, v. 250, 262.

content pervaded the whole population of the kingdom; that every man longed to free himself from the rule of Mary; and that, at the first call, multitudes would unsheath their swords against her. But whenever the trial was made, the result proved the contrary. Men displayed their loyalty, by opposing the traitors; and Henry, by attempting to embarrass the queen, provoked her to lend to her husband that aid which it was his great object to avert.

Hitherto Philip had discovered no inclination for war. Content with the extensive dominions which had fallen to his lot, he sought rather to enjoy the pleasures becoming his youth and station, and, during his residence in England, had devoted much of his time to the chase, to parties of amusement, and to exercises of arms.[1] The bad faith of Henry awakened his resentment, and compelled him to draw the sword. But, though the armistice had been broken in Italy, he was careful to make no demonstration of hostilities in Flanders, hoping by this apparent inactivity to deceive the enemy, till he had collected a numerous force in Spain, and engaged an army of mercenaries in Germany. In March he revisited Mary, not so much in deference to her representations, as to draw England into the war with France. It is no wonder that the queen, after the provocations which she had received, should be willing to gratify her husband; but she left the decision to her council, in which the question was repeatedly debated. At first it was determined in the negative, on account of the poverty of the crown, the high price of provisions, the rancour of religious parties, and the condition in the marriage treaty, by which Philip promised not to involve the nation in the existing war against France. When it was replied, that the present was a new war, and that, to preserve the dignity of the crown, it was requisite to obtain satisfaction for the injuries offered to the queen by Henry, the majority of the council proposed that instead of embarking as a principal in the war, she should confine herself to that aid to which she was bound by ancient treaties, as the ally of the house of Burgundy. At last the enterprise of Stafford effected what neither the influence of the king, nor the known inclination of the queen, had been able to accomplish. A proclamation was issued, containing charges against the French monarch, which it was not easy to refute. From the very accession of Mary he had put on the appearance of a friend, and acted as an adversary. He had approved of the rebellion of Northumberland, and supported that of Wyat: to him, through his ambassador, had been traced the conspiracies of Dudley and Ashton; and from him these traitors had obtained an asylum and pensions; by his suggestions, attempts had been made to surprise Calais and its dependencies; and with his money Stafford had procured the ships and troops with which he had obtained possession of the castle of Scarborough. The king and queen owed it to themselves and to the nation, to resent such a succession of injuries, and therefore they warned the English merchants to abstain from all traffic in the dominions of a monarch against whom it was intended to declare war, and from whom they might expect the confiscation of their property.[2] Norroy king-at-arms was already on his road to Paris. According to the ancient custom, he defied Henry, who coolly

---

[1] Noailles, v. 221.

[2] Transcripts for Rymer, 359. Godwin, 129. Holins. 1133.

replied that it did not become him to enter into altercation with a woman; that he intrusted his quarrel with confidence to the decision of the Almighty; and that the result would reveal to the world who had the better cause. But, when he heard of the proclamation, he determined to oppose to it a manifesto, in which he complained that Mary had maintained spies in his dominions; had laid new and heavy duties on the importation of French merchandise, and had unnecessarily adopted the personal enmities of her husband. The bishop of Acqs was immediately recalled; at Calais he improved the opportunity to examine the fortifications, and remarked that from the gate of the harbour to the old castle, and from the castle for a considerable distance to the right, the rampart lay in ruins. At his request Senarpont, governor of Boulogne, repaired in disguise to the same place, and both concurred in the opinion that its boasted strength consisted only in its reputation, and that, in its present state, it offered an easy conquest to a sudden and unexpected assailant. The ambassador, when he reached the court, acquainted his sovereign with the result of these observations; but at the same time laid before him a faithful portrait of the exiles and their adherents. The zeal of his brother had induced him to magnify the importance of these people. Their number was small, their influence inconsiderable, and their fidelity doubtful. Experience had shown that they were more desirous to obtain the favour of their sovereign by betraying each other, than by molesting her to fulfil their engagements to Henry.[1]

Philip was now returned to Flanders, where the mercenaries from Germany, and the troops from Spain, had already arrived. The earl of Pembroke followed at the head of seven thousand Englishmen;[2] and the command of the combined army, consisting of forty thousand men, was assumed by Philibert, duke of Savoy. Having successively threatened Marienberg, Rocroi, and Guise, he suddenly halted before the town of St. Quintin, on the right bank of the Somme. Henry was alarmed for the safety of this important place; but it occurred to him that a supply might be sent to the garrison over the extensive and apparently impassable morass, which, together with the river, covered one side of the town. On the night of the ninth of August, the constable Montmorency marched from La Fere, with all his cavalry and fifteen thousand infantry; and, about nine on the following morning, took a position close to the marsh, in which it was calculated that he might remain for several hours, without the possibility of molestation on the part of the enemy. The boats, which had been brought upon carts, were now launched, and men, provisions, and ammunition were embarked. But the operation consumed more time than had been calculated; and the Spaniards, making a long detour, and crossing the river higher up, advanced rapidly by a broad and solid road. Their cavalry, a body of six thousand horse, easily dispersed a weak force of reistres, the first that opposed them, then broke the French cavalry, and instantly charged the infantry at a moment when they were falling back on the reserve. The confusion was irremediable. The constable himself, the marshal St. André, and most of the superior officers, fell into the hands

---

[1] Noailles, 33, 35.
[2] To equip this army, the queen had raised a loan by privy seals, dated July 20, 31, 1556, requiring certain gentlemen in different counties to lend her one hundred pounds each, to be repaid in the month of November of the following year.—Strype, iii. 424.

of the conquerors; and one-half of the French army was either taken or slain. The Spanish cavalry claimed the whole glory of the day. Their infantry did not arrive before the battle was won; and the English auxiliaries guarded the trenches on the other bank of the river.[1]

It was but a poor consolation to Henry for the loss of his army, that many of the boats on the marsh had contrived to reach the town, and that the garrison with this supply was enabled to protract the siege for another fortnight. On the arrival of Philip, who was accompanied by the earl of Pembroke, the mines were sprung, the assault was given, the defences after an obstinate resistance were won, and the English auxiliaries, as they shared in the glory, shared also in the spoil of the day. It was the only opportunity which they had of distinguishing themselves during the campaign; but by sea the English fleet rode triumphant through the summer, and kept the maritime provinces of France in a state of perpetual alarm. Bordeaux and Bayonne were alternately menaced; descents were made on several points of the coast; and the plunder of the defenceless inhabitants rewarded the services of the adventurers.[2]

When Mary determined to aid her husband against Henry, she had made up her mind to a war with Scotland. In that kingdom the national animosity against the English, the ancient alliance with France, the marriage of the queen to the dauphin, and the authority of the regent, a French princess, had given to the French interest a decided preponderance. From the very commencement of the year, the Scots, for the sole purpose of intimidation, had assumed a menacing attitude; the moment Mary denounced war against Henry, they agreed to assist him by invading the northern counties. The borderers on both sides recommenced their usual inroads, and many captures of small importance were reciprocally made at sea. But to collect a sufficient force for the invasion required considerable time; before the equinox the weather became stormy; the fords and roads were rendered impassable by the rains; and a contagious disease introduced itself into the Lowlands. It required considerable exertion on the part of the queen regent and of D'Oyselles, the ambassador, to assemble the army against the beginning of October; and they found it a still more difficult task to guide the turbulent and capricious humour of the Scottish nobles. When the auxiliaries from France crossed the Tweed to batter the castle of Wark, the Scots, instead of fighting, assembled in council at Eckford church, where they reminded each other of the fatal field of Flodden, and exaggerated the loss of their ally at the battle of St. Quintin. The earl of Shrewsbury lay before them with the whole power of England; why should the Scots shed their blood for an interest entirely French; why hazard the best hopes of the country without any adequate cause? The earl of Huntly alone ventured to oppose the general sentiment. He was put under a temporary arrest; and, in defiance of the threats, the tears, and the entreaties

---

[1] Cabrera, 157. Mergez, Mém. xli. 24. Tavannes, xxvi. 164.
[2] Noailles, i. 17—19. The success of the combined army at St. Quintin irritated the venom of Goodman, one of the most celebrated of the exiles at Geneva, who, in his treatise entitled "How to obey or disobey," thus addresses those among the reformers, who, "to please the wicked Jezebel," had fought on that day: "Is this the love that ye bear to the word of God, O ye Gospelers? Have ye been so taught in the gospel, to be wilful murtherers of yourselves and others abroad, rather than lawful defenders of God's people and your country at home?" —Apud Strypo, iii. 441.

of the regent, the army was disbanded. "Thus," says Lord Shrewsbury, "this enterprise, begun with so great bravery, ended in dishonour and shame."[1] It produced, however, this benefit to France, that it distracted the attention of the English council, and added considerably to the expenses of the war.

At the same time, the queen, to her surprise and vexation, found herself involved in a contest with the pontiff. Though Pole, in former times, had suffered much for his attachment to the Catholic creed, the cardinal Caraffa had, on one occasion, ventured to express a doubt with respect to his orthodoxy. That this suspicion was unfounded, Caraffa subsequently acknowledged;[2] and after his elevation to the popedom, he had repeatedly pronounced a high eulogium on the English cardinal. Now, however, whether it was owing to the moderation of Pole, which, to the pope's more ardent zeal, appeared like a dereliction of duty, or to the suggestions of those who sought to widen the breach between Philip and the Holy See, Paul reverted to the suspicions which he had before abjured. Though he wished to mask his real intention, he resolved to involve the legate in the same disgrace with his friend the cardinal Morone, and to subject the orthodoxy of both to the investigation of the Inquisition. It chanced that Philip, in consequence of the war, had made regulations which seemed to trench on the papal authority; and Paul, to mark his sense of these encroachments, recalled his ministers from all the dominions of that monarch. There was no reason to suppose that Pole was included in this revocation; but the pontiff ordered a letter to be prepared, announcing to him that his legatine authority was at an end, and ordering him to hasten immediately to Rome. Carne, the queen's agent, informed her by express of the pope's intention, and in the mean time, by his remonstrances, extorted an illusory promise of delay. Philip and Mary expostulated; the English prelates and nobility, in separate letters, complained of the injury which religion would receive from the measure; and Pole himself represented that the control of a legate was necessary, though it mattered little whether that office was exercised by himself or another.[3] This expression suggested a new expedient. Peyto, a Franciscan friar, eighty years of age, was the queen's confessor: him the pope, in a secret consistory, created a cardinal; and immediately transferred to him all the powers which had hitherto been exercised by Pole.[4] In this emergency, Mary's respect for the papal authority did not prevent her from having recourse to the precautions which had often been employed by her predecessors. Orders were issued that every messenger from foreign parts should be detained and searched. The bearer of the papal letters was arrested at Calais; his despatches were clandestinely forwarded to the queen; and the letters of revocation were either secreted or destroyed. Thus it happened that Peyto never received any official

---

[1] See the long correspondence on the subject of this intended invasion in Lodge, i. 240—293. [2] Pol. Ep. iv. 91; v. 122.
[3] These letters may be seen in Pole's Ep. v. 27; Strype, iii. Rec. 231; Burnet, ii. 315. In them great complaint is made that the pope should deprive the cardinal of the authority of legate, which for centuries had been annexed to the office of archbishop of Canterbury. It would appear that this was a mistake; for soon afterwards Pole, though he no longer styled himself legatus a latere, assumed the title of legatus natus, and kept it till his death.—Wilk. iv. 149, 153, 171. Pol. Ep. v. 181.
[4] Pol. Ep. v. 144, ex actis consistorialibus. Paul says that he had known Peyto when he was in the family of Pole; that from the first he had determined to make him a cardinal; and that he considered him worthy of the honour, both from his own knowledge and the testimony of others.—Ibid.

notice of his preferment, nor Pole of his recall. The latter, however, ceased to exercise the legatine authority, and despatched Ormanetto, his chancellor, to Rome. That messenger arrived at a most favourable moment. The papal army had been defeated at Palliano; the news of the victory at St. Quintin had arrived; and peace was signed between Paul and Philip. In these circumstances, the pontiff treated Ormanetto with kindness, and referred the determination of the question to his nephew, the cardinal Caraffa, whom he had appointed legate to the king.[1] When that minister reached Brussels, he demanded that both Pole and Peyto should be suffered to proceed to Rome; Pole, that he might clear himself from the charge of heresy; Peyto, that he might aid the pontiff with his advice. Philip referred him to Mary, and Mary returned a refusal.[2] At Rome proceedings against the English cardinal were already commenced; but Pole, in strong, though respectful language, remonstrated against the injustice which was done to his character;[3] Peyto soon afterwards died; and the question remained in suspense, till it was set at rest in the course of a few months by the deaths of all the parties concerned.

The disgrace which had befallen the French arms at St. Quintin had induced Henry to recall the duke of Guise from Italy, and to consult him on the means by which he might restore his reputation, and take revenge for his loss. The reader has seen that he had formerly attempted, through the agency of the exiles, to debauch the fidelity of some among the inhabitants, or the troops in garrison, at Calais. There is reason to believe that he had at present his secret partisans within the town; but, however that may be, the representations of the bishop of Acqs and of the governor of Boulogne had taught him to form a more correct notion of its imaginary strength; and the duke of Guise adopted a plan originally suggested by the admiral Coligni, to assault the fortress in the middle of winter, when, from the depth of the water in the marshes, and the severity of the weather, it appeared less exposed to danger. In the month of December, twenty-five thousand men, with a numerous train of battering artillery, assembled at Compiegne. Every eye was turned towards St. Quintin. But suddenly the army broke up, took the direction of Calais, and on New Year's Day was discovered in considerable force on the road from Sandgate to Hammes. The governor, Lord Wentworth, had received repeated warnings to provide for the defence of the place, but he persuaded himself that the object of the enemy was not conquest, but plunder. The next day the bulwarks of Froyton and Nesle were abandoned by their garrisons; and within twenty-four hours the surrender of Newhaven Bridge and of the Risbank brought the assailants within reach of the town. A battery on St. Peter's Heath played on the wall; another opened a wide breach in the castle; and the commander, in expectation of an assault, earnestly solicited reinforcements. Lord Wentworth was admonished that the loss of the town must infallibly follow that of the castle; but he rejected the application, ordered the garrison to be withdrawn, and appointed an engineer to blow up the towers on the approach of the enemy. That same evening, during the ebb tide, a company of Frenchmen waded across the haven; no explosion took place; and the

---

[1] Beccatello, 390.
[2] Pallavicino, ii. 500, 502.

[3] Pol. Ep. v. 31–36.

five thousand men in the vicinity of Dourlens; and Henry lay with a force scarcely inferior in the neighbourhood of Amiens. Instead, however, of a battle, conferences were opened in the abbey of Cercamp, and both parties professed to be animated with a sincere desire of peace. It was evident that, if the king should yield to the demands of France, Calais was irretrievably lost. But Philip was conscious that he had led the queen into the war, and deemed himself bound in honour to watch no less over her interests than over his own. He resisted the most tempting offers; he declared that the restoration of Calais must be an indispensable condition; and, at last, in despair of subduing the obstinacy of Henry, put an end to the negotiation.[1]

But the reign of Mary was now hastening to its termination. Her health had always been delicate; from the time of her first supposed pregnancy she was afflicted with frequent and obstinate maladies. Tears no longer afforded her relief from the depression of her spirits; and the repeated loss of blood, by the advice of her physicians, had rendered her pale, languid, and emaciated.[2] Nor was her mind more at ease than her body. The exiles from Geneva, by the number and virulence of their libels, kept her in a constant state of fear and irritation;[3] and to other causes of anxiety, which have been formerly mentioned, had lately been added the insalubrity of the season, the loss of Calais, and her contest with the pontiff. In August she experienced a slight febrile indisposition at Hampton Court, and immediately removed to St. James's. It was soon ascertained that her disease was the same fever which had proved fatal to thousands of her subjects; and, though she languished for three months, with several alternations of improvement and relapse, she never recovered sufficiently to leave her chamber.

During this long confinement, Mary edified all around her by her cheerfulness, her piety, and her resignation to the will of Providence. Her chief solicitude was for the stability of that church which she had restored; and her suspicions of Elizabeth's insincerity prompted her to require from her sister an avowal of her real sentiments. In return, Elizabeth complained of Mary's incredulity. She was a true and conscientious believer in the Catholic creed; nor could she do more now than she had repeatedly done before, which was to confirm her assertion with her oath.[4]

On the fifth of November, the day fixed at the prorogation, the parliament assembled at Westminster. The ministers, in the name of the queen, demanded a supply; but little progress was made, under the persuasion that she had but a short time to live. Four days later the Conde de Feria arrived, the bearer of a letter to Mary from her husband. It was an office which decency, if not affection, required; but Philip had the ingenuity to turn it to his own account, by instructing the ambassador to secure for him the good will of the heir to

---

[1] See the official correspondence in Burnet, iii. 258—263.

[2] Memoir of the Venetian Ambassador, fol. 157.

[3] These libels provoked the government to issue, on the 6th of June, a proclamation, stating that books filled with heresy, sedition, and treason, were daily brought from beyond the seas, and some covertly printed within the realm, and ordering that "whosoever should be found to have any of the said wicked and seditious books should be reputed a rebel, and executed according to martial law."—Strype, iii. 459.

[4] MS. Life of the Duchess of Feria, 156. "She prayed God that the earth might open and swallow her up alive, if she were not a true Roman Catholic."—Ibid. 129. See also Paterson's Image of the Two Churches, 435.

the crown. Though the queen had already declared Elizabeth her successor, Feria advocated her claim in a set speech before the council; and then, in an interview with the princess at the house of Lord Clinton, assured her that the declaration of the queen in her favour had originated with his master. A few days later, Mary ordered Jane Dormer, one of her maids of honour, and afterwards duchess of Feria, to deliver to Elizabeth the jewels in her custody, and to make to the princess three requests: that she would be good to her servants, would repay the sums of money which had been lent on privy seals, and would support the established church. On the morning of her death mass was celebrated in her chamber. She was perfectly sensible, and expired a few minutes before the conclusion.[1] Her friend and kinsman, Cardinal Pole, who had long been confined with a fever, survived her only twenty-two hours. He had reached his fifty-ninth, she her forty-second year.[2]

The foulest blot on the character of this queen is her long and cruel persecution of the reformers. The sufferings of the victims naturally begat an antipathy to the woman by whose authority they were inflicted. It is, however, but fair to recollect what I have already noticed, that the extirpation of erroneous doctrine was inculcated as a duty by the leaders of every religious party. Mary only practised what *they* taught. It was her misfortune, rather than her fault, that she was not more enlightened than the wisest of her contemporaries.

With this exception, she has been ranked, by the more moderate of the reformed writers, among the best, though not the greatest, of our princes. They have borne honourable testimony to her virtues; have allotted to her the praise of piety and clemency, of compassion for the poor, and liberality to the distressed; and have recorded her solicitude to restore to opulence the families that had been unjustly deprived of their possessions by her father and brother, and to provide for the wants of the parochial clergy, who had been reduced to penury by the spoliations of the last government.[3] It is acknowledged that her moral character was beyond reproof. It extorted respect from all, even from the most virulent of her enemies. The ladies of her household copied the conduct of their mistress; and the decency of Mary's court was often mentioned with applause by those who lamented the dissoluteness which prevailed in that of her successor.[4]

The queen was thought by some to have inherited the obstinacy of her father; but there was this difference,

---

[1] MS. Life of the Duchess of Feria, 128. Even the merit of sending the jewels was claimed for Philip; who moreover added a present of his own, a valuable casket which he had left at Whitehall, and which he knew that Elizabeth greatly admired.—Memorias, vii. 260.

[2] Elizabeth, in her conference with Feria on the 10th, spoke with great asperity (malissamente) of the cardinal. He had paid her no attention, and had been to her the occasion of great annoyance.—Ibid. 255, 257. Pole appears to have been aware of her displeasure; for he sent from his deathbed the dean of Worcester with a letter to her, requesting her to give credit to what the dean had "to say in his behalf," and doubting not that she would "remain satisfied thereby."—Hearne's Sylloge, 157. Collier, Records, 88. The moment his death was known, she sent the earl of Rutland and Throckmorton to seize his effects for the crown.—Memorias, 257, 259.

[3] Princeps apud omnes ob mores sanctissimos, pietatem in pauperes, liberalitatem in nobiles atque ecclesiasticos nunquam satis laudata.—Camden, in Apparat. 23. Mulia sane pia, clemens, moribusque castissimis, et usquequaque laudanda, si religionis errorem non spectes.—Godwin, 123.

[4] MS. Life of the Duchess of Feria, 114. Faunt, Walsingham's secretary, says of Elizabeth's court, that it was a place "where all enormities were practised; where six reigned in the highest degree."—Aug. 6 1583. Birch, i. 39.

that, before she formed her decisions, she sought for advice and information, and made it an invariable rule to prefer right to expediency. One of the outlaws, who had obtained his pardon, hoped to ingratiate himself with Mary by devising a plan to render her independent of parliament. He submitted it to the inspection of the Spanish ambassador, by whom it was recommended to her consideration. Sending for Gardiner, she bade him peruse it, and then adjured him, as he should answer at the judgment-seat of God, to speak his real sentiments. "Madam," replied the prelate, "it is a pity that so virtuous a lady should be surrounded by such sycophants. The book is naught: it is filled with things too horrible to be thought of." She thanked him, and threw the paper into the fire.[1]

Her natural abilities had been improved by education. She understood the Italian, she spoke the French and Spanish languages; and the ease and correctness with which she replied to the foreigners, who addressed her in Latin, excited their admiration.[2] Her speeches in public, and from the throne, were delivered with grace and fluency; and her conferences with Noailles, as related in his despatches, show her to have possessed an acute and vigorous mind, and to have been on most subjects a match for that subtle and intriguing negotiator.

It had been the custom of her predecessors to devote the summer months to "progresses" through different counties. But these journeys produced considerable injury and inconvenience to the farmers, who were not only compelled to furnish provisions to the purveyors at inadequate prices, but were withdrawn from the labours of the harvest to aid with their horses and waggons in the frequent removals of the court, and of the multitude which accompanied it. Mary, through consideration for the interests and comforts of the husbandman, refused herself this pleasure; and generally confined her excursions to Croydon, a manor belonging to the church of Canterbury. There it formed her chief amusement to walk out in the company of her maids, without any distinction of dress, and in this disguise to visit the houses of the neighbouring poor. She inquired into their circumstances, relieved their wants, spoke in their favour to her officers, and often, where the family was numerous, apprenticed, at her own expense, such of the children as appeared of promising dispositions.[3]

During her reign, short as it was, and disturbed by repeated insurrections, much attention was paid to the interests of the two universities, not only by the queen herself, who restored to them that portion of their revenues which had devolved on the crown, but also by individuals, who devoted their private fortunes to the advancement of learning. At a time when the rage for polemic disputation had almost expelled the study of classic literature from the schools, Sir Thomas Pope founded Trinity College, in Oxford, and made it a particular regulation, that its inmates should acquire "a just relish for the graces and purity of the Latin tongue." About three years later, Sir Thomas White established St. John's,

---

[1] This anecdote is told by Persons in one of his tracts, and by Burnet, ii. 278.
[2] Nella latina daria stupir ognuno con le risposte che da.—Michele's Report, MSS. Barber. 1208. He adds, that she was fond of music and excelled on the monochord and the lute, two fashionable instruments at that time. English writers also praise her proficiency in the Latin language. She had translated for publication the paraphrase of Erasmus on the gospel of St. John.—Warton's Sir Thomas Pope, 57.
[3] MS. Life of the Duchess of Feria, p. 120.

on the site of Bernard's College, the foundation of Archbishop Chicheley; and at the same time, the celebrated Dr. Caius, at Cambridge, made so considerable an addition to Gonvil Hall, and endowed it with so many advowsons, manors, and demesnes, that it now bears his name, in conjunction with that of the original founder.

Though her parliaments were convoked for temporary purposes, they made several salutary enactments, respecting the offence of treason, the office of sheriff, the powers of magistrates, the relief of the poor, and the practice of the courts of law.[1] The merit of these may probably be due to her council; but of her own solicitude for the equal administration of justice, we have a convincing proof. It had long been complained that in suits, to which the crown was a party, the subject, whatever were his right, had no probability of a favourable decision, on account of the superior advantages claimed and enjoyed by the counsel for the sovereign. When Mary appointed Morgan chief justice of the court of Common Pleas, she took the opportunity to express her disapprobation of this grievance. "I charge you, sir," said she, "to minister the law and justice indifferently, without respect of person; and, notwithstanding the old error among you, which will not admit any witness to speak, or other matter to be heard, in favour of the adversary, the crown being a party, it is my pleasure, that whatever can be brought in favour of the subject may be admitted and heard. You are to sit there, not as advocates for me, but as indifferent judges between me and my people."[2]

Neither were the interests of trade neglected during her government. She had the honour of concluding the first commercial treaty with Russia. Edward died long before Challoner returned from Archangel;[3] but the letter which he brought was delivered to the queen, and the report of the wonders which he had seen excited an extraordinary spirit of enterprise throughout the nation. A new company was formed, with the same Sebastian Cabote for its director, and was incorporated by Philip and Mary under the title of "Merchauntes Adventurers of Englande for the Discoveryes of Lands, Territories, Isles, and Signories unknown." The list of shareholders exhibits the names of the lord high treasurer, and all the high officers of state, of all the officers of the household, of lords, knights, barristers, and individuals of every rank, with the exception of clergymen and the judges. By their charter they were empowered to discover unknown countries by sailing "northwards, north-westwards, or north-eastwards; to erect the banners of England thereon, to subdue all maner of cities, townes, isles, and mayne lands of infidelity" so discovered, and to acquire the dominion thereof for the king and queen, and their heirs and successors for ever. Moreover, the trade with Russia, and all the countries which might be discovered in virtue of this charter, was granted to the company exclusively, and the intruder, if he were

---

[1] On the subject of taxation, the Venetian ambassador has the following passage:— "The liberty of this country is really singular and wonderful; indeed there is no other country in my opinion less burthened, and more free. For they have not only no taxes of any kind, but they are not even thought of: no tax on salt, wine, beer, flour, meat, cloth, and the other necessaries of life............Here every one indifferently, whether noble or of the common people, is in the free and unmolested enjoyment of all he possesses, or daily acquires, relating either to food or raiment, to buying or selling, except in those articles which he imports or exports in the way of traffick."—See the translation by Mr. Ellis, ii. 234.

[2] State Trials, i. 72. [3] See p. 180.

an English subject, was made liable to fine and forfeiture; if he were an alien, they were authorized to resist him as an open enemy. This was the origin of the Russian Company.[1]

Challoner was now sent back with a letter to the czar. Sailing up the Dwina, he traversed the country to Moscow, obtained from that prince the most flattering promises, and returned with Osep Napea Gregorivitch, as ambassador to Mary. They reached the bay of Pitsligo, in the north of Scotland; but during the night the ship was driven from her anchors upon the rocks. Challoner perished; the ambassador saved his life; but his property, and the presents for the queen, were carried off by the natives, who plundered the wreck. Mary sent two messengers to Edinburgh to supply his wants, and to complain of the detention of his effects.[2] No redress could be obtained; but she made every effort to console him for his loss. On the borders of each county the sheriffs received him in state; he was met in the neighbourhood of London by Lord Montague with three hundred horse; and during his stay in the capital the king and queen, the lord mayor, and the company, treated him with extraordinary distinction. He appeared, however, to mistrust these demonstrations of kindness; and it was not without difficulty that he was brought to accede to many of the demands of the merchants. At length a treaty was concluded by the address of the bishop of Ely and Sir William Petre; and Napea was sent back to his own country, loaded with presents for himself, and still more valuable gifts for his sovereign. The trade fully compensated the queen and the nation for these efforts and expenses; and the woollen cloths and coarse linens of England were exchanged at an immense profit for the valuable skins and furs of the northern regions.[3]

Mary may also claim the merit of having supported the commercial interests of the country against the pretensions of a company of foreign merchants, which had existed for centuries in London, under the different denominations of Easterlings, merchants of the Hanse Towns, and merchants of the Steelyard. By their readiness to advance loans of money on sudden emergencies, they had purchased the most valuable privileges from several of our monarchs. They formed a corporation, governed by their own laws: whatever duties were exacted from others, they paid no more than one per cent. on their merchandise; they were at the same time buyers and sellers, brokers and carriers; they imported jewels and bullion, cloth of gold and of silver, tapestry and wrought silk, arms, naval stores, and household furniture; and exported wool and woollen cloths, skins, lead and tin, cheese and beer, and Mediterranean wines. Their privileges and wealth gave them a superiority over all other merchants, which excluded competition, and

---

[1] See charter of incorporation in the Transcripts for the new Rymer, p. 350.

[2] Lord Wharton, in a letter from Berwick of February 28th, says, "A great nomber in that realme ar sorye that they suffered the imbassador of Russea to departo owte of the same; he may thanke God that he escaped from their crewell covetouse with his lief."—Lodge, i. 224.

[3] Legatorum nemo unquam quisquam (sicut autumo) magnificentius apud nostros acceptus est.—Godwin, 129. The presents which he received for himself and his sovereign, from the king and queen, are enumerated by Stowe, 630. Among them are a lion and lioness. All his expenses, from his arrival in Scotland to the day on which he left England, were defrayed by the merchants. I may here observe, that at this time, according to the report of the Venetian ambassador, there were many merchants in London worth fifty or sixty thousand pounds each; that the inhabitants amounted to 180,000; and that it was not surpassed in wealth by any city in Europe. Si puo dire per vero que puo qualla città senza dubio star a paragone delle piu ricche d' Europa.—MSS. Barber. 1208, p. 137.

enabled them to raise or depress the prices almost at pleasure. In the last reign the public feeling against them had been manifested by frequent acts of violence, and several petitions had been presented to the council, complaining of the injuries suffered by the English merchants. After a long investigation, it was declared that the company had violated, and consequently had forfeited, its charter; but by dint of remonstrances, of presents, and of foreign intercession, it obtained, in the course of a few weeks, a royal license to resume the traffic under the former regulations.[1] In Mary's first parliament a new blow was aimed at its privileges; and it was enacted, in the bill of tonnage and poundage, that the Easterlings should pay the same duties as other foreign merchants. The queen, indeed, was induced to suspend, for a while, the operation of the statute;[2] but she soon discerned the true interest of her subjects, revoked the privileges of the company, and refused to listen to the arguments adduced, or the intercession made in its favour.[3] Elizabeth followed the policy of her predecessor; the Steelyard was at length shut up; and the Hanse Towns, after a long and expensive suit, yielded to necessity, and abandoned the contest.[4]

Ireland, during this reign, offers but few subjects to attract the notice o the reader. The officers of government were careful to copy the proceedings in England. They first proclaimed the lady Jane, and then the lady Mary. They suffered the new service to fall into desuetude; Dowdall resumed the archbishopric of Armagh; the married prelates and clergy lost their benefices; and Bale, the celebrated bishop of Ossory, who had often endangered his life by his violence and fanaticism, had the prudence to withdraw to the continent. When the Irish parliament met, it selected most of its enactments from the English statute-book. The legitimacy and right of the queen were affirmed, the ancient service restored, and the papal authority acknowledged.[5] But though the laws against heresy were revived, they were not carried into execution. The number of the reformers proved too small to excite apprehension, and their zeal too cautious to offer provocation.

The lord deputy, the earl of Sussex, distinguished himself by the vigour of his government. He recovered from the native Irish the two districts of Ofally and Leix, which he moulded into counties, and named King's County and Queen's County, in honour of Philip and Mary. He was

---

[1] Strype, ii. 295, 296.
[2] Rymer, xv. 364, 365. [3] Noailles, iv. 137.
[4] Mary's will has been published for the first time by Sir Fred. Madden, in his "Privy Purse Expenses of the Princess Mary," App. No. iv. She states that she made her will being in good health, "but foreseeing the great dangers which by Godd's ordynance remaine to all women in ther travel of children" (30 March, 1558). Then follow several bequests, some of which are highly honourable to her memory. She appears to have intended to do that which was not accomplished till the reign of Charles II. She orders her executors to provide a house in London, with an income of the clear yearly value of four hundred marks, "for the relefe, succour, and helpe of pore, impotent, and aged soldiers, and chiefly those that be fallen into extreme poverte, having no pensyon or other pretense of lyvyng, or are become hurt or maymd in the warres of this realm, or in onny service for the defense and suerte of ther prince, and of ther countrey, or of the domynions therunto belonging" (p. cxci.). Some months later (28 October, 1558), when she no longer hoped for issue to succeed her, she added a codicil confirmatory of her former will, with an admonition to her successor to fulfil it "according to her treue mind and intente, for which he or she will, no doubt, be rewarded of God, and avoid his divine justice pronounced and executed against such as be violaters and breakers of wills and testaments." It is unnecessary to add that no attention was afterwards paid to any part of the instrument.
[5] Irish Stat. 3 & 4 Philip and Mary, 1, 2, 3, 4.

also careful to define, by a new statute, the meaning of Poyning's act. It provided that no parliament should be summoned, till the reasons why it should be held, and the bills which it was intended to pass, had been submitted to the consideration, and had received the consent, of the sovereign; and that, if anything occurred during the session to make additional enactments necessary, these should in the same manner be certified to the king, and be approved by him, before they were laid before the two houses. By this act the usage was determined of holding parliaments in Ireland.

APPENDIX.

NOTE T, p. 5.

It is singular that there are still extant two copies of the archbishop's letter, both dated on the same day, both written with his own hand, both folded alike, addressed in the same words to the king, sealed with the archbishop's seal, and bearing marks of having been received; and yet, though they are the same in substance, they differ greatly from each other in several important passages. A careful comparison of the discrepancies between them will, however, disclose the whole mystery. It will show that the first letter did not satisfy the expectation of Henry. It was not conceived in language sufficiently submissive; it did not fully state the extent of the authority solicited by the primate from the new head of the church; nor did it declare that the motive of his petition was solely the exoneration of his own conscience. It was as follows:—

"Please yt your Hieghnes—that wher your Graces grete cause of matrimony is (as it is thought) through all Christianytee dyvulgated, and in the mowthes of the rude and ignoraunte common people of this your Graces realme so talked of, that feawe of them do feare to reporte and saye, that thereof ys liklyhode hereafter to ensue grete inconvenience, daungier, and perill to this your Graces realme, and moche incertentie of succession; by whiche things the saide ignoraunte people be not a litle offended;—and forasmoche as yt hathe pleased Almightie God and your Grace of your habundant goodnes to me showed to call me (albeyt a poure wretche and moche unworthie) unto this hiegh and chargeable office of primate and archebisshope in this your Graces realme, wherein I beseche Almightie God to graunte me his grace so to use and demeane myself, as may be standing with his pleasure and the discharge of my conscience and to the weale of this Your Graces saide realme; and consydering also the obloquie and brute, which daylie doith spring and increase of the clergie of this realme, and speciallie of the heddes and presidentes of the same, because they, in this behalve, do not foresee and provide suche convenient remedies as might expell and put out of doubt all such inconveniencies, perilles and daungiers as the saide rude and ignoraunte people do speke and talk to be ymmynent, I, your most humble Orator and Bedeman am in consideration of the premisses urgently constrained at this time most humbly to beseche Your most noble Grace that, (1) when my office and duetie is, by Yours and Your predecessours sufferance and grauntes, (2) to directe and ordre causes spirituall in this Your Graces realme, according to the lawes of God and Holye Churche, (3) *and for relief of almaner grieves* and infirmities of the people, Goddes subjectes and Yours, happening in the saide spiritual causes, to provide suche remedie as shall be thought most convenient for their helpe and relief in that behalf; and because I wolde be right lothe, and also it shall not becom me (forasmoche as Your Grace ys my Prince and Sovereigne) to enterprize any parte of my office in the saide weightie cause (4) without Your Graces favour obteigned and pleasure therein first knowen—it may please the same to ascerteyn me of Your Graces pleasure in the premisses, to thentent that, the same knowen, I may procede for my discharge afore God to th'execution of my saide office and duetie according to his calling and Yours : (5) beseching Your Hieghness moost humbly uppon my kneys to pardon me of this my bolde and rude letters, and the same to accepte and take in good sense and parte. From my manour at Lambith, the 11th day of Aprile, in the first yere of my consecration.

"Your Highnes most humble
"Bedisman and Chaplain,
"THOMAS CANTUAR."

If the archbishop thought that this letter was sufficiently comprehensive and submissive, he had deceived himself. The king was dissatisfied with it on three grounds:—1. He had asked to know the royal *pleasure*. Henry meant him to ask the royal *permission* or *license*. 2. He had spoken of *ordering* and *directing* spiritual causes: Henry insisted on having *his* cause *judged and finally determined*. 3. He had indeed said that he wished to perform his said office for his *discharge afore God;* but Henry required something more, words which would exclude all idea of a previous compact between them, and would enable him to show afterwards, if ever there were need, that the whole proceeding originated with the new primate. Accordingly we find, that in the second copy the following corrections have been made. At No. 1, "*my office and duty*" is changed into "the office and duty *of the archbishop of Canterbury.*" At No. 2, after "to direct and order" are added the words "to judge and determyn." At No. 3, the whole passage in italics is omitted. At No. 4, after favour, "*license*" is inserted, and "*your pleasure first knowen,* and it may please the same to ascerteyn me of *your graces pleasure,*" are omitted. Then the following passage is substituted. "It may please therefore your most excellent majestie (considerations had to the premisses, and to my moost bounden duetie towardes Your Highnes, your realme, succession, and posteritie, and for the exoneration of my conscience towardes Almightie God) to *license* me according to myn office and duetie to procede to the examination, *fynall determination, and judgment* in the saide grete cause touching your Heighnes." At No. 5, as if the archbishop were not low enough "on his knees," he is made to substitute the following:—"Eftsones, as *prostrate at the feet* of your majestie, beseching the same to pardon me of thes my bolde and rude letters, and the same to accept and take in good sense and parte, *as I do meane; which, calling Our Lorde to recorde, is onlic for the zele that I have to the causes aforesaide, and for none other intent and purpose.*"—See State Papers, 390, 391.

It may be asked, how it appears that what I have called the second and corrected letter, was in reality such. I answer, from the license granted to the archbishop.—Ibid. 392. That license is founded on the second letter, and not on the first. It embodies the second with all its corrections; it reminds the archbishop of the oath with which that letter concludes, and of his "calling God to his recorde," of his only intent and purpose; it commends that intent and purpose, and states that therefore the king, inclining to his humble petition, doth license him to proceed in the said cause, to the examination and final determination of the same. This instrument places it beyond a doubt that the first petition did not satisfy the king; and that the archbishop was compelled to write the second. How deeply must he have felt himself degraded, when he submitted to this mandate of his imperious master!

NOTE V, p. 29.

On account of its relation to the funeral of Catherine, I add the following letter from Henry to Grace, the daughter of Lord Marny, and wife of Sir Edmond Bedingfeld. The original is in the possession of Sir Henry Bedingfeld.

"HENRY REX.
"BY THE KING.

"Right dear and welbeloved, we grete you well. And forasmuch as it hath pleased Almighty God to call unto his mercy out of this transitorie lyfe the right excellent princesse our derest sister the Lady Catharyne, relict, widow and dowager of our natural brother Prince Arthur of famous memorie, deceased, and that we entende to have her bodie interred according to her honour and estate, at the enterrement whereof, and for other ceremonies to be doon at her funerall, and in conveyance of the corps from Kymbolton, wher it now remayneth, to Peterborough, where the same shall be buryed, it is requisite to have the presence of a good number of ladies of honor, You shall understand that we have appoynted youe to be there oon of the principal mourners, and therefore desire and pray you to put yourself in redynes to be in any wise at Kimbolton to aforsayd the 25th daye of this monthe, and so to attende uppon the sayd corps tyll the same shall be buryed, and the ceremonies to be thereat done be finished. Letting you further wite that for the mourning apparaill of your own person we send you by this bearer   yards black cloth, for 2 gentlewomen to waite upon you   yards, for 2 gentlemen   yards, for 8 yeomen   yards; all which apparaill ye must cause in the meane tyme to be made up as shall appertaine. And as concernying th' abiliment of Lynen for your head and face we shall before the day limitted send the same unto youe accordingly. Given under our signet at our manor of Greenwich the 10th daye of January."

In another hand. "And for as moche as sithens the writing herof it was thought ye should be enforced to sende to London for making of the sayd apparail, for the more expedition we thought convenient to   you immediately on receipt of this to sende your servant to our trusty and welbeloved councellor Sir Wn. Poulet knt comptroller of our household, living at the freres Augustines in London aforesaid, to whom bringing this letter with you (*him*) for a certen token that he cometh from you, the said cloth and certein Lynden for yr head shall be delivered accordinglie.

"To our right dere and Welbeloved the Ladye Benyngfeld."

NOTE W, p. 57.

Of so great importance was it deemed to conceal from public knowledge the grounds on which the marriage of Henry with Anne Boleyn was pronounced null and void, that, even in the record of the judgment, the place which they ought to occupy is supplied by the phrase, "quos pro hic insertis haberi volumus."—Wilk. iii. 804. In like manner, in the new act of settlement, though the real ground of the archbishop's judgment with respect to Henry's first marriage is openly stated, that for the same prelate's judgment respecting the nullity of the second is merely said to have been "certain just and true causes." What could have been the motive of such concealment, but a desire to spare the king's reputation?

To my conjecture that the true cause was the previous cohabitation of Henry with Mary, the sister of Anne, it has been objected by a distinguished writer, 1. That in such case "both the statute and sentence must have stated as their main ground a notorious falsehood; for the commerce, if at all, must have been before the act of settlement." I do not see how this inference can be drawn. Neither the one nor the other assert that there was no such cohabitation. The archbishop in his judgment says only that the causes had lately been brought to his knowledge; the parliament, that the impediments were unknown at the passing of a previous statute, but since *confessed* by the lady Anne before the archbishop, "sitting judiciously for the same." This, plainly, is not a denial of the fact of cohabitation, but only of that fact having been officially brought before the archbishop and the legislature; which, in both cases, was true. Moreover, we are ignorant whether the unlawful commerce between Henry and Mary Boleyn was publicly known or not; but it is certain, —1. that, in order to marry her sister, Henry had obtained from Clement a dispensation to marry within the first degree of affinity, ex quocumque licito seu *illicito* coitu proveniente, provided the woman were not the relict of his own brother; and 2. that such dispensation had hitherto been considered valid according to the decision of Cranmer himself under his own hand,—Affinitatem impedientem, ne matrimonium contrahatur, induci quidem et nuptiali fœdere et carnali copula, illam jure divino, hanc jure ecclesiastico; wherefore the pontiff could not dispense in the first case, but could in the last.—Burnet, Rec. xxxvi. As long as Henry was attached to Anne Boleyn, this doctrine prevailed; as soon as he wished to be disengaged from her, a new light burst forth, and it was found that both affinities were of divine right, and, consequently, that the impediment arising from either was beyond the reach of the papal authority.

In the next place it is objected, that if the impediment arose out of the intercourse between Henry and Mary Boleyn, it could not, as the statute says, have been *confessed* by Anne. But it is plain that the word *confess* means nothing more than that she, by her proctors (she was not present herself), admitted in the archbishop's court the allegation that such commerce had taken place, and that such impediment had been the legal consequence.

But, though the ground of the divorce from Anne is not openly stated in the new act of settlement, it is obviously implied. By that statute it is enacted,—1. That, forasmuch as it was proved in the court of the archbishop, that the lady Catherine was carnally known by the king's brother, her marriage with the king shall be deemed against God's law, and utterly void and adnichiled: 2. That, forasmuch as the king's marriage with the lady Anne hath been adjudged by the archbishop of no value or effect, it shall be deemed of no strength, virtue, or effect: 3. That, since certain impediments of consanguinity and *affinity*, according to God's law, arise from the intercourse of the two sexes, "if it chance any man to know carnally any woman, then all and singular persons being in any such degree of consanguinity or affinity to any of the parties so carnally offending, shall be deemed and adjudged to be within the cases and limits of the said prohibitions of marriage:" and 4. Since no man can dispense with God's law, all separations of persons, of whatever estate or dignity, heretofore married within such degrees, made or to be made by authority of the bishops and ministers of the church of England, shall be firm, good, and effectual, notwithstanding any dispensation granted by, or appeal made to, the court of Rome.—Stat. of Realm, iii. 6589.

The reader will see how ingeniously the latter part of the statute was framed, so as to apply equally to the two marriages of the king. 1. By extending the scriptural prohibition to the affinity arising from any carnal knowledge of a woman, whether lawful or *unlawful*, it opposed the same impediment to the marriage of Anne Boleyn with Henry as to the marriage of Henry with Catherine; 2. by declaring such impediment indispensable by any power on earth, it made the dispensation granted by Clement to Henry, to marry any woman, even in the second degree of affinity (which was the case of Anne Boleyn), provided she were not the relict of his brother, of no more force than the dispensation previously granted to him by Julius, to marry the relict of his brother: and lastly, by declaring all separations of persons so married, made by the bishops of the church of England, firm, good, and effectual, it gave the sanction of the legislature both to the divorce from Catherine, notwithstanding her appeal, and to that from Anne, notwithstanding the dispensation which had been solicited by Henry himself.

NOTE X, p. 186.

The history of their interview is interesting. Ridley waited on Mary, September 8, 1552, and was courteously received. After dinner he offered to preach before her in the church. She begged him to make the answer himself. He urged her again; she replied that he might preach, but neither she, nor any of hers, would hear him. *Ridley.*—" Madam, I trust you will not refuse God's word." *Mary.*—" I cannot tell what you call God's word. That is not God's word now which was God's word in my father's time." *Ridley.*—" God's word is all one in all times; but is better understood and practised in some ages than in others." *Mary.*—" You durst not for your ears have preached that for God's word in my father's time, which you do now. As for your new books, thank God, I never read them. I never did, nor ever will do." Soon afterwards she dismissed him with these words: " My lord, for your gentleness to come and see me, I thank you; but for your offer to preach before me, I thank you not." As he retired, he drank according to custom with Sir Thomas Wharton, the steward of her household; but suddenly his conscience smote him; "Surely," he exclaimed, "I have done wrong. I have drunk in that house in which God's word hath been refused. I ought, if I had done my duty, to have shaken the dust off my shoes for a testimony against this house."— Fox, ii. 131.

NOTE Y, p. 186.

It has been asserted, on the authority of Fox (iii. p. 12), that the Protestants of Suffolk, before they would support the claim of Mary, extorted from her, as an indispensable condition, a promise to make no alteration in the religion established under Edward. Is this statement correct?

Fox himself has preserved a document which seems to show that it is not. During the persecution, these very persons presented to the queen's commissioners a long petition in favour of their religion. It was certainly the time for them to have urged the promise, if any had been given. But they appear to have no knowledge of any such thing. They do not make the remotest allusion to it. They speak, indeed, of their services; but, instead of attributing them to the promise of the queen, they insinuate the contrary, by asserting that they had supported her claim, because their religion taught them to support the rightful heir.— Fox, iii. 578—583. To me their silence on this occasion seems conclusive.

It has been thought a confirmation of the assertion of Fox, that Cobb presented to the queen, soon after her accession, a supplication in favour of the reformed creed, signed by one hundred persons, from Norfolk. But we know not the contents of the supplication; and it was proved that Cobb was an impostor, and that the signatures were forgeries. For the offence he stood in the pillory, November 24, 1553.

A better confirmation may be found in Noailles (iii. 16), from whom we learn that Wyat and his accomplices charged the queen with having broken two promises; one, not to make alterations in religion; another, not to marry a foreigner. Yet little credit can be given to reports circulated by rebels to justify their rebellion. One was, both probably were, fictions, the object of which was to irritate the people.

It should, however, be observed, that the emperor had advised her to make such promise, if she found it necessary. In his instructions to his ambassadors during Edward's illness, he says: "Et pour autant qu'il est vraisemblable qu'ils (the lords of the council) ne voudront admettre notre cousine à la couronne qu'ils ne soient assurés de deux choses, l'une qu'elle ne fera changement ni au gouvernement, ni es choses de la religion, l'autre qu'elle pardonnera tous que pourroient avoir commis ceux qui gouvernent, il sera de besoin que en ce elle ne fasse difficulté, puisque c'est chose en quoi elle ne peut remedier; conservant toutefois quant à soi sa religion entière inviolablement, et attendant que Dieu donne opportunité de peu à peu reduire par bon moyen le tout, que sera ce en quoi elle devra autant veiller, si Dieu lui fasse cette grace de parvenir à la couronne."— Renard, MS. iii. 6. Hence, though there is no evidence of any specific promise being made by the queen, it is not improbable that her partisans held out such expectations to allure men to her standard.

On July 22, as soon as Charles had heard of her success, he advised her to do nothing to shock the opinions of her subjects: "Qu'elle s'accommode avec toute douceur, se conformant aux definitions du parlement, sans rien faire toute fois de sa personne qui soit contre sa conscience ot sa religion, oyant seulement la messe àpart en sa chambre sans autre demonstration. . . . Qu'elle s'attende jusques elle aye opportunité de rassembler parlement."—Ibid. 24.

It was probably in consequence of this advice from Charles that, when she admonished the lord mayor on occasion of the tumult at St. Paul's Cross, she said that "she meaned gratiously not to compell or straine other men's consciences otherwise than Gou should, as she trusted, put in their heartes a perswasyon of the truth thorough the openinge of his worde unto them."—Council Book, Archæol. xviii. 173. However, as if she were apprehensive that advantage might be taken of these words, in a few days she published a proclamation, in which she repeated the same, but with this addition: "untill such time as further order by common consent may be taken therein."—Wilk. Con. iv. 86.

NOTE Z, p. 200.

The principal persons restored were Gertrude the widow, and Courtenay the son, of the marquess of Exeter; Thomas Howard, son of the earl of Surrey; and the two daughters of Lord Montague, who had suffered under Henry; Edward Seymour, son to the duke of Somerset; and the heirs of Arundel, Stanhope, and Partridge, who had been beheaded with Somerset, under Edward. The duke of Norfolk, who was supposed to have been attainted on the last day of Henry's life, did not ask for the same benefit. He denied the validity of the attainder. The case was argued before the judges at Serjeants' Inn. The duke produced the original act, and the commission to give to it the royal assent. His counsel remarked, that, contrary to custom, the king's signature was placed, not above, but below the title; and that the letters were too perfect to have been made by a person at the point of death; whence they inferred that there was no sufficient evidence of the royal assent having been given, and that of course the attainder was of no force. For greater security, however, a bill was passed, "to avoid" the attainder. When it was sent to the lower house, Lord Paget appeared as a witness, and declared on his honour that the king did not sign the commission, but that a servant of the name of William Clark impressed on it the royal stamp; and that this was the fact appears now from Clark's own list of instruments to which he had affixed the stamp, in State Papers, i. p. 898. The patentees, who had purchased some of the duke's property, petitioned to be heard by counsel; but they afterwards referred the matter to arbitration, and the bill passed.—Journals, 32. Dyer's Reports, 93. The duke had, however, taken the precaution to obtain a general pardon of all offences from the queen.—Rymer, xv. 337.

NOTE AA, pp. 239 and 243.

It may be asked why I have omitted the affecting martyrdom of the three women of Guernsey, and the preternatural death of Gardiner. My answer is, that I believe neither. 1. The first rests on the doubtful authority of Fox, whose narrative was immediately contradicted, and disproved by Harding. Fox replied, and Persons wrote in refutation of that reply. I have had the patience to compare both, and have no doubt that the three women were hanged as thieves, and afterwards burnt as heretics; that no one knew of the pregnancy of one of them, a woman of loose character; and that the child was found dead in the flames after the body of the mother had fallen from the gibbet. The rest we owe to the imagination of the martyrologist or of his informer. — See Fox, iii. 625; and Persons' Examination of Fox, part ii. p. 91.

2. Fox, on the authority of an old woman, Mrs. Mondaie, widow of a Mr. Mondaie, some time secretary to the old duke of Norfolk, tells us that Gardiner, on the 16th of October, invited to dinner the old duke of Norfolk; but so eagerly did he thirst after the blood of Ridley and Latimer, that he would not sit down to table, but kept the duke waiting some hours, till the messenger arrived with the news of their execution. Then he ordered dinner; but in the midst of his triumph God struck him with a strangury; he was carried to his bed in intolerable torments; and never left it alive.— Fox, iii. 450. Burnet has repeated the tale.—Burnet, ii. 329. Yet it is plainly one of the silly stories palmed upon the credulity of the martyrologist: for,

1. The old duke of Norfolk could not have been kept waiting; he had been twelve months in his grave. He was buried October 2nd in the preceding year.

2. Gardiner had already been ill for some time. Noailles (v. 127) informed his court, on the 9th of September, that the chancellor was indisposed with the jaundice, and in some danger.

3. On the 6th of October he was worse, and in more danger from the dropsy than the jaundice. There was no probability that he would live till Christmas (v. 150). From the 7th to the 19th he was confined to his chamber; and left it for the first time that day to attend the parliament. These dates are irreconcilable with the story in Fox; according to which, he must have been seized with his disease on the 16th, and could never have appeared in public afterwards.

END OF VOL. V.

www.ingramcontent.com/pod-product-compliance
Lightning Source LLC
Chambersburg PA
CBHW031935230426
43672CB00010B/1933